IRON, FIRE
AND
ICE

THE REAL HISTORY THAT INSPIRED
GAME of THRONES

ED WEST

Skyhorse Publishing

Skyhorse Publishing books may be purchased in bulk at special discounts for sales promotion, corporate gifts, fund-raising, or educational purposes. Special editions can also be created to specifications. For details, contact the Special Sales Department, Skyhorse Publishing, 307 West 36th Street, 11th Floor, New York, NY 10018 or info@skyhorsepublishing.com.

Skyhorse® and Skyhorse Publishing® are registered trademarks of Skyhorse Publishing, Inc.®, a Delaware corporation.

Visit our website at www.skyhorsepublishing.com.

10 9 8 7 6 5 4 3 2 1

Library of Congress Cataloging-in-Publication Data is available on file.

Cover design by Rain Saukas

Print ISBN: 978-1-5107-3564-4
Ebook ISBN: 978-1-5107-3565-1

Printed in the United States of America

CONTENTS

INTRODUCTION

A young pretender raises an army to take the throne. Learning of his father's death, the adolescent—dashing and charismatic and descended from the old kings of the North—vows to avenge him in combat. Despite his youth, he has already won several battles and commands the loyalty of many of the leading families of the realm; he is supported in this war by his mother, who has spirited away her two younger sons to safety far from the rampaging armies of their father's enemies. Against them is the queen, "passionate and proud and strong-willed"[1] and with more of the masculine virtues of the time than most men. She too is battling for the inheritance of her young son, not yet fully grown but already a sadist who takes delight in watching executions.

This tale will sound familiar to fans of George R.R. Martin's *A Song of Ice and Fire* series, and its HBO television adaptation *Game of Thrones*, but this is not the story of Westeros; rather of the real-life realm of England in 1461. On March 29 of that year, the deadliest battle ever fought on British soil took place on a spot now called Bloody Meadow in Yorkshire, deep within what was once the old kingdom of the north. Lasting into the night, despite a thick blizzard, the Battle of Towton was marked by extreme brutality, and by the end of the fighting some twenty-eight thousand men lay dead, many executed after the battle's end.[2] It was the climax to six years of violence and would decide which family ruled the kingdom.

On one side was an army led by Edward, Earl of March—the name was pronounced "Eddard" at the time[3]—the eighteen-year-old heir to the House of York, who had claimed the throne that year following the beheading of his father, Richard of York. Facing him were the forces of the House of Lancaster, fighting in the name of the queen, Margaret of Anjou, and her husband, the mad King Henry VI, whose weak mind had been the cause of York's rebellion.

Edward had recently won a victory at Mortimer's Cross, close to the Welsh border, weeks after his father and brother Edmund were slain at Wakefield. Richard of York, a descendant of the great warrior king Edward III through both his mother and father, had emerged in the 1450s as the most powerful man in the kingdom, but he would not win the throne. Instead his head was stuck on a pole in the city of York with a paper crown placed on top in mockery of his ambitions; his son Edward had sworn vengeance and would get it. Still barely a grown man, he went on to win a series of battles before his success was imperiled by his choice of bride.

By the time the conflict between the Houses of York and Lancaster had burned itself out, the bones of three or even four generations of some families would be scattered across the battlefields of England, the Plantagenet line destroyed in the fury of the Cousin's War. During this period, 25 percent of male aristocrats in the kingdom died violently, and some houses were entirely wiped out in a cycle of vengeance that came to break all the laws of warfare.[4]

The story would fascinate future generations, retold in the plays of William Shakespeare and later by the nineteenth-century novelist Walter Scott, who popularized the name "the War of the Roses" in reference to the emblems of the two families. It was this dynastic conflict that would provide much of the historical inspiration for George R.R. Martin when he wrote his fantasy series. Martin, a keen fan of popular history, has spoken on occasions about the people and periods that he drew on. A *Song of Ice and Fire* is set in "the Realm," or Seven Kingdoms, a country comprising the southern half of the island of Westeros. These books tell the story of the struggle to win the Iron Throne by a number of competing families: among them are the Lannisters, the richest clan in the Realm, who have gained control of the capital, King's Landing, in the southeast of the island; the Starks, who are the leading family of the old northern kingdom; and the Baratheons, who trace their roots to an ancestor who helped a great conqueror several generations earlier. It is a brutal and tragic world, one where the only options for those playing the game of thrones are victory or death.

As well as being an epic fantasy in its own right, *Game of Thrones* is also a fantastic (in both senses of the word) retelling of the story of the real Realm—England. It was inspired, in the author's own words, not just by "The Wars of the Roses . . . but also the Hundred Years War, the Crusades, the Norman Conquest,"[5] and along the way the story takes in a sweep of European and Near Eastern history, from the ancient worlds of Egypt, Rome, and Greece, through to the flowering of medieval civilization and beyond to the Renaissance and the birth of the early modern world. And the struggle for the throne of England, from the Saxon invasion in the fifth century to the downfall of the House of York a millennium later, is as fascinating as any fiction on earth.

George R.R. Martin first laid out the concept for his novel A *Game of Thrones* in a letter to his agent in 1993. He called it "a cycle of plot, counterplot, ambition, murder and revenge, with the iron throne of the Seven Kingdoms as the ultimate prize."[6] Westeros was to be, in the words of one historian, "a loose tribute to the British Isles at some unfixed point in the Middle Ages, where the mood of the Anglo-Saxon heptarchy is mashed together with the merciless family feuding that engulfed England during the [fifteenth]-century War of the Roses," a mixture of fantasy and history that delighted in squalor "torture, prostitution, incest, sodomy and rape."[7]

Or as novelist John Lanchester wrote of the series: "The Wars of the Roses, in this reimagining, are—as they surely were in real life—a blood-soaked, treacherous, unstable world, saturated in political rivalries, in which nobody is safe . . . It's not a world any sane person would want to live in, not for a moment."[8] The show is also utterly amoral. There is no right or wrong. And that is the attraction.

History is the underlying inspiration, but *Game of Thrones* is also influenced by the genre of medieval heroism that originated with the tales of King Arthur and Chrétien de Troyes, epic stories from the birth of medieval Europe that informed how people thought of the world. But unconstrained by a need for accuracy, fantasy allows the author and reader far greater freedom, so what we have is an "epic retelling of the War of the Roses without the burden of history."[9] Any historical comparison can only go so far, and no character exactly matches a real historical figure, and yet most of what takes place in Westeros can be found in a specific period of European history that historians refer to as the Crisis of the Late Middle Ages, when England and France were ruined by war, famine, plague, and social and religious upheaval. It is this period, 1315 to 1461, that this book will mostly cover, telling the backstory of European history as the narrative progresses.

═══════

The medieval realm was a delicate political body that depended on a strong king who could unite the aristocracy, but tragically, and within half a century, England was ruled by two monarchs who were mentally unbalanced; firstly, Richard II, a boy-king whose paranoia and sense of personal majesty bordered on the pathological, and later the feeble minded, and possibly schizophrenic, Henry VI.

Likewise, *Game of Thrones* begins in the aftermath of a rebellion against a violent and paranoid monarch who has alienated the great magnates of the land. In Westeros, the rebel lords overthrow the mad king Aerys II Targaryen, a revolt led by Robert Baratheon, who in turn takes the crown and marries Cersei Lannister, a beautiful, cunning, and ruthless individual from the country's leading house. Like many powerful women of the late medieval period, she is accused of being unfaithful, although in this case the allegation is true; her twin brother, Jaime, is the real father of her three children, including the eldest, Joffrey, a monster in the making.

The usurper Robert Baratheon is the eldest of three brothers; of his siblings one is cold and calculating, the other jovial but facile; and with Robert gorging himself to an early grave, the two maneuver for power. Simmering conflict is emerging between the Lannisters and the Starks, the latter descendants of the old rulers of the North and the most powerful family in that kingdom. Eddard Stark had been Robert Baratheon's childhood friend, his comrade-at-arms and then his Hand, charged with administering the Realm on behalf of the monarch. Drunk and bloated, King Robert is killed in a hunting accident before his fortieth birthday, mauled to death by a boar; it is this event, not entirely an accident, that triggers a fresh conflict, with the succession of Joffrey opposed by his uncles, the claimants Stannis and Renly Baratheon.

Ned Stark, having learned the truth of Joffrey's parentage, gives his support to Stannis, only to be arrested by Cersei Lannister and then executed on Joffrey's orders. This is despite the new king being betrothed to Sansa Stark, Ned's daughter. After Stark's death, his son Robb declares himself the King of the North, as his ancestors were before they bent the knee, while Ned's bastard son Jon Snow has joined the Night's Watch, the body of men sworn to guard the wall that protects the Seven Kingdoms from the wildings to the north.[10]

Within King's Landing various figures jostle for power: Varys, a eunuch nicknamed "the Spider" because of his network of spies; Petyr Baelish, a moneylender and brothel-keeper who has risen to the council from a relatively lowly station; Tyrion Lannister, the dwarf brother of Jaime and Cersei; and their father Tywin Lannister, an imposing and brutal aristocrat warrior whose sole motivation is to further the interests of his house, whatever the costs. The War of the Five Kings begins, pitting the

Lannisters, with their powerbase in the south, against the pre-eminet family in the north, the Starks.

And so it was in real life—sort of. Edward IV, as the Earl of March became, was in Martin's words an inspiration both for Robert Baratheon and Robb Stark. Like the Starks, March was descended from the old ruling family of the most northerly of Anglo-Saxon England's seven kingdoms, Northumbria, a distinctive, independent land, tougher and poorer than the south, before the realm was united in the tenth century. Like Robb, he never lost a battle during his successful adolescent military career; like Robb, too, he faced a formidable and fearsome queen whose machinations had already cost his father his head.

This conflict marked, in British history, the end of the medieval period and the start of a new era. An era of new weapons capable of killing on an awesome scale, a technology that arrived from the east and was far more terrifying than dragons: gunpowder. It was a dangerous new world, of increasing instability around the throne and of worsening violence in politics, for as one historian put it, "a deposed monarch has nowhere to fall but into the grave."[11] Or as Cersei tells Ned Stark: "This is the game of thrones, you win or you die."[12]

This great crisis starts in the year when the long winter came.

1
THE REALM

Dead history is writ in ink, the living sort in blood.

—RODERICK HARLAW

Alnwick Castle was the first line of defence if ever the wild men from beyond the wall poured over the border. A forbidding fortress built on a slope and controlling the only passable road on the English side of the Cheviot Hils, it was built to hold the North. The only way in to the citadel was via the barbican, the intimidating gateway overlooked by a tower, and through this narrow passage, with thick wooden doors at either end, the daily traffic of horses and men would bring supplies to the castle. When the invaders came to rape and pillage the villages of the North, as they had done for centuries, men and women would swarm into the castle seeking the protection of their lord.

Built in the eleventh century, Alnwick is deep inside Northumberland, England's most northerly county, and just twenty miles from the border with Scotland, inside a frontier country that had become increasingly lined with fortresses. The castle had been enhanced over the years with a solid portcullis gate protecting the entrance, with heavily-defended battlements, a twenty-one-foot drop below the drawbridge and walls seven feet thick, as well as a moat. Looking down at the surrounding area was an octagonal tower decorated with thirteen stone shields representing the families who had married into the House of Percy down the generations.

If the outer door of the barbican was ever penetrated by invaders, it still presented a dauting prospect, overlooked by four high towers from which loyal northern men could fire at the enemy below—using arrows or missiles, boiling water or fat. Inside the barbican, an attacker would be surrounded by high, thick walls and arrows firing down at them from all sides. Below them they would feel the mesh that led to the dungeons.[1] If the barbican fell, the castle still had two courtyards, or baileys, from which last gasp fighting could be carried out. The fortress of House Percy had been built to keep them in the North.

Just as in Westeros the King's Road heads from King's Landing to Winterfell and to beyond the wall, so in real life the Great North Road led all the way from London to Edinburgh—Castle Rock, as its fortress was called—passing by the stronghold of Alnwick. Whoever controlled Alnwick therefore controlled the main route from Scotland to the South, and by the catastrophic year of 1314 this was the House of Percy. From Alnwick, the Percys dominated the frontier with the Scots beyond the great wall once built by the Romans (although in reality Alnwick, like a tiny portion of England, lies north of the wall).

The Percys were the leading house in the North, and if the Scots came it was their burden to raise men from five northern counties to repel them. They had rivals, of course, so while Henry de Percy, the First Baron Percy, was recognized as the strongest northern lord, there was also Neville, Lord of Raby, Clifford, Lord of Westmorland, Lucy, Lord of Cockermouth, Dacre, Lord of Gilsland and Umfraville, Lord of Redesdale. They were all proud families with their own pedigrees, but the Percys were kings in the North. In the words of historian Alexander Rose, "In that tumultuous place, the Westminster-based, Southern king's writ hardly ran. In Percy country, there was Percy law backed by a Percy army paid for by Percy money."[2]

Like most of the country's leading clans, they had not always been from the island. The Percy histories claimed as their oldest ancestor Mainfred, or Manni, who in the year AD 896 arrived in France after pillaging in England. He was a Dane, or as we would call him now, a Viking, and like many of his kind, settled in a region of Francia that came to be called Normandy. From the Percy lordship in Pays de Caux, northwest of Rouen, one of their number had arrived in England alongside William the Conqueror in 1066 when England's ruling class was ruthlessly eliminated and replaced by a French-speaking elite.

From minor lords in the wilder, rougher north of the country, which the Normans had treated with special brutality, the Percys had risen to become the most powerful family in the region. Just eleven generations after arriving on the island, a Percy was made Earl of Northumberland.

Although they had marched with the hated conqueror, the Percys had over time made themselves true men of the North. First settling in Yorkshire, they were a minor family who, in 1166, were still only the seventh largest tenant-in-chiefs in that county.

However, Henry de Percy had that year married Isabel, daughter of Adam de Brus II, Baron of Skelton; it was an advantageous marriage, in return for which de Percy and his heirs swore to every year ride to Skelton Castle "to lead the lady of the castle from her chamber to the chapel for Mass, and then escort her back to her chamber and take meat with her before withdrawing."[3] This they did, honoring their debts, until the Reformation in the sixteenth century swept away such ancient traditions.

They were not just powerful and rich, but well loved too. Northern men followed them with their arms and their hearts, and at their command thousands would appear in the field, men to whom the king in London was a distant figure who spoke a strange dialect: "To them, the last man standing between Northerners and destruction was not the faraway king, but a Percy. He was their commander, their protector, their judge and their sheriff."[4]

And the Percys had always looked after their men. The records down in London show Henry de Percy writing to the chancellor on behalf of a valet: "Aleyn, son of Sir Thomas de Heton, who might have lost his land"[5] had his lord not defended his corner. Percy's son would speak on behalf of attainders who had fought loyally for the crown so that they might be spared punishment for the violent crimes they had committed at home. The Percy soldiers were paid out of his own pocket, knowing that silver promised from the crown might take an age to reach men with hungry families, a level of diligence to vassals few southern barons would have bothered with.

The Percys came to dominate the local honors, among them Warden of the East March, whose role it was to secure the eastern portion of the border with Scotland. They were in charge of justice, too. In Westeros, "the man who passes the sentence should swing the sword,"[6] and executions are carried out in the king's name without any sort of trial. It was not quite the case in real life, although local lords were tasked with the grim task with punishing lawbreakers after their guilt was determined, for "he who prosecutes shall carry out the judgement," as the twelfth century code of Preston in Lancashire goes.

The most recent Henry de Percy had, in 1294, adopted the lion as the symbol of his house, having married Eleanor, daughter of the Earl of Arundel. The Arundels, an Anglo-Norman family with their base on the Welsh border, had for generations displayed a golden lion on a red field, and could trace their ancestry back to Adeliza, widow of King Henry I. Percy now adopted the animal to show his Arundel blood, and in tribute to a founder of the Percy dynasty, Joscelin de Louvain—*leeuwen* being Flemish for lion.

Their new heraldic symbol—called sigils in Westeros—was appropriate for the Percys' rising status. The art of heraldry was in its infancy, reflecting the importance of lineage and the most important thing to a man in the medieval world: *who your father was*. And just as the ruling houses of Westeros traced their lineage back to obscure and semi-mythical kings, in medieval England those of royal blood descended from the rulers of Wessex, Mercia, and Northumbria, the ancient kingdoms of the island, which were eventually united before being conquered in 1066 by Normandy's Duke William. Families placed great importance on their pedigree, in particular a link to the Conqueror and his companions, and through him to the ultimate forefather of medieval Europe, Charles the Great, King of the Franks, who in AD 800 had been crowned Emperor of the West in Rome.

And so heraldry was more than just about team colors; it was a reminder of who your father was, and his father before him, and what would be passed onto the next generation. It gave courage in battle, so that "a knight of good lineage would be emboldened in the field by recollection of his ancestors' brave deeds and spurred on in bravery himself by a desire to add to the family roll of honour."[7]

Henry de Percy, First Baron Percy, had been born in 1273, from a family that almost went extinct after his six paternal uncles all failed to produce children and his two brothers died without issue. His maternal grandfather was John de Warenne, the powerful Earl of Surrey who, back in 1278, had been served with a royal writ of *quo warranto* ("by what right"). King Edward I, determined to learn which subjects had usurped royal privileges in order to claim them back, demanded of each man proof of how he came by his property. De Warenne, approached by the king's men, drew his rusty sword and declared that *this* was his warrant, for "My ancestors came with William the Bastard, and conquered their lands with the sword, and I will defend them with the sword against anyone wishing to seize them."[8]

Alnwick had been erected during an intense period of castle-building following the Norman Conquest, during which five hundred such fortresses were erected in a generation. Raised as a show of strength against the Scots across the river Tweed, it was a motte-and-bailey castle, the standard type of the period used by the Normans, characterized by a raised and defensible central keep, the motte, surrounded by a courtyard (bailey) with a ditch around it. De Percy had now added a heavily fortified barbican, as well as new circular towers, more efficient than the older square towers as they could not be battered at the corners or easily undermined (that is, dug under and set fire to). A moat was added, along with a well, a portcullis, a drawbridge, and eight semicircular bastions to the keep, castle-building technology reaching its apex during this period. Erected on a peninsula, with the River Aln to the north and a ravine to the east and south, Alnwick was almost invulnerable, for a garrison of sixty men within could easily defend such a castle against six hundred outside.

Which was just as well, as in de Percy's lifetime relations between the kingdoms of England and Scotland had deteriorated sharply, and he had spent almost twenty years fighting on the border, leading raids into enemy territory and defending the north from attack. De Percy had been knighted by King Edward in March 1296 while besieging Berwick, Scotland's largest city; three years later he became the first Lord Percy as his reward.

The border wars came at great cost; in March 1307 Percy and three hundred of his men were at Turnberry Castle in Carrick when they were attacked by the Scottish leader Robert the Bruce. The fighting was so horrific it was rumored afterwards that Percy was afraid to go into Scotland again. In the autumn of 1314, as the harsh Northumbrian winter approached, Percy was forced to defend nearby Newcastle and lead a raiding party north. He died in early October, most likely fatally wounded while fighting Scottish raiders.

He died, but his house survived. As Tywin Lannister put it, "Before long I'll be dead, and you and your brother and your sister and all of her children, all of us dead, all of us rotting underground. It's the family name that lives on. It's all that lives on. Not your personal glory, not your honor . . . but family."[9] Of 136 barons summoned to Westminster between 1295 and 1300, only sixteen of their houses were left in 1500, and the Percys were among the survivors. In fact, they still survive today, and still live in Alnwick six months of the year, the other half of which it is used as a film set to fund its maintenance. Fans of the Harry Potter films will recognize it as Hogwarts School of Witchcraft and Wizardry.

THE NORTH

The Great North Road is still there too, this real-life King's Road now going by the less romantic name of the A1 and M1 motorway, and still following mostly the same route, one of four ancient paths in Britain dating to Roman times and beyond. The Gough map, commissioned during this period, shows three thousand miles of main roads by 1360, 40 percent of which were built by the Romans.

The map was ordered by a king intent on extending his power beyond the south of the island, outside of which most monarchs had little experience. Southern kings had often had only fragile control over the North, a naturally distinct region of England defined as the area between the great Humber river and the Scottish border. It has "older, harder rocks and hillier terrain,"[10] compared to the flatter and more fertile South. The narrow width between the vast stretch of the Humber and the hills of the Pennines made the region hard for southern armies to control. Even thirty-five miles inland the great river is a mile across, and so dominance of just one small gap between river and mountain allowed an army control of York, the largest city in the region, as well as the rivers Ouse, Ure, Aire, Don, Derwent, and Trent—and so the whole North.* Any army arriving from the South would find themselves in a corridor between the Humber swamps and the Pennines, the mountain range that forms a spine down northern England, removing any numerical advantage southerners had.

People of the North were different: "When the earl and his Northern retinue travelled to London, locals would stare at the foreigners," as one historian put it. "The Northerners were poorer and rougher, and it showed. Northern soldiers, overdressed for the summer climate," had "outmoded armor; even the earl's warhorse was a feeble creature compared to the splendid steeds favoured by Southern magnates. The Northerners were permanently wary and clannish."[11]

Yorkshire, the largest of the northern counties, formed the southern extent of this region. Beyond that, the four most northerly shires, Northumberland, Westmorland, Cumberland, and Durham, were a patchwork of miniature fiefdoms run by warring families in which the laws passed in Westminster were of lesser importance than ancient traditions and local custom, including long-held vendettas.

The North of Westeros "is like its Warden: stark, unforgiving, masculine and wild."[12] Likewise William Camden, who in the Tudor period wrote the first geographical study of the British Isles, described a "rough and barren" land: "You would think you see the ancient nomads, a martial sort of people," he concluded.

Geoffrey of Monmouth, in his *History of the Kings of Britain*, wrote that "it was a frightful land to live in, more or less uninhabited, and it offered a safe lurking place to foreigners. Indeed, by its very geographical position it lay open to the Picts, the Scots, the Danes, the Norwegians and anyone else who came ashore to ravage the

---

*The Trent roughly occupies the same point of the map of England as the Trident does in Westeros.

island."[13] According to the twelfth century chronicle, the *Gesta Stephani*, "the root and origin of all evil arose in that part of England called Northumbria to produce plunder and arson, strife and war."[14] Or as a fifteenth century writer put it: "The north, whence all evil spreads."[15] But then, of course, these men were all from the South.

Long ago it had been a kingdom in its own right, Northumbria, one of seven in early medieval England, a chaotic and violent time commonly called the Dark Ages. Its two warring kings brutally killed by Viking invaders in 865, Northumbria had been heavily settled by Norsemen, a Scandinavian legacy still reflected in Yorkshire dialect today. A century later it had been the last region to come under the sway of the southern kings of Wessex who had united the country, and retained a distinctive, semi-Scandinavian identity for far longer. Reluctant to help the southern lords fight off the Norman invaders in 1066, the northern men had afterwards most ferociously opposed the conqueror and been crushed as a result. Hundreds of thousands died, whole villages were destroyed, and the region never recovered.

Border life was still tough, centuries later, as it always had been. The Flemish chronicler Froissart wrote of men there forced to consume "small poor wine" and "bread evil baken in panniers" which "was sore wet with the sweat of horses."[16] Up in the North, saddles were "all rotten and broken, and most part of their horses hurt on their backs . . . nor they had nothing to make fire but green boughs, the which would not burn because of the rain."[17]

In the North, some traditions held on longer: stories of shapeshifters that dated back at least to Saxon times before the conquest. Beyond lay the terror of Scotland, a barren, cold land with its folk tales of *sith*, or *aes sídhe*, supernatural undead beings who lived in the Land of the Dead, having been driven into remote areas by invaders.[18] In Scottish folklore, these creatures formed the *slaughe sidhe*, the "fairy horde," an army of the undead. Few on the English side of the wall believed that anymore; the living Scots were terrifying enough, and that year the army of the realm headed deep beyond the wall to fight them—only to meet with disaster, a catastrophe that would plunge the kingdom into civil war.

But worse still, people across the Realm and beyond had noticed that the weather was turning. On the colder fringes of the known world those on the margins felt it first as the temperatures plunged; they did not know it yet, but the following year the cold rains would begin, and the crops would fail. Winter was coming.

KING'S LONDON

As the fifteenth century chronicler Polydore Vergil observed, "The whole Countrie of Britaine . . . is divided into four partes; wherof the one is inhabited of Englishmen, the other of Scottes, the third of Wallshemen, and the fowerth of Cornishe people. Which all differ emonge them selves, either in tongue, either in manners, or ells in lawes and ordinaunces."[19]

The Realm of England had grown out of several small kingdoms carved out by three Germanic tribes, the Angles, Saxons, and Jutes, arriving on the island as Rome's control of western Europe collapsed. The kingdom, united four centuries before Henry de Percy's time, shared the island of Britain with various peoples beyond a wall on its northern frontier, speaking a mixture of tongues, as well as surviving British speakers on two peninsulas in the west and south-west.

The island's thriving economic hub had for many years been London, settled on the north bank of the River Thames by the Romans, and with access to the continent, especially the rich markets of Flanders, northern France, and the German "free imperial cities" across the North Sea. Here the king of England sat in Westminster Hall, once part of a tiny island a mile upstream from Lundenberg (as the Saxons called it) but now a western suburb of the city. Like the Great Hall of the Red Keep, this is where the monarch kept court.

The throne sat at the south end of the hall by a twelve-foot-long marble slab, the King's Table, which long symbolized the monarch's power. The current King's Table dated to the reign of Edward I's father Henry III, replacing a far older wooden slab that once would have travelled around the country with the monarch. The throne itself, the King's Seat, was modelled on the Biblical throne of Solomon and carved with lions, emblems of the kingdom. Marble thrones had become symbols of great imperial prestige, used by the still surviving eastern Roman emperors in far-off Constantinople and by Charlemagne, Emperor of the West. The palace of Westminster had also recently become home to semi-official meetings of lords and commons now called the Parliament ("to talk" in French, from where English also gets "parley", to talk with an enemy).

London, from where the king ruled his realm, was perhaps home to sixty thousand people, far smaller than Granada, Seville, Venice, or Milan, or countless other cities to the south. London's merchant elite were English-speakers, as they always had been, although the kings and higher aristocracy had spoken French for two and a half centuries. A teeming, bustling, and squalid city, London was surrounded on three sides by a Roman wall with seven gates and on the other by the river (these gates were not pulled down until 1760). The city had by now long sprawled out of its ancient wall and extended from the Tower in the east to the River Fleet to the west.

The Tower of London, built by the Normans in order to control the city and intimidate it, was a royal fortress, apartment block, and even zoo, home to an elephant and leopard during the reign of Henry III. It was also a prison, from which only one man had ever escaped, Ranulf Flambard in 1101, a bishop notorious for scamming both rich and poor out of their wealth. The Tower also had a library of 160 volumes, one of the biggest in England[20]—although in real life people's reading tastes were rather lowbrow, fifty-nine of these books being trashy romances, with the Queen of England among the keenest borrowers.[21] In Westeros, The Citadel, headquarters of the Order of Maesters in Oldtown, has the "largest library in the Known World"[22] but in England at the time even the greatest book collection scaled into insignificance compared to their ancient equivalents, and would do so until the seventeenth century.

London was grotesquely unhygienic, a city drowning in its own filth. One Londoner complained of the slaughterhouse nearby that had made his garden "stinking and putrid," another that blood from animals filled nearby streets "making a foul corruption and abominable sight to all dwelling near."[23] A complaint against William E. Cosner, resident of the ward of Farringdon Without, stated that "men could not pass" by his house "for the stink [of] horse dung and horse piss."[24] It was not unknown for men to drown in shit, or for the smell and squalor to drive people to murder, hardly surprising when they lived and worked in "lanes barely wide enough for a fat man to turn around in."[25] It was not until later that century that slaughterhouses and other unhygienic places were forced to locate outside of the crowded city.

Across the river Thames, Southwark was famed for its very strong beer made from brownish Thames water, but also for its large numbers of brothels—"stews"—most of them, strangely, owned by the Bishop of Winchester. Many of the women were Flemish, relatively exotic migrants from across the sea, working in Cock Lane and Gropecuntlane, among the many colorful street names in the city (there was also a Shitbrook Street and Pissing Alley). Londoners in trouble with the authorities could always run off to Southwark and because it was a separate jurisdiction, they often escaped justice; later this seedy underbelly would become host to the city's most famous playhouse, William Shakespeare's Globe Theatre.

Even a century earlier the city was home to over 350 ale houses, taverns, and inns, notorious dens of vice and crime. Across the sea in Flanders, beer was already made with hops, but it was not until the Hundred Years' War that Englishmen would first taste this drink, recognizable to modern palates as beer. The "beer" consumed at that time would have had a texture more like porridge, muddy and foggy, although it had its enthusiasts and lasted well into the Tudor period. A later poet described his love of the native ale:

> Ich I am a Cornish man, and ale I can brew
> It will make one to cacke also to spew
> It is thick and smokey and also it is thin
> It is like wash of pigs had wrestled therein[26]

Like with all significant towns in the fourteenth century, London's citizens could entertain themselves with plays, although before the first theaters they would have been done by travelling amateurs on major feast days. These performances were very bawdy, featuring sex, sadism, rape, nudity, drunkenness, and torture (with entrails from local butchers as props). But the violence on stage reflected the violence off it, with murder rates comparable to modern central America.[27] At night, the bell in the church of St Mary-le-Bow would sound the start of nightfall, and while this was no longer the signal for the curfew, as it had been in William the Conqueror's day, men and women were wise to head indoors.

HERE BE DRAGONS

London's dominance of Britain was due to its position on the Thames, giving its large class of merchants—considerable even in Roman times—access to the markets of Europe's richest regions: Flanders, France, the Rhineland, and northern Italy. This interconnected economy, once abysmally poorer and more primitive than the East, had begun to catch up and even surge ahead economically; already Flanders and Holland showed signs of the economic advances that would later lead to the seventeenth century Dutch invention of modern capitalism. This Catholic Christian world would have been familiar to educated Englishmen, but beyond that it would be a matter of "here be dragons." (The phrase is not a myth, for there are indeed two recorded incidents of maps bearing the Latin phrase *HC SVNT DRACONS*, "here are dragons," both from the 1500s.)

Martin's world is composed of four known continents: Westeros, Essos, Sothoryos, and Ulthos, the latter two of which we've heard little of in the first books, although Sothoryos is supposedly filled with steaming jungles and tropical diseases and is presumably a bit like Africa. Between Westeros and Essos lies the Narrow Sea, on the other side of which are a group of city-states called the Free Cities, and to the south and east of them fallen civilizations as well as nomadic peoples such as the Dothraki, who cross the vast expanses of the continent on horse, occasionally terrorizing and enslaving the continent's cities, and sometimes trading with them instead.

Westeros is nine hundred miles long, with a wide range of climates and peoples: the southernmost kingdom, Dorne, is Mediterranean-like, warm and dusty and filled with "scorpions and sand," and noted for its hot-blooded people who hail from various, racially-diverse invaders. The North is snowbound, even in summer, while beyond the wall the climate is arctic. The Realm itself covers only the southern portion of the island, and is protected by a three hundred-mile wall, beyond which are the Free Folk, or wildlings, descendants of the original inhabitants of the island, as well as other less savory and more fantastical beings. At the very far north is the Land of Always Winter, from where the feared White Walkers are supposed to hail, although the existence of these ghost-like creatures is disputed by many.

To Western Europeans at the time, just as in Martin's fantasy, there was the known world, of Europe and the near East, and the unknown world beyond. Distant lands such as Persia and India were, in historian Barbara Tuchman's words,

> seen through a gauze of fabulous fairy tales revealing an occasional nugget of reality: forests so high they touch the clouds, horned pygmies who move in herds and grow old in seven years, brahmins who burn themselves on funeral pyres, men with dogs' heads and six toes, 'cyclopeans' with only one eye and one foot who move as fast as the wind, the 'monoceros' which can be caught only when it sleeps in the lap of a virgin, Amazons whose tears are of silver, panthers who practice the caesarean operation with their own claws, trees whose leaves supply wool, snakes 300ft long, snakes with precious stones for eyes, snakes who so love music that for prudence they stop up one ear with their tail.[28]

Most people in the realm of England would never have met anyone from these far-off lands, although some might have seen their exotic exports, of silk, gold, and ivory, among other things. Even further away than Persia or India, as far as the world reached, Western European maps at the time feature "Seres," a land so-called because its people wear silk, a precious material grown by worms, which these Eastern people had tried to prevent foreigners from acquiring (until a monk sneaked a pair of silk worms to Byzantium). Yet little was known of this Seres, "China," or the rumors that a sophisticated island-kingdom lay even beyond it.

People thought India covered half the world, while others believed that there were three Indias, one ruled by Prester John: a legendary central Asian king Europeans believed would help them win the Crusades. Letters supposedly from the magnificent ruler circulated in the twelfth century stating, "I, Prester John, am the lord of lords, and I surpass all the kings of the entire world in wealth, virtue and power . . . Milk and honey flow freely in our lands; poison can do no harm, nor do any noisy frogs croak. There are no scorpions, no serpents creeping in the grass."[29] This exotic faraway kingdom was filled with diamonds, emeralds, and other precious stones, as well as peppers and elixirs that would cure all sorts of ailments.

Men dreamed of huge and unfeasible wealth in the East: "gem-bearing trees and mountains of gold" guarded by snakes and Ophir, a land filled with "giants, pigmies, dog-headed men, a river that flowed to Paradise, precious stones, a fountain of youth, a sea of sand, a river of stones, beyond which lived the Ten Lost Tribes of Israel, also tributary to Prester John."[30] There were other magical lands—"Atlantis, El Dorado, Rio Doro, the River of Gold, the Empire of Monomotopa, Island of the Seven Cities of Cibola, discovered by seven bishops and St Brendan's Isle discovered by the Irishman during the 6th century."[31] St Brendan the Navigator, well into his seventies when he went on his outlandish journey, and trusting in God rather than any navigational tools, may have ended up in the Azores or Iceland.

People at the time knew of three continents and believed that across the great ocean there was the *Terra Australis Incognita*, the unknown southern land. It was too hot for men, but among the races that could be found there were the Sciopods, monsters with one large foot; when it became too hot they simply lay on their back and used their feet as shade. Also expected to be found in this faraway land were the Antipodes, whose feet point backwards; the Amazons, who had a single breast; Cynocephales, men with the head of a dog; Panoti, men with elephant trunks; and

Blemmyae, who have no heads at all but faces on their chests. Outside of the known world there could also be found Headless Men, or Ethiopian Troglodytes, and some groups in the east supposedly ate their parents—although there were certainly canni-bals in remote parts of Asia, even until relatively modern times. Of these Marvels of the East, a twelfth century manuscript now at the Bodleian Libraries in Oxford included two-headed snakes, centaurs, and unicorns, this worldview influenced by classical mythology.

Perhaps nothing better captured the imagination than dragons. Faraway Sri Lanka, to the south of Prester John's empire, was full of them, according to popular belief, but these terrifying creatures featured as objects of fascination in almost every culture. Carl Jung, founder of analytical psychology, saw the dragon as the arch-enemy of the archetype hero, the monster that had to be defeated in order for good to triumph—by the Norse hero Sigurd, the Anglo-Saxon Beowulf, or the Christian St George—but also the monster within us.

Great men of the thirteenth century such as Albert the Great and Roger Bacon thought that the equator was incapable of sustaining life because of its heat, and so men only inhabited the northern hemisphere; this was believed until the fifteenth century when Portuguese explorers proved it wrong by sailing all the way around the Cape of Good Hope. Little was really known of the world beyond, and European maps were still primitive compared to those of antiquity; typically, they showed a T-shape of the world with Asia at the top, Europe and Africa below. In contrast, in the more advanced Chinese model, the equator is seen as a circle around the globe, an idea the Europeans would borrow from the East one day, along with eyeglasses, paper, and gunpowder. *Ptolemy ?*

Before the mid-thirteenth century, no European had gone further east than Bagh-dad and returned. Then, between 1276 and 1291, an explorer from Venice called Marco Polo had reached the court of the faraway Mongol Emperor Kublai Khan. The Polo company had on their travels reached Lop, an "immense, dry, salt-encrusted lake bed covering extreme northwestern China, the wasteland . . . notorious for its special hazards" and which was "synonymous with the edge of the unknown."[32] In the Desert of Lop, it was said, merchants often heard malignant spirits calling out to them to follow, never to be heard of again.

Polo found many cultures utterly alien to Europeans. The women of Kamul, now Hami in western China, had a custom whereby "the stranger stays with his wife in the house and does as he likes and lies with her in a bed just as if she were his wife, and they continue in great enjoyment," with the approval of their menfolk.[33] In Burma, in contrast, Polo found people who poisoned strangers, inviting them to lodge in the house and then killing "him by night either by poison or by other things so that he died."[34] That way their soul would never leave the house and so bring it good fortune. Polo found Buddhists in south China who "eat all coarse things and they also eat human flesh very willingly, provided that he [the deceased] did not die a natural death"—they preferred those who died by this sword as they had "very good and savoury flesh."[35]

Polo had also visited Russia, where he saw dog sledding and wrote that the people "have all their houses underground because of the great cold that is there." In this icy land "these are sables and ermines and squirrels . . . and black foxes" from which they make skins and furs. After this he found another region in Russia, the "the land of shadows," where men "live like animals . . . and it's so cold that people's urine gets frozen."[36]

London's merchants had recently begun trading with this far-off country which they called their "land of darkness." It was still at the very edge of their slowly expanding consciousness; centuries earlier Alfred, King of Wessex, had received a visitor who had travelled to the far north of Norway where reindeer herdsmen scraped a living, and told fantastic tales. Beyond that, in the frozen wastes of the Arctic, there lay a land where it was forever winter, sailed only by hardy Viking adventurers three centuries earlier and named, with some irony, Greenland. As one approached the coast of this vast landmass, a visitor would find "rising out of the frigid, white-capped sea" a land of always winter that "gazed up at monstrous cliffs of silvery ice shimmering in the brilliant, bitter sunlight."[37]

The people here lived on the very edge of existence, dependent on supplies from across the sea, and towards the end of the last century they would have been among the first humans to notice that the winters were getting harsher. People in London or Alnwick might not have known it yet, but the world was getting colder and a great disaster was unfolding.

2
THE IRON KING

No matter how much I make up, there's stuff in history that's just as bad, or worse.

—George R.R. Martin

It could take up to half an hour for a burning man to die. The Flemish chronicler Froissart's description of a criminal going to the flames during the reign of France's Mad King Charles captures the horror of the punishment:

> They hustled him on. The fire was ready. A gibbet had been set up in the square, and at the foot of it a stake with a heavy iron chain. Another chain hung from the top of the gibbet with an iron collar attached. This collar, which opened on a hinge, was put round his neck, then fastened and hauled upwards so that he should last longer. The first chain was wound round him to bind him more tightly to the stake. He was screaming and shouting. As soon as he was secured to the stake, great heaps of woods were piled against it and set on fire. They flamed up immediately. So was he hanged and burned, and the King of France could have seen him from his window if he had wanted to.[1]

The stake was a terrifying and agonizing way to die, and so reserved for the most heinous of crimes—and there were few as abominable as heresy. And so, in March 1314, the people of Paris had gathered on an island in the center of the city to watch four old warriors being led to their deaths for such a crime. The men were members of the Knights Templar, an order of sworn brothers founded two centuries earlier to protect Christian pilgrims to the Holy Land. Over the years the Templars had grown into a military power fighting a holy war, the most famous order of brothers sworn to take no wives and to defend civilization, recognizable by their white tunics. And yet the brothers had become more than that; with their reputation for honesty and their muscle, and with bases across Europe and the Near East, the group had also begun handling large amounts of money, growing into a sort of international banking organization, enormously powerful and wealthy. But like bankers through the ages they had become resented—and so when the Crusades were lost in 1303, they were inevitably vulnerable to rival powers.

And there was no one more powerful in Europe than the King of France, the country being at that point by far the leading state in the Christian world. France was "supreme," in the words of one historian, "her superiority in chivalry, learning, and Christian devotion was taken for granted, and as traditional champion of the Church, her monarch was accorded the formula of 'Most Christian King.'"[2] French was the language of the ruling class in England, Flanders, and much of Italy, the language of law as far away as Jerusalem, and everywhere in Europe the language of scholars and poets. Kings of French blood sat on thrones from the eastern Mediterranean to the rocky Atlantic coast of Ireland; French words in their thousands found their way into languages across the continent.

Tracing descent from the barbarian Frankish kingdom founded in the ruins of Roman Gaul, the kings of France sat in the royal court in Paris, the center of the Western world. And the current monarch, Philippe *le bel*, "the handsome," was a domineering and icy-cold man intent on expanding his power.

Philippe IV, also known as the Iron King, was likened to a statue for his coldness, or an owl who says nothing but simply stares (the bishop who made that remark soon regretted it). Philippe was a pious man who wore a hair shirt and regularly whipped himself, and "those who met him found his fixed stare, his long silences and his mysterious manner disconcerting."[3] But for all his religious devotion, he was not a man to be crossed, and the punishment dished out to the Templars was not even the worst of his cruelty; other enemies he had flayed alive.

The head of the Capetian dynasty, Philippe's line had begun with Hugh Capet in 987; further back the Franks had once been a Germanic tribe who overran the northern part of Gaul and accepted the submission of the Gallo-Roman population there. Embracing Christianity soon after the fall of the empire, they had steadily adopted the language of the native Latins, a tongue that had evolved into Old French.

The Iron King had been crowned at the cathedral in Reims, north of Paris, like his forefather Clovis eight centuries earlier, where the archbishop handed him the sword once wielded by his ancestor Charlemagne, fastening it to the king's side and reciting "Accipe hunc gladium cun Demi benediction"[4]—Accept this sword with God's blessing. Philippe had now ruled for thirty years and foresaw a strong and long dynasty ahead of him, with three sons grown to manhood and one surviving daughter married to the king of England. They had just two years earlier produced a grandchild for him, a boy called Edward.

Yet the august and sovereign kingdom of France was in financial trouble, and Philippe's ruinous spending led him to search for new sources of revenue. So without even asking the Pope, Clement V, Philippe conspired to have the brotherhood destroyed and to take their wealth. In 1307, he sent secret orders to arrest all fifteen thousand members of the brotherhood in France for crimes, in the words of Philippe's secret orders, "horrible to contemplate, terrible to hear of . . . an abominable work, a detestable disgrace, a thing almost inhuman, indeed set apart from all humanity." Only two dozen escaped that day, Friday the thirteenth.*

Numerous men who had been thrown out of the Knights Templar were brought forward as witnesses, happy to make all sorts of allegations against them. The Templars were accused of selling their souls to the devil, sex with each other and with *succubi*—female demons who supposedly had carnal relations with men—and various other sordid activities. They were also supposed to have drunk a powder made from the ashes of dead comrades and their own illegitimate children.

The crimes were totally implausible even to a credulous public, although most of the Templars confessed to their guilt—but then most people probably would admit to sex with demons after prolonged torture by the Holy Inquisition. Among the methods authorized were the rack, in which the victim was horribly stretched until they confessed; the *strapedo*, whereby a man was raised over a beam by a rope tied to the wrists bound behind his back, until he confessed; or rubbing fat on the soles of the victim's feet and placing them before a fire, until he confessed. Sometimes, as with one knight called Bernardo de Vado, this went wrong and his bones fell out, which was not the intention.

With the *strapedo*, weights were sometimes added to the testicles to make the experience even more painful. Many others were strapped to the rack, and their ankles

---

*The theory that this is the origin of the superstition was only first mentioned in the historic novel *The Iron King*, which was published in 1955, and further made popular by the *Da Vinci Code*. It's probably not true.

and wrists dislocated by a device that slowly pulled joints from sockets. By January 1308, 134 of the leading 138 Templers arrested in Paris had admitted their guilt to a range of charges, among them blasphemy, various sexual degredations, and a ceremony where they worshipped a demon who took the form of a cat. They were also accused of negotiating with the Muslims over the Holy Land, the Christian world being desperate for some explanation for their failure in war.

Grand Master Jacques de Molay eventually confessed to blasphemy but denied sodomy, and a month after this admission the reluctant Pope Clement V sent letters to all European rulers instructing them to arrest Templers in their countries. In Paris, some fifty-four knights were soon put in carts and taken out of the city and burned to death, and the finale came on March 18, 1314 when Molay and the other leading Knights were executed in dramatic style on Paris's Island of Jews (now renamed the "Island of Templars").[5] They had spent seven years in dungeons suffering various tortures by that point.

The knights had built their first Temple in Paris the previous century, and by the time of their destruction it was a fortress in itself, a vast *donjon*, or keep, flanked by four towers just beyond the city walls, and rivalling the Palais Royal in its grandiosity.

Paris was home to as many as 210,000 people, the largest in the Christian West and perhaps four times as big as London (which did not overtake its rival until the eighteenth century). The city boasted six paved streets, including its main thoroughfare Le Grand Rue, as well as Les Halles, where farmers brought produce on Fridays, and St Jacques-la Boucherie, the butchers' quarter, where "fierce Paris wind made little ripples in the pools of animal blood."[6] Nearby was the Champs-Dolet—the "field of suffering and cries,"[7] where the animals were slaughtered, while the Parisian tradition of roasting stray cats alive on Place de Greve lasted until the seventeenth century.

Medieval Paris was a dangerous, noisy, and malodorous place, but the city now boasted its first hospital, the Hôtel-Dieu, where patients slept three or four to a bed and the clothes of the dead were sold at monthly auctions. Its great cathedral Notre-Dame had been completed on the site of a temple to Jupiter dating to the Roman city of Lutetia (although most of the interior today is a nineteenth century restoration, much of the original having been vandalized in the Revolution). Then there was the stunning Sainte-Chapelle, built by Philippe's grandfather Louis IX and containing many of the most priceless relics in Christendom, taken from the Middle East by crusaders. The city's Left Bank was already a student quarter, and home to the famed Paris University, the second oldest in Europe.

Toward the end of the early medieval period, around the turn of the millennium, the Italian cities of Venice, Naples, and Milan were the first to reach population levels seen in antiquity, followed by Florence and the Hanseatic port towns of Germany. But Paris was by now supreme, economically and culturally, and the flowering of what was later called Gothic architecture is testimony to the dominance of northern France, soon imitated across England, Germany, and the rest of Europe.[8]

English medieval history is impossible to understand without France, which exerted a huge cultural influence over its northern neighbor well into the modern era, and so the story of the Seven Kingdoms is not just that of England but rather Britain, France, and Spain in one. In Martin's words, "Westeros is much much MUCH bigger than Britain. More the size (though not the shape, obviously) of South America."[9] Although the Seven Kingdoms all speak the same language, they are varied in their ancestry and racial appearance, while the geography varies hugely; so, while the five most northerly kingdoms correspond to Britain, the Reach strongly resembles France and Dorne is Moorish Spain. Paris is the model for King's Landing, and in the books appears far less tropical than in the television series, which is filmed in Malta and Croatia.[10]

The Reach is:

a vast and fertile land, with a more pleasant climate than much of the rest of the country. It's home to an island called The Arbor that, like the French regions of Burgundy and Bordeaux, makes what is widely considered the best wine in the world. The city of Oldtown is the biggest and most sophisticated in Westeros, much as Paris was for some time the biggest and most sophisticated city in Europe. And the inhabitants of The Reach are invested in chivalry, art and culture to a significantly greater extent than those in the rest of Westeros.[11]

France is big, roughly the area of Texas, while England is about the same as New York state, a quarter of its size. Before modern technology, it took twenty-two days to cross from the north of France to the south, and sixteen from east to west, making it extremely hard for one man to rule.[12] Historically it had therefore been controlled by dukes and counts, with the king in Paris only as overlord.

The Reach is a highly fertile area that provides its neighbors with wheat and wine, just as France did; it is also the home of courtly love and courtly manners, and the trendsetter in fashion, as France was. Northern France, aside from Brittany and western Normandy, is a huge wheat-growing region, among the most fertile areas for this staple on earth, along with England and Denmark.[13] Wheat is the best natural produce for state-formation, being easy to tax and record, so it aided the creation of strong centralized authorities with functioning revenue-raising powers. The Île-de-France, the region around Paris, became a state earlier than almost anywhere else in Europe, although as the country expanded it became harder to maintain control over its more Latin south and Celtic west. France's castles were spoken of being held "in the hand of the crown of France," and French writers specifically used the metaphor of a hand to describe the monarch's power.[14]

According to Carolyne Larrington in *Winter is Coming*: "The Reach is a land of rolling hills and terraced vineyards; the huge river Mander runs through, watering its fertile fields and nurturing the fruit for which the region is renowned."[15] It is "the garden of the Seven Kingdoms, famous for its vines and the wine," with the Sunset Sea to the west and Red Mountains of Dorne to the southeast, and it also produces numerous crops and flowers as well as supplying grain, wine, and livestock. France has eight wine producing regions, mostly in the south (although Champagne, its most northerly, is beyond Paris) and whereas in England wine was an expensive drink reserved for the aristocracy; in Paris even the low born might enjoy it.

The forefathers of the king resided at the royal mausoleum at St Denis, just outside Paris; Philippe's grandfather Louis had had the tombs in the necropolis rearranged, and on one side resided his ancestors the Capetians and on the other his more distant forefathers, the Carolignian dynasty of Charlemagne and the even more ancient Merovignians, who dated all the way back to Clovis, the first of the Franks to abandon the old gods.

The Iron King had constructed a new assembly hall in the city, the Grande Salle, a cavernous room with a gilded ceiling on eight columns with windows colored with the *fleur-de-lis*, the arms of France, and several gigantic fireplaces with seating along the walls. Statues of previous kings looked down on the visitors who came to seek the king's support.

Nearby was the Conciergerie prison, attached to the Palais de Justice and where witnesses were "put to the question," that is brutally tortured; there they endured prolonged sleep deprivation, immersion in cold water, and having water forced down the throat to the point of suffocation. North of the city walls was Montfaucon Hill, where felons were hanged "by the dozen on great stone gallows nearly forty feet high, their rotting corpses left to dangle for weeks as a warning to others."[16] Witnesses and heretics condemned to be burned often wore black, as did the executioner, to mark the gravity of the situation.

Medieval Paris had been largely built by King Philippe Auguste in the late twelfth and early thirteenth century, and much of it lasted until the 1860s and the age of photography. The Palais de la Cité had four great defensive towers, one of them known as the Tour Bonbec, or Blabbing Tower, because that's where people talked after they were put to the question. It was here that, in 1307, Philippe had twenty-eight rioters tortured and then hanged on the eve of Epiphany from elm trees at four entry points to Paris. Philippe also had counterfeiters boiled alive.

Nearby the Grand Chatelet had been founded to keep out the Norsemen and now it became the offices of the *prevot*, or governor, and later regarded as the most sinister of the city's many prisons, the thick walls blocking out the screams of the tortured.

Philippe had put up a large donjon, complete with turrets, on the river, on the center of which was a great tower, forty-five meters in circumference and thirty meters high. It became known as the Louvre, perhaps from *louve*, a female wolf;[17] rebuilt in the eighteenth century, it is today the largest and most visited museum on earth. Opposite the Louvre, on the Left Bank, was the Hôtel de Nesle, a fenced tower that later became a palace. The Iron King turned it into apartments for his three sons and their families, and it was here in the old towers that two of their wives took lovers, sparking a series of disastrous events that reverberated around the kingdom.

Medieval cities were, by our standards, grim. There was a famous story "told of the peasant in the city who, passing a lane of perfume shops, fainted at the unfamiliar scent and was revived by holding a shovel of excrement under his nose."[18] This is no doubt a joke, told by the early moderns to congratulate themselves, but many Parisian streets still testify to the large amounts of excrement once found there—rue Merdeux, rue Merdelet, rue Merdusson, Merdons, Merdiere—and the city reeked with the waste of tanneries and butchers. When he was twenty, Philippe Auguste had gone to the window of his palace and was so appalled by the stench, the roads being little better than open sewers, that he ordered for the first streets to be paved.

Having human fecal matter dropped on your head was an ever-present danger, and it was obligatory for city-dwellers to shout "look out below" three times before dumping the contents of their waste. At ground level there was barely any sunlight, each story of the surrounding buildings jutting out over the one below so that on the fifth-floor people might even shake hands with those on the other side of the street; this method, called jettying, was used to maximize space.

Violence was an ever-present concern for Parisians, and at night the town was sinister and frightening, "despite being patrolled by watchmen who, once clocks arrived, would call, 'One o'clock and all's well!'—and heavy chains were stretched across street entrances to foil the flight of thieves."[19] The area by Notre Dame was assigned as the red-light district, "the warren of mean hovels becoming a bastion of vice, bawds, whores and ponces."[20] Parisian street names such as L'Ecorcherie, or knacker's yard, and Pute-y-Muce, "whore in hiding," described their purpose before the development of modern niceties.

Entertainment came from the *jongleurs* who played a *viele*, a sort of triangle-shaped proto-violin; jongleurs would have travelled all around the known world at a time when most hardly left their village, telling fantastic tales of the east. Under Philippe's grandfather, there had been a cultural flourishing, expressed most strongly in the poem *Roman de la Rose*, an allegorical story told in the form of a dreamy vision. It was the most widely read work of the fourteenth and fifteenth century, and condemned by many for its carnal overtones, the rose symbolising female sexuality.

The poem concerned the "wheel of fortune," an idea that fascinated the medieval mind, at a time when people were helpless in the face of catastrophes, whether from acts of God or princes: "The image of Fortune's wheel took root in the collective consciousness, turning faster and faster as it raised some and secured the downfall of others. The key themes were destabilization and emulation, and 'winning' (*gagner*) became a watchword for the period."[21] The wheel of fortune became a theme obsessing the European mind as the twelfth century gave way to the thirteenth, talked of in men's battles over trade, land—and war.

As the old knights were taken to the stake, there were shouts of "heretic" and "blasphemer," and out of the crowd someone threw a stone at them. The wind from the river had aggravated the mob's anger at the condemned men, but once the fire was lit there was only silence. Then, as the flames lapped up, Jacques de Molay issued a summons to King and Pope ordering them to join him within a year, and put a curse on the king's house.[22] Over the screams and burning embers, he shouted: "Pope Clement, iniquitous judge and cruel executioner, I adjure you to appear in forty days' time before God's tribunal. And you, King of France, will not live to see the end of this year, and Heaven's retribution will strike down your accomplices and destroy your posterity."[23]

The following month the pope died suddenly, aged just fifty; his body was taken to a church to lie in state when lightning struck the building, almost burning it down. In November, Philippe was hunting just outside Paris when he suffered a stroke; he was taken to bed to rest, but succumbed a few days later. Chancellor Guillaume de Nogaret, Philippe's main minister, had expired the previous year of mysterious causes, his tongue thrust out, according to one story.

Philippe the Fair's fateful decision to destroy the Templars and burn their leading men became linked in the popular mind with a period of disaster for the royal family and for France. This was the story behind the popular French historical series, *Les Rois Maudits* (The Accursed Kings) written in the 1950s by Maurice Druon, which Martin credits as a big influence.[24] The books feature Philippe's daughter Isabella, a beautiful, blonde princess commonly known in English history as the She-Wolf of France, a strong-willed and cunning queen who is forced to compete against cruel kings: in this case, her brother Louis and husband Edward, a weak man who is only in his position on account of his birth and sex. Isabella, who takes a lover and loathes her husband, is nevertheless loyal to her own blood relations and will do everything for her young son who must take the throne.

The Templar's curse would also plunge France and England into a bitter, horrific conflict, which, in the Victorian age, became known as the Hundred Years' War, costing three million lives. The century that followed was one of unmitigated tragedy, marked not just by war but by the Black Death, the schism in the Catholic Church, and the first international banking crisis. This Crisis of the Late Middle Ages would culminate, for the English, with defeat and destruction in France at the hands of explosive, terrifying new technology called gunpowder and the country's descent into a dynastic conflict later called the War of the Roses.

But more immediately something more sinister threatened. In the spring following the Iron King's death, temperatures plunged across the known world; in April the rains came down and would not stop, a downpour that lasted until August without pause. The crops failed, and France—and Europe—faced a long winter that would last centuries.

3
THE LION OF ENGLAND

A lion does not concern himself with the opinions of sheep.

—TYWIN LANNISTER

T he Iron King had another enemy more dangerous than the Knights Templar—his cousin Edward, King of England, Duke of Gascony, Hammer of the Scots, and one of the most brutally effective medieval monarchs. *Game of Thrones* is not history, and as historian Dan Jones put it: "It is alt-history, not a reconstruction of a known past. It is historically literate without ever claiming to be history."[1] And yet there are some clear and obvious historical parallels, and one that George R.R. Martin has spoken of is between Tywin Lannister and King Edward I.

Like Tywin Lannister, Edward "Longshanks" was the ultimate medieval warlord, unafraid to inflict any misery when pursuing a war, and using relatives in power games that would further his goal. And yet his cruelty always had a purpose, and though he used torture and murder to further his aims, drove bankers to extinction, and caused misery for the small folk of Wales and Scotland, his violence was never mindless; indeed, he reprimanded those around him who committed atrocities for their own sake.

In the television series, Tywin is played by English actor Charles Dance, who specialises in portraying cold-hearted aristocratic types lacking in sympathy for the lower classes. King Edward was certainly in that bracket, and is probably best known in the popular imagination as the villain of the Mel Gibson historical epic *Braveheart*. In reality, both Edward and his Scottish enemy, Robert the Bruce, were French speakers, and the film is not exactly pedantic in its accuracy—but the king was every bit as brutal as it makes out.

Both Tywin and Edward were very tall; Edward was 6'3", a giant for a time when the average man was no more than 5'7", which is how he got the nickname

Longshanks. He was one of the finest swordsmen of the age, and the earliest Robin Hood stories have him in single combat with the outlaw, such was his renown. Historian Michael Prestwich argued that his "long arms gave him an advantage as a swordsman, long thighs one as a horseman. In youth, his curly hair was blond; in maturity it darkened, and in old age it turned white. His speech, despite a lisp, was said to be persuasive."[2]

The king was described as having "a sinking, or dip, between the chin and under-lip" which "was very conspicuous. Both the lips were prominent; the nose short, as if shrunk . . . there was an unusual fall, or cavity, on that part of the bridge of the nose which separates the orbits of the eyes."[3] He inherited the drooping eyelid of his weak father, King Henry III, although not his temperament.

Quite the opposite, for Edward was famous for his ruthlessness. As a young man, he ordered his attendants to put out the eyes and cut the ears of an adolescent who angered him.[4] Archbishop Corbridge of York had an interview with the king and was so shaken that afterwards he took to his bed and died. In another famous story attached to Edward, a cleric dropped dead with fear upon approaching the king with a request for lower taxation.

Unlike his gentle father, Edward had the characteristic violent rage of the House of Plantagenet. The dynasty originated with Geoffrey of Anjou in the mid-twelfth century, whose descendants later earned their name after the *planta genista* broach he wore.[5] Geoffrey came from a line of warlords in western France so brutal they were considered by some to be descended from Satan himself. His father Fulk IV Rechin, count of Anjou, was excommunicated for abusing his authority by keeping his brother in a dungeon until he went mad. Geoffrey's great-grandfather, Fulk III the Black, son of Geoffrey Greycloak, was a violent pervert of "fiendish cruelty" who had his first wife burned at the stake in her wedding dress and later tortured his own son. Legend had it that that Fulk's grandmother had been Melusine, a dragon disguised as a woman who was one day exposed during Mass, only to fly off shrieking with two of her children.

Melusine was a popular figure of early medieval folklore in western and northern France, often appearing as a fish or snake, seductive and supernatural, but a bringer of evil (like her near-namesake Melisandre, the red woman of Westeros). Melusine often appears in "spinning yarns," stories told by ladies as they spun cloth, and was most likely once a pagan-era water fairy: magical creatures believed to be capable of bringing all sorts of disasters, and who sometimes swapped people's children with changelings. (In the tales of King Arthur, the "Lady of the Lake" is supposed to be a water fairy.)

In reality, the Plantagenet line originated with the earliest counts of Anjou, a region to the south of Normandy that was the birthplace of medieval cavalry; with lush, fertile lands growing wheat and wine in abundance, it was the most heavily contested territory in western Europe, and only the most belligerent of warlords emerged to becomes its rulers. The House of Anjou was one such, as were their bitter enemies the Dukes of Normandy—a rivalry that came to an end with a marriage alliance between Geoffrey of Anjou and Matilda, daughter of Duke Henry. Henry was also King Henry I of England, so the House of Anjou came to rule that land in 1154—but over the next century and a half the line would collapse dramatically with Edward's descendants slaughtering each other.

Lannister and Plantagenet share the same sigil, or as they were called in real life, coat of arms. The Lannister sigil is of one lion rampant, the same as that of the kings of Scotland; in England the symbol of the three lions came about from the union of two duchies, combining Normandy's flag of two lions with the one lion of Aquitaine, the region to the south of Anjou for many years joined to the English crown. By adding two lions to one, Edward's great-uncle Richard the Lionheart had created the famous symbol now most recognizable as that of the England national soccer team and its occasionally marauding supporters.[6]

Lions were well regarded in Europe, and medieval people had strange ideas about the animals, which they believed were heroic and honorable and would not devour injured men.[7] A theory best not tested. The thirteenth century *Bestiary* in the Bodleian Library in Oxford, a sort of medieval guide to the natural world, states that "the merciful nature of lions is confirmed by numerous examples. They will spare men lying on the ground and will lead captives with whom they meet to their home. They will attack men rather than women. They only kill children if they are exceptionally hungry."[8]

This is obviously untrue and anthropomorphizes the animals to give them the qualities most idealized in chivalry—strength, Christian mercy, and deference toward women. But then men would want their family emblems to reflect the traits they hoped to be known for, and so lions appeared on one in six coats of arms, five times as often as the second most popular animal, the eagle. The lion displaced more traditional Germanic imagery, of wolves, bears, and boars, these being the animals most commonly found in the forests of northern Europe. Lions were also popular because of their symbolism in Christianity, especially with the gospel-writer St Mark, a link which continued in the Arthurian legend when Yvain rescues a lion, and most recently in the *Chronicles of Narnia*, in which Aslan represents Christ.

Lions in heraldry were sometimes also referred to as leopards, which at the time were believed to be a cross between a lion and the mythical pard. Edward was regularly compared to both. The *Song of Caerlaverock*, written in praise of Edward's military adventures in Scotland by one of his soldiers, told that "the king confronting his enemies was like the three lions embroidered in gold on the red of his banner—dreadful, fierce and cruel."[9] More commonly he was known as the Leopard because the animals were believed capable of changing their spots, just as Edward would switch sides or do anything to win.

Like Tywin, he was shaped by having witnessed a weak father troubled by unruly vassals. Tytos Lannister faced a rebellion from two houses, Reyne and Tarbeck, and so his elder son Tywin raised an army to defeat Lord Robert Reyne. As Tywin's brother Kevan stated: "Our own father was gentle and amiable, but so weak his bannermen mocked him in their cups. Some saw fit to defy him openly . . . At court they japed of toothless lions."[10] In real life Edward would do the same to take on those who humiliated his father, with brutal effectiveness.

Henry III had become monarch at the age of nine during a civil war between his father King John and the country's leading magnates, in particular a group of Northerners who objected to the king's cruelty and rapaciousness. Unlike John, who openly mocked religion and would sit in church fidgeting, Henry was an extremely holy man who went to Mass several times a *day*, a gentle soul described as "simple" by a chronicler. He was "pious, amiable, easy-going, and sympathetic,"[11] and he cried during religious sermons. He also rebuilt Westminster Abbey, the equivalent of the Great Sept of Baelor, and idolized its founder Edward the Confessor, even naming his first son after him.

But Henry could not inspire fear or respect among his people. One day he and his half-brother Geoffrey de Lusignan and some other noblemen were walking through an orchard when they were pelted with "turf, stones, and green apples" by one of Geoffrey's chaplains, a man "who served as a fool and buffoon to the king . . . and whose sayings, like those of a silly jester . . . excited their laughter."

The chaplain pressed "the juice of unripe grapes in their eyes, like one devoid of sense."[12]

Desperately short of money, Henry III began to meet the most powerful subjects in the realm for informal talks, where they would discuss their grievances and in return grant him money. The meetings were given the name of Parliament in 1236, but between 1248 and 1249, four such parliaments refused Henry any money, complaining about corruption, and the influence of foreigners. Then, in 1258, the country was hit by famine and disease, and while Henry went on a tour of East Anglian shrines, order seemed to be breaking down. A group of rebellious barons were led by the king's brother-in-law, Simon de Montfort, a French nobleman who had arrived in England at the age of twenty-two to claim his peerage after a youth spent fighting a particularly bloodthirsty crusade, this one against heretics in the south of France.

The de Montforts originally hailed from the House of Reginar, a Frankish dynasty of the tenth century who had been dominant in Lothringia, today's Lorraine. And despite his own origins, de Montfort was able to exploit the xenophobia directed at the family of Henry's queen, Eleanor of Provence, who were widely hated. Young de Montfort displayed a terrifying ability to lead and a ruthlessness in battle, as well as religious fanaticism extreme even for the age; he drove the Jews from Leicester with as little pity as his father had slaughtered the Cathar heretics, and Henry III was known to fear him greatly. Simon had even married the king's sister Eleanor despite the monarch's objections.

De Montfort had demanded that the realm should be governed only by "native-born men," and under his radical proposals, Parliament would meet annually, and would not need to be summoned by the king. These terms were unacceptable to the monarch, and, in 1260, the conflict descended into full-on civil war, with de Montfort close to controlling the country—but for Edward.

Henry's elder son had once been close to his uncle, but as de Montfort had become more power-crazed, he had switched sides. At one point, rebels held both the king and his son prisoner, but the prince escaped after asking his jailors if he could try out the horses in the yard, before riding off on one. As he sped off Edward shouted: "Lordlings, I bid you good day. Greet my father well and tell him that I hope to see him soon."[13]

He then negotiated the king's release, and Henry went away for recuperation in Gloucester castle, while Edward arranged negotiations with rebel leader William de

Clare at his camp, with an offer of a compromise. The next day de Clare woke up with severe stomach pains and died, while his brother lost all his hair, fingernails, and toenails. In 1264, the two sides came to blows at the Battle of Lewes, where the royalists flew the dragon banner "that signalled the intention of fighting to the death, taking no prisoners."[14] At the battle were London infantry volunteers described by chroniclers as "bran-dealers, soap-boilers and clowns," and utterly destroyed by Edward's cavalry.[15] However, the battle proved inconclusive, so the following year the two sides met again at the Battle of Evesham, at which Edward displayed a shocking ruthlessness.

Although the rebel leader did not know it, Edward had engaged de Montfort's son in battle and defeated him. De Montfort's barber, an expert at recognizing heraldry, saw Simon's banners in the distance at the front of a large army and informed him that his son was arriving with his men. As it got closer, though, and too late, it became clear that the Leopard was using trickery, and as Edward's forces came closer, the barber panicked and shouted: "We are all dead, for it is not your son as you believed." De Montfort replied calmly, even gleefully: "By the arm of St James, they are advancing well. They have not learned that for themselves but were taught it by me."[16] (Again, this was similar to a trick used by Tywin Lannister in Robert's rebellion, as related in *A Game of Thrones*, when the gates of King's Landing were opened to Tywin in the belief he had come to help. "So the mad king had ordered his last mad act," Ned told Robert.)

Henry, helpless in combat during the battle, was almost killed by his own side who did not recognize him, until his son came to his rescue; but de Montfort was seized from behind by a royalist knight and stabbed to death. His two eldest sons were also killed, and afterwards thirty of his knights were executed on the spot. Edward had his uncle's testicles cut off and hung around his nose, his body cut up into four pieces and sent around the country, and his head delivered to a noblewoman who had helped him escape from de Montfort's imprisonment, as a token of appreciation. In coldly killing his defeated opponents, Edward had broken the rules of medieval warfare, where aristocrats were ransomed, executions were rare, and it was condemned as murder by one contemporary. Edward had begun a precedent, and by the end of this period, the rules of war had disappeared completely, and rival barons were only intent on exterminating their enemies.

And yet just as *The Rains of Castamere* immortalised Tywin's eradication of House Reyne, so *The Song of Lewes* praised the royal heir and compared him to a lion, "because we saw that he was not slow to attack the strongest places, fearing the onslaught of none, with the boldest valour making a raid amidst the castles." It also gave warning to any other uppity house that "if Fortune's moving wheel would stand still for ever; wherein let the highest forthwith know that he will fall, and that he who reigns as lord will reign but a little time."[17]

Unrest continued in much of the countryside for the next couple of years, and it was during this period, when defeated aristocrats known as the "Disinherited" were blamed for numerous atrocities, that the Robin Hood legend was first set. Yet soon the realm was pacified, and the monarch and his son in any case gave the rebels much of what they wanted; in 1275, the new king Edward signed the Statute of Westminster formalizing Parliament, and for the first time, commoners—knights and burgesses (city men)—were allowed into the Privy Council, the king's inner circle of advisers.

Like Tywin, Edward was a dedicated husband who did not even have mistresses; Tywin is devoted to his wife, his cousin Joanna Lannister, and their wedding day is supposed to be one of few in which he smiled openly. After she died giving birth to their son, Tyrion, he never smiled again. Likewise, Edward and his beloved Queen Eleanor were cousins, both great-grandchildren of her namesake Eleanor of Aquitaine. The couple were betrothed when he was fifteen and she just nine, a marriage brokered to make an alliance with Castile, to the south of France, but it was an enduring romantic attachment unusual for the age. When she died, in 1291, he was so devastated that he had twelve "Eleanor crosses" built by the route her coffin had taken from Lincoln down to the village of Charing, three of which still survive. (Although today's Charing Cross, by Trafalgar Square in London, is a replica.)

And like Tywin, Edward would have a violently difficult relationship with his son, who was an outcast in medieval life.

The royal couple's marriage was marked by tragedy. In *Game of Thrones*, Cersei reflects on losing her child, who unlike her later offspring is actually Robert's, and such misery was the norm. In medieval Europe infant mortality was widespread—indeed it was very unusual for a couple to not lose a child or two. Edward and Eleanor had sixteen, of whom only six survived childhood and just four outlived the king; of these, seven died in their first year. Even for the wealthiest of aristocrats, life was unbearably tragic.

Until the early eighteenth century, when infant mortality rates began to fall in western Europe, childhood was bleak and often short; indeed, child death rates in seventeenth century Europe were no better than in hunter-gatherer societies.[18] In this period, between 30 and 50 percent of people died before the age of five, the bulk of those being in the first year of life.[19] Today the rate in the industrialised world is 0.1 per one thousand.

And even queens were not immune to such horror. Edward's mother Eleanor of Provence had nine children, of whom just five survived, and Margaret Tudor, wife of Scotland's James IV, had just one child make it out of six, and her daughter-in-law Mary of Guise saw only one in five live to adulthood. The most luckless monarch was Queen Anne, who died in 1714, after enduring seventeen pregnancies, but giving birth to only five live children—of whom none survived childhood.

When the couple were young, Eleanor made a present to her husband of a French translation of *De Re Militari*, the Roman writer Vegetius's treaties on war. The most popular and well-read martial manual of the time, this *Concerning Military Matters* was required reading for anyone who wished to be a warrior and, in 1270, Edward duly went off on crusade, taking his wife and two young children with him. While there he almost died in Haifa, in modern-day Israel, after being seriously wounded by an Assassin, a member of a secretive death-cult; the dagger was poisoned, and his life was only saved when his wife sucked out the poison.[20] Edward was in Sicily in 1272, on his return, when he learned that his father had died, but it took the new king almost two years to get home, stopping off in France along the way to take part in a tournament that almost killed him.

Edward was a terrifying figure whose men feared and respected him, even if they did not love him. Unafraid to get his hands dirty, he would sleep out in the cold with his troops on campaign; in one later offensive, while besieging Conwy in Wales, he shared his one barrel of wine with his soldiers: Edward was in his fifties or sixties by then, an old man for the times.

His long reign would be dominated by wars across Britain, first in Wales and then in Scotland, although the simmering hostilities with France also intensified. Conflict had begun in the west after the Prince of Wales, Llywelyn ap Gruffydd, refused to turn up to Edward's coronation because the King of England had given shelter to his arch-enemy, Dafydd, who also happened to be his brother. Wales was for most Englishmen still a wild and strange place; Anglo-Normans had been encroaching on the south of the country for two hundred years, but in deepest Wales where Llywelyn's rule held sway, the old laws called *Hywel Dda* still applied, with disputes settled by blood feuds. The country was extremely poor, even compared to England let alone France or Italy, and its mountainous terrain made it difficult to unite, and yet Llywelyn had come to extend his lordship over most of the land.

Edward raised an army and marched west, crushing opposition and building a series of castles, most of which still stand, among them Caernarfon, Flint, Rhuddlan, Conwy, Criccieth, and Aberystwyth. These fortresses could be defended by as few as twenty soldiers and, with stairs that led directly to the sea, could withstand a siege for several years. Slowly, but steadily, they ensured English domination of the country, which had already been heavily colonized under the reigns of Edward's predecessors.

Llywelyn had married Edward's cousin Eleanor without his permission and so in response Edward kidnapped her, then allowed her to wed the Welshman when it became expedient; but after she died in childbirth he had her daughter Gwenllian jailed, in case she might be used by his enemies. She remained a prisoner her entire life, dying at the age of fifty-four—but with the royal blood of Wales and England in her veins she was a threat to Edward. Also imprisoned with her in far-off Lincolnshire, on the North Sea coast, were the daughters of Llywelyn's brother Dafydd. His two young sons were not so lucky: they were sent to Bristol castle where one, another Dafydd, died after four years and the other, Owain, was placed in a cage of wood bound with iron. He was never released.

By the end of 1282, all Welsh resistance was over; Llywelyn himself died in December that year, at the hands of an English soldier in Powys but Dafydd had a more gruesome fate.

For many centuries the first thing that would have greeted visitors to London was the sight of decapitated heads, either at the Tower or at the southern entrance of the bridge, a reminder of the king's dreadful power. It was Edward who had built a moat around the Tower and also erected its most notorious spot, Traitor's Gate, where heads were placed on spikes.

Among those now on display was Dafydd, captured in 1282 and convicted of treason, murder, sacrilege, and plotting against the king. As punishment, the Welshman underwent four corresponding punishments for his four crimes, respectively dragged by horses, hanged, disembowelled, and quartered. Before he was dead, his intestines were slashed from his body and burned in front of him, and his corpse was then sent to various English cities, leaving only his head to rot at the Tower of London, along with his brother's.

In 1284, Edward formally absorbed Wales into the Realm, ending its independence forever. To celebrate, the king held an Arthurian-style Round Table celebration, presenting himself as heir to the mythical British king and the rightful ruler of all Britain. It is recorded that the party was so popular, with attendees coming from all over the country and keen not to snub the Leopard, that the floor gave way, killing many.

Dafydd's grim fate was a sort of joke, a mockery of ancient Welsh tradition. For almost a millennium, since the Angles and Saxons had crossed the North Sea and driven the native Britons into the mountainous west, there had been prophecies about a Welsh king once again looking over London. Finally, to Edward's grim amusement, it had proven true.

4
THE FIRST MEN

Past a certain point, all the dates grow hazy and confused, and the clarity of history becomes the fog of legend.

—HOSTER BLACKWOOD

The island of Britain had once been settled by three brothers, the eldest of whom, Locrinus, had been given what is now England. This was at least Edward's argument for why he, as successor to Locrinus, should rule all Britain, although the myth was largely the work of twelfth century cleric Geoffrey of Monmouth. Geoffrey had also chronicled the story of a great king named Arthur, who had led the Britons against the Saxons, but of much else of their origins people knew very little.

Lying off the far western edge of a gigantic super-continent, the island of Great Britain is just a thousand miles from the Arctic Circle, and to the first civilized people who made the journey across the chilly English Channel it must have appeared inhospitably cold, wet, and covered in fog; to others who heard of it the land was filled with monsters and Cyclops or even cannibals. Much of this folklore would remain in the collective subconscious long after the forests had been cleared and roads and cities laid down where paths and villages had once stood.

Great Britain is by far the largest island in an archipelago often called the British Isles and which consists of over six thousand islands in total, of which 132 are inhabited, the least populated being St Kilda, off the Outer Hebrides, which has a summertime population of just fifteen.[1] Britain is defined by two geographic regions, the low lying terrain of the south and east, similar in geology to the adjacent land on the continent, and suitable for arable farming and crops, especially wheat, and possessing the vast bulk of the island's good farmland; and the upland, mountainous regions of Scotland, Wales, and the north and west of England, the highlands and islands, where the rock is much older and the climate harsher. Battered by the storms of the Atlantic Ocean, here hardy races clung on, etching out a living in fishing, sheep-raising, or occasionally raiding, and exporting excess population, often to fight in other peoples' wars. Many of these distinctive cultures, or traces of them, survived into the modern era, always facing an onslaught from the dominance of London and the south. This division has defined British history.

To those living through the cousins' war, the history of the island stretched back into a distant and murky past. Men knew of different peoples who had once walked the land, and that a great race called the Romans had conquered it, supermen capable of every feat imaginable. These Latins had left large stone buildings across Britain, but many people considered them to have been a breed of giants, and some actively avoided Roman buildings as they thought them haunted.

It was known that the original inhabitants of the island were the Welsh, who still occupied the mountainous western regions, in many parts of it living by their old laws; people knew that their ancestors had once worshiped many gods but had been successively converted to the new faith, first during the Roman period and later when the Saxon invaders abandoned their old gods.

Beyond that any common understanding of the past would have been told by men like Geoffrey of Monmouth. In the more remote parts of the realm, they might have believed legends of green men and fairies and dwarves and other such creatures that had been passed down in folklore. It was only with modern technology, as well as modern historical methods, that we have come to know more extensive details about ancient Britain and some of the people who lived there.

We know of one young man, no older than his mid-twenties, who died from repeated blows to the head from a blunt instrument, the killers leaving his body in a secluded place where it could not be found. Of the victim's life we can tell very little, except that he had eaten horsemeat on his last days on earth, and that he died a rather unpleasant death. He lived in Britain in the seventy-second century before Christ, ending his days in the deep underground Gough's Cave in Cheddar Gorge, Somerset sometime around 7150BC.

As the man's body was not buried or burned, it's possible his family never found him, and there it remained, for nine thousand years, while above the cave the world transformed in an unimaginable way, night falling and sun rising over and over again, some three million times, before he would be discovered. Six millennia later he would have found the people using materials he might find incomprehensible but which we would recognise as iron or bronze; another millennium and people would have spoken a language totally alien to him but which a linguistic expert would identify as Brythonic, the ancestor of modern Welsh; another thousand years and he would perhaps see two-story buildings and men and women living in settled groups of dwellings that might properly be called villages. The tongue would have been mystifying to him, but we might pick up the odd word and understand it as something vaguely Germanic—*Anglisc*, or Old English. Their language, technology, and worship would have been utterly alien to Cheddar Man, but these people were his descendants nonetheless, and the ancestors of modern Britons.

The gorge had been formed one million years before when melting glaciers dissolved the underground limestone to create a chasm almost 450 feet deep. Gough's Cave had not been discovered, or at least rediscovered, until 1837, when a man called George Cox was digging out limestone close to his water mill and came across an underground world filled with stalactites and stalagmites, some of them brightly colored due to the iron oxide in the water that formed them. Because of their unique properties the caves are lit in a particular way, with pools also reflecting the rocks above them. Close to the seaside town of Weston-Super-Mare, Gough's Cave became a popular tourist spot from the Victorian era, and among the many people who visited were a couple on honeymoon in 1916; the groom, a young man about to set off for the western front named John Tolkien, was so affected that he used the gorge as the inspiration for Helm's Deep in his later masterpiece *The Lord of the Rings*.

Thirteen years earlier workmen in the area had stumbled upon some bones in the cave, and these remains turned out to be the oldest complete skeleton in Britain. They were brought to the Natural History Museum in London, where they lie today. However, the story did not end there; in the 1950s came the invention of carbon dating, which allows scientists to pinpoint the age of fossils, as well as the discovery of DNA in 1951. But it was the isolation in the 1980s of mitochondrial DNA, a particular type of the genetic material that is passed unaltered from mother to daughter, which proved the most interesting insight into Cheddar Man's place in British history. In 1996 a team making a documentary about the ancient corpse carried out blood tests in a nearby school and found two locals carrying the exact same mDNA, suggesting a direct descent in the female line from a recent ancestor of the caveman. Cheddar Man died, but his family lived on.

This corpse and its unlikely afterlife offer a glimpse of the first men who came to Britain, and the British history and folklore that inspired George R.R. Martin and his creation. In the back story, recalled in passages during the first five books, various characters explain that the first inhabitants of the island were the Children of the Forest, a human-like species who dwelled in caves and lived off the land; they were said to have magical powers and believed the weirwood trees were deities, "the nameless gods," whom they would join in death. The Children were smaller than men, "dark and beautiful," freckled and with large ears, and came to the island during "the dawn age" at the very beginning of time. In this era there were also giants, around twelve feet in height, who "knew of no better tools or weapons than branches pulled from trees," and "had no kings and no lords, made no homes save in caverns or beneath tall trees, and they worked neither metal nor fields."[2] The Children worked with a metal, *obsidian* or dragonglass, a form of frozen glass used to kill white walkers.[3] Their religious caste, called the Greenseers, were "the wise men of the children" who could supposedly see through the eyes of the carved weirwood. Educated Westerosi at the time of the War of the Five Kings are skeptical of this claim, just as they are of much ancient tradition and lore.

War began when the First Men arrived on Westeros twelve thousand years before the current era, via the Arm of Dorne, a land crossing linking the continents. The First Men used weapons of bronze and brought with them strange new animals such as horses, and over a period of decades or maybe centuries migrated north and increased in number, spreading across the continent. They chopped down the forest, including the sacred weir trees of the indigenous people, and in a doomed attempt to stop the migration, the Children of the Forest used dark magic to flood the world, but to no avail; the invaders burned the weirwoods and the two groups went to war. This is what some people in Westeros supposedly believe at any rate; better-educated chroniclers suggest that flooding the Arm would have been beyond the capabilities of the Children, and that it was mostly a natural cataclysm similar to the Doom of Valyria.[4]

Armed with bronze swords, the First Men triumphed, but eventually a pact was reached in which the Children stayed in the forest and the First Men had the rest of the island, agreeing not to burn any more weir trees; the treaty was signed in the presence of the sacred trees as witnesses. For four thousand years, the two groups were said to have lived in peace, and the newcomers even adopted their tree gods. Under the rule of the First Men, Westeros was divided into seven kingdoms, which survived even after newcomers conquered all but one.

The First Men used runes and spoke a harsh-sounding language, the Old Tongue, that survives beyond the Wall and in given names. Although much of their culture was lost, it is known that they followed the laws of hospitality, that justice was meted out by a blood price, and that they worshipped the Lady of the Waves and the Lord of the Skies, who made thunder.

However, the less educated people also believe that among the First Men were skinchangers who could communicate with the beasts and control them; in Martin's world, myth and magic are rarely in people's everyday lives, but sit somewhere in the back of their minds. There is also the legend of the green men, old tales about creatures with dark green skin and horns.

The pact between the Children and the First Men was ended after four millennia by the arrival of the Andals, blond-haired people who hailed from a peninsula in the north of Essos by the Shivering Sea. They used iron, and conquered six of the kingdoms, destroying the last remnants of the Children; only the North held out, and although part of the Realm, it still maintains much of the culture of the First Men, including aspects of its religion.

In turn, new invaders came to Westeros, the Valyrians, also originating in Essos, who had crossed the sea after their homeland was destroyed in a cataclysm. They were led by Aegon I Targaryen and his two sister-wives, with the aid of three dragons, and began their conquest with Dragonstone, a small island off south-east Westeros. Alongside Aegon on his daring and risky invasion was his half-brother Orys Baratheon, ancestor of King Robert. Aegon allowed lords who bent the knee to keep their land, but those that didn't he destroyed, and he won Westeros with extreme brutality. The conqueror established King's Landing, which developed into a bustling, if squalid, city between the conquest and the current era, although its population had at one point been depleted by the Great Spring Sickness, which had killed four in ten. Four centuries later, the Targaryens and Baratheons would be on opposing sides in the War of Five Kings.

Just as the people of Martin's world live on an island with memories of strange and mysterious peoples who still inhabit the wilder edges of their world, so did the people of medieval England.

Anatomically modern people had inhabited the island before the Ice Age arrived 10,000 years before Christ—the oldest human remains in Britain belong to the Red Lady of Paviland, which were found in south Wales and date to 33000BC. The bones were discovered in 1823 by a vicar who sent them to William Buckland, a professor of geology at Oxford; Prof Buckland was a noted scholar, but also a creationist who believed the world to be no more than a few thousand years old, and so seeing the remains covered in red ochre (a naturally colored type of dirt) and adorned with what looked like elephant-bone jewelry, he concluded it to be the remains of a Roman-era prostitute. In fact, it was not elephant bone, but mammoth, and the Red Lady was a man who lived long before the dawn of history, as DNA tests from the 1990s finally established.

But these first inhabitants left nothing but their bones. Around eleven thousand years ago the earth cooled down and life became impossible for the inhabitants of Britain; if any survived, it would have been by moving south to beyond the Alps. North of that no human life could exist.

Giant glaciers arose and for thousands of years, until 6000BC, Great Britain was joined to the continent by a peninsula known to us as Doggerland (from the Dutch *dogger*, fishing boat), stretching from East Anglia to what is now the coastline of Denmark, Germany, and the Netherlands. It was over this stretch of land, and the ice sheet that covered the Channel, that small bands of people arrived from the tenth millennium BC until the first, their obscure tongues clinging on to rocky outposts much later; today, ships in the North Sea still occasionally pick up the bones of mammoth and other animals that once walked this land. (British people will recognize "Dogger" as one of the shipping regions mentioned on BBC public radio.)

The village of Thatcham in Berkshire, in the Thames Valley to the west of London, lays claim to be the oldest continually-inhabited place in Britain, with the remains of a settlement dating back as far as ten thousand years being found, and evidence of continued later Iron Age inhabitation.

The most outstanding—and most famous—monument of ancient Britain is Stonehenge, built on Salisbury plain and completed around 2600BC. It is possibly a sundial (or a burial site), but remains enigmatic, and whatever its purpose, it was important. It

was a very violent world, according to the evidence from skeletons,[5] and in among
hunter-gatherer peoples studied in the modern era the proportion of males who die as
a result of homicide is usually between 15 and 60 percent, as opposed to about 0.4 for
Americans today.[6]

Over the millennia, several waves of people crossed over, nine groups in total, some
up the coast of Iberia and France and others from across the North Sea. Agriculture
first reached Britain around 4000BC, and by 3700BC had penetrated into every region
of the British Isles.[7] Cheddar Man's people used flint, but newcomers arrived with
bronze in approximately 2500BC, a group now called the Beaker People. Current
genetic research suggests that, since the Beaker people replaced 90 percent of the gene
pool of Britain, they probably did not make very accommodating neighbors.[8]

The Beaker People were part of the Megalithic Culture of the Atlantic; those living along a stretch of coastal Europe from Portugal to Denmark, and across southern
Britain and Ireland, shared a way of life that involved the erection of standing stones,
for what purpose we cannot tell; one can still walk among them in deserted parts of
south-west Ireland in spots that feel vaguely haunted.

When one people replace or assimilate another, they often keep the original names
for rivers, hills, and other natural features, and many topographical words are the last
surviving remnants of the indigenous European languages that faced the onslaught
from the east, although sometimes terms from different languages would be joined to
form a place name. Torpenhow Hill in Cumberland on the border with Scotland is a
good example, believed to be a quadruple tautology—*Tor* and *penn* both mean hill in
ancient British languages, as does *howe* in Old Norse.

Aside from these few place names, the languages of Cheddar Man and the Beaker
People and all the other British dialects that would have been spoken are lost to us. It
is estimated that nine successive groups colonized the island before the arrival of the
Romans, at least based on DNA evidence, and each would have spoken their own
language, probably a number of them.

From 4000 BC Indo-European speakers began to sweep across Europe, reaching
its western shores around 1000 BC. The Indo-Europeans were pastoralists—
cattle-herders—from what is now southern Russia and may even have developed a
genetic advantage over the natives through a mutation that allowed adults to ingest
milk (today this phenotype is found in almost all western Europeans, but is rare in
many other parts of the world). These new people, who brought iron to Britain, were

later called the Celts, and archaeological evidence suggests they arrived by 600 BC at the latest, on an island which already had up to one million people.

They were possibly small in number, but as their language came to dominate one can assume that they did too; they built fortresses and conducted warfare with great ferocity, as the evidence from such sites as Fin Cop in Derbyshire shows.[9] The different groups may have shared regions, as we know later peoples did, villages of indigenous people on one side of the river and newcomers on the other. They could have co-existed for many years, perhaps even centuries, but at some point, the indigenous people were absorbed by the Celtic speakers and their culture vanished.

By the time of the Romans' arrival, there were two major and related Celtic linguistic groups on the archipelago, the Brythonic and Goidelic, the former's language being the ancestor of Welsh, Cornish, and Breton, and the latter of Irish, Scots, and Manx Gaelic. There was also Pictish, spoken in what is now central and northern Scotland, which remains a mystery; it was perhaps a mixture of Celtic and a pre-Indo-European language now extinct.[10] The Picts wore paint and for this reason the Irish called them "the people of the designs," or *Cruithni*.

Most of what we know of pre-history is through bones and stones, but at the time the Houses of Lancaster and York were fighting over the realm, people had a very different idea of the past, and this is reflected in the chronology of Westeros. In *The History of the Kings of Britain*, written by Geoffrey of Monmouth in 1138 during a previous war between two houses, it is explained that the first inhabitants of the island were giants; they were followed by Trojans who fled that city after its destruction, led by Aeneas's descendent Brutus, who sailed all the way from the eastern Mediterranean to Britain, landing on the southern coast and dividing the island between his three sons. His eldest son Locrinus ended up ruling the whole island, followed by ninety-eight successors, until the arrival of the Romans. Geoffrey was, to put it kindly, rather liberal with the truth.

And so in Martin's world, the chronology may be mythical, too; people talk of family rivalries going back thousands of years, yet in real life it was commonly believed in Tudor England that the Romans had built the Tower of London 1,500 years before; in fact, the Normans had, only four centuries previously.[11] So when members of the Stark family claim they have been in conflict with the Boltons for thousands of years, it is possible that they mean hundreds.

Likewise, the Wall of Ice is believed to be eight thousand years old, but it probably isn't. Samwell Tarly finds there have only been 674 commanders of the Night's Watch, not 997 as is commonly believed, suggesting the chronology is all mixed up. He says that, "The First Men only left us runes on rocks, so everything we think we know about the Age of Heroes and the Dawn Age and the Long Night comes from accounts set down by septons thousands of years later. There are archmaesters at the Citadel who question it. Those old histories are full of kings who reigned for hundreds of years, and knights riding around a thousand years before they were knights."[12] History in Westeros is full of anachronisms, just as real folk memory is.

Educated Westerosi believe their ancestors to be credulous, just as some Renaissance humanists did in late medieval Europe. So while educated people in the Middle Ages would not have known about the Beaker People, they understood that stories told of Brutus and one-eyed giants were most likely untrue. Some of Geoffrey of Monmouth's contemporaries, highly-educated men with access to a wide range of sources, believed him to be an outright liar. William of Newburgh, a twelfth century monk from Yorkshire, said that "only a person ignorant of ancient history would have any doubt about how shamelessly and impudently he lies in almost everything." And yet Geoffrey's work was by the far the most read account of the time, and informed people's views of the past; there are two hundred surviving manuscripts of his Latin-edition *History of the Kings of Britain*, more than all English and French texts of the period combined, an indication of how popular it was.

And it is only with the Greeks and Romans that Britain emerges from pre-history. The Brythonic peoples referred to their country as *Alban*, or Albion, a Celtic word meaning white, but to the civilized Phoenicians and Greeks, the most technologically advanced people of the time, they were the *Cassiterides*, or Tin Islands, a strange and foggy land located on the very edge of the known world (although "the Cassiterides" may not have referred to Britain but somewhere in France or Spain, no one entirely knows). Although the fifth century BC historian Herodotus referred to them, the first civilized man to actually visit was Pytheas, a Greek sailor from what is now Marseilles. In 330BC Pytheas travelled all the way to the coast of northern Scotland, a fantastically risky voyage in which he saw whales in the ferocious "dead sea" (as the shivering North Sea was called by Mediterranean people) and a land where the sun shone just a few hours a day. Pytheas had come into contact with some of the natives, virtual savages in comparison to the Greeks, and it was their fondness for tattoos that inspired him to give it a new name, Pretani, Pretannike or Brettaniai—Britain.

5
"YOU'RE NO SON OF MINE"

Why is it always the innocents who suffer most, when you high lords play your game of thrones?

—VARYS

In Scotland a child sat on a throne, and not just a child but a seven-year-old girl, Margaret, "Maid of Norway." Raised in her mother's bitterly cold homeland in the far north, in 1290 the young queen finally made the perilous journey from Scandinavia to Scotland to claim the throne, as the last surviving grandchild of Alexander III. Margaret's mother, another Margaret, had died in childbirth while both her uncles had perished young, and then her grandfather had broken his neck four years earlier riding home to spend his first night with a young French wife.

Life at sea was grim and terrifying. On board no one washed or shaved, everything was damp, and the cabin stank of urine, excrement, vomit, and rat.[1] According to historian Laurence Bergreen, "Even a peaceful voyage was remarkably distasteful, uncomfortable, and dangerous. The dank, crowded ships stank of rotting food and human waste. Vermin ran riot, and passengers . . . had to coexist with cockroaches, lice, and rats."[2] It was unbearably hot in summer and cold in winter, and always cramped. If you were very rich you might have a panelled cabin with a hammock; if you were poor the journey was not going to be fun. There was always water in the hold, and the onboard urinals, made of terracotta, often overturned, although many chose to relieve themselves overboard, and it was not uncommon for men to fall into the sea during the night. Since few could swim at the time, most were never seen again.

Sailing after sundown was especially dangerous as lighthouses were extremely rare, there being only one in fourteenth century England, at St Catherine's Oratory on the Isle of Wight, built in 1313; in fact, people in coastal areas were more likely to put out false signals in order to purposely wreck a boat and steal all its cargo rather than help. But as the average speed of a land journey was eight to ten miles a day, and brigands were more of a problem than pirates, sea travel was more practical, even within Britain. Travellers from Cambridge to York, a 150-mile land journey between two inland cities, were known to travel by boat up and down rivers and via the North Sea, hugging the coast.

Seafaring was most of all dangerous; as a matter of course, voyagers would make an offering to a saint before setting off, most commonly St Christopher, patron of travellers, and many wore pendants of the saint. Men would normally make wills before going on a boat, even for relatively short journeys, as no one could tell what the sea gods had in store. Sailors were especially superstitious and might throw someone overboard if convinced they were unlucky.

Alas fate was cruel to the young Maid of Norway and near the Orkney Islands, then still ruled by Norway, she fell ill from seasickness, and died, even before she had set foot in her new kingdom. This brought to an end a house that had ruled Scotland for two and a half centuries, and threw the crown into chaos, with thirteen different claimants.

Edward had planned for Margaret to marry his youngest son, another Edward, and thereby unite the crowns. After a two-year inquiry in which the King of England assumed leadership, Edward helped impose one claimant, John Balliol, Lord of Barnard Castle in Durham, an important point which blocked any Scottish invasion from Cumberland to Yorkshire. The Balliols were more English than Scottish, which was indeed the whole point of choosing him. His rival was Robert the Bruce, fifth Lord of Annandale, who had once fought with Edward against de Montfort; when he died in 1295, the cause was taken up by his son of the same name. Like many aristocrats even north of the border, the Bruces were once Normans, originally from Brix, south of Cherbourg, the name being de Brus at the time. However, unlike in England where the Normans came as conquerors, successive kings of Scotland had invited them to settle as a new aristocratic military caste.

Bruce's young son and namesake, the seventh Lord of Annandale, was still an adolescent but already considered one of the best tourney knights in Britain. He would have grown up trilingual, speaking the Norman French of the aristocracy and the Scots dialect of English spoken in the south of Scotland, as well as the Gaelic of the north. Unfortunately, the newly-installed council under Balliol was dominated by the Bruce's hereditary enemies, the Comyn family, a clan from the central Highlands—originally from Bosc-Bénard-Commin in Normandy—and in 1295 they used their power to seize all the Bruce castles.

Yet trouble was brewing for King Edward at the other end of his realm. His inept grandfather John had lost most of his continental possessions to Philippe Auguste, but the two kingdoms had enjoyed good relations since, largely because the wives of England's Henry III and France's Louis IX, Eleanor and Margaret of Provence, were sisters. However, those decades of peace were shattered in 1295 when the Iron King attacked Gascony, and when Edward demanded the Scots help him fight his war they instead rose up, storming Carlisle Castle. The young Bruce, despite his father's warnings, joined the rebellion.

Edward, with loans from the Riccardi and Frescobaldi families of Florence, invaded Scotland with five thousand heavy cavalry and ten thousand footsoldiers. First the English stormed Berwick, where Edward had several hundred of the city's people massacred, with countless bodies hung by the city's walls as an example to any other would-be rebels. The king paid the townsfolk a penny a day to bury the numerous victims.

After defeating Balliol at Dunbar, Edward forced him to undergo a ceremonial "degradation" at Montrose with the Lion of Scotland torn from his surcoat, after which Scotland was ruled by a series of guardians. The king took with him back to London the Stone of Scone, or Stone of Destiny, a rock which was supposed to have been brought from Ireland by the first Scots king, and on which Scottish monarchs were crowned. It remained in London, inside a wooden coronation chair, for the next seven centuries.

The Scots were not only weaker than the English, but were also far more clannish and divided, and yet from time to time a charismatic leader will emerge in such a society, a sort of Mance Rayder figure; the Gauls had Vercingetorix to lead them against the Romans, and from 1297, the Scots had William Wallace. From the southwest of the country, Wallace's family had originally been Britons—Wallace is related to "Welsh"—but little else is known about his origins except that he had been involved in criminal activity of various sorts. And yet he was to launch a guerrilla war that took a huge toll on the southern invaders, and at the Battle of Stirling Bridge in late 1297 inflicted a crushing defeat on the English.

Wallace probably devised the "schiltrom" which involved a tight circle of soldiers crammed with 1,500 spearmen—the front rank knelt down with twelve-foot spears held at a forty-five-degree angle, and those behind pointed theirs forward at chest height. At Stirling Bridge, the English were also caught with the river Forth at their backs, hemmed in and isolated in small pockets where they were surrounded by a hundred Scottish spearman. The Earl of Surrey, watching the massacre, panicked and retreated; another English commander, the hated Hugh de Cressingham, was killed and Wallace afterwards had him flayed—as he had supposedly done to Scottish prisoners—and turned his skin into a belt.

The English had ravaged crops across the south of Scotland and so with starvation overcoming them in 1298, Wallace led his men across the border to raid Northumberland. However, Philippe the Fair had now been bought off and deserted his allies, and the Scots were soon defeated at Falkirk; Wallace abdicated his leadership role and disappeared into the countryside.

As Edward's war progressed the young Bruce had been drawn to the rebels, despite his father's disapproval; then, in 1299, his feud with John Comyn accelerated with Comyn seizing him by the throat in an argument. But when Edward invaded again in 1301, his sixth excursion north, Bruce submitted, and by the time Edward launched his largest invasion yet, in 1303, all the leading Scots had bent the knee—with the exception of William Wallace.

Edward needed to capture Stirling, the largest town in the center of Scotland, giving whoever held it control over the whole country. In 1304, he laid siege to Stirling castle where he unveiled "Warwolf," one of his trebuchets, terrifying war machines which also appear in Westeros, where they have names such as the Six Sisters. (In real life they also had colorful titles, and during the Third Crusade Richard the Lionheart had two trebuchets which he named "God's Own Catapult" and "Bad Neighbor.") Siege machines in the tenth and eleventh century were basically giant catapults, but by the start of the thirteenth they had been replaced by the trebuchet, first in northern Italy and then elsewhere in western Europe. Trebuchets had a range of up to three thousand feet (three hundred metres) and could fire weights up to 750 lbs (sixty kilograms). First used in China, they were brought to western Europe via Byzantine Greece, and are mentioned by the *Strategikon* military manual of Emperor Maurice in AD539.

This period also saw the development of battering rams, cats and other machines designed to storm castles, as well as mobile sheds called tortoises which would give attackers some measure of protection from arrows. (Battering rams often had the head of a ram painted on them.) Besiegers would also use a tall wooden tower to overlook and attack a castle, requiring some very brave men to jump across and hope that they made it and that their comrades did not leave them. Siege or "counter-castles" were also built next to castles; Henry I besieged Arundel in the south of England in 1102 with such a temporary building.

At one point, a crossbow bolt went through Edward's clothes while he was riding around the walls, and stones from a trebuchet scared his horse which threw him. And yet, even when the Scots submitted, he refused to accept their surrender for four days, so he could continue battering its walls with his machines, all the while threatening its defenders with disembowelment. As the war went on, Edward's ruthlessness and cruelty toward the Scots intensified, to the point of mania. The king even had his own version of Gregor Glegane, a man-mountain called Sir John Fitz Marmaduke, and up in Scotland commanded him: "You are a bloodthirsty man, I have often had to rebuke you for being too cruel. But now be off, use all your cruelty, and instead of rebuking you I shall praise you."[3]

Wallace was captured the following year, betrayed by Sir John Menteith, a fellow Scotsman, who apparently blamed him for the death of his brother (and considering Wallace's record, that is not implausible). According to legend, Menteith revealed his enemy's location to English soldiers by turning a loaf of bread upside down in a tavern where Wallace was staying.

Wallace's execution was even more gruesome than Dafydd's. Dragged through the streets of London, he was half-strangled in a noose before being castrated and disembowelled, his guts and genitalia burned in front of him. Finally, his suffering was ended with the axeman's swing and his body hacked to pieces, his bloody remains sent north to the border towns of Newcastle and Berwick, as well as Stirling and Perth in Scotland. Only his head remained in London, mounted on the bridge as an expression of the king's power.

The elder Robert the Bruce had died in 1304, but Edward deeply distrusted his son; and while a truce was agreed between John Comyn and young Bruce, Edward had already ordered his arrest. However, Edward's son-in-law Ralph de Monthermer, a friend and admirer of Bruce's, warned him with a poetically coded message, a silver shilling bearing Edward's image, as well as some spurs; this he correctly interpreted as a warning and with his family and retainers headed further north. Along the way Robert's party came across a Scotsman riding in the other direction and searched him to find a letter from Comyn promising Edward his support. Bruce now sent a message to John Comyn asking for a meeting in Dumfries, and the two men cast eyes at each other at the altar of Greyfriars Church, where Bruce stabbed him. Bruce fled, but hearing that Comyn was still just about alive, two of his followers went in and finished the job. The rebel lord now declared himself king.

King Edward responded with characteristic brutality. As revenge, Robert's sister Mary Bruce and another woman Isabella, the Countess of Buchan, who had offended Edward by helping to crown Robert, were taken prisoner. Against all the rules of warfare, they were stuck in wooden and iron cages and then attached to the walls of Berwick and Roxburgh castles as a public warning. For four years they endured the indignity of Edward's imprisonment, something unknown in the French-speaking world of which they were all part, where aristocrats were by custom treated quite well, even lavishly, in captivity. Mary Bruce's appointed servants in jail, all of them elderly, were ordered never to smile at her.

Edward had also wanted Bruce's adolescent daughter Marjorie caged at the Tower of London but changed his mind, and she was instead put into the custody of the Percy family, much to her relief. Robert's wife Elizabeth Bruce escaped punishment because she was the daughter of the Earl of Ulster, an English aristocrat, but she was kept under house arrest for eight years.

And now dozens of men were rounded up and executed; Simon Fraser, a knight who fought with Wallace and then Bruce, got the full traitor's death—hanged, drawn, and quartered—an innovation introduced by Edward. Also killed were Bruce's friend Christopher Seton and two of Bruce's brothers, Neil and Alexander, the latter a highly-respected scholar. John of Strathbogie, Earl of Athol, was hanged and burned, and his head displayed on London Bridge, the first earl to be executed in England for over two centuries, heralding a new era of savagery.

The Scots responded with what is now called a scorched earth policy, denying the enemy supplies by destroying everything in their wake. This form of warfare, brutal but effective, went back to the ancient Greeks and was used by the Celts against the Romans. Byzantine Emperor Maurice's *Strategikon* recommended a policy of destroying crops, fields and trees, and poisoning wells, and similar tactics, while in the twelfth century, Count Philip of Flanders advised laying waste the land: "by fire and burning let all be set alight, that nothing be left for them, either in wood or meadow, of which in the morning they could have a meal."[4]

It was the peasantry who suffered most, both in Scotland and the north of England. Taxable revenue in the border areas fell by more than 90 percent,[5] and it was said in 1317 that "no man nor beast was left between Lock Maben and Carlisle," a distance of twenty-five miles.[6] As Varys put it: "Why is it always the innocents who suffer most, when you high lords play your game of thrones?"[7]

After April 1306, Edward's army headed north again toward Galloway where he directed his men "to burn and slay and raise the dragon banner"—that is, to take no prisoners.[8] His son Edward was even worse, and "would spare neither sex nor age. Wherever he went, he set fire to villages and hamlets and laid them waste without mercy."[9] The father chastised his son, not on humanitarian grounds, but because he should spare "the penalty for their betters, as the rich had taken to flight."[10] It was bad strategy to attack the poor but not the rich, and however brutal King Edward was, he was never brutal just for the fun of it.

Before leaving for Scotland, the king held a grand ceremony in Westminster where his son and 260 other young men pledged to follow him into Scotland and on crusade, after which they were knighted—alongside the young prince were Piers Gaveston, Hugh le Despenser, and Roger Mortimer, three men whose fate would be tied up to the young heir and his disastrous reign to come.

There was a fresh Scots revolt in 1307, and Edward, now sixty-eight, marched north once again. He never made it, and near the border he came down with dysentery and expired. Even with his dying breath, the king demanded that servants carry his bones around Scotland until the rebels were crushed.

"We will never see his like again," said Ser Loras Tyrell to Cersei at Tywin's wake, and many people were similarly devastated by the English king's death, poems lamenting that the Lion had gone. He had surpassed "not only Arthur and Alexander but also Brutus, Solomon and Richard the Lionheart," one writer said with great sadness: "We should perceive him to surpass all the kings of the earth who came before him."[11]

And yet there was one man who did not regret the lion's passing, the outcast who had brought shame on him—his own son.

THE KING'S ARRIVAL

In 1284 while on campaign in Caernarvon, north Wales, Queen Eleanor gave birth to her sixteenth and last child, christened Edward. He was their fifth son, but none of his brothers would survive childhood and he grew up an isolated, lonely figure, his parents having left him in England when he was very young, moving to Gascony where they spent three years without their boy. His mother died when he was seven and his father was already an old man, and often away on campaign.

Longshanks was a brutal and unsympathetic father, and once threw his daughter's crown in a fire in a rage, while on another occasion he ripped out his son's hair. And so, when, just before the old king's death, his son Edward told him of his plans to award land to his close friend Piers Gaveston, the father exploded in anger: "You baseborn whoreson! Would you give away lands, you, who never gained any?"[12]

Like the Lannisters, Plantagenet father and son hated each other. Edward was not a dwarf, but another type of medieval outcast, a homosexual, and his attachment to Gaveston provoked fury in his father. Gaveston's influence would prove disastrous to his reign, as would that of a later lover; more important than his sexual preferences, which most regarded with disdain but considered a private matter, it was the largess he dispensed toward favorites that alienated the aristocracy, and eventually his own wife.

To broker peace, Philippe IV and Edward I had arranged a marriage between the heir to England and Philippe's daughter Isabella, while at the same time the widowed Longshanks was to be married to Philippe's young sister Margaret. She was eighteen and he sixty, but such age gaps were not unknown, nor such double marriage-alliances that led to complex familial relationships, especially if they brought peace between hostile neighbors. Isabella, the Iron king's sixth child but only surviving daughter, was promised to Edward when she was four and so all her childhood was spent knowing she would one day become queen of England; however, such were the political complications that Longshanks only finally agreed on the match soon before he died, the bride bringing an enormous dowry of land, gold, jewels, and silver.

The marriage took place in January 1308. When Edward arrived for the wedding in Boulogne-sur-Mer, in the very north of France, the Channel crossing took three days, due to the unusually cold weather, and during the ceremony it fell well below freezing, 30–40°F colder than what was normal for that time of year.[13] It was an ominous sign.

After a wedding, traditional medieval custom dictated that the bride and groom were ceremonially put to bed, but on this occasion, on account of her young age, that didn't happen. At the time Isabella was just twelve, but as she grew into a woman, the queen became noted for her fierce intelligence and cunning. Her father King Philippe was a strangely unemotional man and her mother also died young, and she grew up to be hard, and feared and disliked among many in France. She was more popular in England, at least until she took a lover, although there were plenty of contemporaries willing to hurl insults at her: Geoffrey le Baker calling her "that harridan", "that Virago" and "Jezebel."

In later chronicles her name was blackened, and in the most famous phrase the poet Thomas Gray wrote of her: "She-Wolf of France, with unrelenting fangs, that tear'st at the bowels of thy mangled mate."[14] Indeed, Maurice Druon describes her in his series as "having small, sharp, pointed carnivore's teeth, like those of a she-wolf."

In reality, Isabella was by all accounts exceptionally attractive, even at a time when men were prone to exaggerate the beauty of powerful women. Godefroy de Paris called her "the most beautiful woman in the kingdom and the Empire," and Walter of Guisborough said she was "one of the fairest ladies in the world." She had thick blonde hair and large blue eyes, one portrait of her showing curls escaping from under her wimple. (Art was tantalizingly close to giving us an image of Isabella—her successor and daughter-in-law Philippa of Hainault was the first queen of England of whom a realistic likeness was drawn.)

She was also lavishly attired, so that at her wedding her wardrobe contained "dozens of dresses" just for her own personal use and seventy-two headdresses; indeed Isabella had inherited her father's rapaciousness and her spending was phenomenal. As queen she enjoyed many conventional pursuits that fitted her role as an aristocratic lady, such as hunting, hawking, and romances, and could be charitable, once arranging for a boy orphaned in the Scottish war to be adopted. She could also be cruel and vindictive, and became a master at dissembling, hiding true feelings that could prove dangerous. She was much more intelligent than her husband, and when their fairy-tale marriage proved bitterly empty he was no match for her, politically.

When Edward and Isabella first met, at their wedding, her husband must have appeared a prince straight from a *chanson de geste*, the romantic poems told by the trouvères of her native France.* King Edward II was tall at six feet and "a fine figure of a handsome man' and "one of the strongest men in his realm."[15] He was well spoken in his native Norman French and dressed well, and yet knowing how to dress and how to smile did not make him fit to be king.

People often complained that the new king's countenance was unregal, that he preferred gardening to soldiering and liked to mingle with "harlots, singers and jesters." Worst of all was his poor judgement in people, and that he was weak and easily influenced. Before his father's death, Edward had developed a close friendship with Gaveston, who was a Gascon from the minor aristocracy. His father had banished Gaveston, but after the old king died, and even before he was buried, Edward had reinstated his friend and elevated him to Earl of Cornwall. And yet there was something more to their friendship.

A chronicler of the period wrote that when Edward Longshank's son saw Piers Gaveston, "he fell so much in love that he entered upon an enduring compact with him and chose and determined to knit an indissoluble bond of affection with him, before all other mortals."[16] Thomas Burton, a Cistercian monk at the Abbey of Meaux, put it more crudely when he said that Edward was "too much given to sodomy."

Openly gay rulers were unusual in the medieval period, and for obvious reasons; homosexual acts were considered a serious sin, and so the allegation was only made against unpopular rulers. William II (1087-1100) was accused of indulging in various vices, one chronicler complaining that the court was full of "prostitutes and parasites" of both sexes. Anselm, the Archbishop of Canterbury, wrote of William's followers that many had abandoned themselves to homosexuality, their long hair and effeminate clothes having encouraged this abomination. And yet Anselm and King William had violently fallen out by this stage, so he was not an impartial source; the only circumstantial evidence is that William did not marry, nor father any bastards.

After their marriage, Edward had put Gaveston in charge of his coronation that same year, a heavily symbolic event with ancient origins in which all the leading magnates of the realm had a role. The ceremony represented the mystical bond between God, the king, and his people, an inviolable pact that blessed the ruler with divine approval; it was this relationship that made the slaying of kings the most heinous of crimes.

---

*This was the northern French rendition of the southern *troubador*, singers of epic tales and romances.

The king and queen stayed at the Tower until the day before the ceremony, when they rode across London; in the morning they walked from Westminster Hall to the Abbey, with the king's cousin Thomas, Earl of Lancaster, carrying Curtana, the sword of peace that symbolized royal authority. His brother Henry carried the rod, while the Earl of Hereford held the sceptre with the cross, the Earl of Lincoln the royal staff, and the Earl of Warwick the three swords of state. All of these treasures meant something, as did the act of Earl of Arundel, Thomas de Vere, Hugh le Despenser, and Roger Mortimer carrying the royal robes on a board covered with a checkered cloth.

And yet, during the ceremony King Edward and Gaveston stunned Isabella's two uncles by outward signs of physical affection, touching and caressing. The upstart Earl of Cornwall was dressed in purple sewn with pearl, a regal outfit unsuitable for a courtier and which could only be interpreted as an insult. A London chronicler said that "rumors circulated that the king was more in love with this artful and malevolent man than his bride, that truly elegant lady, who is a most beautiful woman."[17] After the ceremony, Gaveston angered many noblemen by carrying Curtana, and the banquet following the coronation almost ended in murder. When Piers, in his imperial purple, beckoned the king to join him at his seat, one earl drew his sword and had to be restrained. The queen's uncles stormed off, furious at the humiliation of their kin.

Isabella grew to hate her husband's favorite, but still a child, endured this insult without complaint; yet, the leading barons would not take such an upstart usurping their power. Edward and Gaveston even wore the same clothes when they were holding court, and the king's favorite made enemies by giving powerful barons acidic nicknames, "whoreson" for the Earl of Gloucester, "the fiddler" for Leicester, and "the black hound" for Warwick. To further anger them, Gaveston, like the Knight of the Flowers, was also an accomplished and skilled tournament fighter, and defeated a number of leading magnates with whom he had already made enemies.

Soon an opposition formed, a group of barons solely committed to removing Gaveston. They were led by the king's cousin Thomas, Earl of Lancaster, who set up a committee of twenty-eight men, called the Lords Ordainers; Lancaster was the son of Edward I's brother Edmund and was the wealthiest magnate in the realm, the House of Lancaster being tremendously rich on account of owning large amounts of land in the northwest. In fact, Lancaster was far wealthier than any of the other twelve earls in England, with an annual income of more than eleven thousand pounds, as well as a large private army and a fiery temper.

Tall and imposing like his uncle Edward, he was also deeply unpleasant, "haughty, selfish, treacherous and vicious" and "a sulky, quarrelsome and vindictive man . . . quick to resort to violence."[18] Dressed flamboyantly, "his speech was coarse, and he was promiscuous to excess."[19] A chronicler at the time said that Lancaster had "defouled a great multitude of women and gentle wenches," and rather unsurprisingly he had a deeply unhappy marriage. Among Edward's other enemies, the Earl of Hereford was "prickly and quick-tempered, but also intelligent with a sense of humor," while Warwick was very cultured and owned numerous books, but he was also a "thug." Another, Surrey, was "a nasty, brutal man with scarcely one redeemable quality";[20] both Lancaster and his father-in-law, the more moderate Earl of Lincoln, especially detested him.

In 1309, his opposition to the crown intensified after one of Lancaster's dependents was humiliated by Gaveston. By February the following year, many earls refused to attend court while the Gascon upstart was there, but the next month Edward agreed to allow twenty-one Lord Ordainers to help rule the country, among them eight enemies of Gaveston. For a second time, in 1310, the opposition told the king to exile Gaveston, and this time Edward made him Lord of the far-away Isle of Man, but he soon turned up again. By now Lancaster had become quite open in his contempt for the king and when the two men met, across the River Tweed in 1311, Lancaster made the monarch come to him, a hugely disrespectful act. Yet Guy de Beauchamp, Earl of Warwick, hated Gaveston with an unmatched intensity and after the king's lover surrendered to the moderate Earl of Pembroke, Warwick waited for the magnate to leave for London and, in June 1312, dragged his prisoner out of Pembroke's home. Gaveston was brought to Warwick castle, first on foot at the end of a rope and then on an old horse; he was then taken to a nearby hill where one Welshman ran him through with a sword and another hacked his head off. The king was devastated.

Yet in November Isabella gave birth to a son, christened Edward, following a difficult labor, and after the birth and the celebrations across the kingdom Edward declared peace with Gaveston's killers and publicly dined with Lancaster. Isabella returned to France the following year, and again the year after, with an entourage of twenty-seven ships and thirteen barges. Back home she spent time with her father, her three brothers Louis, Philippe, and Charles, and their wives; the two younger boys had married two sisters, Blanche and Joan of Burgundy, and the eldest, Louis, was wed to their cousin Margaret of Burgundy. As a token of friendship, Isabella had given three distinctive purses to her three sisters-in-law. Her father would have been presented with his grandson, the future Edward III, and in Druon's series the old king ponders what might happen if the baby inherits his force of will, and whether this could be disastrous. We can never know the Iron King's thoughts, but Edward would indeed grow up to become the greatest king of the period, and bring horror to France.

The Queen spent eight weeks in her homeland, hunting with her greyhounds—of whom she had fifteen—and giving hugely generous gifts at various holy shrines. Even for the standards of the higher aristocracy Isabella was lavish, overspending by as much as ten thousand pounds a year and maintaining a household of two hundred servants.

Isabella had arrived the day after the Templar Jacques de Molay was burned, and the chain of events leading to France's tragedy now unfolded. The Queen of England, a naturally suspicious individual, soon learned that not all was well with her three brothers and their brides; there must have been troubling rumors, or perhaps she had a sixth sense, and the presents she so generously gave to her sisters-in-law had been designed to find the truth.

So when the gifts were found in the possession of two young brothers, Gautier and Philippe d'Aulnay, the consequences were horrific. Soon Margaret and Blanche confessed to their adulterous relationships with the young Norman knights, and the third bride, Jeanne, admitted to having concealed the liaison. Isabella's three sisters-in-law were thrown in a dungeon, and Marguerite and Blanche made to wear "the cowled garb of a penitent" and their hair shaved as an act of public shaming. For their lovers, who had confessed after torture, a far, far worse fate awaited them.

In front of a baying mob both d'Aulnay brothers were castrated, and as the executioner raised in his hands the severed genitals of the two men the crowd cheered, before the penises and testicles were fed to dogs. Worse was to follow, as the two men were then flayed alive in front of the screaming small folk of Paris, spread-eagled on a wooden cartwheel, where their arms and legs were broken with iron cudgels as the wheels turned. After they were decapitated, their torsos were hung by their armpits in a gibbet where birds would eat them.

Flaying was a particularly gruesome form of execution that involved cutting off the skin, which a skilled torturer could keep intact; it was spectacularly painful, and it could take the victim days to die, either from blood loss, infection, or even hypothermia, the skin being vital for heat regulation. The practice dates back to the ancient

Assyrians of what is now Iraq, who boasted about this punishment in their monuments, some of which can still be found in the British Museum in London. Even in the harsh Middle Ages, this was a rare punishment reserved for the most abominable of offences, and the cruellest of rulers; and so naturally Edward I also did it, back in 1303 when three monks were convicted of stealing from the treasury of Westminster Abbey. Their skin was left hanging on its door as a warning to others. (Unsurprisingly, no one attempted to rob it again.)

Marguerite and Blanche were made to watch this ordeal; Blanche, wife of the eldest son, Louis, was taken to a castle, Château Gallard in Normandy, where according to one account her husband sent his brutish cousin Robert of Artois to offer a pardon if she admitted her daughter was not his. Robert, an enormous, thuggish, and sometimes charming man, then tried to rape her, but she successfully persuaded him of the dire consequences he might face for violating the king's daughter-in-law, even a disgraced one.

Jeanne, the wife of middle brother Philippe, had only been guilty of concealing her sister and sister-in-law's adultery, and was eventually allowed back to her husband's side, thanks to her scheming mother Mahaut, who many believed to be a witch and a poisoner. Philippe gave her the l'Hôtel de Nesle to live in, the same spot her sister and cousin had taken their lovers, where "stories persisted down the ages that Jeanne, watching from her window in the tower, would send for passing students and, having exhausted their virility, would then have them tied in sacks and thrown from the top of the tower to drown in the Seine below."[21] Neither adulterous princess would ever see freedom again; indeed they both died within weeks of their husbands ascending the throne, rather conveniently.

Perhaps, some wondered, Isabella may have wanted to make her own son the king of France, and by discrediting her female relatives would also tarnish the blood of their offspring, who would always now be suspected of bastardry. If this was the true motive, rather than fraternal loyalty, then she had helped bring disaster to her country.

That year, just months after executing the Templars, Philippe the Fair died, replaced by his son Louis X "Le Hutin"—the Quarrelsome. Some months later a comet passed over the city and was visible for three nights, an event almost always considered an ill-omen.

6
"WE BOW DOWN BEFORE NO MAN"

The Unsullied are not men. Death means nothing to them.

—MISSANDEI

Herodotus wrote his *Histories* during the high point of Classical Greek civilization, the fifth century, but by the time Pytheas sailed to Britain it had waned with the collapse of Athens and Sparta and the rise of the Macedonians, a semi-barbaric mountain people to the north fond of excessive drinking. A *Song of Ice and Fire* takes place in a world filled with the memories of a far greater civilization across the Shivering Sea, and so it was in medieval Europe with Greece and Rome. Although most Englishmen of the fifteenth century would not have travelled far from their villages, let alone crossed the perilous water, which might involve three days of seasick-filled misery, the ghosts of ancient peoples lingered in the minds of the more educated.

The first great civilization was Old Ghis, a city in Essos built on slavery. Long before Westeros had emerged out of barbarism, the Ghiscari had developed heavily-disciplined military units using tall shields, called lockstep legions. In this they resembled the hoplite tactics of classical Greece, and in particular Sparta, but in its giant pyramids built on slave labor, Ghis could be Egypt; and in their destruction at the hands of rivals, in this case Valyria, they resemble Carthage, defeated and razed by Rome in 146BC.

The Ghiscari colonized and subjugated their neighbours, but after a thousand years their power in turn faded and they were replaced by the Valyrians, who reduced Ghis when they built their own empire. After the Doom of Valyria, Ghis rose again, although nowhere as powerful as it once was, and they now bought and bred slaves rather than winning them by conquest. They had also stopped speaking their native Grazdan tongue and come to use High Valyrian instead. This can happen in real life: the ancient Assyrians eventually adopted the language of their neighbors, the Arameans, having conquered them, so that today some of their descendants in Iraq and Syria still speak Aramaic, also the mother tongue of Jesus Christ.

At its peak, Valyria was the greatest city in the world, surrounded by shining walls within which a number of rival houses competed for dominance, rising and falling in bloody internal conflicts.[1] Like with Rome, the Valyrians had no monarchs and called their empire "the Freehold," rather than the kingdom; their rulers were termed archons (a name borrowed from ancient Greece, meaning "lord" or "prince")[2] and were chosen by the ruling families, although one clan might dominate for periods, as in Rome.

After the fall of Old Ghis and Valyria these old civilizations were succeeded by the present-day slave cities Astapor, Yunkai, and Meereen. The latter is ruled by an elite class calling themselves the Great Masters while Astapor has an army of eunuchs, the Unsullied. Yunkai, the yellow or "Great city," is ruled by the Wise Masters but is regarded by Westeroi as being filled with corruption and financed by the selling of "boy-whores."

The Valyrians learned slavery from Ghis but they increased its use hugely as their empire, like Rome, expanded in all directions. They needed copper and tin for the bronze used in weapons and monuments, and iron for the steel to make swords; the number who died in the Valyrian mines is said to be "so large as to surely defy comprehension."[3] One of their great advantages was their use of Valyrian steel, created by folding iron numerous times to balance and remove impurities and the use of spells, or at any rate arts unknown to men of Westeros. Swords of Valyrian steel are highly prized, and while the smiths of Qohor claim to know the art of making them, no one is entirely sure how to do it anymore.

Curiously, something very similar did exist in real life: Damascus steel, which was developed in India before the time of Christ and used in swords in the Islamic world during the medieval period. There are many stories attached to Damascus steel, such as its ability to cut through rifle barrels or that a hair falling on the blade would be chopped in half, but even rigorous scientific analysis has shown it to be extraordinary for its time. Yet by 1750, due to the loss of trade routes between India and the Middle East, the technique had been forgotten. And despite modern technological advancement, the exact science behind the making of this remarkable and versatile material is lost.

Before classical Greece there were the ancient Minoan and Mycenaean peoples, who lived during the Homeric Age of Heroes which ended around 1100BC with the start of the Greek Dark Ages. This civilizational collapse destroyed numerous societies across the eastern Mediterranean; around this period the worlds of the Egyptians, Trojans, Hittites, Syrians, and Canaanites all fell or suffered serious calamities, the product either of a natural cataclysm or uncontrollable piracy by groups collectively known as the Sea Peoples. Some modern historians even believe that there was a giant "World War Zero" around the time between the Near Eastern powers, or that they were overwhelmed by northern barbarians.[4]

From the palaces of the Mycenaean era the landscape of Greece reverted to one of isolated villages, from which emerged in the eighth century BC the *poleis*, or city-state (from where we get "politics" and "police"). Culturally Greece would lay the foundations of Western civilization, but the core of Greek power was, as with Old Ghis, military. The hoplite system involved units of troops in tight formation whose shields collectively protected the group and who engaged in the extremely bloody wars Greeks fought against each other.

Western civilization begins with the abduction of a woman, although as with King Robert's war, it is ambiguous as to whether it is indeed force, or love. In *The Iliad*, an epic poem probably written sometime in the ninth century BC but relating to a far older war between Greeks and Trojans, Paris snatches Helen from her husband Menelaus, but as with Lyanna Stark, it not entirely clear whether she has been taken against her will. Until the twentieth century, the Trojan war was believed to have been entirely fictional, or at best highly metaphorical, but archaeological evidence has since provided convincing signs that it contained elements of truth; there certainly was a city in Ilium, now in north-west Turkey, and it was sacked around the time Homer's story was set. Even the central storyline, the kidnapping of a noble woman by a rival, was always assumed to be about something else, like trade or land— but recent analysis of pre-agricultural societies points to the very high level of warfare conducted over the kidnapping of females, so it's not at all improbable.

The Iliad and its sequel *The Odyssey* were passed down from generation to generation, sung by bards at feasts until, some four hundred years after the historical event, it was written down. Memorized by heart, it would initially have been sung; Homer's opening words are "Sing, Goddess, Achilles' rage, Black and Murderous." Stories and epics were originally told in song form, and so Martin's epic is rightly *A Song of Ice and Fire*.[5]

Classical Greece reached its zenith in the fifth century BC, but it was perilously weakened by a ruinous thirty-year conflict now called the Peloponnesian War, the origins of which lay in the rivalry between the region's two greatest city-states, Athens and Sparta. During the fifth century, Athens, the largest of these *poleis*, had been at the forefront not just of military and economic power but of political development, too, becoming the first state to give every free, adult male a say in government—rule of the people, they called it, or *dēmokratia*. It also developed the great philosophical schools of the ancient world, which were to last centuries, as well as inventing the theatre.

City-state politics was marred by factional conflict, usually between groups favoring oligarchy ("rule by a few") and democracy. Volantis, in the Free Cities, is divided between two parties, the Tigers and Elephants, the latter representing merchants and moneylenders and the former the traditional military-aristocratic elite. Likewise, Cleon, the populist in Astapor, takes his name from the Athenian general who represented the commercial class of the city and demanded renewed war against Sparta. (The playwright Aristophanes painted him as a demagogue.)

And yet for all Athens's achievements, it is Sparta that has always fascinated both historians and the wider public. While Athens gave the world theatre, philosophy, and science, Sparta was the ancestor of all authoritarian regimes and suppressed art, culture, and finance; almost all activities bar warfare, which was for this city-state the very reason for its existence. The Spartans also had some similarities to the Unsullied, the brutalized slave army of Astapor.

Like the Unsullied, the Spartans were famed and feared warriors; during the Persian Wars from 490 to 479BC, when the city-states of Greece temporarily united to drive away the Empire of King Darius and his successor Xerxes, the Spartans performed one of the most famous acts of heroism in history when they sent three hundred warriors to the mountain pass of Thermopylae to block the way of the enormous Persian army, which numbered in the hundreds of thousands. It was a suicide mission, and these men went to their deaths with a stoicism that inspired the ancients and moderns alike, falling after thirty-six hours of brutal fighting. (Likewise, "The Three Thousand of Qohor" were a heavily outnumbered Unsullied force who fought the Dothraki.)

Yet the differences between the Unsullied and Spartans also highlight their odd-ness to us: while the Unsullied were eunuchs, the men chosen for Thermopylae had to have fathered a child so that their line might survive. And whereas Athenians wore their hair short in what they saw as the civilized manner, the Spartans, like the Dothraki, saw long hair as a symbol of masculinity and strength.

Sparta's unique social structure had its origins in the eighth century BC, a time of unrest across Greece as the newly emerging city-states faced conflict between rich and poor. In many of these *poleis* this led to the replacement of kings by "tyrants," that is usurpers who usually lasted two or three generations (the word did not have an entirely negative connotation at the time). However, the Spartans chose to avoid inter-nal conflict by designing a system that would maximize equality between free males. According to legend, a powerful king, Lycurgus, received a Delphic oracle called his "Great Rhetra," which contained the laws of Sparta. And the Spartans obeyed the law, without question.

The system he devised was highly egalitarian. Indeed, Spartans called each other *homoio*, equals, and the key to their military success was the strong sense of comrade-ship the men shared; they all wore the same modest clothing and ate the same food, which was rationed strictly. But there was an extremely dark side to this settlement.

THEIR CHOICE MAY BE BETWEEN BONDAGE AND DEATH, BUT THE CHOICE IS ALWAYS THERE.

"The magnificence that is the Queen of Cities rests upon the back of slaves," as Daenerys is told by Xaro Xhoan Daxos, one of the creepy men of Qarth. "Ask yourself, if all men must grub in the dirt for food, how shall any man lift his eyes to contem-plate the stars? If each of us must break his back to build a hovel, who shall raise the temples to glorify the gods? For some men to be great, others must be enslaved."[6] This was the unchallenged belief throughout ancient Greece and Rome, where slavery was universal, and indeed slavery had been the norm in Europe until around the eleventh century, when under pressure from the Catholic Church it began to be abolished. Anglo-Saxon England, for example, had a slave population of at least 10 percent, and as high as a quarter in poorer, more remote areas, until the practice was abolished by William the Conqueror and his successors, replaced by the almost-as-awful serfdom. But enslaving non-Christians remained acceptable, and later the bloodstained profits of the Atlantic slave trade made the institution more racialized and on a far more horrifying scale; during the fourteenth and fifteenth centuries, slavery would have existed on the fringes of the Western consciousness, in the Middle East, but few would have experience of it, except if they were unlucky enough to be kidnapped by North African pirates—a menace until the eighteenth century in coastal areas.*

In Rome, slaves might be freed and rise in society, but in Greece they were doomed to remain slaves forever, as were their children. But alone in antiquity, Sparta created a system of institutionalized racial slavery; the Spartans, having subjugated their Messenian neighbors in the southern Peloponnese, made them their Helots ("the captured"),[7] that is eternal slaves. Every year Sparta would formally declare war on its neighbor so that any Spartiate (as full citizens were called—only the child of two Spartiates might become one) could commit murder legally; junior members of the Krypteia, an ancient secret police force formed to terrorize the slave population, would abduct and kill Helots just as the Unsullied of Essos were expected to murder babies in front of their mothers. It was, to put it mildly, not a very pleasant place.

Helots belonged to the state, not to individual Spartiates, and so unlike in other slave-owning societies emotional ties did not develop between master and bondsman. Almost all slave-owning societies have devised some way of signaling the unfree out. While in Athens visitors noted with disgust that one could not tell slave and free men apart, in Sparta Helots had to wear a dog skin cap and leather tunic at all times. It was decreed by law that they "should be beaten a fixed number of strokes annually, besides any offence they committed, so that they would never forget that they were slaves,"[8] something they were unlikely to do. If a Helot started to look too physically strong, they were executed and the Spartiate assigned them was fined.

It was a remarkably cruel society—but not especially fun for the Spartiates either. At birth a Spartiate was selected by the elders, and those deemed to be weak were exposed to die, although exposure was fairly common in all pre-Christian European societies. If they made it that far, then at seven a Spartan boy joined the education system and lived with other young males, where they were trained to be obedient soldiers. The boys were led by a *paidonomos*, who was assisted by young men carrying whips and dishing out punishments. Boys were encouraged to steal food, but harshly

---

*In 1631, over one hundred people in the Irish village of Baltimore were kidnapped by North African slavers and taken away to the Middle East. Over time, one million Europeans were kidnapped and taken into slavery in the Middle East in total. The gung-ho song *Rule Britannia*, with its lyrics "Britons never will be slaves," refers to the Royal Navy having by the mid-eighteenth century eliminated this menace.

punished if caught—not because they had committed theft but because they had not gotten away with it; the aim was to teach them cunning. Children were also to some degree shared communally, to such an extent that a man could discipline any other's son for wrongdoing (their notion of child discipline, unsurprisingly, was rather harsh).

The Spartans were also forced as young boys to listen to songs extolling the glory of the military. Their only poet, the seventh-century Tyrtaeus, celebrated war as glorious fun, the boys being told to "stand up to men of the spear, with a terrifying din, as the adversaries clash rounded shield against rounded shield; awful will be the screams as they fall on one another, thrusting spears through the breasts of men."

Spartiates were expected to fight until the age of sixty, and constant training was compulsory—punishment for refusing to fight was death. However, a man who fathered three healthy sons was exempt from military service; after four he no longer had to make financial contributions to the state. On the other hand, Spartiate men were penalized for not marrying or marrying too old or for doing so with the wrong woman.

Everything about their society had a military rationale, including their unique constitution, under which there were two kings, from two dynasties, the Agids and the Eurypontids; the idea being that neither would become too dominant, and one could always remain at home while the other went to war. Some other surviving aspects of their laws paint a puzzling picture of paranoia. Spartiates were not allowed to carry a light around in the dark, for example, so that they would be on full alert all the time. Presumably this caused lots of accidents, but there was a logic, as Sparta was vulnerable to rebellion by the Helots, including a major revolt that occurred in 464BC following an earthquake. This ended in failure and bloody reprisals, as slave revolts of the ancient world almost always did.

In 490BC, Greece faced its greatest crisis when the Persian Empire sought its conquest, and Sparta would be instrumental in beating them back. At Plataea in 479, the Spartans helped drive the Persians out of Greece, "bristling like a wild animal at bay" in Plutarch's words.[9]

Told at Thermopylae that the Persians they faced had so many men that their arrows would block out the sun, one soldier, Dieneces, famously replied "then we shall fight our battles in the shade."[10] This was an example of the dry Spartan sense of humor, from which we get the word laconic, Laconia being the name for the region around the city (such was its popularity that the Roman Plutarch even assembled a book of laconic sayings). Dieneces, like Leonidas and 298 or so others, was killed after the gruelling thirty-six-hour battle against the Persians.[11]

Another word still in use, Spartan, reflects their plain and simple tastes. A wit once commented on their food that "Now I know why the Spartans don't fear death," and their famous disgust for luxury attracted admirers throughout the ages, from their Greek rivals to the nineteenth century German educationalists who established boarding schools based on their way of life.

Hoplite warfare (which the Unsullied tactics are clearly based on) was an extremely bloody affair, and foreigners were shocked by the level of brutality in Greek conflict. Herodotus quoted a Persian, Mardonius, who noted that in Greece's wars "even the victors suffer extreme fatalities. Needless to say, the losing side is annihilated." Even Greeks realized this was a costly way of settling disputes, and Xenophon's description of a battle between Thebes and Sparta in 394 gives some idea of the ferocity: "The earth was stained with gore, with the bodies of friends and enemies strewn alongside one another, shields shattered into pieces, spears smashed in two, swords pulled out of their scabbards—some on the ground, some in cadavers, some still clutched in the hand."[12] It must have been terrifying.

Tyrtaeus, describing hoplite warfare with barely concealed homoerotic glee, wrote: "Everyone must bite his lip and stand firm, his feet firmly planted bestriding the ground, using his broad shield to cover his thighs and shins below, and breast and shoulders above. He must shake his mighty spear in his right hand and wave the crest frighteningly on his head."

The phalanx, about eight to ten men deep, was a rectangular form, with the best fighters at the front and back. Into battle each man carried a large and heavy convex shield, the *aspis*, and a spear with an iron tip and a spike on the other end, as well as a short sword and helmet, and armor covering the trunk. As the battle began trumpets blared and phalanxes moved forward and attacked: "Let each warrior get up close to the one of the enemy, wound him and take him down with long spear or sword," Tyrtaeus sang. "He must fight his opponent placing foot against foot, pressing shield against shield, crest beside crest and helmet beside helmet—fight breast to breast gripping his word or long spear."

The battle would end when eventually one side gave way, the blood-letting rarely lasting more than an hour. As in all conflict, cowardice was looked down upon, for if anyone fled the battle everyone in his line was immediately in lethal danger, exposed to the enemy's spears. Running away without one's shield, in order to make escape quicker, was considered a disgrace, leading to the famous Spartan mother's wish that her son return "with his shield, or on it."[13] In some battles the violence would end with every single one of the defeated dead on the battlefield; sometimes it would go down to fighting with teeth and nails, as with the Spartans at Thermopylae.

Although poorer and smaller than its rival, Sparta won the Peloponnesian War because of its enemy's hubris; Athens alienated its allies in the Delian League by pushing its weight around and, in an act of sheer madness, attempted to invade Syracuse in Sicily, the largest city in the known world with over a quarter of a million people, and part of the Greek-speaking area of southern Italy called Greater Greece.

After initially taking the mantle of dominance, Sparta was badly beaten in battle by Thebes at Leuctra in 371BC, but it was ultimately destroyed internally by the low birth rates that became endemic; but considering that brides on their wedding night were forced to shave their heads, it was perhaps not entirely surprising that its people were not that keen on having children. Eventually both Athens and Sparta, along with the rest of Greece, were conquered by Macedonia, a sort-of-Greek kingdom to the north inhabited by a race of people who spoke a dialect of their language. (Greek itself was known as *koine*, literally "the common tongue," as the language of Westeros is known to its speakers.) With the Macedonian king Alexander the Great conquering most of the known world, these semi-Greeks spread the Hellenic language and culture across the Near East and Asia, in much the same way that American dominance in the twentieth century helped spread English beyond those regions that had been settled by British colonists.

SISTER-WIVES

Among those lands conquered by Alexander was Egypt, home to a much older and, to us, far more exotic and strange civilization. Egypt's Old Kingdom was as distant from Alexander's time as his was from us—millennia before Greece emerged, the gigantic Nile River nourished a long, thin fertile strip upon which a civilization grew. Its crop production allowed a centralized state to emerge, ruled by leaders with semi-divine status, and like the gods, the royal family practiced incest.

Among the earliest recorded evidence of such behavior concerns the Pharaoh Ahmose, who back in the sixteenth century BC was one of a dozen children born to full brother and sister, his parents both children of the Pharaoh Tetisheri. Ahmose also married his full sister, Ahmose-Nefertari, who went by numerous titles, including King's Mother, King's Daughter, King's Sister and King's Great Wife, although the last two applied to the same king, and she also called herself "God's wife."

The reasons for the practice are unclear; it was possibly to emulate the gods, who indulged in brother-sister marriages, or more prosaically to shut out any potential rivals, or to increase clan solidarity—still a reason for widespread cousin marriage in the Middle East today. The Pharaohs were not the only people to practice the same marriage patterns as the Targaryens, although they are the most famous; the Incan and Hawaiian royal families both indulged in it. However, it came with obvious downsides, for the Theban rulers of the seventeenth and early eighteenth dynasties eventually became so inbred they were unable to have healthy children. Amenhotep I and his sister-wife were the product of a brother-sister marriage, and their parents before them, so the royal couple had only two great-grandparents, rather than eight.[14] The most famous of Egyptians, Tutankhamun, was married to his sister, and they had two stillborn daughters before his untimely death at nineteen from a bone disorder; both his children are mummified and buried beside their father in the Valley of the Kings.

After Alexander, Egypt was ruled by a Greek family, the Ptolemys, who continued the practice, repeatedly marrying siblings. In the mid-270s Ptolemy II divorced his Macedonian wife Arsinoe so he could marry his sister, another Arsinoe; their images were issued jointly on coins and when she died in 270 BC he declared her divine. Incest continued within the dynasty—confusingly, all of whom were called Ptolemy—right up until their fall in the first century BC. They were a cruel family, but rulers of Egypt were expected to be so, this country being an obvious inspiration for Slavers' Bay, with its grand pyramids and endlessly suffering legions of slaves.

Ptolemy VIII married his brother's widow, who was also his own sister, and allegedly had her son by his/her brother Ptolemy VI murdered during their wedding party. Then he began a relationship with his sister-wife's younger daughter (his double-niece) before marrying her in 141BC, making her queen; mother and daughter became rivals, as did Ptolemy and his son by his first wife/sister. Fearing his son's ambitions, Ptolemy had him kidnapped and murdered in front of him, before the body was cut up and sent to the boy's mother just in time for her birthday celebrations.

The last Ptolemaic ruler of Egypt died in 30BC, having married first her brother Ptolemy XII and fallen out with him, later being wed to two foreigners in succession and poisoning herself with snakes. Her name was Cleopatra, one of the most famous female rulers in history, and by this stage the world was dominated by a different sort of power, indeed a true superpower. For by the third century BC a new city-state had been emerging north of Greater Greece, an expanding empire built on slavery that would shape Europe like no other—Rome.

7
WALLS OF ICE AND BRICK

Many worthy fighters have died trying to make it to the Great Games.
When most of you worthless scum join them in death this afternoon, it
will represent a significant rise in your station.

—YEZZAN ZO QAGGAZ

T he games began with the sound of trumpets and horns ringing out, then a loud roar erupted and the dust on the floor rose as the gates opened. The largest stadium in the imperial capital held tens of thousands of people and the noise would have been deafening, and terrifying, to men from faraway lands who had never seen two-story buildings before. All the fighters entering the arena would have known one thing—that many of them would die that day, not for a cause, or a country or for a woman, but for sheer entertainment.

The Roman crowd was enthralled by this bloodthirsty spectacle, screaming words of encouragement for their favorite fighter: *verbera, iugula, ure* (whip, slice, burn). Often, after the fight had been concluded, the people chose whether the loser lived or died, his fate depending on whether the shouts of *mitte* (free him) or *igula* (cut his throat) were loudest—although the ultimate decision came down to the *editor*, the citizen who had paid for the games, or the emperor if he was in attendance. An effective means of buying popularity, leading Romans often put on games at great expense; Julius Caesar, for his father's funeral games, paid for 320 pairs of gladiators to fight in his memory.

After this horrific spectacle, the winner would leave by the victor's door, the loser dragged off to the exit opposite, the *libitinaria*, door of Libitina, the goddess of death. There the body was brought to a room with rounded corners—it was easier to wash off the blood—stripped, and if still alive, finished off with a sharp knife. Little was wasted: the blood of gladiators might then be sold off as an aphrodisiac.

All this seems cruel, but ancient Rome was a cruel place. When a slave revolt erupted, led by a Thracian called Spartacus and including up to seventy thousand desperate men, the Romans dealt with it by crucifixion, a fantastically inhumane method of execution that could take days to kill its victims. Likewise, in the Slavers' Bay city-states Astapor and Meereen, crucifixion is used as a way to discipline slave populations. In Meereen, Daenerys Targaryen also visits Daznak's Pit, where for political reasons she is obliged to attend the games in the slaving city, part of their Valyrian heritage. There the Queen watches as tens of thousands of people come to see men fight to the death, an elephant take on a pack of six red wolves, and see a bull pitted against a bear. For the audience's amusement there is also a mock battle, with six men on foot against six horsemen, the latter dressed as Dothraki; on top of this there is a fight between jousting dwarves, lions against people, and a woman fighting a boar. The new queen is horrified by the violence, but the people love it, enthralled, aroused, and amused by the day's events. Rome witnessed such horror countless times.

The city that became master of the world had been founded in the eighth century BC when a number of villages in Latium, central Italy, joined together; to the south the Greeks had colonized most of the peninsula while to the north lay the somewhat mysterious Etruscan civilization. From 616BC until 495BC Etruscan kings ruled Rome until their overthrow and the establishment of the Roman Republic. They left their mark on the Latin tribes to the south, including a belief that breaking mirrors brought bad luck and a number of words such as *people, arena, palace, military, element,* and *letter.* Another innovation they gave the Romans was the games, which first began at funerals.

Having thrown off Etruscan rule, Rome began a period of expansion, and by 300BC they controlled most of Latium; a century later they ruled almost all of Italy, and a hundred years after that they were effectively in control of the Mediterranean.

Rome's two most obvious influences on Martin's world are the games and its horrendously murderous court politics. At the city's Colosseum, officially known as the Flavian Amphitheatre, an astonishing number were sent to their deaths for the crowd's amusement; in AD107 the emperor Trajan, having captured fifty thousand prisoners in the conquest of Dacia (today's Romania), staged fights between ten thousand gladiators, likely prisoners of war; two years later, some 9,800 people died in the arena during games that lasted 117 days. Then in AD115, another 2,400 perished for sport.

Even the low-end estimate for the total number of deaths from the time of its opening in AD80 to the abolition of gladiator fights by the Christian emperor Constantine in the fourth century is 270,000, with as many as one million perishing for sport; it is a place of death.

Daenerys orders that only criminals should be forced to fight, for just as in Rome, previously in Essos the innocent and guilty alike were made to die for the pleasure of the mob. In Rome many of those pushed into the Colosseum were lawbreakers but most were simply luckless slaves, usually foreign prisoners now sent to agonizing deaths in this bewildering, monstrous, terrifying arena, with its ninety feet statues, watched by a crowd larger than their tribe. That being said, a small minority of gladiators were volunteers who took on the risks for the money and glory. Some even made it to the end of their careers and retired, and these skilful, lucky men were given a wooden *rudis*, a miniature wooden version of the *gladius*—the sword with which they fought—to symbolize the end of their service.

Many were honored, respected men, and when two gladiators, Priscus and Verus, fought such a long and gruelling contest that they conceded at the same time, placing their swords down out of respect for one another, Emperor Titus—seeing the crowd's approval—gave them each a *rudis*. Some weren't that keen on freedom—Flamma, a Syrian slave, was offered his liberty four times but chose to continue fighting, winning most of his thirty-four contests until his predictable death at age thirty. He lost four bouts before his final, fatal fight, but then not every gladiatorial event ended in death—in fact only between 13 and 19 percent were lethal, but even this meant that at a rate of two or three battles a year most gladiators would not expect to last a decade.[1]

There were twelve different types of gladiators, among them the *retiarius* (net fighter), who battled with a net and trident, usually pitted against a *secutor* (chaser), armed with a large rectangular shield, an arm guard and an egg-shaped helmet. The gladiators also wore feathers on their helmets, a throwback to the archaic headdresses worn by ancient Italic peoples before the Romans rose to power.

Rome had been a republic since 510 BC, but in the first century BC it would come under strain as a series of powerful generals fought for control; one of them, Julius Caesar, had become too strong and so a senatorial conspiracy brought about his murder. On top of many offences, on his travels to Egypt he had fallen in love with its ruler, Cleopatra, much to the disgust of Rome's elite who distrusted the foreign queen.

Later his leading supporter Marc Anthony and his nephew Octavius would become enemies, but not before the former had also fallen for the Egyptian beauty.

The civil wars of the first century BC would lead to the downfall of the Roman Republic and the rise of an imperial family, followed by almost five centuries of rule by emperors, the first being Octavius Caesar, or as he now styled himself, Augustus. The first five Caesars, of the Julio-Claudian family, are clearly an inspiration for the intrigues of Westeros, in particular the third emperor, Caligula, and his nephew Nero, who succeeded as the fifth. Both were sadists who indulged in sexual depredations but also enjoyed vast spectacles to impress the poor of Rome.

Caligula had grown up in a poisonous world full of intrigue. Born Gaius Julius Caesar Augustus Germanicus, he had spent much of his childhood following his father Germanicus on campaign in Germany, where the soldiers nicknamed him Caligula, or "little soldier's boots," after the footwear he sported. Later his mother Agrippina the Elder fell into a bitter dispute with the emperor Tiberius, her father-in-law, which resulted in the murder of her two eldest sons. And so when Tiberius died in 37AD, Caligula was almost the last member of Augustus's family left, and assumed the role of emperor, aged just twenty-five.

A sadist of great cruelty, he was immature and bestial but also obsessed with spectacle; indeed, the comparisons with Westeros's own boy-tyrant even extend to a strong resemblance to the actor Jack Gleeson. At one of Caligula's events in the Bay of Naples, bonfires were lit on the surrounding high ground to illuminate the party goers feasting on boats anchored together to form a bridge across the bay. There the emperor had his companions and even relatives pushed into the sea, and "Finally, determined that the celebrations not end in anti-climax, he ordered that some of the vessels where his men lay feasting be rammed. And as he watched the action, so his mood was all elation."[2] Caligula also had the children of senators act out the role of prostitutes on his private island, mostly to humiliate them as well as arouse himself.[3] Although the story that he made his horse a senator is probably a myth, there is more truth to the tale that he once declared war on the sea, after a failed attempt to launch an invasion of Britain in which his troops merely collected seashells on the coast.

Eventually Little Boots was murdered, and the throne passed to his uncle Claudius, who had a crippled leg and a stammer and had always been somewhat despised by his family. Claudius, however, eventually succumbed, most likely by poison at the hands of his wife Agrippina, and the throne passed to his stepson Nero, the very epitome of the mad king, who soon disposed of Claudius's fourteen-year-old son Britannicus, or so it was said.

Nero, just an adolescent, was a mixture of Joffrey and Ramsay Snow. He enthralled the people with shows, pandering to their desires and worst excesses, thrilling them with spectacles beyond their dreams, such as recreating great sea battles off the coast—but this frivolity came with a very dark side.

As he was growing up, Nero seduced boys and married women alike, and also raped a Vestal Virgin, the priestesses of Rome whose chastity was considered so sacred that intercourse with one was a capital offense. He also indulged in incest—with his own mother—and it was said that whenever he and Agrippina rode together in the same litter they would act on their passions and "the stains on clothes when he emerged proved it."[4]

As emperor, he had men and women tied to stakes and himself released from a "den" and, while dressed in wild animal skins, he rushed at them and attacked their genitals. Suetonius wrote that "after working up sufficient excitement by this means, he was dispatched—shall we say?—by his freedman."[5]

After a great fire destroyed much of Rome that in AD64, Nero used the disaster as an excuse to greatly expand his palace and gardens by knocking down the slums and pinned the blame on a small and eccentric religious cult who followed a rabbi put to death thirty years earlier. As well as famously putting Christians in the arena with lions, he also had them installed as candles at his garden party, so that as evening fell the poor victims were nailed to crosses and then burned to light up the party. There he walked and talked among his guests while dressed as a charioteer, which left even the not especially humanitarian Romans shocked and filled with pity, since "the Christians' annihilation seemed to arise not from public utility but from one man's brutality."[6]

Eventually Nero grew tired of his mother and had her murdered. After the emperor deliberately had her boat sunk, a friend of hers, struggling in the water, frantically tried to get one of her rescuers' attention by calling out "I am Agrippina"—and was immediately beaten to death with oars and poles. Agrippina silently swam away from the wreck, but not long after her son had assassins stab her to death.

Ignoring scandal, Nero revelled in his depravity. After he kicked his wife Poppaea to death by accident, he ordered his minions to find a doppelgänger, and ended up with Sporus, who was perfect in every way except that he was a boy; and so, he was dressed up in Poppaea's robes, his hair styled to resemble her, and the same makeup applied. Afterward, the emperor toured Greece with his new "wife" who was carried in the litter reserved for Caesar's spouse, attended to by maids. He then held a mock wedding with his bride dressed in saffron and with grand celebrations, as well as traditional prayer that the gods might grant them children.

Nero went too far eventually. In March 68, the governor of northern Gaul rebelled and was joined by Galba, governor of Hispania; soon the head of the Praetorian Guard—the elite body of men charged with protecting the monarch—turned against the mad emperor, too. Cornered, Nero asked his private secretary to finish him off, his last words being *Qualis artifex pereo*, "What an artist dies in me." The Julio-Claudian dynasty was at an end—and the country fell into a civil war known as the Year of the Four Emperors.

THE HILL FOLK

Julius Caesar's rise and fall would ultimately lead to the republic's dissolution, but before that he added to victory in Gaul by planning his next conquest—Britain. In 55BC, Caesar led a force across the sea, arriving in Cantium, which was home of the Cantiaci tribe whose name is preserved in Kent, which would become one of the seven Anglo-Saxon kingdoms. (In Westeros the seven kingdoms originate with the First Men, but Kent was the only kingdom definitely known to have pre-dated the Saxons' arrival in Britain.) The following year Caesar returned, but again after a few days left for Rome, and in 50BC the empire descended into chaos.

It was Claudius who eventually conquered the island of Britannia. At the time the journey was daunting for many, as it was variously believed that the Britons were either cyclopses or practiced human sacrifices. Certainly, various mass burial sites suggest a country not unacquainted with extreme violence, but as for written evidence we only have the Romans' word for it. (In Martin's world, contemporary educated people are sceptical of their ancestors' belief that the First Men did this.)

As in Westeros, where the Valyrians arrive after an invitation from a native king, so too a British tribe sought assistance from Rome, and in AD45 a force of forty thousand men under Aulus Plautius assembled at Boulogne for the crossing. Among the twenty or so tribes they encountered on the island were the Hammerers, the Hill Folk, and the People of the Deep, although we know them better by the names given to them by their conquerors—the Ordovices, Brigantes, and Dumnonii respectively.

Their gods carried clubs and were mysterious even to those who followed them: Dagda the lord of knowledge, Lugh the god of arts and crafts, and Lud (or Nud) the closest thing the barbarians had to a supreme deity, and whose temple may have been on or close to the current site of St Paul's cathedral (now Ludgate Circus). Some traditions have lasted a very long time: in ancient Britain it was believed that a cockerel defended against thunderstorms, which is one explanation for why cocks are still found on top of weathervanes.

The Britons, like their near relations further west in the even more mysterious Hibernia, or Land of Winter, celebrated Samhain during the time of year when the animals were slaughtered before the cold set in; this later evolved into Halloween, which was brought to America by Irish immigrants, where it became the child-centered celebration it is today.

Although the Romans easily overran the flat south of the island, it was not long before rebellion erupted, led by a woman who became a military leader after the death of her husband, and was known for her striking hair.[7] According to the contemporary Roman historian Tacitus, Boudicca was "possessed of greater intelligence than often belongs to women,"[8] while Cassius Dio said that she had "a harsh voice and piercing glare, and habitually wore a large golden necklace (perhaps a torc), a many-coloured tunic, and a thick cloak fastened by a brooch."[9] With her distinctive appearance, this woman, with her freed slave army hell-bent on revenge against their masters, must have been a terrifying figure.

Boudicca's Iceni tribe, from the east of the country, had been allies of the Romans until their king Prasutagus died in AD60. As was the custom, Prasutagus left half his possessions to the Roman Emperor, while the other half of his estate went to his wife Boudicca. But the Roman officials took Boudicca's land and had her whipped, and also raped her two daughters—and the Iceni erupted, joined by others as the rebellion snowballed. It was only eventually put down with great bloodshed, and after three cities had been sacked, including Londonium.

Yet in the coming years the south of the island—Britannia Superior—was easily tamed. In these flat pastures, the Romans cut roads out of forests; the natives were introduced to exotic luxuries such as olive oil and ate Mediterranean fruits and vegetables. The north, or Britannia Inferior, was far tougher, and the Romans distinguished between the semi-Romanized *Britanni* of the south and the belligerent *Brittones* of the north, with its rocks and crags and hills. The Britanni almost certainly

came to speak a form of Latin like their cousins in Gaul, who had become Roman-
ized after many years; although French contains a number of Celtic words, some
of which have come into English, such as *brave, bribe, galon/gallon, greve/gravel,
mouton/mutton, petit,* and *piece.* The Brittones mostly still spoke the native Brythonic
language.

Further north, the even stranger peoples of Caledonia were a different proposition
altogether. These dark Picts, uniquely in Europe, traced their lineage through their
mothers, not fathers, and were a terror to the people of the south.[10] The indigenous
people of Scotland are thought to have arrived from Iberia several thousand years
earlier, and their language was a mixture of Indo-European and older, ancient tongues
of which we know little. They maintained a hunter-gatherer lifestyle until far later
than the Britons, and so may have been dark skinned; a protein-rich diet from hunting would not have favored mutations for pale features, which only became advantageous when Europeans turned to cereals, and so rickets became a problem (pale skin
converts Vitamin D from the sun more efficiently and so reduces the risk of the disease). Cheddar Man was certainly dark-skinned and it's likely Britons would have
remained so until the arrival of agriculture.[11]

In 83AD, the Romans headed north and defeated the natives at Mons Graupius,
deep into the north of Caledonia. The contemporary historian Tacitus recorded a
speech by the Caledonian leader Calgacus telling his enemies: "We, the most distant
people of the earth and of liberty, our very isolation and the obscurity of our renown
have protected us up to this day: now the farthest boundary of Britain lies open, and
everything unknown is considered marvellous, but now there are no people further
on, nothing except waves and rocks." He concluded it, in the famous phrase used to
condemn empires: "they make a desert, and call it peace."[12]

Despite this victory, in which as many as ten thousand natives died as opposed to
just 180 or so Romans, Caledonia remained a wild and forbidding place. Among the
stories told about their untamed homeland was that of the famous Roman IX Legion,
which disappeared in the 120s after an expedition beyond Britannia. Their fate
remains unknown.[13]

The Picts continued to menace the north of Britannia until Emperor Hadrian
resolved to solve the problem by building a wall to keep them out. Work began in
122AD, taking fifteen thousand men six years to build, and at its completion Hadrian's
Wall was eighty miles along, eight feet thick, and 15 feet high, with forts every fifteen

miles and a ditch on each side, sufficient to keep out the wild Picts beyond. Martin's creation is four times as long and seventy times as high, being three hundred miles in length and seven hundred feet tall (even the Great Wall of China was only twenty-six feet at its highest point, and the world's tallest wall today is 164 feet, a climbing wall in Nevada). However it's likely that, like the wall of Westeros, it was once white, painted by the Romans to maximize its visual impact.

After Hadrian's death in 138AD, his successor Antoninus Pius built a second wall further north, in the narrowest spot in the central lowlands of Scotland—although this was abandoned soon after. (Aerys the Mad King also proposed building a second wall further north before other things got in his way.)

Much of Hadrian's Wall was subsequently taken away over the years to build roads and was only saved by a nineteenth century lawyer called John Clayton, without whom it might have been lost. It now attracts many sightseers from around the world, including George R.R. Martin, who made a trip there during his visit to Britain in the early 1980s. As the slow northern twilight crept over, he pictured himself as a legionary, at the edge of the known world and facing barbarians outside of civilization:

We climbed to the top of Hadrian's Wall and I looked north and tried to imagine what it was like to be a Roman soldier stationed there in the first century. At the end of the known world staring at these distant hills and wondering what lived there and what might come out of it. You were looking off the end of the world. Protecting the civilized world against whatever might emerge from those trees.[14]

And then, he asked himself, "What if the legionaries were facing something worse than barbarians?"

At its peak, about ten thousand troops were stationed on this northern frontier of civilization, and each fort could hold as many as six hundred men, with cavalry units of up to one thousand at each end. Northumbrian winters are harsh, and the Roman soldiers stationed here wore woollen cloaks, trousers, and sheep-skin boots, but life on Hadrian's Wall was not as grim as one might expect—records show that many soldiers had heated baths, toilets, a hospital, and a wide selection of food, as well as plenty of holiday time, and there was little daily threat from beyond the wall. For the officers, they even had a form of under floor heating called a hypocaust. In fact, some historians believe the wall may have been as much a question of prestige as anything else, but the structure lasted as a manned fortress for three hundred years, even some time after Rome abandoned Britain in 410.

It was garrisoned with soldiers from across the Empire, men who hailed from as far as Syria.[15] Among those who travelled to this most militarized part of the *imperium* were 5500 horsemen from Sarmatia, steppe nomads from what is now Ukraine who spoke an Iranian language. They were described by historian Cassius Dio as "a savage uncivilized nation . . . naturally warlike, and famous for painting their bodies to appear more terrible in the field of battle. . . . They lived upon plunder and fed upon blood mixed with the blood of horses."[16]

These Sarmatians were eventually settled in a temporary colony in what is now Lancashire, in the northwest of England, but which became permanent. Today the Ossetians, who live in the Caucasus mountains in the very south of Russia, trace their descent from the Sarmatians and speak an Eastern Iranian language. Among the legends of Ossetian folklore is the story of a dying warrior who asks his friend to throw his sword in a lake lest it fall into the hands of his enemies; the man cannot bear to be rid of such a magnificent weapon and twice lies, only for the hero somehow to know. Eventually he flings the weapon into the water and it is caught by a woman's hand coming out of the lake. That this strange tale exists nowhere else but among the Ossetians and Welsh suggests that Sarmatians may have brought the idea of King Arthur to late Roman Britain or that, as the 2004 film *King Arthur* suggested, he was a Sarmatian.[17]

More fatefully, from the third century the Romans imported as soldiers Angles and Saxons from across the cold German Sea.

A GOLDEN CROWN

Perhaps the height of Roman civilization was the period of the Five Good Emperors, from Nerva in 96AD to Marcus Aurelius, who died in 180AD. The last of these was a philosopher as well as a warrior, but his unhinged son Commodus would begin what in retrospect was the rot.[18] Commodus insisted on taking part in the games, and this became a regular event; on one occasion "he killed a hundred lions with a hundred javelins."[19] The emperor then started decapitating ostriches, at which point some senators started to question whether he was entirely suitable for the role and decided to poison him; that failed, and so they found an athlete to strangle him. The emperor was finished, although as he had recently appointed the athlete in question governor of Syria, might have felt he was rather lacking gratitude. Commodus and his father have famously been portrayed in two films, *The Fall of the Roman Empire* and *Gladiator*, although neither are considered accurate portrayals of Commodus by serious historians, something that would surely vex him.*

In 193AD came the "year of the five emperors'" and in the third century civil wars sparked up between rival generals, often splitting the empire. During a fifty-year period of the third century, twenty-six emperors and more usurpers claimed power. Real power now rested with the Praetorian Guard, tasked with protecting the emperor, but more often prone to killing him and installing a successor. Without a legitimate structure for passing on authority, power did indeed reside where people believed it resided.

In 260 a Roman emperor, Valerian, was captured by the Persians, a great shock and humiliation to the empire; he never came home, and according to one theory was used as a human footstool by the Emperor Shapur. One source suggested that after Valerian offered large amounts of money for his release, Shapur forced him to swallow molten gold and then had him skinned alive and his skin stuffed with straw and placed as a trophy in a temple.[20]

The Doom of Valryia was a natural cataclysm, caused by a rupture in the earth that literally sinks the capital of the empire, leading to a century of chaos. It is recalled that every city within five hundred miles was incinerated and even dragons in the sky burned, red clouds raining down "the black fire of demons," causing water three hundred feet high to drown the land.[21] This has some historical resonance with the disaster that struck the late bronze age societies, and which may have been responsible for the Biblical flood myth.

The doom that faced Rome, however, was man-made. The Romans had been concerned about barbarian birth rates from at least the first century; a Roman *milite* might spend twenty-five years in the profession and soldiers stationed along the frontiers that lined the Rhine and Danube would have heard from older comrades that the number of barbarians seemed to grow and grow each decade (although by now most of his comrades might be barbarians themselves). From the fourth century,

---

*Father and son were played by Alec Guinness and Christopher Plummer in *The Fall of the Roman Empire* and by Richard Harris and Joaquin Phoenix in *Gladiator*. Maximus was fictional.

Germanic tribes began to settle in the western Empire, often to protect its frontiers from other tribes, for the Romans had run out of men willing to fight for them. On December 31, 406, a number of barbarian groups led by the Vandals and Alans crossed the Rhine and walked into Gaul, almost unopposed; they were refugees, and also invaders.

Across the continent enormous war bands of German nations moved into imperial territory, the Visigoths, Ostrogoths, Vandals, Franks, Saxons, and Angles among them. From the late fourth century, Saxon ships were being sighted in twos and threes off the coast of Britannia, but as the years went by they came back in greater numbers. Looking east out to the North Sea from the flat, eastern coast of Britain—what is now Essex and East Anglia—one looks into the ice-cold vastness of what was once called the German Ocean and can imagine the terror the natives must have felt upon seeing the Saxon ships make their way along the coast of continental Europe and across to this poorly-defended island.

In Britannia, pirate attacks become more frequent; in 367, they suffered raids from the east and west, from Saxons and Irish; a later raid is attribiuted to Ireland's high king, Niall of the Nine Hostages. According to legend, he found his beautiful wife when a group of his friends were stopped by an old hag guarding a well and had to kiss her in exchange for water. Only Niall satisfied the crone, after which she turned into a beautiful maiden and they produced an abundance of sons who became the heads of many successful clans. This is the legend, but in 2006 geneticists discovered that one in twelve Irishmen are descended from one very fecund individual directly through the male line, and 2 percent of New York men, and numerous other Americans such as Stephen Colbert, Bill O'Reilly, and Henry Louis Gates.* Certainly Niall, or some other figure at the time, had a large number of surviving sons who in turn were hugely successful in producing offspring.

In 407 the Roman legions pulled out of Britain. Sometime later, and desperately under threat from German tribes now attacking in much larger numbers, the British leaders appealed to Rome again: "To Agitius, thrice consul: the groans of the Britons . . . The barbarians drive us to the sea, the sea drives us to the barbarians; between these two means of death, we are either killed or drowned."[22] The empire, or

---

*The *Game of Thrones* backstory has its equivalent, Garth Greenhand, first lord of First Men to cross to Westeros who is supposed to have had an improbable number of children and descendants.

what was left of it, replied that the Britons must take care of their own affairs, for Rome could no longer help. The city itself would not be spared the cataclysm: the last emperor, the boy Romulus Augustulus, stepped down in 476, deposed by a barbarian king.

A century later, when Pope Gregory the Great established papal control of the city, one that would bring it a new empire—this one spiritual—it was home to just a few thousand souls nestling in the ruins of a millennium of greatness, a ruin of goatherds and livestock. To a visitor from Rome's past it would have looked like a cataclysm had befallen the city even if, unlike in Martin's world, it was one created by men.

And then came the ten years without summer.

8
BEYOND THE WALL

I met some wildlings when I was a boy. They were fair thieves but bad hag-
glers. All in all, they seemed like any other men, some fair, some foul.

—DAVOS SEAWORTH

By the sword's edge or the spear's point they slaughtered the sick in their beds, women who were pregnant or in labor, babies in their cradles or at their mothers' breast and sometimes they killed the mothers too. They slaughtered worn-out old men, feeble old women . . . They killed husbands in front of their wives. Then they carried off their plunder and the women, both widows and maidens, stripped, bound and roped together they drove them off, goading them with spears on the way. Their fate was either to be kept as slaves or sold on to other barbarians in exchange for cattle.

So wrote the northern English chronicler Richard of Hexham in 1138 after the Scots had piled over the border, causing mayhem and terror.

The Wildlings are a diverse bunch, speaking seven different languages and varying culturally, from tribes who are very similar to the people of the North, to out-and-out savages who eat human flesh. Likewise, the raiders of 1138 would have spoken a number of tongues, including variations of Gaelic, Pictish, Brythonic, the Anglian dialect Lallands and, among their leaders, Norman French. This elite of two hundred Norman noblemen led an array of archers and spearmen from across the different tribes of Scotland, including Picts, Scots, Gaels, Lowlanders, Highlanders, and Islanders, but worst of all the notorious Galwegians, who still fought naked.

In the words of one historian: "No doubt all the motley host of Scots and English [English-speaking Scots], of Norwegians from Orkney and the Isles, of Normans and even Germans and Danes contributed to this orgy of cruelty, but all accounts agree that the Picts of Galloway, 'those bestial men,' were the perpetrators of the worst and most unspeakable horrors of this grim campaign."[1]

The Scots were regarded with horror in England, just as the Wildings were in the Realm. The men of the North in particular hated those beyond the wall, and to them the only thing worse than the Scots' love of violence was their habit of raiding for slaves.

When the northern English army came to meet them, on August 22, 1138 at the Battle of the Standard, they faced the terrifying spectacle of the nude Galwegians, from the part of Scotland facing Ireland and "renowned for such habits as braining babies on doorposts."[2] Behind them were spearmen from Cumbria, speakers of the old Brythonic language that elsewhere evolved into Welsh, as well as Lowlanders and fighters from Aberdeenshire on the northeast coast, most of them fishermen. The battle began with the blowing of Scottish horns, followed by three howls, the spur for the Galwegians to charge, the naked savages drumming their spears on their shields. The English fired at them with their bows, and "the arrows flew like the densest rain, rushing into the breasts of those who stood in the way, sticking into their faces and eyes."[3] One Galwegian could be seen "bristling all round with arrows and nonetheless brandishing his sword and in blind madness rushing forward [to] smite a foe [and] lash the air with useless strokes."[4] Soon the Galwegians fled and the Scottish king was dragged away by his knights, while the rest of his army ran off, now the prey of the local populace.

Raiding from beyond the border dated back to at least the eleventh century, and one writer recorded a 1070 attack in which King Malcolm "commanded them no longer to spare any of the English nation, but either to slay them all or drive them away under the yoke of perpetual slavery . . . Old men and women were either beheaded by swords or stuck with spears like pigs destined for the table . . . Babes were tossed high in the air, and caught on the spikes of spears. Malcolm watched all these things without pity; merely ordering his slave-drivers to make haste."[5] King Malcolm "Canmore" (Great Chief) raided England five times from 1058 to 1093, until killed in the last invasion.

The Scots came to burn and steal and enslave, one contemporary lamented, so that "the young men and the young women and whoever seemed suitable for work and toil were driven bound before the enemy . . . Scotland was filled with English slaves and handmaidens, so that even now no little village, nor even homestead, is without them."[6] When the wild men turned up, northern villagers would make for a safe refuge, a church being an obvious choice, where the monks' prayer would compete with the cries of newborns and the sound of livestock.

However, the Norman Conquest of England led to a great increase in the number of castles going up across the country; the first in the north was Durham, built in 1072, and the New Castle followed in 1080, erected on the River Tyne following one of Canmore's raids and giving its name to the region's largest city. Soon after came Carlisle, on the western edge of the Wall. Otherwise people would hide in the hills or forests. Aware of this ploy, the Scots might pretend to leave, only to wait for the English to come out, as they did in 1070.

Although Wildings can speak the Common Tongue used south of the wall, the equivalent of English, some groups—such as the Thenn—still converse in the Old Tongue. Likewise, Gaelic culture and language flourished in the mountains and islands of Scotland until the eighteenth century and the Highland clearances, at which point their clannish society was crushed forever.

Hadrian's Wall had been put up by the Romans to keep out Caledonian tribes and today is close enough to serve as a metaphor for the Anglo-Scottish border. However, although the walls in both fiction and reality remain central psychological barriers between rival cultures, in real life it was not Hadrian's Wall that remained culturally significant, but the more northerly Antonine, built over the thinnest point in Scotland's central belt. Although little of the actual structure survives, and it was in fact abandoned after only a few years, it better (although not perfectly) marks the division between the historically English and Celtic-speaking areas of northern Britain.

After the fall of Rome, a Germanic tribe, the Angles, overwhelmed the land on both sides of Hadrian's Wall. Further north Alba, or Scotland, had been united in the ninth century, through a marriage alliance between the Gaelic-speaking Scots of the west, who originally came from Ireland, and the indigenous Picts in the northeast. Lothian, the south-east of Scotland, had been part of the Anglian kingdom of Northumbria, and stretched as far as Din Eidyn, which became Edinburgh in the seventh century; the court of that city had always spoken the Anglian tongue, developing into the English dialect called Lallands ("lowlands"). Northumbria and Lothian were "linguistically, socially, and economically indistinguishable,"[7] and the latter was described as being "in the land of the English and in the kingdom of the Scots."[8]

In the tenth century, the southern kings of Wessex had conquered all the English-speaking kingdoms from the Vikings but, finding it too far out of their sphere, conceded Lothian to the Scots instead. It included the strategic point of Castle Rock, the site of a former volcano that controlled the Firth of Forth and which became Edinburgh Castle. Castle Rock was at the very end of the Great North Road from London, and whoever controlled it effectively controlled central and southern Scotland.

So the division between the Wildlings and the knee-benders is inspired not just by the difference between Scots and English, but between Scots Highlanders and English-speakers—both Scots and English—of whom Highlanders made no distinction. The Scots Gaelic word for the English, *Sassenach*—literally "Saxon"—originally applied to both.

In return, the English-speaking people of the Scottish Lowlands regarded the Highlanders with terror and disgust. Andrew Wyntoun called them "wyld wykkyd Heland-men"[9] while John of Fordun, writing in the fourteenth century, said: "The lowlanders are home-loving, civilized, trustworthy, tolerant and polite, dress decently and are affable and pious. The islanders and highlanders are a wild untamed people, primitive and proud, given to plunder and the easy life, clever and quick to learn, handsome in appearance but slovenly in dress."[10]

But the people of Northumberland were terrified of both the Lowlanders and Highlanders, and their occasional raids against the "Southrons". This term, once used by northern English as a term for southerners, was also used by the Scots for the English generally, just as it is used in Westeros by people from the North for those south of the Neck, and by Wildlings for anyone south of the Wall.

In the wilder terrain north of the border wolves were still common; they had once been widespread across the island, but were now in retreat after determined attempts to eliminate the animals. Anglo-Saxon kings as far back as the tenth century would demand wolf skins as tribute, while criminals might escape execution in return for a certain number of the dead beasts. Edward I embarked on a policy of exterminating wolves from his kingdom, although it was not until the Tudor period when they were finally driven out of England.

The wolf is "an enduring symbol of terror in the Western European imagination. The wolf howl in the dark forest, the noiseless padding of the creature around the winter homestead, even the big, bad wolf of fairy tale all speak to an ancient fear of what awaits us in the wilderness."[11] As well as being a danger to children and livestock, wolves also often scavenged over the corpses left by men in war; at the Battle of Water-firth in the eleventh century, fought between Gaels and Norsemen, the poet Arnor sang that afterwards "There I saw the grey wolf gaping, O'er the wounded corse of many a man."[12]

They survived beyond the wall for longer; up until the early modern era large areas of Scotland were densely wooded forests in which wolves were abundant, and it was not until these woods were cleared in the seventeenth century that they were driven to their doom. Indeed, in the Highlands wolves were such a menace that people were often buried on small islands where the animals could not dig up the corpses. Dire wolves also really existed, once found in North America before their extinction ten thousand years ago; *canis dirus* were bigger than other species of wolves, although not quite as gigantic as the creatures in Westeros, and their interaction with humans was brief and painful.[13]

"THERE SITS THE ONLY KING I MEAN TO BOW MY KNEE TO, M'LORDS. THE KING IN THE NORTH!"

Scottish royal politics had always been absurdly violent. King Duncan was slain by his uncle Donald the White in 1094, while Donald was killed and mutilated in 1097 when the exiled Anglo-Saxon leader Edgar the Atheling helped put his Scottish-born nephew Edgar on the Scottish throne. Before them all Macbeth had taken the crown through victory in battle, not by murder as in Shakespeare's telling, and his end was also predictably bloody.

Things somewhat improved after the Scottish monarchs began to intermarry with the English and French aristocracy, bringing them more into the European main-stream. Malcolm Canmore's English wife Margaret, later made a saint, insisted that slaves be ransomed by their families. Her son King David returned his own slaves.

By the fourteenth century, the border was heavily militarized, with hundreds of "pele" towers, small fortified houses with walls seven to ten feet thick, as well as a number of castles. The people in northern villages would bring their goods into the castle for safe keeping when attacks came. However, whereas previously the Scots could only plunder the north, with the invention of castles they might conquer it, if they could capture the fortresses. David I had done just that, occupying five castles after crossing the border with a great army. His grandson William the Lion had invaded England in 1173 and tried to take Northumberland, before eventually being repulsed. By this time, Scotland had come heavily under the influence of the French, and their armies included mercenaries from continental Europe, mainly Flanders. So now the Scottish and English knights, both of Norman origin, fought each other under the laws of chivalry, having duels and being ransomed when captured. And yet the wild Galwegians regarded the knights leading them as no different to the enemy, so that when King William was captured at Alnwick they immediately headed back to their native land and destroyed all the castles he had built and killed all the "new-comers," Frenchmen, they could find.

Other parts of the isles took longer to come into the European mainstream. In the thirteenth century, the royal Scottish army defeated "unarmored and naked" Manxmen, the last part of the isles where war was done *au naturel*.

And in the far north of Britain, things would not have been remarkably different from a millennium before. According to the thirteenth century *Chronicle of the Kings of Man and the Isles*, the inhabitants of the Isle of Lewis lived "mostly by hunting and fishing, for the land is mountainous and rocky, almost all of it unfit for tillage" The Gaelic speakers shared this region with Vikings, some of whom still lived by raiding as late as the twelfth century. Svein Asleifarson, lord of Orkney, would sow his seed in the spring and, "that done, he would go off plundering in the Hebrides and Ireland on what he called the 'spring trip.'" He returned in time to gather in the harvest, then he would raid for his "fall trip."[14] Warned by the local leader to put an end to this rather old-fashioned behaviour, Svein ignored him and headed off to Dublin for a raid—where he was brutally killed.

And despite considerable advances, Scotland at the time of the cousins' war in England was certainly less developed than the lands further south. In the 1430s, papal envoy Aeneas Silvius Piccolomini, the future Pope Pius II, visited what was then still a place on the edge of civilization. He wrote: "It is a cold land, of few fruitful plants and is, for the most part, barren of trees. In the earth there is a sulphurous rock which they dig up to feed their fires. Their communities have no surrounding walls and their houses are most often constructed without mortar and have roofs covered with turf, while in the countryside the doorways are shut off with ox hide. The people, who are poor and uneducated, fill themselves up with meat and fish but only eat bread as a delicacy . . . They do not have wine, other than what they import . . . It is said that there are two Scotlands, one cultivated, the other wooded and without fields. The Scots that live in the wooded part speak in a different tongue and sometimes eat

tree-bark."[15] The meat-eaters he met would have been the very richest of the aristocracy; for the vast majority of people, oats were their daily fare, if they were lucky.

The country increasingly became Anglicized and might have been absorbed were
it not for King Edward's invasion; instead, there was written a national story of resistance to unite the disparate tribes north of the Wall. And the climax came in the year
of 1314, when the Scots defeated an invading army, one of three crucial battles that
heralded the beginning of the end for the medieval world.

The old order in Europe had in fact begun to crumble on May 18, 1302 when
Philippe the Fair's army marched north to crush the Flemish, confident of an easy
victory against a small but industrious people on the kingdom's edge. Across the cold
North Sea from southern England, Flanders was low-lying and not naturally rich in
resources—*Vlaanderen* comes from the old Dutch word for flooded—but despite
poor soil and a very high-water table, the Flemish had turned swamps into towns and
sheep pastures, building a cloth industry that brought them great rewards. Along with
northern Italy, Flanders was now the wealthiest part of Europe, its GDP per capita 20
percent greater than France and 25 percent better than England. Unusually, some
40 percent of its people lived in towns, one of the effects of which was that their mili-
tias could regularly drill together, unlike the mostly rural French.

For centuries the European order had rested on knights, aristocratic warriors who
fought on horseback. This form of warfare had been mastered by the Franks from
about the seventh century, and later the Normans perfected the cavalry charge, a
terrifying prospect to anyone facing it. Against mounted cavalry the infantry stood
little chance—as the English discovered to their cost at the Battle of Hastings in 1066.
From the time of the First Crusade (1095-1099), horsemen also carried lances thirteen feet long with very sharp leaf-shaped steel blades, which caused terror among
infantry soldiers.

A man was nothing without his horse, and a mount with the right traits was highly
prized. It was said that a horse should have fifteen qualities, three each of a man,
woman, fox, hare, and ass—so like a man bold, proud, and hardy, and like a woman
fair breasted, fair of hair, and easy to lie upon. A war horse, or *destrier*, cost thirty-six
times as much as an average farm animal, weighed up to 1400 lbs and could carry 300
lbs on their backs.

This strength was required when battle harness weighed up to sixty pounds, a mass
of heavy and highly-expensive metal. A knight's outfit would include not only a shield,

sword, lance, and maybe an axe, but a vast array of protective clothing: mail hauberks and mail leggings and plate armor above their lower legs and forearms; steel gauntlets, kneepads, and steel plates over the forearms; steel skullcaps to which they attached an aventail, and a curtain of mail hung over the neck and shoulder, as well as the various paddings worn underneath, including the gambeson, a thick, woollen padded jacket similar to that worn by dog handlers, as well as breastplate and backplate.

Cavalry had also led to chivalry, from *chevalier* (horseman), the code of conduct that defined how medieval men viewed the world and themselves; the laws of chivalry demanded that enemy prisoners were captured rather than killed, and in fact fatalities among knights were low. In Flanders during the whole twelfth century only five knights died on duty, and only one of them in battle; one of the others was killed after blowing his horn too vigorously. Yet that all changed suddenly at the fateful Battle of Courtrai in 1302, when hundreds of French *chevaliers* were cut down in one day by ten thousand Flemish infantry.

Many of the Frenchmen were hacked to death by a long spear called a *geldon*, from *goedendag*, "good day," a sort of Dutch joke—essentially a baseball bat with spear points, which the defenders used to lethal effect after digging hundreds of ditches to lure French horsemen to their doom in the mud. However, the decisive Flemish weapon was the arrow—an old weapon but used in numbers not seen before.

An infantry soldier cost one-tenth as much as a horseman, and so anyone could fight, while any state with sufficient tax-raising abilities could gather large armies, especially from cities filled with men for hire. The Flemish discovered that sufficiently large numbers of archers and infantrymen could overpower a cavalry force, especially if well-drilled and disciplined. The Flemish victory was a military revolution, and led to the expansion of infantry, so as a result battles became bigger and bloodier, dwarfing anything seen before. It was the beginning of the end for chivalry—afterward, so many spurs were taken from the dead that it became known as the Battle of the Golden Spurs.

This was one of three battles that shocked the European order. On November 15, 1315, archers from the Swiss Confederacy, calling themselves the Everlasting League of the Three Forest Cantons, defeated an Austrian army at the Battle of Morgarten, so confirming Switzerland's independence. Swiss history reached its most exciting phase, although that is admittedly quite a low bar, and the only well-known figure who emerges from this period is William Tell, although whether he actually existed, let alone fired an apple above his son's head, is open to question.

The third was the Scots victory at Bannockburn, where an English army was wiped out in 1314. In March that year the Scots had captured Edinburgh castle, the force led by William Francis, a local who had become skilled at climbing the castle scarp in order to visit his girlfriend. In response, King Edward summoned a huge army of 21,640 men from England and Wales and 4,000 from Ireland. Although his internal enemies, among them Lancaster, Warwick, Surrey, and Arundel, had sent the bare minimum of soldiers, so confident were the English that before invading Edward II hired a troubadour to "write an ode commemorating the coming victory."[16] Alas, it did not go to plan.

Edward's army also consisted of 2,500 cavalrymen, including more than 1,000 knights (the highest rank of cavalry soldier), and 3,000 archers. They crossed into Scotland on June 17, 1314 and soon met a Scots force half the size on a spot close to Stirling called Bannock Burn. This now-famous location lies just a few miles away from Doune Castle, which was partly destroyed during this war and substantially rebuilt in the 1380s and is where Winterfell is filmed (it was also used in *Monty Python and the Holy Grail*).

The Scots were outnumbered, and they were also arrayed in less effective armor as they lacked metal-forging capabilities (another similarity with the Wildlings); most Scots also had a lighter type of horse, a courser, than their English opponents. Before the battle, the English knight Henry de Bohun, nephew of the fantastically rich Earl of Hereford, was yards ahead of the rest of the army when he saw Robert the Bruce on a gray horse inspecting his divisions about one hundred yards ahead. There was an old grudge between the men, the de Bohuns having been given Bruce family lands when he was a fugitive, and now Henry couched his lance and charged at his enemy with the full momentum of his powerful horse. And yet by the time he had covered the boggy slope on top of which Robert waited, his horse was exhausted; King Robert, on a lighter animal, swerved and dodged the blow, turned around, and, with one swing of his axe, split de Bohun's skull open.

Bruce addressed his men: "You could have lived quietly as slaves, but because you longed to be free you are with me here, and to gain that end you must be valiant, strong, and undismayed . . . You know what honor is. Bear yourself in such fashion as to keep your honor."[17]

The Scots were arranged in four schiltroms, walled in by shields and with hedges of eighteen-foot pikes facing each direction. The battle was fought in "an evil, deep and wet marsh," and by its end one thousand Englishmen were already dead, many drowned in the mud, and many more would perish in the pursuit that followed. Twenty-two English barons fell, along with sixty-eight knights; the Scots lost just two knights and five hundred pikemen.

In the course of the battle, Edward had one horse killed underneath him, but despite "fighting like a lion," eventually Pembroke grabbed the reins of the king's second mount and dragged him away to Stirling Castle, alongside five hundred surviving cavalrymen, eventually heading to Edinburgh and Berwick. Edward had left his shield, arms, and the privy seal, symbol of his power—a humiliation. The Earl of Hereford was captured, to be exchanged for Bruce's queen, sister, and his daughter Marjorie. It was a huge shock to the realm of England, and many blamed the king.

But worse was to follow. Much worse.

9

THE OLD GODS AND THE NEW

Earth and water, soil and stone, oaks and elms and willows, they were here before us all and will still remain when we are gone.

—JOHEN REED

The Romans were horrified by the religion of the Britons, one that involved the worship of nature but also— if they are to be believed—human sacrifices. It was a clash of cultures that has strong parallels in Westeros, which borrows from aspects of British folklore, early nature-worship, anthropomorphic paganism, and the Middle Eastern religions that came to replace all of them. Although the world of *Game of Thrones* is polytheistic, inhabited by people worshipping many different gods, from the second book there emerges an alien religion proclaimed by a sinister foreign woman from the east who's rather keen on burning people alive. However, in real life the mysterious eastern faith spread by women across the British Isles proclaimed the end of sacrifices, and certainly not human ones.

There are four main religions in Westeros—the Old Gods, New Gods, the Lord of Light's faith, and the Drowned Gods worshipped by the Iron Born. In the earliest days, the Children of the Forest believed spirits could inhabit the bodies of animals or inanimate natural objects. The Children followed a faith that resembles the first religions found on earth in that it had few formal rules, no organized belief system, and no temples to worship; the Old Gods are similar to the deities usually found in pre-agricultural societies, being attached to elements. The closest thing there is to formal religion are the forests with weirwood trees, which members of the Stark family still go to visit. (Cut a weirwood tree and they appear to bleed, one of many rather strange aspects of the religion that has parallels in Celtic folklore.) The singers of the forest had no books and no writing and when they died, it was believed only the trees remembered their actions. Likewise ancient Britons saw the natural as sacred, including rocks, mountains, and trees. Pliny the Elder, writing in the first century AD, said of the Celts: "They choose oak-woods for their sacred groves, and perform no sacred rite without using oak branches."[1]

Druidic ceremonies were held in such sacred groves, and the Celts "also revered yew, rowan, and mistletoe, whose red cones and berries echo the red leaves of the weirwood groves."[2] Likewise, in one of his visions, Bran Stark sees his ancestors offering human sacrifices in the godswood, as was most likely carried out in ancient Britain, judging by various mass graves dating from the Iron and Bronze Ages. Since the eighteenth century, hundreds of well-preserved bodies have also been found in marshes across northern Europe, suggesting humans killed for ritual purposes, either by garroting, hanging, beating, or drowning.[3]

The White Walkers resemble creatures from Celtic folklore, such as the *Sidhe* or *Aos Sí*, a fairy-like race that lived in burial mounds in ancient Irish mythology. Among the most frightening of the *Sidhe* are the banshees, bearers of bad omens and messages from beyond, noted for their piercing cries (in the west of Ireland the howling wind at night can make one understand how such stories would have sent a chill down the spine).

One theory is that much of Irish mythology has its origins in the migrations of different peoples to the island; folk tales about leprechauns, or the little people, stemmed from older beliefs in the Tuatha Dé Danann, mythical short and dark fairy-like creatures with magical powers. The Tuatha Dé Danann may be lingering folk memories of the country's pre-Christian gods, although another theory is that such creatures represent indigenous inhabitants who moved to the hills when later Bronze Age Celtic newcomers with superior technology settled in the valleys.

The Walkers also bear a resemblance to the ice giants of Scandinavian mythology, thought to be a big influence on Martin. In the Norse epic *Ragnarök*, the world is plagued by a long winter, known as a *Fimbulvetr*, during which the gods Loki, Odin, Thor, and Hel (Queen of the Dead, from which our word Hell comes) do battle.[4] Loki lives out in the wilds with a group of animals, and has the ability to take on their consciousness, using his third eye. This is repeated in Westeros where Bran Stark is taken on by Brynden Rivers, known as the Three-Eyed Crow, who can warg into a variety of animals, including crows, and is played by Scandinavian actor Max von Sydow.

The Vikings believed in *draugr,* or walking dead, who would be cursed to tread the earth if not given a proper burial.[5] Later medieval Europeans were similarly terrified of *revenants,* "the returned," and although part of folklore, this fear was sometimes encouraged by the Church, which was keen that everyone have a proper burial.

Twelfth century abbot Geoffrey of Burton wrote a striking account in his *Life and Miracles of St Modwenna* about two peasants living in Stapenhill, Derbyshire; trying to escape serfdom, they ran away to a nearby village, Drakelow, but the next day the two men dropped dead and their bodies were returned to their home village for burial. However, "soon one evening they appeared to villagers in Drakelow, while the sun was still up, carrying on their shoulders the wooden coffins in which they had been buried. . . . The following night they walked through the paths and fields of the village, now in the shape of men carrying wooden coffins on their shoulders, now in the likeness of bears or dogs or other animals. They spoke to the other peasants, banging on the walls of their houses and shouting."[6]

This terrifying spectacle was repeated each night until soon an unexplained disease spread through the village, killing all but three people. The lord of the manor, Count Roger the Poitevin, gave money to the abbey in compensation for having accepted runaway serfs, and the Church exhumed the bodies of the two men. So Geoffrey records:

They found them intact, but the cloths over their faces were stained with blood. They cut off the men's heads and placed them in the graves between their legs, tore out the hearts from the corpses, and covered the bodies with earth again. They brought the hearts to the place called Dodecrossefora and there burned them from morning until evening. When they had at last been burned up, they cracked with a great sound and everyone there saw an evil spirit in the form of a crow fly from the flames. Soon after this was done both the disease and the phantoms ceased.

Of course, a serf who fled his home could become a free man on another manor or a city, where his labor was often in demand, and so there was social pressure for lords not to accept runaways. One might see this ghost story as a convenient cautionary tale: try to escape your miserable life as a serf, and something even worse will befall you. Employ a fugitive serf, and you'll bring bad luck on your manor.

Orderic Vitalis tells the story of his dead brother who, as punishment for a life of fighting, had to travel with an army of the dead "bearing red-hot weapons and wearing spurs of fire."[7] His near-contemporary Walter Map recalled a wicked man in Herefordshire who came back from the dead and took to wandering through the village at night, calling out the names of villagers who all fell ill and died within three days. Eventually the local bishop had the man's body dug up and the head cut off with a spade sprinkled with holy water, and then reburied.[8] William of Newburgh described a similar case in Berwick of a reanimated corpse where: "the simpler folk feared that they might be attacked and beaten by the lifeless monster, while the more thoughtful were concerned that the air might be infected and corrupted from the wanderings of the plague-bringing corpse'."[9] Everywhere there was "widespread acceptance of the idea that the dead, especially the wicked dead, could return to do harm."[10]

Shape-changing was also widely believed. Gervase of Tilbury, writing in Essex in the years either side of 1200, thought werewolves not uncommon—although he also believed women could turn into snakes. There was a popular French tale, *Bisclavret*, about a werewolf, and *Yonec*, a Breton *lai*—a short-rhymed play, usually about love and the supernatural—concerning a lover who comes to a woman in the form of a hawk.

Other mythical beings abounded: the *grant* was a long-legged, bright-eyed creature that looked like a foal, and its appearance in villages warned of fires. There were *portuni*, small creatures with wizened faces who wore tiny clothes and were fond of humans, and who toasted frogs on a fire; they helped around the house but would sometimes cause mischief, snatching a rider's reins late at night so their horse went into the bog, after which it would run off laughing. And there were giants. Ralph of Coggeshall, a well-educated man with access to a growing body of literature, nevertheless wrote "what is read in old histories about the bodies of giants" is true.[11]

However, by the late medieval period there was far more scepticism about such folklore, and most chroniclers would have agreed with Tyrion that the Watch are there to defend Westeros from "grumkins and snarks and all the other monsters your wet nurse warned you about."[12]

The presence of birds in Martin's books is another northern European influence, crows and ravens being prominent in Celtic as well as Nordic mythology. Badb, the Celtic goddess of war, turned herself into a raven or crow and, like real birds, followed armies into battle; intelligent crows have long been known to do this, in the expectation of juicy corpses to eat in its aftermath. The *Anglo-Saxon Chronicle* records that, after the Battle of Brunanburh in 937, in which the Saxons beat a combined army of Vikings and Scots, King Athelstan left the "corpses for the dark black-coated raven, horny-beaked, to enjoy."[13] Which they surely did. Across the North Sea, the Scandinavians believed that ravens served as messengers between this world and the "Otherworld," with Odin, the head of the gods, having two ravens as pets, Thought and Memory.

Likewise with other beasts. In the first book, *A Game of Thrones,* Jon Snow notices a white wolf cub hidden in the snow that will become Ghost, mirroring Celtic myths in which white animals from the Otherworld appear: "from King Arthur's white deer to Pryderi and Manawydan's gleaming white boar and the mysterious White Hound of the Mountain" in the words of one author.[14]

Celtic legend and folklore also included shapeshifters, called *faoladh* or *conroicht,* just as is believed to exist in Westeros. There were tales of strange tribes of werewolves out in the remote countryside of County Tipperary, beings that were called on by ancient kings to help them in battle. Gerald of Wales records one story,[15] after his visit to this strange wild country with the future King John in 1185, a trip that ended disastrously when the mentally unbalanced playboy prince spent all his soldiers' wages on alcohol and prostitutes.

Gerald recalled a tale that took place a number of years before, about a priest and a young boy, a novice in training. They were on their way from Ulster in the north to Meath in the midlands and traveling along side roads. With night falling they made a camp at the edge of the forest, and soon they were surrounded by darkness. The older man became aware of a strange noise and gathered his courage to approach; a voice called out, warning the priest that if he were to see the man with his eyes he would be terrified. After some time, the priest convinced the owner of the voice that he was protected by God, and so a wolf-like figure emerged from the dark. He told the priest and the novice he had been cursed for seven years to appear as a wolf, and there were others like him; his tribe, the Clan Allta, had been jinxed by an Abbot Natalis soon after the time of St Patrick (a whole six centuries earlier). These creatures would often find the urge to attack sheep but once disturbed would run away and return to human shape.

Likewise, the Anglo-Saxons had their own monsters, the *Scaedugengan* (literally "shadow-going"), shapeshifters who are neither alive nor dead, and who can take the form of children, often moving in on a compassionate family who take them in. They feature in the epic poem *Beowulf*, and this belief lasted long after the arrival of the Christians, especially in the north.

THE LORD OF LIGHT

Folk religions developed in relatively small, rural cultures, but as human societies became bigger and more complex, and with the need to cater for larger communities of more distantly related peoples sharing more important resources such as wells and rivers, their religions necessarily became more moralizing and their gods more anthropomorphic. And so, in sophisticated polytheistic societies such as Greece and Rome, human-like deities would punish wrongdoers in this life or the next, even if the gods themselves acted in a way we might find less than perfect, trying to impregnate everything in sight and using devious and eccentric means to achieve this goal.

But the Romans rarely had any problem with foreign religions, and simply co-opted alien gods and pasted them onto their own, a system that worked surprisingly well until they came across a group in Judea who took the progression to its next logical step by proclaiming that there was just one god. These beliefs would inevitably come into conflict.

While the First Men have the nature-based Old Gods, the Andals follow anthropomorphic deities called the Seven: the Mother, the Warrior, the Maiden, the Smith, the Crone, the Stranger, and the Father Above, the last being head of the gods as well as god of justice, depicted as a bearded man who carries scales (the gods are also described as being seven aspects of one god).

Many religions in real life have worshipped a mother figure. The Romans revered a Mater Matuta, or Great Mother, "the mother of good auspices," who was also the goddess of fertility, of beginning, and of dawns.[16] In Christianity, especially among Catholics and Greek Orthodox, the Virgin Mary is worshipped as the Mother of God, in many ways more revered than her son.

The book of the Seven is called the Seven-Pointed Star, and seven is a number with significance in almost all religions; the Catholic and Orthodox churches have seven sacraments, seven deadly sins, and seven archangels, while in Islam there are the seven circuits of the *Kaaba* and seven destructive sins. The Babylonians had seven gates of hell, and in Greek mythology there were seven daughters of Atlas; the Hindus have seven stages to their wedding and the Bahai seven "valleys" or experiences.

Today the Yazidi minority of northern Iraq follow a religion strongly resembling Martin's New Gods; they believe in one deity who had entrusted the world to seven holy beings, the "Heptad," most pre-eminent of whom is Melek Taus, the "Peacock Angel" whom they worship. Melek Taus is also known as Lucifer, but to the Yazidi, although Lucifer was an angel who rebelled against God, he has since repented and is now restored to his favor. However, the Yazidi worship of Lucifer is often used as an excuse for persecution by Islamic fundamentalists (as if they needed one). This horror gained worldwide attention in the summer of 2014 when the Islamic State of Iraq and the Levant (ISIL or ISIS) drove the Yazidi out of their homes in Nineveh, murdering more than four thousand and enslaving twice as many.

The faith of the Yazidis is rooted in ancient Iranian folklore, mixed with elements of Christianity and Islam, as well as Babylonian religions. The ancient Babylonians, like them, prayed toward the sun, sacrificed a bull every year and had taboos about wearing blue or killing fish. (The Babylonians also worshipped birds.)

Religious violence is evident in fantasy, too, and there are allusions to past conflict in the books, between the followers of the Old and New Gods, between more traditional nature-worship, and anthropomorphic religions. In Westeros, the New Gods are themselves challenged by R'hllor, the "Lord of Light," a faith spread by Melisandre, a priestess who has converted Stannis Baratheon to her new faith. Her religion is dualist, with the priests believing in two gods at war. It has many influences from Gnosticism and Manicheanism, religions that emerged in the Near East that saw the world divided into light and darkness. Manicheanism, was founded by the Iranian Mani who lived in the third century and taught that life is a constant struggle between a spiritual world of light and an evil world of darkness. Mani was martyred by the Iranian Zoroastrian hierarchy in 274, but afterwards his ideas spread to the Roman empire.

Gnosticism, a word that covers a range of pre-Christian and Christian beliefs, holds that an evil false god, the *demiurge*, created our imperfect world and therefore brought chaos to the universe; so for Melisandre sacrificing people was actually freeing them from this awful world. Although the Gnostics were driven out by mainstream Christians, they later influenced the Cathars, a heresy that emerged in the south of France during the twelfth century and whose adherents believed that all material things were essentially evil. Indeed, some Gnostics thought the universe itself was a mistake.

There are still some dualist religions around today, among them Mandaeism, whose followers believe in a world separated between darkness and light, with spirits guiding the righteous to the world of light after their deaths. They originated at around the time of Christianity and hold John the Baptist in esteem, but reject Jesus as well as Abraham and Moses, and speak an obscure dialect of Aramaic. This faith still barely clings on in Iraq, with a few thousand believers remaining, although their numbers have been devastated since the 2003 invasion; there are now as many Mandeaens in Sweden as in their native land.

But the most fitting parallel with the faith of R'hllor is Zoroastrianism, the native religion of Persia and the oldest surviving faith on earth. Zoroaster lived around the year 1000 BC and taught that the universe was divided into two principles, Ahura Mazda (Illuminating Wisdom) and its opposite, Angra Mainyu (Hostile Spirit). To Zoroastrians, Ahura Mazda is the lord of light and wisdom, who created the universe and brings "goodness from evil, light from darkness"; this is in contrast to Angra Mainyu, lord of darkness, who created the evil in humankind. This Great Other is a dark god "whose name must not be spoken."[17] Until the Arab conquest brought Islam to the country, Zoroastrianism was the official religion of Persia, although they constitute only a small minority today.

The most telling similarity is the emphasis on fire. In Persia, followers of Ahura Mazda worshiped it, believing fire was the son of their god, and its sacred fire brought joy to believers and destruction to the lovers of evil. In comparison, R'hllor's priests call him "the Heart of Fire, the God of Flame and Shadow." Ancient Persians also used fire for purification and healing, as does Melisandre, for as she said, "The night is dark and full of terrors . . . but the fire burns them all away."

Zoroaster talked of a future battle and a crisis in the world that would bring about its rebirth, and after a miraculous virgin birth, a hero called Saoshyant would lead the final battle, and the mountains will melt into a flaming river; again, this is similar to Melisandre's search for Azor Ahai and his flaming sword. Likewise, the use of the word *Maegi* in the Red God's religion, which echoes the Zoroastrian *Magi* who "performed certain rituals and ceremonies connected with fire, sacrifices and burials" and "may have claimed supernatural knowledge and acted as fortune-tellers, astrologers, magicians, sorcerers, tricksters, and charlatans."[18] Magi is where we get "magician," and is the name given to the wise men who arrived soon after the birth of Jesus.

It should be pointed out that Zoroastrians did not practice human sacrifices, and that while the religion was at time intolerant—apostasy could be punished by death—in more recent years they have been a small and vulnerable minority suffering persecution (and whose most famous recent adherent was the Queen singer Freddie Mercury).

There are other gods in Martin's world. The Dothraki worship horses, and their religion has some similarities with Tengrism, the faith of central Asian horsemen that mixed shamanism, monotheism, and ancestor worship, and was once the religion of Mongols, Turks, and Hungarians. The Tengric book, the *Irk Bitig* or Book of Omens, was written in the ninth century and discovered in a cave in China in 1907. Most of the omens inside concern animals, primarily horses: "A horse that is lost in the desert finds grass to eat and water to drink" is considered a good omen, while "A blind foal tries to suckle at a stallion" is considered bad. "Heaven decrees that a slave girl becomes a queen" is good, as is "A man encounters a god who wishes him plentiful livestock and long life." A culture that divided the world into things that were either good or evil, many of the horse peoples eventually adopted Manichaeism and later Islam.

Then there are the Faceless Men, worshiped by assassins from Braavos in the Free Cities. These killers follow the confusingly abstract "Him of Many Faces," or simply "death." The Faceless Men believe death is an act of worship and carry out assassinations; they began as a cult among slaves who wished for their own deaths, such was the horrendous conditions many faced, until one day they heard a slave praying not for his own end but his master's. As horrific and insane as it sounds, there were groups like this in real life, most of all the Ḥashshāshīn, or Assassins, a cult that began in the eleventh century during the First. The Assassins were Islamis, that is "Seveners" who followed a more esoteric and mystical interpretation of Islam. Their founder Hassan-I Sabbah was a popular figure in the Middle East who recruited followers from around the region and established a fortress in Alamut in Persia. There he built up his secret society, which carried out numerous murders, calling them the *Asasiyun*, or "people close to the faith."

Bitterly opposed to the Sunni Seljuq dynasty, the Assassins spent most of their energy fighting other Muslims rather than Christians, although they killed a number of high-profile crusaders using poisoned daggers (Edward I narrowly became one of them). Sometimes merely leaving a dagger on the victim's pillow, with a threatening letter attached, did the job; the great Saladin, the celebrated Muslim leader during the Third Crusade, conceded all their demands after such a visit.

Assassin "self-sacrificing agents" were trained to infiltrate the target's entourage, blend in, and gain their trust before striking, and Sabbah's men would be educated both in religion and war; they were well trained and well informed, which made their behavior all the more frightening. They often also talked their victims into one-on-one meetings before revealing their true intentions. According to Venetian traveller Marco Polo, the Old Man of the Mountain was able to convince his followers by having them ingest hashish; however, Polo, who was born in 1254, may have been mixing Sabbah (who died in 1124) with another old prophet who lived in the mountains, of whom there seemed to have been quite a few at the time; in fact, the etymological confusion between assassin and hashish was due to Arabic writers and was taken on board by western travelers.

Another, even stranger, death cult was the Thuggee, a Hindu group who worshipped Kali, goddess of destruction and death, and who would strangle travelers as they made their way across India. They are first mentioned in 1356 and would terrorize the country for centuries.[19]

A group straight from *Indiana Jones and the Temple of Doom*, Thugs could be initiated into the sect by a guru, or sometimes Thugs would abduct the children of their victims and turn them into Thugs. They would overpower larger bands of travelers by joining a group one by one, so that at the moment of execution the victims would suddenly find themselves attacked from all sides, unaware that all the newcomers were in fact working together. Anywhere between fifty thousand and two million people were killed by the cult, until the nineteenth century when the British set up a Thugee Department to track down and destroy them. Yet many Thugs claimed they believed they were saving mankind. As one explained, Kali demanded the sacrifice: "God has appointed blood for her food, saying *khoon tum khao*, feed thou upon blood. In my opinion it is very bad, but what can she do, being ordered to subsist upon blood!"[20]

The cult was suppressed, though *thug* became one of numerous Indian words to enter English through the British Raj, along with *pyjamas, bungalow, pundit, shampoo, yoga, karma,* and *blighty.*

10
WINTER IS COMING

Fear is for the winter, my little lord, when the snows fall a hundred feet deep and the ice wind comes howling out of the north.

—OLD NAN

Farmers in the Saastal Valley in Switzerland were probably the first to notice the changing weather, back in the 1250s, when the Allalin glacier began to move down the mountain.[1] Or perhaps the Norse colonists in bitterly-cold Greenland, already on the edge of survival, may have felt the pressure starting to tell. Ivar Baardson, a Norwegian priest of the time, wrote: "The ice now comes . . . so close to the reefs none can sail the old route without risking his life."[2] But across the known world more and more people would have noticed the weather, as four cold winters in a row hit from 1308; the Thames even froze, dogs chasing rabbits across the icy surface, and nobody could remember that ever happening.

And yet no one in Europe could have had any inclination of the approaching disaster. *The Chronicle of Guillaume de Nangis*, written by a monk at the Abbey of Saint-Denis outside Paris, recorded that in April 1315 the rains came down hard—and didn't stop. The deluge continued day after day until August, one account stating that it rained for 155 days continually, everywhere in Europe north of the Alps and west of the Urals.[3]

The rain flooded the fields and, drenched and starved of sunlight, the crops failed. The price of food doubled and then quadrupled, and desperate bands of starving country people could be heard groaning in despair; the poor "gnawed, just like dogs, [on] the raw dead bodies of cattle" and "grazed like cows on the grasses of the field."[4] There was misery "such as our age has never seen," a chronicler recorded sadly.[5] As many as a tenth of the population of England starved to death over the next two years, and some parts of the continent suffered even worse. It was the worst famine Europe had ever known.

The climate is always at the mercy of faraway events, and human catastrophes often arise as a result of volcanic eruptions in distant continents. Explosions in Tambora, Indonesia in 1815 and Laki in Iceland in 1873 caused severe famines around the world, and back in 1257 a huge volcanic eruption in Indonesia led to widespread hunger in Europe; one of the consquences of this was the popular discontent that led to Simon de Montford's rebellion and the establishment of Parliament.

But this was on an altogether new level. The years from 1303 to 1328 were the coldest twenty-five-year period ever recorded. Four of those years were "severe," the worst winters in four centuries, with snow from fall to spring and rivers and lakes frozen for at least a month across the continent. It became so frigid that horsemen could travel on the frozen sea all the way from Denmark to Sweden, a distance of two miles at its shortest.

In historical times, the planet went through a number of extended periods of relative warmth and cold, rather similar to the long winters of Westeros, and cold spells, it was always known, brought hunger. In pagan times, Germanic people would hang evergreen trees outside their houses to ward off the winter, and Ded Moroz, the Slavic equivalent of the Germanic Santa Claus, has its origins in Zimnik, the pagan god of winter (transformed into a benevolent figure by Christians). Christmas trees may be a modern-day hangover from that ancient terror.

For a number of reasons relating to atmosphere, the earth intermittently goes through ice ages, of which there have been four major ones in the last billion years. We are technically within one right now, but within these large ice ages there are warmer periods called interglacials and colder periods called glacials, colloquially also known as "ice ages." For four hundred years Europe experienced the Medieval Warm Period, something we know because of the amount of radioactive isotope Carbon-14 found in tree rings. This is formed by cosmic-ray interaction with nitrogen and oxygen in the upper atmosphere, so the less solar activity, the more Carbon-14. Victorian historian H. H. Lamb was the first to suggest the idea based solely on chronicles that, he noted, referred to strange phenomena, such as vineyards in the north of England. He was right, and since then a huge variety of different measurements have proved him correct, among them not just tree rings, but also the height of tree-lines and pollen in peat bogs.

This long summer started in the ninth century, and for many years vineyards were scattered across England, including such areas as Ely in East Anglia and the Vale of

Gloucester in the west. William of Malmesbury, a twelfth century chronicler, wrote that "In this region the vines are thicker, the grapes more plentiful and their flavor more delightful than in any other part of England. Those who drink this wine do not have to contort their lips because of the sharp and unpleasant taste, indeed it is little inferior to French wine in sweetness."[6]

The increased warmth led to an extra twenty days growing season in Europe, and as a result far more food was available. England's population went from one and a half million in 1000 to five million in 1300, France's from under six million to between seventeen and twenty-one million in the same period. In Europe as a whole, the number of people increased fourfold.

And yet as the population grew, so did the number of people scratching a living on poor-quality, marginal land. Calorie intake went into decline, and surviving skeletons show that the average height in England fell from about 174cm (5'7") at the turn of the millennium to 168cm (5'5") in the fourteenth century.[7] And so when winter arrived suddenly between 1310 and 1330, millions starved.

The first signs of the coming winter came in the thirteenth century, when pack ice in the North Atlantic began to advance south, as did glaciers in Greenland. Surviving plant material from Iceland suggests an abrupt decrease in the temperature from 1275—and a reduction of one degree made a harvest failure seven times more likely. As the spring of 1316 approached, there were prayers for the return of the sun. They were not heard. In April, the grey skies turned black and the rain came down again: "Cold, hard, and pelting; it stung the skin, hurt the eyes, reddened the face, and tore at the soft, wet ground with the force of a plough blade."[8]

In October, four mills along the river Avon in the west of England were swept away, as were fourteen bridges on the Mur in Austria. In Saxony more than 450 entire villages, along with their people, cattle, and houses, were submerged, with huge numbers of casualties. Dykes and bridges disintegrated, and buildings were flooded and collapsed.

Wood and peat became too wet to burn, and no crops could be planted nor harvested. In England, a quarter of wheat or beans or peas sold for twenty shillings, four times its price in 1313, and barley, oats, and salt saw similar rises in the region of 300 percent. In May and June 1316, crop production in England was down by up to 85 percent and there was "most savage, atrocious death" and "the most tearful death."[9]

Hopeless townsfolk walked the fields, searching for any bits of food; men wandered across the country to work, only to return and find their wife and children dead from starvation. Bodies were seen face down in flooded fields, weak from hunger. At one point, on the road near St Albans, no food could be found even for the king.

An observer in Flanders wrote that "the cries that were heard from the poor would move a stone."[10] In Ireland the starving "extracted the bodies of the dead from the cemeteries and dug out the flesh from their skulls and ate it." A German monk wrote: "Certain people . . . because of excessive hunger devoured their own children. In many places, parents, after slaying their children, and children their parents, devoured the remains."[11]

At the time most people received between 80–90 percent of their calories from crops; the Normans who conquered England, for instance, got 80 percent of their calorific intake from just one type of bread. Meat was rare, and lamb was a great luxury eaten by aristocrats once a year, while the poor would never see it on their plates. Most people at the time of the famine already lacked protein, and even during good years, the diet of at least half the population was deficient in calories and also calcium, Vitamins A, C, and D, magnesium, and zinc.

Rye bread was widespread in northern Europe, but it was vulnerable to ergotism, a fungus that has the same essential property as LSD; some blame the various demonic possessions of the period on ergotism, although people at the time often attributed it to the Devil. Eating mouldy rye would lead to the fungus attacking the nervous system, and it can even cut off circulation and cause gangrene. There was also gastrointestinal anthrax caused by eating infected meat.

Fish was also essential to many people's diet, but the trade relied on salt for preservation, again dependent on the weather. England's long coast held huge seaside salt pans, depressions built between lines of high and low tide in which salty water was captured until it evaporated. But because of the lack of sun there was a huge shortage of salt from 1315, so between 1315–1319 fish prices rose to a record level.

The production of wine was also devastated, as grapes require one hundred days of sun a year, which is why today Saxony is the most northerly wine-producing region in Europe. In 1316 "there was no wine in the whole kingdom of France," much to their obvious distress, and Germany's great Neustadt vineyard produced "a trifling quantity" the following year. Wine production in England declined, although it continued to be produced for some time, but of far inferior quality; by the Victorian age a popular magazine joked that drinking English wine requires four people—one to drink it, two to hold him down, and the other to force it down the victim's throat.

As well as starvation, many after 1315 died from scurvy, dementia, or blindness, caused by such things as pellagra (a niacin deficiency) or xerophthalmia (a lack of vitamins). Malnutrition in youth also often leads to problems with the immune system in later life, and this would have very serious consequences later on when an *even* worse catastrophe befell Europe.

Crime shot up, and there was widespread (if understandable) theft of grain, while rioters took over towns such as Douai in Flanders. Landless knights and men-at-arms took to extortion, and mobs from the countryside flooded into Paris, "an assortment of unemployed youths seeking adventure, brigands, thieves, unfrocked priests, beggars and whores."[12] They seized the Grand Châtelet, the city's main stronghold, pillaged abbeys and also attacked Jews, who were thrown into a fiery pit. In fact, there is a correlation between medieval European temperatures and the intensity of anti-Semitic violence, as resources became scarcer.[13] Starvation does not bring out the best in people.

From 1317 gangs of *schavaldores*, a local word meaning robbers, terrorized Northumberland, robbing people at home and in the fields, stealing their cattle and pigs, and often killing them—perhaps a mercy, as they would surely starve otherwise. In the north of England, desperate Scots were more of a menace than ever.

There was also cannibalism, which occurs during all periods of hunger (during a famine in China in the third century BC, the emperor had even officially allowed parents to eat their own children). In Estonia, "the mothers were fed their children," while an Irish chronicle wrote that people "were so destroyed by hunger that they extracted bodies of the dead from cemeteries and dug out the flesh from the skulls and ate it; and women ate their children out of hunger." In Poland and Silesia there were reports whereby "parents devoured their children and children their parents."[14] Some also ate the bodies of hanged criminals. The somewhat sinister fairy tale Hansel and Gretel comes from the famine years, when sending children off to the forest was not an unknown way for desperate parents to avoid watching their children starve.

The winter of 1317–8 was the harshest of all, with cold weather lasting almost until May. The Baltic froze in 1318, the third time since 1303, and rivers feeding it turned to ice too, isolating coastal cities.

There were now a series of huge storms in the North Sea basin, caused by the growing temperature differences between the Arctic Ocean and Gulf Stream. These tempests became more severe in the English Channel, a funnel between two seas and so more dangerous; Dunwich in East Anglia, one of the largest towns in England at the time was devastated by one flood after another, losing 269 buildings. It never really recovered, and today is home to just eighty-six people. The Chronicler of Salzburg described how in 1317, floodwaters in the Mulde River near Leipzig were so violent that a church was lifted off its foundations and drifted away.

Most estimates of the Great Famine suggest that between 5 and 12 percent of Europe's population died, mostly from starvation. This disaster was followed by a disease of cattle and sheep; the parasitic worms *Fasciola heaptica*, known as sheep liver fluke, reduced sheep and goat numbers by 70 percent from 1321, while flocks were likewise hit by sheep pox, also known as the Red Death. The cattle disease murrain hit the country in 1319, devastating the population—it was the same disease that afflicted Egyptian-owned cattle but spared the Hebrews during the time of Exodus. What more obvious sign of God's displeasure could there be?

A LANCASTER ALWAYS PAY HIS DEBTS

Just six weeks after Bannockburn, the Scots, led by Bruce and "Black" James Douglas, were piling into the counties of Northumberland and Durham, and the following year the raids were even worse. Over the summer of 1316, they reached as far as Yorkshire, led by the courageous but ruthless Douglas. Back in 1308, Black Douglas had become notorious when his men attacked an English garrison on Palm Sunday, entering a church and shouting "Douglas!" Prisoners were taken to the castle larder where they were beheaded and their corpses put on a pile, which was then set on fire, after which the Scotsmen poisoned the wells with salt and dead horses. Douglas also removed the right hand of the captured archers, hated and feared across the border, for as the proverb stated, "every English archer carried 24 Scottish lives in his belt."[15] It became known as the Douglas Larder and made Douglas more notorious "than the devil in hell."[16]

By 1318, the city of Berwick was slowly starving and surrounded by Scots, the English reduced to eating their horses. The edge of the town fell in March after street fighting, but it was another three months before Berwick Castle surrendered to Black Douglas, whose father William had handed it over to the English twenty-two years earlier. The Scots now penetrated deeper into English territory, at one point controlling almost all the north, yet the realm was crippled by conflict between King Edward and his enemies. In 1319, the king summoned twenty-three thousand soldiers to muster at York, but only eight thousand appeared, and further disaster occurred with a horse epidemic, the pathogen *burkholderia mallei*, killing half of all the animals between 1320–1322. Edward invaded Scotland with a cavalry force but returned with infantry.

And with Gaveston out of the way things, perversely, got worse. Opposition continued to revolve around Lancaster, but there were also deep divisions, made worse when Thomas's father-in-law, the Earl of Lincoln, the most moderate of the king's critics, died in 1311. Meanwhile after the death of Gaveston, Edward had found solace in an even more venal favorite Hugh le Despenser, a brutal, violent bully who became Edward's lover.[17] Despenser had recently murdered a captive, Llewelyn Bren, a shocking crime that broke the laws of chivalry, but it was certainly not the only one, and on another occasion "one John de Sutton was held in prison until he had surrendered the castle of Dudley," while a wealthy heiress called Elizabeth Comyn was kidnapped and held hostage for a year until she handed over her estates.[18] Despenser was particularly notorious for preying on widows with desirable houses; one of his victims, Lady Baret, was tortured so much that her four limbs were broken and she went insane as a result. And yet he had a hold over the king—much to the queen's distress.

Queen Isabella had in 1322 given birth for the fourth time, to a girl, and as she grew into her role she had been handed more power and responsibility at court, the king valuing her advice. Her relentless acquisitiveness and love of luxury remained unbated, however, and despite the country's hardships, she still kept sixty seamstresses to ensure her household kept up with the latest fashions, as well as 180 servants, including "an almoner, whose only job was to dispense alms on feast days and holy days, using 'the Queen's great silver alms dish.'"[19] A Queen was expected to show pity to the poor.

Such was Lancaster's unpopularity that there had also formed a middle party, opposed to both the royal cousins, led by Bartholomew Badlesmere—an MP, baron, and veteran of Edward I's wars—whose home was Leeds Castle in Kent. Other magnates had remained loyal to the king, despite his faults, among them the marcher (border) lord Roger Mortimer, whose family had held the title of Baron Wigmore since 1074. Mortimer was "tall, swarthy of complexion, and strongly built . . . tough, energetic, decisive, and versatile in his talents." He was also "arrogant, grasping and ambitious" and proud of his family pedigree and background.[20] He had refined tastes and had turned his castles in Wigmore and Ludlow into palatial properties worthy of his grand name.

And yet the brutality of the Despensers was too much even for him. On top of this, the Despenser and Mortimer families also had an old grudge that went back to the 1260s, when Roger's grandfather, another Roger Mortimer, had killed Hugh's grandfather, also his namesake, at the Battle of Evesham. Despenser, ever greedy for land, preyed on his rival's territory and so, in the spring of 1321, Mortimer mobilized a group of marcher lords where they attended a meeting in Yorkshire with Lancaster and other northern rebels.

The more moderate Pembroke, seeing that the king's relationship with Despenser was destroying him, warned Edward: "He perishes on the rocks that loves another more than himself."[21] The queen had begged her husband on her knees to remove Despenser from court, but to no avail. Isabella had been a mere child when her husband had humiliated her with Gaveston, but now she was a grown woman, had borne her king two sons and two daughters, and deserved respect. Yet King Edward was as much under the spell of Despenser as he had been of his previous obsession, and his favorite was intent on ruining and, if possible, removing the queen.

To add to Isabella's humiliation, Edward also had an interest in low-born men; records showed that he made payments to various individuals, including Wat Cowherd, Robin Dyer, and Simon Hod. This may have been an ongoing feature of their marriage, for back in 1314, Edward and Isabella had spent Christmas apart, the king "rowing in the Cambridge Fens with a great concourse of simple people, to refresh his spirit" and swimming with "silly company."[22]

In August 1321, Lancaster turned up in Parliament with a force of five thousand armed retainers, ordering that Despenser and his father Hugh le Despenser the Elder be banished. The younger Despenser fled to his vessel and became a pirate, capturing a Genoese ship and killing the entire crew, and stealing five thousand pounds worth of treasure—but he soon returned.

As Despenser became more powerful and ingrained at court, moderate men like Badlesmere turned increasingly toward Lancaster. The king responded by having Badlesmere banned from his county of Kent, and in October 1321, while he was away in Oxfordshire, the queen was sent, en route to London, to stop at Leeds Castle. When Isabella arrived, however, and demanded entry, Lady Badlesmere instead ordered her archers to fire on the queen's retainers, killing six men in front of her eyes. The queen headed back to London, shaken, to inform her husband.

Things came to a head the following March when an army loyal to Edward met Lancaster's force at Boroughbridge where the northern barons' cavalry was overwhelmed by the king's archers. Lancaster's ally the Earl of Hereford was stabbed by a pike-thrust from below his horse and died horribly, bowels hanging out.[23] Lancaster was taken prisoner and condemned to death by being hanged, drawn, and quartered, but out of respect for his royal blood this was commuted to beheading; Lancaster was forced to ride to his execution on an old mare, wearing a ripped hat, while locals pelted him with snowballs. Alice de Lacy, the earl's unhappy wife, afterward married her lover, Eubulo L'Estrange.

This was followed a week later by the killing of six of Thomas's leading followers. On March 22, another twenty-four of Lancaster's associates were executed in various horrible ways, and over the next month 118 in total were put to death, including six leading noblemen. For his role in the rebellion, Baron Badlesmere was dragged through the streets of Canterbury before being decapitated, and afterward "his head spread on a pike and set to stare down, hollow-eyed, on the cowed townspeople from the city's east gate."[24] Edward also hanged the constable of Leeds Castle along with thirteen others, and imprisoned Lady Badlesmere and her children in the Tower of London. Also jailed was Lancaster's elderly mother-in-law, the countess of Lincoln, whose husband had been a loyal, if critical, subject. The king's troops also captured Mortimer, who was sentenced to death, but with the bloodlust burning out he was instead locked up in the Tower indefinitely.

This ruthless purge of his enemies made Edward appear strong, although his temporary popularity did not last. Europe's barley harvest collapsed, worse in 1321 than even in 1315, and the following year fifty-two people were crushed at the gates of the Preaching Friars in London, fighting over food. The king became increasingly tyrannical under the sway of Despenser, now more powerful than ever. The Earl of Carlisle, who had loyally defeated Lancaster on behalf of the king, had accepted peace overtures from the Scots, and when the king learned of this, he had him cruelly executed.[25]

In August 1322, Edward II invaded Scotland, but Bruce escaped beyond the Forth and now the Scots chased them back and the Earl of Richmond was captured, yet another humiliation. Worse still, Edward had left his queen at Tynemouth Priory on the Northumbrian coast, at the mercy of the Scots nearby, and made no attempt at rescue her from the Earl of Douglas nearby. This was the second time he had deserted her in this way, the first being when he had fled with Gaveston; the queen and her damsels eventually escaped in a boat, but in their desperation one of her ladies fell overboard and drowned. Her hatred was growing, and the She-Wolf would not take the humiliation forever.

"I HEARD IT SAID THAT POISON IS A WOMAN'S WEAPON."

In August 1315, King Louis's wife Margaret died in a Normandy dungeon, supposedly of a cold, although poison was suspected; at the very least she was heavily maltreated. However, the following year Louis died too, aged just twenty-six, from a chill caught after playing tennis, and many spoke of poison at the hands of his brother Philippe's mother-in-law Mahaut of Artois. A few months later, Louis's heavily pregnant second wife Clemence gave birth to a boy, John, but he succumbed after just six days, and so the crown passed to the Iron King's second son, conveniently for Mahaut.

Poison was often suspected in French court politics, but as forensics was not capable of detecting its presence in a corpse much is just speculation. Mahaut was rumored to be a killer, and some even believed her to have murdered the infant king too to further her daughter's position. Perhaps. Just as poison was prevalent in Essos and Dorne, so courts in France, Italy, and Spain were said to be hotbeds of such trickery. The Normans in particular were notorious for it, and their dukes certainly poisoned at least one Duke of Brittany—their chief rival—but many other rivals died under mysterious circumstances. In Moorish Spain in 1008, Abd al-Malik, ruler of Cordoba, was on his way to fight the Christians when he collapsed, apparently after his brother had offered him an apple laced with deadly poison. This Spanish tradition was maintained by the caliphate's Catholic successors and, in the fourteenth century, Blanche of Bourbon, Queen of Castile, was fatally drugged at the behest of her husband, King Pedro the Cruel.[26]

Many believed unicorn horns were an antidote to poison, and these were bought at markets across Europe; although as unicorns don't actually exist, what they were being sold was the horn of the narwhal, a type of whale found in the cold, northern seas. In reality, there were no known cures for most types, and so the French court kept a Master of the Stomach to protect the monarch from anyone who might wish to remove him. Being a royal food taster to the king of France, however, would not have been the worst job, as the Valois kings helped to invent what we now think of as cuisine. They employed one of the most important figures in the history of the culinary arts, Guillaume Tirel, who was *enfant de cuisine* (kitchen boy) to Charles IV's queen Jeanne. Later he became head chef to Philippe VI, and wrote *Le Viandier*, the first cookbook of the medieval period, which details the food of northern France; it is because cuisine was first developed formally in Paris that, even today, to become a chef is to learn, firstly, about French food.

Philippe V had been able to claim the throne because of the suspicions of illegitimacy hanging over his brother's surviving daughter; it was instead decreed that the crown could only be inherited through the male line, using a dubious historical precedent, the "Salic Law" of the Franks. In just a few years, this legal dispute would explode into a war costing millions of lives, but this was all in the future. Tragically, however, Philippe died aged just twenty-nine, further proof of the curse of the Templars in some people's minds, and the crown in turn passed to his youngest brother Charles in 1322.

As well as the throne, Charles IV had inherited the dispute with the English over the border region between Gascony and French-controlled Aquitaine. When the kings of England and France had met in June 1320, Philippe V had demanded Edward do fealty for Gascony. Edward had already done homage, which involved the surrender of a particular fief, or property, by a vassal to a lord where he swore to become his man, from the French *homme*; the lord then returned it, symbolically handing him an item associated with the property, often something that grew on the land. Fealty was something different altogether, an oath of fidelity to serve against all others, something that Edward as king could not do; he exploded in anger.

Then in November 1323 conflict broke out when some Gascons tore down a fortress that a French lord had built on disputed territory. The following year King Charles declared Edward's land in Gascony forfeit and the countries were now sliding into war.

For Despenser, this was the perfect pretext to undermine the queen; all French nationals were dismissed from the court, depriving Isabella of her closest friends and confidents, and all their goods confiscated. It got worse, with the queen's children taken away from her, the girls being sent to live with Despenser's family while

Despenser's wife Eleanor de Clare—also the king's niece—was appointed as the queen's housekeeper to follow her everywhere. She was also, quite obviously, a spy who kept the queen's seal on her person and reported everything back to her husband and his clan.

Isabella must by now have hated her husband's lover, and yet the queen was more skilled at the art of court politics than her enemies, perhaps having learned it in Paris. One element of court life represented by Margaery Tyrell in Westeros is the art of dissembling, because for a woman at the center of court no one should ever really know her true feelings. Isabella mastered this skill, and never gave away any signs of her real, burning hatred toward Despenser and, increasingly, her husband.

The impasse with King Charles threatened to descend into all-out war, and it was now that Queen Isabella, outwardly forgiving to her dear husband and his trusted advisor, suggested that she take their son Edward over to do homage for Gascony in Edward's place. This would satisfy the king of France without humiliating the king of England and, for Despenser, remove an irritant from the king's presence.

When the queen left for France, Edward wrote, "on her departure, she did not seem to anyone to be offended" and gave a farewell kiss to Despenser: "towards no one was she more agreeable, myself excepted." He noted "the amiable looks and words between them, and the great friendship she professed for him on her crossing the sea."[27] Despenser had been unsure about the queen's suggestion and her motives, but when at last he realized how they had been outwitted and placed in check, it was too late.

Meanwhile Roger Mortimer had been languishing in the Tower of London, a fortress from which only one man had ever escaped. And yet the earl could be persuasive and had managed to turn the captain of the dungeon, who therefore arranged to drug all the guards on the night of a banquet held once a year to honor the Tower's patron saint. Mortimer made a daring escape, dug his way through a passageway and in the darkness climbed down to the river where a waiting boat took him away. The king sent out search parties, expecting him to head toward his stronghold in the border region, but in fact he had gone in the opposite direction, to France, where his wife had relatives.

Mortimer went to Picardy, and from there to Paris—where he and Isabella fell in love. The marcher lord was an extremely domineering and masculine man, already had ten children by his wife, and for a woman in a loveless marriage with a man who did not desire her, he may have been irresistible.[28]

Romance runs through Martin's world, with the young Sansa Stark epitomizing the naive idealization of honorable knights and damsels in distress, at least until the grim reality of the world sinks in. At the start of the epic she believes in the idea that a handsome prince such as Joffrey must by definition have the qualities attached to his class, such as nobility and gentleness (both of these words originally meant "high-born"); unlike her sister she enthusiastically adopts the traditional roles expected of an aristocratic lady, in particular courtesy.[29] However, a fondness for such a romantic idealization did not suggest weakness or even naivety. Isabella, as strong-willed as her father, was nevertheless obsessed with romance books—indeed, that is one thing she had in common with her lover, who also saw himself as a latter-day King Arthur, and they both "possessed an inordinate fondness for dreadful, bodice-ripping chivalric romances of heroic derring-do."[30]

Isabella regularly borrowed books from the Tower of London library, all of them romance stories that we might think of as somewhat corny. For all that she had seen and experienced, and understood how weak and devious men could be, she still believed in the ideal.

Now the queen, in possession of her son Edward, was extremely dangerous to her husband, for she presented not just an opposition but an opposition with a viable replacement. The king directed her to return, and when she did not, he cut off payment, continuing to send letters to his wife and son; and yet her brother was not going to allow her to go hungry. Edward also wrote to his son, now thirteen, who was put in a very difficult position; he, no doubt, hated Despenser and what he'd done to the family, but he had no love for Mortimer either, a domineering bully who was now openly the queen's lover.

King Charles, especially with his own history, was also uncomfortable at the openly adulterous relationship and so Isabella, Mortimer, and Edward had to flee north, to the Count of Hainault in what is now Belgium. Here she was forced to do what many desperate exiles have done down the years—arrange a marriage alliance in return for a foreign army. Pledging her son Edward to the count's daughter Philippa, she was provided with troops with which to sail across the sea (it so happened that Edward and Philippa had spent time together and had already grown fond of each other).

The Queen of England had now been declared an enemy alien and her lands had been confiscated for the safety of the kingdom, but her rival court abroad began to attract leading noblemen from England, among them the king's half-brother Edmund, Earl of Kent. She now planned her crossing to England.

Gathering her forces, she made land in East Anglia, and of two thousand soldiers sent to contest Isabella, only fifty-five turned up, and they switched sides. London collapsed into chaos and the invasion was met with widespread support, and soon Edward and the younger Despenser were isolated in Caerphilly Castle in south Wales. They should have stayed there, one of the strongest in Europe, with thirty-foot-high walls that were twelve feet thick, and well supplied. Instead they made a dash for the sea but were stuck for six days in torrential weather before being forced to return.

Hugh le Despenser's father, aged sixty-five, had been condemned to die as a traitor and hanged. Afterwards his torso was suspended by the arms with two strong ropes for four days, after which it was chopped up and thrown to some dogs. The younger Despenser's fate would be far worse; after being condemned by a group of barons, including Mortimer and Lancaster's brother Henry, Earl of Leicester, he was sentenced to be executed in London, but tried to starve himself to death. Instead, now desperately weakened by hunger, he endured an agonizing death in Hereford, as the authorities worried the journey to the capital would kill him. Dressed in a reversed coat of arms—symbol of treachery—a crown of nettles was placed on his head, with mocking biblical verses about hubris carved into his skin with knives. He was dragged through the city by four horses, to the sound of trumpets and bagpipes, and half-hanged on a fifty-foot-tall-gallows so that all might see. At one point he fell unconscious but was cut down and slapped awake before his intestines were cut out; likewise, "his member and his testicles were cut off, because he was a heretic and a sodomite, even, it was said, with the king." A fire was lit under the scaffold, and Despenser's genitals were thrown in, followed by his intestines and heart, the dying man watching everything. Then the crowd cheered as his head was cut off.

Mortimer declared that the magnates had deposed Edward because he had not followed his coronation oath and was under the control of evil advisers. And so, in January 1327, Parliament was called in the name of Edward's son, with Mortimer appointed Keeper of the Realm. Edward II witnessed Sir Thomas Blount, steward of the household, break his staff of office to show the household had been disbanded.

The king was moved to Berkeley Castle in Gloucestershire, but after a rescue attempt by supporters he was found dead. A story soon circulated that he had been killed with a red-hot poker inserted in his anus so that no signs of violence would show on his corpse.[31] Almost certainly Mortimer was responsible.

Just a few weeks later, in April 1327, an army was sent north to battle the Scots again, but it ended in failure once more. The English force had gone to Percy-controlled Topcliffe in Yorkshire and onto to Durham, which French chronicler Jean le Bel, a soldier in this army, called "the last outpost of civilization."[32] Believing the Scots to be attacking through Cumberland, the English were tricked, sending their men onto the western approach to the border, while Black Douglas and his men went east and burned and pillaged Northumberland, sending terrified villagers into fortresses and woods. The Scots could not be defeated, and so a treaty was signed in 1328 recognizing their independence formally, much to the fury of the boy king Edward, whose sister Joan was married off to Bruce's son David. Robert the Bruce died the following year, of leprosy, but the king beyond the wall had succeeded.

11
THE SEVEN

They watch over all of us, ready to dole out mercy, or justice.

—LANCEL LANNISTER

R eligion evolves as societies change and eventually, in the most complex of Middle Eastern civilizations in the first millennium BC, there developed what evolutionary psychologist Ara Norenzayan called "Big Gods"— all-powerful deities who were concerned with how people lived and behaved. Previously the spirits people worshipped did not especially care what men did with their lives, but increasingly they acted in a moralistic way, even if the behavior of the Old Testament God appears to us cruel at times. The sophisticated Assyrians worshipped a number of deities but were perhaps the first to raise the lead god, Ashur, to such importance that the others almost lost their divinity in comparison. Between the tenth and sixth centuries BC, the Hebrew pantheon of gods evolved into the worship of just one, Yahweh, but monotheism exploded across the ancient world only when a sect of Judaism began to proclaim that their leader Jesus of Nazareth, crucified by the Romans in Jerusalem, was the promised Messiah, or as it was translated into Greek, *Christos*—and not just for the Jews, but for all humanity.

This new cult promised eternal life for the poor and virtuous and an end to sacrifice, God having made the final sacrifice with His Son. In 34 AD they had their first martyr, Stephen, stoned to death in front of a crowd that included a Greek-speaking Jew called Saul who was at the time zealously hunting down members of the new group. Soon after, in one of the most fateful events in history, Saul was on his way to Damascus when he was struck blind and saw a vision of Jesus, and joined the followers of the "Messiah," these Christians. By the end of the second century, the sect had spread across the eastern and soon the western Mediterranean, the first Latin Christian text appearing in 180 AD.[1] By 200 it had already established a foothold in

Britain, and the island's first martyr, a soldier called Alban, died in 304 after shelter-
ing a Christian priest and converting. The new religion, although sometimes tolerated, suffered periodic persecution from the Roman authorities, among the worst
being the wave of destruction and murder that followed the Emperor Diocletian's
edict of February 24, 303, which ordered the destruction of all churches and the burning of all their scriptures. Countless Christians were burned to death or otherwise
gruesomely murdered in the "Great Persecution" that followed.

The fanatical red priestess Melisandre is extremely intolerant of other religions,
destroying any signs of their worship and indeed killing unbelievers. She convinces
Stannis to abandon the worship of the Seven and burn their effigies, and to also force
conversion on unbelievers; Stannis then goes into battle with the flaming heart of the
Lord of Light on his banner.

And so, in 313 the Roman Emperor Constantine, before a great battle with a rival
for the throne, had seen a vision of a crucifix in the sky with the words "by this sign
you will conquer." He ordered his troops to paint a cross on their shield before the
battle, and soon after this victory he legalized Christianity, and later converted himself. But, having achieved tolerance and then dominance after centuries of persecution, it was not long before the Christians turned persecutors, both of pagans
and—more zealously—other Christians, often over the most pedantic of doctrinal
differences.

One of the most revered saints from the late Roman period, St Martin of Tours,
was also an enthusiastic destroyer of pagan temples in Gaul before his death in 397—
although local people would not allow him to knock down a particular tree, which
remained sacred. St Martin's desecration of pagan shrines was universal. When the
king of Northumbria accepted the new God, the first thing his chief religious leader,
freshly converted, did was throw a spear into the old pagan place of worship, angry
that the gods had not favored him. As Samwell says: "The Seven have never answered
my prayers. Perhaps the old gods will."[2]

But worship of the new God was not spread by conquest, and indeed many conquerors of Christian people took the religion of their subjects, rather than vice versa.
The Targaryens, upon subjugating Westeros, accepted the faith of the Seven rather
than bringing their own religion, which has often been the case with conquering
peoples. At the collapse of the western Roman Empire, many barbarian tribes became
Christian as they overwhelmed Roman lands, if they were not already converted.

Later conquerors of the Middle East adopted Islam as their faith; on purely practical grounds it's far easier to rule people if you share their religion. And after the fall of the western empire, Christianity, once a religion of prostitutes and beggars and outcasts, would become institutionalized under bishops who assumed authority in the crumbling cities.

SEPT AND STATE

The religion of the Seven is more formalized than that of the Old Gods, just as Christianity was more formalized than traditional European religion; they have temples called Septs and their own caste of priests, the Septons. Like with Christianity, the religion has some emphasis on sexual shame and guilt, the Septons playing a leading part in Cersei's humiliation for adultery. The faith of the Seven is linked to the state, with the High Septon anointing the king, and his support is essential for any monarch. Like with western Christianity, the king is expected to follow the religion, with official ceremonies conducted by Septons and Septas, male and female priests respectively. The clergy of the Faith of the Seven are chosen by the Council of the Most Devout, and people take oaths to the Seven, like men and women in medieval Europe took an oath to God. There is also inevitably a clash between church and state, as in real life, where many Church leaders ended their lives violently as a result.

Of the seven Westerosi godheads, three are masculine, representing divine justice, courage, and production; three are feminine, representing fertility, purity, and wisdom. The seventh, the Stranger, is "unknowable and transcendent,"[3] described in *A Clash of Kings* as "less and more than human, unknown and unknowable." There are obvious comparisons here with Christianity, which has a Trinity of Father, Son, and Holy Ghost, three and one at the same time, with the Stranger resembling Christianity's Holy Spirit. The Stranger also provides for outcasts, which is why the dwarf Tyrion Lannister prays to it.

In Martin's own words, "The faith of the Seven is of course based on [the] medieval Catholic church" and the Seven based on the Trinity. The religion of the Seven also contains the physical aspects of European medieval Christianity, such as cathedrals, stained glass windows, church bells, altars in candlelight, and catacombs. The classic western style of cathedral in the popular imagination is Gothic, called the "French style" at the time and which originated in northern France (it was only later called Gothic, originally as an insult, because its pointed arches were seen as the antithesis of Roman architecture, and so more suitable to barbarian Goths). Almost all the best-known cathedrals, such as Notre-Dame de Paris, Chartres, Cologne, and Lincoln, are Gothic, although the Great Sept of Baelor is designed to look more exotic.

That Catholic Christianity came to dominate Europe had much to do with one very successful barbarian tribe, the Franks. Their supremacy began during a period commonly known as the Dark Ages, although this is a term medieval historians dislike for a number of reasons. However, while "dark" historically refers to the lack of historical records of the period, in every measure of progress there was a sharp decline both in western European living standards and intellectual output from 500 to 1000AD.[4]

For some years it was also literally a time of darkness. Just as in Westeros, where there are folk memories of times gone by when the sun disappeared and the crops failed, so on earth the doom of Rome was followed by cataclysm. By the mid-sixth century the imperial city, once a hubristic metropolis that ruled most of the known world, was being fought over by Greeks from the east and Goths from the north, a site that would have stunned Romans from two centuries earlier.

While uncultured tribes from beyond the Alps had swarmed into northern Italy in the late fifth century as Rome collapsed, and the west was overrun by blond-haired barbarians, in the east the empire survived in its new capital, Constantinople, and would do so for another thousand years. This Greek-speaking empire became known to western historians as Byzantium, although the "Byzantines" just called themselves Romans.

In 476, a German tribe called the Goths had subjugated Italy, but the following century the ambitious Byzantine emperor Justinian was determined to win it back for the empire. The greatest Byzantine general, Belasarius, had already conquered the region around old Carthage in North Africa from the Vandals, and in 535 the Byzantines crossed over to Sicily, which had been Greek-speaking since the eighth century BC and would continue to be until the late medieval ages. (Today there are pockets of southern Italy where a form of Greek with Italian influences, called Griko, is still spoken.) The war would ultimately last decades and became something of a pyrrhic victory for the eastern Romans, who remained in control of half of Italy, but were drained and exhausted. Although they could not know it, a force was emerging in the east that would threaten them far more than any westerners could manage.

Across the Latin-speaking half of the former empire, things had become bleak; between the sixth and seventh century western Europe lost between half and two-thirds of its population. The city of Rome had declined from several hundred thousand to just twenty thousand people in 800 AD; after everything it had previously suffered, the Byzantine-Gothic war had led to the ruin of its aqueducts, which permanently destroyed its ability to supply a large population. A chronicler of the time said: "In the middle of the debris of great cities, only scattered groups of wretched people survive." Rome "was moribund, a crepuscular near-wasteland of weeds and wolves and a mere twenty thousand dispirited, malarial residents eking out livings among monuments stripped of marble, public buildings cannibalized for their brick and bronze."[5]

During his travels, the Byzantine historian Procopius, who had arrived in Italy in 536, had noticed something very strange: "The sun began to be darkened by day and the moon by night, while the ocean was tumultuous with spray from the 24th of March in this year till the 24th of June in the following year . . . And, as the winter was a severe one, so much so that from the large and unwonted quantity of snow the birds perished . . . there was distress . . . among men . . . from the evil things."[6] That year the faraway *Annals of Ulster* record "a failure of bread," and food shortages were recorded as far afield as Peru and China. This extreme weather event, which would linger in the historical memory, also occurs in Westeros with "the Long Night," a season of winter that lasted a generation, when, according to some old wives' tales, people never saw daylight for years on end.

The real year without sun is thought to have been caused by a volcano in the South Pacific spreading ash around the world and led to famines and possibly the destruction of a city in Central America. It may have also prompted the migration of Mongolian tribes to the west, which brought further misery to Europe.

At the time there were reports of blood-colored rain in Gaul, of a yellow substance "running across the ground like a shower" in western Britain.[7] The sun dimmed throughout Europe and the Near East, and Flavius Cassiodorus wrote: "We marvel to see now shadow on our bodies at noon, to feel the mighty vigor of the sun's heat wasted into feebleness."

This was the darkest moment in western Europe's history, but as in Westeros, a new age would emerge.[8] In Essos, the Rhoyne is described as the "mightiest river in the world"; there the people, the Rhoynar, built "elegant towns and cities from the headwaters of the Rhoyne down to her mouth, each lovelier than the last."[9] Art and music flourished, and united by blood and culture the people of Rhoyne "were fiercely independent," while in this part of the world women were regarded as equal to the men. The parallel is clearly with the German statelets that emerged in the medieval period, which were centred on the river Rhine, and which indeed were noted for their elegant, beautiful towns (until many were destroyed in World War II).

At the time of Rome's collapse, the Rhine was home to a number of tribes, the most dominant of which were the Franks, who had begun to settle heavily in northern Gaul while allied to the Romans. At the end of the fifth century, a warlord called Clovis put all the Franks under his leadership, establishing the founding dynasty that would one day rule all of France.

Clovis was married to Clotilda, who came from another Germanic tribe to the south, the Burgundians, and who tried her utmost to convert him to her Catholicism. After crying out for the Christian God's help in battle, Clovis gave his thanks on Christmas Day, 496, when he and three thousand of his warriors were baptized at the Cathedral of Rheims in the heart of the Frankish lands north of Paris. And so it was here that the kings of France would be crowned until the nineteenth century.

With this fateful decision, Catholic Christianity was established as the religion of western Europe, and it was Franks who created the union of church and state. They became the pre-eminent tribe in the West, claiming a continuity with the fallen empire; this Germanic tribe, although conquerors, even adopted the language of the people they had overrun, which they called, simply, "Romanz" but would take the name of the conquerors, Frankish or *Français*.

By being crowned by a bishop, representing God, Clovis also raised kingship up beyond something involving mere mortals. King comes from Old German *kuningaz*, and became *cyning* in Old English, the closest modern translation being "leader of the people" or "descended from nobility," although "warlord" would be just as good. However, after Clovis and, especially Charlemagne three centuries later, kings became more than lords; instead they were anointed by God, and this explains the particular horror felt about the killing of a monarch. This majesty was reflected in the pre-eminent game of medieval life, chess, in which the king alone could not be killed. Writing in the thirteenth century, English theologian Alexander Nequam recalled how Louis VI, while running from the army of the English king Henry I, found that one of Henry's knights had seized his reins and so cried out: "Fie upon you! Don't you know that a king may not be taken even in chess?"[10] Killing a king was the ultimate sin against nature.

Clovis and his successors were called the Merovingians, after his father Merovich, and as they wore long hair as a family privilege, they were sometimes referred to as the "long-haired kings" (Latin *reges criniti*) by contemporaries. Like with Dothraki, cutting hair off subsequently became a sign of defeat and deposition, after which men could not rule.

Under Clovis, the Franks conquered almost all of northern Gaul, but they also established effective dominance over the south, although in the regions of Aquitaine and Septimania the people maintained their Latin language and culture, and until recently the two parts of France spoke distinct languages. Despite these differences, the Duke of Aquitaine had always recognized the king in Paris as overlord, although their relationship was difficult—and a new crisis was soon to change all that.

As time passed, the kings of the Franks became less powerful and real power passed to a hereditary "Mayor of the Palace," as these chief ministers were styled. When Pepin of Herstal, mayor of the palace and de facto ruler, died in 714, his widow Plectrude attempted to seize power, exiling Pepin's illegitimate son, a tall, blond, twenty-five-year-old named Charles. She would not succeed, and the young man would not only take power, sending his stepmother to a convent, but lead the Franks to victory in one of the most influential battles in history.

12

DORNISH SPAIN

Dorne is sand and scorpions, and bleak red mountains baking in the sun.

—Reznak mo Reznak

A new threat soon emerged causing terror to both Franks and Latins. To the south of Gaul, the imperial province of Hispania had been conquered in the fifth century by another barbarian tribe, the Visigoths; three hundred years later, they, in turn, were overrun by a new empire that incorporated a third of humanity and stretched from Gibraltar to the Indus—that of Islam. The "Believers," as they styled themselves, had emerged out of the Arabian desert and with their strong social cohesion, or "group feeling"—*asabiyyah*—had conquered much of the Byzantine Empire and overrun altogether the world's other great power, Persia. Converting the conquered with financial as well as heavenly incentives, they had followed their initial capture of the Near East with a second burst of energy along the coast of North Africa.

Then in 711 AD, a huge army crossed the narrow straits of land separating Roman Hispania from Africa, and the Arabs would stay in Spain for another seven centuries, during which time Moorish Spain was far more advanced than its Christian neighbors.

George R.R. Martin has said that Dorne, the most southerly of the Seven Kingdoms, is based on Moorish Spain. Dorne is far drier and hotter than the rest of Westeros, the people more romantic, their food spicier than those to the north. The Dornish are described as "dark-haired, olive-skinned, hot-blooded and passionate";[1] they mostly look different to people in the other kingdoms, who have a northern European appearance, although they descend from three separate races of people, and so there are three types of Dornishmen—Stony, Sandy, and Salty (Stony Dornish are mountain folk and have fair hair and skin, unlike the others). Uniquely in the Seven Kingdoms, the Dornish partly descend from the Rhoynar of Essos, and so maintain many of their customs; the Rhoynish had been led to Dorne centuries back by Nymeria, who burned their ships so that his followers would not head back.

Dorne has "vast deserts of red and white sand, forbidding mountains . . . sweltering heat, sandstorms, scorpions, fiery food, poison, castles made of mud, dates and figs and blood oranges."[2] It has semi-arid hills, deserts, mountains, and coastal areas with large populations, and because it is geographically hard to unite, Dorne has had the largest number of petty kings.

The southern kingdom is different in many ways—tolerant of homosexuality, for example—just as southern Europe has traditionally been more relaxed than the north; France and Italy decriminalised same-sex activity in the eighteenth and nineteenth centuries, long before Britain and Germany. Indeed, until the twentieth century the Islamic world was more kindly disposed towards homosexuality than the West: Islamic poetry often features a beautiful boy as the object of love, while Morocco and Egypt have long had a tradition of same-sex relationships.[3]

Like Dorne, Iberia is hot, and except in its far north receives the most sunshine in Europe, with only pockets of southern Italy, southern Greece, and Provence matching it. It is also large—at 229,000 square miles, around the size of France—and mountainous. After Switzerland and Norway, Spain and Portugal are the most elevated countries in Europe, with five systems over the peninsula, from the Cantabrian in the north-west to the Sierra Nevada in the south. This makes it hard for one central power to control the area.

The Visigoths had ruled Iberia as a separate caste, largely refusing to integrate with the native Ibero-Romans and remaining aloof; so when the Muslims arrived there was little desire to fight for the rulers, and many towns welcomed them. For cities that put up resistance there followed the summary execution of adult males and enslavement of women and children, a fate that befell Cordoba and Zaragoza. Those that surrendered, such as Pamplona, were spared.

Like Dorne, Spain has been invaded by numerous different people, ranging from olive-skinned Arabs to blue-eyed Germans. The invaders of 711 brought a variety of settlers from across the Middle East and North Africa; Tariq ibn Ziyad, the conqueror of Iberia who, upon their landing, ordered for all his army's ships to be burned so that they might not turn back, was Persian or maybe a Berber.

Indeed, most of the invaders were not Arabs but Berber, the native people of north-west Africa. Berber comes from the Greek word barbarian, although why it stuck with just one group is a mystery, and they called themselves "free men," or *Amazighen*. Centralized authorities always saw this freedom in a different light and later rulers of Morocco referred to tribal areas outside of their control as "the lands of insolence."[4]

Some hundred thousand Arabs and Berbers settled in the region, from Syria, Palestine, Yemen, and elsewhere, and left their mark; Spanish, Portuguese, and Catalan all have hundreds of words derived from Arabic, often to do with agriculture and administration, as well as food—sugar, oranges, aubergines, and rice are all Arabic in origin, among the new crops introduced by the conquerors, as well as cotton, lemons, limes, bananas, spinach, and watermelons.

It became a remarkable society; while Christian Europe slept, a magnificent civilization flourished to the south in al-Andalus, as Moorish Spain was now called. Theirs was a culture rich with beauty, and the crown jewel was the city of Cordoba, which at the turn of the millennium was the largest in Europe, home to 450,000 people, ten times more than Venice or Rome and over twenty times that of Paris; the largest Christian city in western Europe, Salerno, had just 50,000. As late as 1330 Islamic Granada, home to perhaps 150,000 people, was possibly the largest on the continent.[5] Ibn Hawqal, the tenth century Arab geographer, wrote that "it has no equal in the Maghreb, and hardly in Egypt, Syria or Mesopotamia, for the size of its population, its extent, the space occupied by its markets, the cleanliness of its streets, the architecture of its mosques, the number of its baths and caravanserais." Islamic Cordoba was centered on the Roman city of Corduba.

Within the old walled town, by the river Guadalquivir to the south, was the governmental quarter that featured the palace of the caliphs, the chancery, barracks, prison, and the homes of the leading officials, as well as the Great Mosque. Beyond that the walled city, which could be entered through seven gateways, was surrounded by dense residential areas, markets, gardens, cemeteries, and bathhouses and further out the *munyas*, the large palatial country retreats of the city's elite, nestling on the southern edges of the Sierra de Cordoba.[6] By the Great Mosque of Cordoba were the public baths, as well as the central market, where one might buy bread, fruit, oil, or lamb, but also "Persian carpets, Damascus metalware, China silks, fine leather and jewellery, slaves, and much else supplied on demand by the Muslim world economy."[7]

The Moors had rebuilt the bridge over the river in the eighth century, replacing a Roman structure; it is also recognizable as the Long Bridge of Volantis over which

Tyrion and Varys walk, although at the time it also featured homes, taverns, brothels, and a market.[8]

Then there was the palace of Madinat az-Zahra, commissioned in 936 by Emir Abd al-Rahman III. It took ten thousand workmen toiling away for years to create the magnificent building—marble was imported from North Africa, while a bishop was sent to Constantinople to collect art as well as craftsmen. The emperor Constantine Porphyrogenitus may have sent 140 columns to help with its construction.

The throne rooms were magnificent, but the most splendid was the Hall of the Caliphs:

> Its roof and walls were constructed out of sheets of variously tinted marble so fine as to be translucent. In the center of the room stood a large shallow bowl containing mercury: it stood on a base which could be rocked, and it was so placed as to receive sunlight from a number of surrounding apertures. When the caliph wished to impress or alarm anyone who had been granted an audience he would sign to a slave to rock the bowl and the sunbeams reflected from the surface of the mercury would flash and whizz round the room like lightning.[9]

The palace of Zahra, which means "blossom" or "flower" was, according to legend, named after the emir's favorite wife, Madinet al-Zahra. When foreign ambassadors went to see the monarch, there was a three-mile-long rank of soldiers two-deep flanking the sides, "their naked swords, both broad and long, meeting at the tips like rafters of a roof . . . The fear that this inspired was indescribable."[10] Inside, the palace contained "colonnaded great halls, geometric gardens, and cascading fountains [that] humbled generations of ambassadors and awed subjects."[11]

There were seventy libraries in Cordoba, and the city's main bibliotheca had something like four hundred thousand manuscripts, mostly paper. In contrast, St Gall in Switzerland, the biggest in the Christian north, had just six hundred, all of inferior calfskin or sheepskin. To a visitor from Christendom the city would have appeared majestic; Hrowswitha of Gandersheim, a Saxon nun, called Abd al-Rahman III's Cordoba "the brilliant ornament of the world."

The city's only rival at the time was Seville, which featured the sumptuous Alcazar Palace. Meaning "Room of the Princes" in the Arabic-Spanish hybrid language of the time, Alcazar was the seat of the Abbadí kingdom, and one of three capitals of the Almohad empire after it was built in the eleventh century. Later it would be used by the Castilian monarchs after the Christians conquered the city, and it is now recognizable as the Dornish royal palace.[12]

Spain was a diverse place in a way France or Britain were not. Abd al-Rahman had a personal bodyguard that consisted of Caucasian infantry from the southern mountains of Russia, complemented by the prince's personal bodyguard of black Africans. Al-Andalus is, in particular, associated with the idea of *convivencia*, the spirit of coexistence, a country in which Muslims, Christians, and Jews managed to live together, although this tolerance was all relative; converting from Islam to Christianity was punishable by death, and the slow but steady trickle of converts the other way reflected the financial penalties for being a non-Muslim.

And yet Jews and Christians were routinely employed at the court. Al-Mu'tamid of Seville used a rabbi as his official astrologer, one Al-Mu'tamin of Zaragoza, who was so skilled he apparently accurately predicted the actual day of his own death, an impressive if admittedly useless trick.

This mixture produced a wide variation of racial appearances still found today in Spain; Abd Rahman III was honorifically referred to as al-Nasir li-dini 'Ilah, "he who fights victoriously for the faith of Allah," but as his father and grandfather had both married captured Christian girls, he was only one-quarter Arab and so had blue eyes, reddish hair and pale skin. He dyed his hair black so he could look more like a Muslim prince was supposed to look.

Dorne's Oberyn Martel plays on a traditional sort of medieval Muslim archetype, the romantic, well-traveled philosopher-poet famed for his prowess with the sword but also noted for mercy and moderation. Many Moorish rulers did indeed fit this model of the sophisticated, smooth-talking Islamic aristocrat, among them Abd al-Rahman II (822-852), the fourth Emir of Cordoba. He collected books, wrote poetry, and brought over the musician Ziryab from Iraq to live in the Munyat Nasr palace.

Ziryab was a fashion leader who introduced many eastern musical traditions into Europe, adding the fifth string to the lute (another Arabic word), as well as helping to popularize toothpaste and introducing eastern hairstyles. Moorish Spain may well have had an influence on bringing Middle Eastern ideas of courtly love to Europe, perhaps originally from Persia; the ultimate source of Europe's romantic tradition, which sprung up in southern France, is a mystery.

Just as Oberyn Martell wrote romantic verse, so did many of Moorish Spain's aristocrats, among them Al-Mu'tadid, King of Seville in the eleventh century, who penned these words:

> My heart met hers, knowing that love is contagious,
> And that one deeply in love can transmit his desire:
> She graciously then offered me her cheek—
> Oft a clear spring will gush forth from a rock—
> I told her, "Let me now kiss your white teeth,
> For I prefer white blossoms to red roses:
> Lean your body on mine"—and then she bent
> Towards me, granted my wish, again, again,
> Embracing, kissing, in mutual fire of desire,
> Singly and doubly, like sparks flying from a flint[13]

His son Mu'tamid also penned some rather corny poems about his youth and the ladies he'd known:

> Many a night I spent, enjoying their shadows,
> With maidens round-hipped, yet slim of waist:
> Their white and brown beauty pierced my heart
> Like white blood-spilling swords and points of brown lances!
> And those nights playfully spent on the river dam
> With a girl whose armband was like the curve of the crescent!

The verse ends with her letting her robe fall and the poet getting to see her "splended form."

One of al-Mu'tamid's favorite wives was a Christian from the north. One day he found her crying because, she said, she would never see the winter snows from her native home—and so he rounded up his best gardeners who overnight planted a forest of northern almond trees in blossom outside her apartment. When she awoke he took her to the window and said: "See my love, there is your snow."[14]

Mumammad ibn Abbad al-Mu-tamid, the ruler of Seville in the eleventh century, was out walking one day and reciting some verses when a girl washing clothes down

by the river Guadalquivir heard him and offered to finish it. She did so, and they were
married, the girl remaining his favorite wife, for whom he wrote many more poems.
Emir Al-Hakam I, who ruled from 796 to 822, was known to keep fine wines in his
cellars and also wrote poetry; when five young beautiful harem women defied him,
he "told them of his right" and yet lamented that he was "subdued" by them "like a
captive,"—a hard life indeed. Two centuries later the polymath Ibn Hazm wrote his
great work of courtly love, *The Ring of the Dove* (*Tawq al-Hamama*) in Cordoba.
Another emir, the tenth century Al-Hakam II, was bisexual and even supposedly had
a male harem, although he eventually produced an heir at forty-six; however, he was
more interested in books, amassing an enormous personal library of six hundred
works and commissioning one of the largest translation projects of the Middle Ages,
turning numerous works from Latin and Greek into Arabic.

More so than romance, a great influential legacy of Moorish Spain in Europe was
Arabic numerals, introduced to the Christian world via Cordoba. This revolutionized
mathematics in the west, reflected in the fact that so many words to do with the subject are Arabic (although Arabic numerals came from India originally). Before this,
attempting multiplication and division using Roman numerals was a maddening process, which is one reason why medieval estimates concerning numbers in battles are
often so far off (though exaggeration is the main cause).

Another innovation brought via this part of the world was chess, which had originated in Persia—checkmate comes from *shah mat*, "the king is helpless"—but taken
up in al-Andalus in the 820s. The king had originally been accompanied by the *vizier*,
the Arabic minister of the king, but in Spain, Jews and Christians began to use a
queen instead, although she was at first a relatively weak piece, only able to move one
square at a time; later the elephant was replaced by a bishop. (The *Game of Thrones*
equivalent of chess, Cyvasse, likewise comes from exotic Volantis.)

With this magnificence and romance came great brutality. Al-Andalus was the last
place to practice crucifixion in Europe; Christians, because of Jesus's death, found
the practice to be in bad taste, although this was hardly on any human rights grounds,
as they were perfectly happy to inflict various other cruelties on people. So in 805,
after a conspiracy in Cordoba against the Amir al-Haken I, seventy-two people were
crucified as punishment; while in 888 the unfortunate leader of the rebellious garrison at Archidona in Andalusia was crucified between a dog and a pig.[15] When Yemeni
soldiers took over Seville, the emir Al-Rahman led a slave army to break them, and

personally presided over the hands and feet of his enemies being chopped off. Afterward, all the heads were put into brine, labelled, and sent off to Mecca as proof of their defeat so that when Caliph al-Mansur saw the gory details he said of his own subordinate: "God be praised for placing a sea between us!" [16]

Moorish Spain never had a good relationship with its Christian neighbors to the north, which is partly why al-Andalus had a standing army of sixty thousand. Between the Muslims and Franks was the *tierras despobladas*, the unsettled frontier zone, with Islamic Spain guarded by an army of soldiers known as "the silent ones" because they could not speak Arabic.

And yet Spain was itself divided, between Arabs, Moors, and its largely eastern European slave population; eventually the caliphate of Cordoba collapsed in 1031, eighteen years after the city had been destroyed in a civil war; most of the library was burned down, and the emir's old residence was destroyed, although the mosque survived.

After this, al-Andalus was partitioned into a number of small emirates, whose rulers became known as "the party kings," not because they could be found by the barbecue wearing a Hawaiian shirt, but due to the literal Arab phrase *muluk al-tawa'if* referring to "partisan" or factional. There were even smaller *taifa* states, independent principalities, among them pirate states such as Denia on Spain's east coast, run by an outlaw of slave origin called Mujahid al-Amirii. Much of eastern Spain came to be ruled by Slavs originally from eastern Europe; so widespread was the subjection of Slavs that the word came to denote an unfree person in many European languages, *esclavo* in Spanish, *esclave* in French, and slave in English.

Slavery was ubiquitous, the trade dominated by Sicilian Arabs, middle men between the Christian and Muslims words who helped bring Lombard and Greek slaves east. At al-Rahman's death in 961 there were an astonishing 3,750 slaves living in the royal palace.[17] By the tenth century, Jewish traders from Verdun in what is now north-east France were running slaves from eastern Europe down to Spain. Irish and English slaves were also found in ninth century al-Andalus, victims of the Vikings. The region was connected to a wider world economy, the trans-Saharan caravan routes that went all the way from Spain to Sijilmasa in southern Morocco and on to the Niger valley near Timbuktu, 1,400 miles away, a route along which gold and men passed.

Moorish Spain also had different religious factions, often with confusingly similar names, so that the tolerant Almoravids were challenged by the Almohads, who were fundamentalists. Often, as with North Africa, relatively obscure but united tribes would seize power and install themselves as rulers before inevitably becoming prone to faction-fighting and decadence. The fourteenth century North African philosopher Ibn Khaldun, who spent much time in Granada, was influenced by the history of al-Andalus in the formulation of the *asabiyyah* cycle; the theory of history that explains the rise and fall of empires, from barbarism to decadence. The early rulers of Moorish Spain were a good example, a desert people who had overrun a whole province and in turn become rich and complacent. Yet so ferocious and brave were their ancestors that they even looked like they would go further and conquer Gaul, and perhaps make all of Europe Islamic.

THE IRON CROWN

In 721, the Arabs had first crossed over the Pyrenees mountain range separating Spain from France when at Toulouse they were defeated by a largely Latin army. A decade later a far larger host crossed the mountains and the Arabs this time reached the Loire river in northern France. There they were stopped near the city of Poitiers by the Frankish duke Charles, who had overcome his stepmother after his father's death to rule the kingdom. His cavalry drove the Muslim invaders back, putting an end to any further Islamic influence in Francia; later chroniclers called him Charles Martel, literally the "hammer."

With their dominance of western Europe, the Franks also wedded church and state in a way similar to that of the Seven; in 752, Charles's son Pepin the Short removed the last of the long-haired Merovingian kings, having his head shaved and sent to a monastery; two years later at the Basilica of St Denis outside Paris, Pope Stephen II anointed Pepin with holy oil, representing God's approval of the monarch, a symbolism that made removal of the king without papal approval an extreme taboo.

The pope gave his support to Pepin's usurping of the throne because Rome was menaced by a Scandinavian tribe who had overrun northern Italy, the Longobards, or Lombards, who came to give their name to a region of the country. The king of the Lombards wore "the Iron Crown," supposedly given to the Emperor Constantine by his mother and made from the nails used on Jesus. Headwear of various sorts had been used by rulers in various cultures, among them ancient Egypt, Greece, and various Asian and European cultures; these were mostly diadems, small headbands worn around the front of the head, or laurels as used in Rome. However, the Iron Crown was the first of its kind, as a modern audience would recognize the concept.

Although the Lombards were ferocious, they were no match for the Franks. Having destroyed them in battle, in 800 Pepin's son Charlemagne—Charles the Great— would be declared Emperor of the West in Rome, the pope placing the Iron Crown on his head.

Charlemagne's family was celebrated in the epic poems *La Chanson de Roland* and *Le Couronnement de Louis*, which alongside the Arthurian sagas were the most influential of the Middle Ages and celebrated the martial qualities of the time. As with Arthur, Roland's sword has a name, *Durendal*, while his enemy's is called *Précieux* (Precious) just as in real life Charlemagne's weapon was called *Joyeuse*. Indeed, lots of people named their swords, as Arya tells the Hound; the Spanish Christian leader El Cid had *Tizona*, still in a Madrid museum; Magnus Barelegs, a Viking king killed in Ireland in 1103, had *Legbiter*. Then there was *Skofnung*, sword of the legendary Danish king Hrolf Kraki, which was supposed to be possessed of supernatural sharpness and contained the spirits of his twelve-strong bodyguard of Viking berserker warriors. This blade also came with lots of superstitions, such as that it should never be drawn in front of a woman.

The coronation of the English king featured the Sword of Mercy, or *Curtana*, a ceremonial object which had its point blunted to illustrate the monarch's clemency, and which featured an emblem of a running wolf down the side. It was of huge ceremonial importance, which is why when Piers Gaveston took it upon himself to carry it in 1308 it caused outrage.[18] The Curtana, or at least a seventeenth century replica, is still used at the coronations of British monarchs.

After their conquest, the Moors had left a tiny sliver of land along the north coast of Spain where a Christian kingdom, Asturias, hung on. Over the coming centuries, a number of Catholic statelets would grow in the north: Castile, Aragon, Navarre, Leon, and Catalonia. Castile had emerged in the ninth century on the frontier, its name literally meaning "castle," and by the twelfth century the Christians had regained control of most of the north of the country. Portugal, formerly a county, had gained recognition as a kingdom from the pope in 1143 and its new capital, Lisbon, had been captured by passing English sailors on their way to the crusades in 1147.

A measure of stability in Moorish Spain ended after the caliph Yusuf II died in 1224, in Marrakesh, after being gored to death by a cow. Authority collapsed and the Christians took advantage, capturing all but a tiny section of southern Spain around Granada. As the poet Ibn Abbad al-Rundi wrote on the fall of Seville to the Christians in 1248: "Oh heedless one, this is Fate's warning to you, If you slumber, Fate always stays awake."[19]

13

SILK RIBBONS TIED ROUND THE SWORD

Loyal sellswords are as rare as virgin whores.

—CERSEI LANNISTER

West of London stood the tree of Tyburn, at the junction of two Roman roads, and close to the river Westbourne, once a tributary of the Thames that is now mostly underground. Tyburn was the location of an ancient monolith pre-dating the Romans and which stood on the site until 1869 when, shortly after an archaeological magazine published an article about it, it disappeared, never to be seen again. For some reason the ancients believed the spot to have had some significance, but in medieval England it had a different meaning, for it was here that men were taken to be hanged from a tree.

From the thirteenth century the condemned were hauled from Newgate prison to the place of execution, a three-mile journey in a cart where along the way he would be given strong liquor to ease his anxiety. Huge crowds would gather to watch these spectacles and on November 29, 1330 an exceptionally large one turned out to witness the demise of Roger Mortimer.

Just eight months earlier people had watched in silence as the late king's half-brother was beheaded. Edmund, Earl of Kent, had been entrapped into taking part in an uprising against the country's new ruler, but so unpopular was his execution that he had to wait five hours on the scaffold until they could find someone to kill him. A condemned criminal did the job, the man a "gonge-fermer" or "shit-scavenger," someone who removed waste from latrines, who in return escaped his own punishment. The earl's assets went to Mortimer, as people had come to expect after three years of the rapacious marcher lord's rule.

The Earl of March, as Mortimer had declared himself after Edward II's death, had alienated almost all the leading men of the kingdom, frivolously spending the crown's reserves with the help of his lover, the queen. And then, in 1330 at Nottingham castle, the de facto ruler of England had gone so far as to accuse the puppet boy-king Edward of complicity in his father's death before a Great Council which Mortimer had rigged with his supporters. He sat wearing lavishly expensive clothes and had become "so ful of pride and wrecchednesse" that he had started holding a Round Table in Wales where he copied "the maner and doyng of Kyng Arthure."[1] The queen, meanwhile, just like Cersei, had grown jealous that her young son's wife would use her feminine charm to bewitch and dominate him and so had delayed her coronation for over two years.

Mortimer had become suspicious of Edward's young friend William Montague, repeatedly asking him about his presence at the castle; Mortimer had every gate and door locked and barred at night, while the queen looked after the keys, and she forbade her son from entering. Yet Mortimer's suspicions were well-judged, for the young Montague's secret mission was to help Edward arrest the earl and his entourage and seize control. As Montague told a friend: "Better eat the dog than let the dog eat you."[2]

On the night of October 19, Edward entered the castle with twenty-five men, killing three courtiers before Mortimer was caught putting on armor behind a curtain. The queen begged her son to "spare gentle Mortimer," but the man responsible for the death of the king's father and uncle was now tried at Westminster while forced to wear a cloak with the phrase *quid gloriaris* emblazed on it—"where's your glory now?" Inevitably he was sentenced to hang, and though spared disembowelment, his body was left for two days at Tyburn. As the Latin chronicle *Vita Edwardi Secundi* put it in 1326: "It is not wise to set yourself in opposition to the King. The outcome is apt to be unfortunate."

The queen was banished to Norfolk, where she spent the rest of her life, well-treated by her son, although history has since judged her harshly, when in truth she was pushed into an impossible position by a weak husband and his sadistic lover.

NO FIGHT IS HOPELESS TILL IT HAS BEEN FOUGHT.

The Prophecy of the Six Kings, appearing soon after the birth of Edward III and supposedly written by Merlin, tells of six monarchs to follow King John, the reign of the last being marked by disaster: "A dragon shall rise up in the north which shall be full fierce and shall move war" and "this dragon shall gather again into his company a wolf that shall come out of the west" and joined by a lion, "and the land shall be partitioned in three parts; to the wolf to the dragon and to the lion, and so it shall be for evermore." The fourth king, it said, would sharpen its teeth at the gates of Paris and win back the land of its ancestors.

King John had ruled an empire that spanned the Atlantic and North Seas, stretching from Scotland to Spain and encompassing all of western France, until he disastrously lost everything but Gascony in 1204. The young Edward was the fourth king to follow him.

On February 1, 1328, the last of the Iron King's sons died, fulfilling the Templar's curse. Charles, cuckholded by his wife Blanche, had refused to take her back and she was sent to a convent; his subsequent marriages produced no surviving sons, and so as the noblemen of France had agreed that the throne could only pass through the male line, it was awarded to Charles's cousin Philippe of Valois.

The following year Edward brought a group of barons with him to France, including Henry Percy, the second Baron Percy who had inherited the title in 1314 at the age of sixteen. The House of Percy continued their rise under the new king, and in 1331 Henry was put in charge of the East March, a position the family would control until 1550.[3] Also with the king was Henry Grosmont, Thomas of Lancaster's nephew, just two years older than Edward but already a champion fighter. A number of aristocrats had turned up at Amiens for this gathering, among them the kings of Navarre, Bohemia, and Mallorca as well as various dukes. Edward departed without saying goodbye to King Philippe, which angered him; already there were signs of tension between Valois, a proud and dominant figure, and the much younger King of England.

In 1333, Edward received his first experience of war, against the Scots at Haildon Hill, where afterwards the field was filled with the Scottish dead, hands sawn off for their rings. Meanwhile the tension in Gascony continued to smolder. Edward, as Duke of Guyenne, was a vassal to the king of France, and so could not take up arms against him without risking excommunication from the pope. Frustrated with continual French aggression, in 1339 Edward instead declared himself king of France, through his mother, a claim that would prove a curse, drawing the English into a war lasting over a century.

George R.R. Martin has spoken of the influence of this conflict on his story, saying in one interview that the armor of the Hundred Years' War was the model for that used in *Game of Thrones*, although "Westerosi armor tends to 'later' styles as you go south. Plate is more common in the Reach say, while mail is more the rule in the North, and beyond the Wall the wildlings have very crude primitive stuff."[4] This would tally with real life, with fifteenth century Scotland being considerably more backwards than France.

At first the English won many victories, a triumph of the king's organizational genius and charisma, and at Sluys in 1340 they defeated a French navy twice as large, with up to twenty thousand Frenchmen left dead after an attack on their fleet in the Flemish port. The sea was choked with corpses.

Edward's biggest logistical problem was that Gascony was very far away, and involved a long risky voyage around Brittany, the western peninsula of France that jutted out into the Atlantic. Brittany had been under the dominance of France for many centuries, but it retained some degree of independence, and had its own Celtic language, brought over by Britons fleeing the Saxons in the fifth century.[5] And yet the following year an opportunity presented itself when Brittany plunged into civil war following the dead of its duke, Jean III. King Philippe supported his niece Jeanne as heir, and so the late duke's half-brother Jean de Montfort called for English assistance.

In November, Jeanne besieged the city of Nantes, and catapulted the heads of thirty knights over the wall, after which the town immediately surrendered. Jean de Montfort was invited to Paris to plead his case, but when he got there, despite promises of safe conduct, Philippe had him arrested and placed in the Louvre. In his place his wife Joanna of Flanders led a rebellion "with the courage of a man and the heart of a lion."[6] Joanna soon found her home of Hennebont besieged by Charles's forces and, dressed in armor, she conducted the town's defenses, urging women to "cut their skirts and take their safety in their own hands." Seeing that the enemy camp was unguarded, she led a force of three hundred men, burning down the French tents and destroying their supplies, eventually securing the town and the nearby city of Brest. A long siege followed, and with morale running low, they finally spied the English fleet in the distance.

But Joanna was not the only ferocious female warrior of this conflict. Yara Greyjoy,* was a sort of pirate queen who commanded a longship called the *Black*

---

*In the novels she is called Asha.

Wind and took Deepwood Motte, a castle in the north. Afterwards she made a claim to the throne, but her cheerfully psychotic uncle Euron beats her to it. However, there was one prominent female pirate in the middle ages every bit as brave.

Nobleman Olivier de Clisson had been among the French soldiers captured when the English besieged the Breton city of Vannes in 1342. Afterward, de Clisson had been the only Frenchman released, in exchange for an English earl, with a very low sum offered as a ransom—and this led the French to suspect he was a traitor. And so in 1343, during a truce, Olivier and fifteen other Breton lords were invited to a tournament where they were arrested, taken to Paris, and after a brief trial beheaded at Les Halles, after being dragged naked to his execution.

De Clisson's widow Jeanne, it was said, carried her loved one's head all the way from Paris to Brittany, where she displayed it before her seven-year-old son and swore revenge, as well as her eternal hatred for the kingdom of France.

Born in 1300 in the Vendée, on Brittany's southern border, Jeanne had already given her first husband two children when she was widowed at twenty-five; she birthed another five by the time her second husband Olivier de Clisson was slain. Fuelled by the thought of vengeance, she set out as a pirate on her ship *My Revenge* where she would capture French crews, sparing only one sailor on each ship to pass on the message. Over a decade, Clisson and her Black Fleet became notorious and feared, earning her the nickname the Lioness of Brittany. Like Greyjoy, she also took an enemy castle, massacring its garrison, in revenge for the violence inflicted on her family. Unusually, de Clisson seems to have retired peacefully, and her story later inspired nineteenth century novels—although later her son played a prominent and particularly horrific part in the war. The Lioness of Brittany also helped to supply the English army for Edward's greatest victory, at Crecy.

A STORM OF ARROWS

In July 1346, the English landed in Normandy and sacked Caen, killing most of the people. Some eight thousand men, half of them archers, had sailed from Portsmouth, marching through Normandy on their way to Paris. North of the capital they turned around to join their Flemish allies, and the French king Philippe VI trudged across the Somme to catch them.

Vegetius's fourth century treatise *Epitoma Rei Militaris*, then the most popular book on warfare, discouraged pitch battles in favor of sieges, arguing that anything was better than battle because so much was down to luck. King Philippe was certainly in agreement, avoiding battle with his young enemy, although partly on the advice of his cousin, the King of Sicily—"a great astronomer and full of great science." In the summer of 1346, however, he chose to take on his young enemy.

It goes without saying that medieval battle would have been a terrifying experience, a sensory overload, the sounds of horns calling men to formation, drums, the rallying cries, the thundering of horses' hooves, the clash of steel on steel, and most of all screams and shouts. But a dominant feature from this point would have been the wusssssshhhh of thousands of arrows arching menacingly into the air before coming down at lethal, high velocity. And at Crecy-en-Ponthieu on August 26, 1346, the piercing sound of metal in flight would have been relentless and dreadful, with as many as twenty-five thousand arrows in the air at one point, coming down "so thickly and evenly that they fell like snow."

During his invasion of Wales, Edward I had discovered a weapon used by the natives which was to revolutionize war, not just in Britain, but across Europe. The longbow weighed between sixty and ninety pounds and could launch twelve arrows per minute, compared to the crossbow's two, with a high rate of accuracy up to 220 yards; if elevated it could go even further, but was less likely to kill. It was lethally effective, able to penetrate a church door at close range and armor far further, and so after crushing the Welsh, Edward had recruited many of their bowmen into his army. At Crecy six thousand English and Welsh longbowmen fired as many as half a million arrows over the day, a mass of lethal weaponry weighing twenty tons lying on the dead and dying. Against them the French cavalry, and their Genoese crossbowmen, stood no chance.

Crossbows had been first recorded in northern France in the tenth century, but did not become widespread until the twelfth, partly replacing the short bow. Byzantine princess Anna Comnena described this "barbarian bow . . . so hateful to God"[7] and crossbows were considered so morally appalling that—like snipers in twentieth century wars—their users were treated as pariahs and outside the normal rules of war. When Rochester castle surrendered to King John in 1215, everyone was ransomed except the crossbowmen who were hanged. Because of this they were well paid, earning twice as much as ordinary foot soldiers.

Crossbows had great force, and corpses found on the site of the Battle of Visby in what is now Sweden, fought in 1361 between Danes and Gotlanders, found skulls with up to six crossbow bolts that had fully penetrated both their helmets and bone. Against this, mail coats were completely ineffective. Yet the Welsh longbow, although in appearance more primitive, had huge advantages, and its impact was horrifying. During the campaign against the Welsh, one Englishman was shot "right through his thigh, high up, where it was protected inside and outside the leg by his iron mail . . . and then through the skirt of his leather tunic", finally penetrating right through the saddle and fatally wounding his horse."[8] Indeed, they were so effective that Edward I had to have forests cleared for a hundred yards either side of Welsh roads because of sniping. And even if an arrow didn't penetrate armor it still wore down the enemy, both physically and mentally, and disrupted their formation.

As offensive weaponry got more lethal, the armor of the period changed with it. The gambeson, the dog-handler style of jacket, was going out of fashion, which is just as well as it could be unbearably hot. The upper legs were still protected by a *cuissart*, armor made of padded leather with strips of steel, and on top of armor knights wore the jupon, a sleeveless garment sometimes padded and finished with expensive cloth—silk or velvet—and embroidered with heraldic arms (this is why it became called a "Coat of Arms"). However, around this time the conical *bascinet* came into use, the helmet with a snout at the front that one normally associates with medieval jousters, and suits of mail were also augmented with riveted steel plates to protect against armor piercing arrows, the first entire plate suit of arms appearing around 1380.

Crecy also saw one of the first uses of cannon and gunpowder in Christian Europe, which the French had acquired from Italy; originally used by the Chinese in the eighth century, this was to alter a European hierarchy based around the castle, impenetrable fortresses that could withstand rebellions or invading armies, but were powerless against the new technology. Gunpowder had been used in Spain during the siege of Algeciras from 1342-1344 and had now come north.

And yet that day the French were destroyed, impetuously riding into battle in the afternoon sun rather than resting the night. They were confident; after all, even their twelve thousand Genoese crossbowmen outnumbered the English armies put together, most of whom were on foot. Yet faced with the storm of arrows, the Genoese ran away and so Philippe called out for his men to attack them: "Quick now, kill all that rabble, they are only in our way."[9] Thousands of Frenchmen were cut down in a storm of arrows, and at the end of the day 1,500 French noblemen and 10,000 soldiers lay dead.

It was an unnatural type of war for the aristocrats of northern France. "For the French, a new era had dawned; for the first time the nobleman on his horse could be struck down by the common man on his feet."[10] This killing was done without crossing swords and so a nobleman wouldn't even know who had hit him, a blow to the traditional ethos of chivalry.

Yet the day is still best remembered for the actions of one man that epitomized chivalry and romance. Among the kings of France's allies was Blind King John of Bohemia, who, despite having lost his eyesight on crusade, insisted on taking part, asking that twelve of his knights tie their horses together so that they might lead him into battle. All but two were killed, and needless to say John did not survive.

Such acts of bravado epitomized the spirit of the age: Eight years earlier some forty English bachelors (the lowest class of knight) had fought at Valenciennes, each with one eye covered with silk, "because, so it was said, they had made a vow among the ladies of their own country that they would not see with more than one eye until they had some deeds of arms in France," as Froissart recorded in his *Chronicles*. Most were killed, unsurprisingly.

After the battle, the pursuit would normally end at the baggage train, which provided the best opportunity for looting. Metal would be stripped from the corpses while the ransomed prisoners were led away; those who were injured most likely faced agonizing death if they were not despatched out of mercy. Some camp followers knew about ointments and balms, and certainly nuns and monks did, but only the richest men could afford surgeons and doctors. There were now medical schools at Oxford and St Barts in London, as well as Bologna, Florence, Paris, and Montpellier, but it was centuries before serious advances were made in treating battlefield wounds. The biggest killer was infected blood and flesh, which is why the most urgent matter was to cut off an infected limb and cauterize the area with fire.

On the same day as Crecy, the English beat the Scots at Neville Cross, and their king David II was captured by John Coupland, a Northumbrian squire. Coupland was made a knight-banneret and given an annuity of five hundred pounds, some manors, and the wardenship of Roxburgh, and was also pardoned for various "homicides and felonies" he had committed. He was also an occasional jailer, as well as murderer, and yet many similar members of his class were basically thugs who had been raised to the gentry by proving themselves in war. In 1332, with the Scottish and English armies waiting to fight, "a gigantic Scottish ruffian" called Turnbull had challenged any Englishman to fight him so Sir Robert Benhale, a Norfolk knight, went up to him, "sliced his black mastiff dog in half, then lopped off his left hand and head."[11] He would end up as Lord Benhale. Criminality was no bar to office either; Sir John Hawley, eighteen times mayor of Dartmouth and Member of Parliament until his death in 1408, was a pirate.

On the other hand, fortune was fickle, and Coupland's luck ran out in 1363 when he was murdered by jealous neighbors.

The victories in France were celebrated back home with the minting of coins celebrating the great warrior king, but in reality the crown was building up huge debts with the real iron banks, all of them based in Italian city-states. His mother had run overdrafts with the Bardis of Florence, perhaps Europe's largest bank, and Edward had borrowed another 900,000 florins from the family, along with 600,000 from another bank, the Peruzzis. In 1345, the king had defaulted, causing Europe's first ever banking crisis, but then the mundane business of finance never did interest the king.

Edward celebrated the victories at Crecy and Calais by founding an order of knights, the Garter, on St George's Day, 1348, inviting twenty-four leading men to become part of a brotherhood. According to one theory, the order had begun as an in-joke between Edward and one of his oldest friends; from his earliest days, including the daring raid to capture Mortimer, Edward had established a band of close friends and the "garter" may have been a reference to their wild and care-free younger days of womanizing. (In A Game of Thrones, Robert Baratheon and Eddard Stark recall their youth fighting and wistfully reflect that such times are gone.)

Perhaps the most celebrated knight among Edward's band was his second cousin, Henry Grosmont. Thomas of Lancaster's title had passed to his brother Henry, and although he helped in the overthrow of Despenser, he was by then going blind and increasingly withdrawn. His son, the "wiry, tight-lipped, high-cheekboned" Henry, had first seen action in Scotland in 1333, and successfully led the Anglo-Gascon forces in 1345. While on campaign, he learned that his father had died, making him earl. And for the next thirty years he took part in almost every war in Europe, often taking leave when there was peace in France to head as far as Lithuania, Greece, Cyprus, and the Middle East. He never missed a war if he could help it, and attracted an entourage of aristocratic followers, the sons of lords from across France and Germany who served under him. When he went to Avignon in 1354 to visit the pope he was mobbed by crowds.

Lancaster in many ways epitomized the medieval thirst for life, in spite of—or because of—the horrors around it. He took pleasure in hunting, feasting, and seducing peasant girls, but it was also said that he "loves the song of the nightingale and the scents of roses, musk, violets and lily of the valley."[12] A heroic figure admired across Europe, in 1350 he rescued the Black Prince and his ten-year-old brother John of Gaunt at the Battle of Winchelsea, when he rammed a Castilian ship closing in on them. Young John went on to marry Grosmont's daughter Blanche.

In 1351, Edward made Henry duke, only the second in the country, giving him palatinate control over Lancashire in the north-west, allowing him to rule like a small kingdom in its own right. He went on crusade to Prussia that winter, but fell out with his fellow crusader, Otto, and they had a duel in Paris, in which his rival lost his nerve and humiliatingly shrunk in terror. Lancaster also wrote a racy book, *Le Livre de Seyntz Medicines*, about his own personal failings, which detailed his fondness of busty peasant girls, despite finding the poor malodorous.

A Knight of the Garter wore lace on his left shoulder until he had earned the right, by his deed, to remove it, adding further kudos. The aim of the order was to glorify and honor the cult of chivalry and war, at a time when a man's sword and his ability to wield it was almost everything. That this life offered death, injury and misery only added to the attraction, for as Sir Geoffroi de Charny wrote in 1352 as advice to young knights: "You will have to put up with great labour before you achieve honor from this employ: heat, cold, fasting, hard work, little sleep and long watches, and always exhaustion."[13] When battle comes, de Charny wrote: "You will needs be afraid often when you see your enemies bearing down on you . . . and you do not know best how to protect your body. Now you see men slaughtering one another . . . and your friends dead whose corpses lie before you. But your horses are not killed, you could well get away . . . If you stay, you will have honor ever after: if you flee you dishonor yourself. Is this not a great martyrdom?"[14]

And yet chivalry was four-fifths illusion, in the words of historian Barbara Tuchman, for what mattered ultimately was strength, the ability to fight wearing fifty-five pounds of steel armor, crashing full gallop into the enemy, giving blows with swords or axe and taking them.[15] Or as Sandor Clegane puts it: "A knight's a sword with a horse. The rest, the vows and the sacred oils and the lady's favors, they're silk ribbons tied round the sword. Maybe the swords are prettier with ribbons hanging off it, but it will kill you just as dead."[16]

RAPERS AND SELLSWORDS

The reality for the ordinary people of France was as far from any chivalric romance as could be possible.

One major difference between modern and medieval societies is that in the former the vast bulk of crime is committed by men from lower socio-economic classes, while in earlier periods those higher up the social ladder were as likely, and sometimes more likely, to do it. When, in 1317, the papal legates Cardinals Gaucelin of Euaze and Luca Fieschi were sent by Pope John XXII to install the new bishop of Durham, they were attacked by a Sir Gilbert Middleton, a knight who used his castle at Milford as a base for robbery, and his "gang of desperadoes." In the following decade, England was plagued by outlaw gangs, often led by gentry families, and known variously as *compaignies*, *conspiratours*, or *confederatours*. This crime wave took place in an already violent society in which roads were very dangerous, and it was extremely unwise to travel except in large groups; the forests, home to countless outlaws, were even worse.

The most notorious gang were the Folvilles, six brothers from the English midlands and their accomplices, among them a village parson, a clerk, and a constable of Rockingham castle. The Folvilles robbed countless people as well as kidnapping a judge of the king's bench and murdering a baron of the exchequer.

Some of these gangsters had connections at court. Roger Bellers, a confederate of the criminal Zouche brothers, had been protected by Despenser, at least from the authorities—but on the road between Melton Mowbray and Leicester he was murdered by the Folville brothers. Over the course of 1327, while violence spiked in the face of crumbling royal authority, the Folville gang cruised the highways looking for victims. One of the brothers, Eustace Folville, was personally accused of four murders and a rape, yet in the chaos of Mortimer's takeover, the Folvilles were above the law.

They once again received a pardon in 1328 after helping Mortimer, after which they went on a crime spree, robbing people across Leicestershire of another two hundred pounds. The eldest brother was a keeper of the peace and probably provided information to the others. A sword for hire called Roger de Wensley was employed to track down the Folvilles and an associated gang, the Coterels, but so impressed were the latter family with him that they offered him a cut and he ended up joining them.

In 1331, the canon of Sempringham Priory hired the gang to destroy a water mill belonging to a rival; they then teamed up with other criminal families with the aim of kidnapping a judge, Sir Richard Willoughby, and ransomed him for 1,300 marks, a huge sum. Finally, Richard Folville was beheaded after a local bigwig, Sir Robert Colville, caught up with him, the two men engaging in a medieval shoot-out with arrows at a church. However, despite a big taskforce being sent out and charged with arresting two hundred known outlaws, most criminals escaped, and indeed many served in Edward's war; Eustace Folville was eventually knighted, after having fought at Crecy; Robert Folville also served in Flanders.

Until modern times, soldiers were always hated figures, for they "ate and drank at the common people's expense, uncontrolled by their officers, they . . . took what they chose, including sexual favors, paid for nothing and, if opposed, tortured and killed."[17] Yet the English in France were especially loathed and feared, largely because a large proportion were criminals. Troops were raised by local commissioners of array, who, when given the task of deciding which local men should be sent to the war, naturally chose the most anti-social and violent. At Halidon Hill there were robbers, poachers, and murderers in the army, and during the Scottish campaign of 1334-5 there were over two hundred men who had received royal pardons for serious crimes.

Arya's journey with criminals destined for the Wall would have been not unlike life with soldiers of the Hundred Years' War. As Tyrion said of the Men of the Night's Watch, they are "sullen peasants, debtors, poachers, rapers, thieves and bastards."[18] In the words of one historian, France was "ravaged by the scum of England and the worst mercenaries of Europe."[19]

Of the archers in Edward's army, about one in ten were released felons, three quarters of them in jail for murder or manslaughter. The force raised by Percy in the Northumbrian army "contained a far greater than average proportion of killers, rapists, thieves and outlaws."[20] Among them were Robert atte Kirke of Brantingham, who had murdered the cooper Robert Plumton; Richard de Aclyngton who killed John Taullour in "hot conflict and not of malice," according to Percy, who defended him.[21] There was John Plummer, who killed Robert Epworth and stole his horse and saddle, but did "good service in the wars of France" for Percy.[22] Over 1339-40, some 850 charters of pardon were issued nationally for men serving in the war,[23] and, in 1390, there was even protest in the Commons about convicted rapists and murderers being allowed off.

Worse than the criminals were the sellswords, the mercenaries, also known as écorcheurs, which translates as "Flayers" or "Skinners." Chroniclers describe these men as "adventurers"—but Froissart said they were "really brigands and thieves."[24] In Westeros, the Brave Companions were nicknamed the Bloody Mummers because of their brutality and are also called the Footmen because they cut off feet. The "Second Sons" name reflects the position of many medieval younger brothers who, "with no hope of inheriting under primogeniture, leave home to make their fortunes by their sword."[25] Likewise with bastards, the Golden Company being founded by a bastard Targaryen called Bittersteel.

In real life, free companies such as the White Company or Tard-Venus were equally brutal, if not worse. "Defiled by bloodshed, corrupted by money and by the gratification of their voracious appetites," in the words of French historian Georges Duby, "these sacrilegious ruffians caroused from the chalices they had stolen from churches. Recruited from the very dregs of society and frequently illegitimate, they had known only penury and destitution."[26]

Mercenary groups had existed since the twelfth century, composed of exiles from all across Europe; Walter Map described these men who "armored from head to foot in iron and leather, armed with clubs and with steel...reduce monasteries, villages and towns to ashes, commit violence and joyless adultery, saying in the fullness of their heart, 'There is no God.'"[27] However, there was a difference between professional mercenaries on the one hand and *routiers* on the other, who were just desperadoes without any sense of honor: "They lived for fighting and plunder; they spared neither sex nor age, neither the clergy nor the peace-loving trader; their ruthless cruelty and wanton destruction made them objects of universal detestation and fear."[28]

Most mercenaries came either from heavily populated urban areas such as Flanders and Brabant, or from tough, poor, remote regions like Brittany and Wales. So many mercenaries came from Brabant that "Brabanters" became a generic name for all sellswords from the twelfth century.

Welshmen, in particular, were greatly feared, and in 1305 the future Edward II sent a letter to his cousin Louis, Count of Evreux, stating that "If you care for anything from our land of Wales, we will send you some wild men, if you like, who will know well how to give young sprigs of noblemen their education."[29] The mercenary market had grown with the rise of Italian city states in the thirteenth century, which had more money than men to defend them.

Among the major free companies in France were the Tard-Venus or "Latecomers" led by the notorious "Archpriest," a former clergyman by the name of Arnaud de Cervole whose own men eventually hanged him. Two of the most famous and notorious of English mercenaries were Sir High Calveley and his half-brother Sir Robert Knolles.[30] The Cheshire born Sir Robert's mercenary army was three thousand-strong and he had grown so rich that back home was able to built a dyke around his house to keep out "clerks and apprentices" begging for his large fortune; when that failed he laid down potentially fatal caltraps to get the message across.[31] Froissart's phrase, to "better himself in the profession of arms" was a euphemism for getting rich from *plunder*, a new English word imported from Italy during this time, and lots of Englishmen bettered themselves in the war.

Of Knolles it was said: "Such was the terror of his name that at one place, it was said, people threw themselves into the river at word of his approach."[32]

The combined free companies force was eventually sixteen thousand strong, larger than Edward III's army, and the biggest and perhaps most frightening was led by John Hawkwood. Raised in Essex, Hawkwood had been a tailor's apprentice, fought at Crecy and after the 1360 treaty of Brétigny went to Burgundy to join a mercenary company who were then in control of much of the region. He ended up in charge of his own group, the White Company, many of his troops also coming from Essex. After France became less profitable, they moved into northern Italy, where they fought for the Visconti family of Milan against Florence; Hawkwood won the hand of one of the leader's numerous illegitimate daughters. He then fought for the pope against the kingdom of Naples, and afterwards Hawkwood was hired by Florence and, despite previously terrorizing the city, he ended up commander-in-chief of its armies for seventeen years until his death in 1394, showered with gifts of land and money. There is still a monument to "Sharp John," as the Italians called him, in Florence's Doumo.

And yet, while sellswords had no sense of honor, and were despised by the traditional aristocracy, they were usually better at fighting. In contrast, the French military was constrained by the desire to win glory, which hindered discipline and organization in the thick of battle. The free companies offered men a chance to rise up and the mercenary captains did represent a form of brutal and immoral social mobility; although many mercenary leaders were from the lower ranks of the aristocracy, usually younger sons, others came from modest backgrounds, while regular armies were totally constrained by class, and only noblemen could command.

As the war dragged on, with large amounts of territory outside of any central control, these routiers became addicted to destruction, spreading misery across the country. Roving gangs of desperados would seize a castle en masse and use it to gain control of the countryside, before moving onto a nearby town and robbing everything in sight, raping the women and murdering the men. As always, it was the innocent who suffered while princes played their games of thrones.

14
THE SEVEN KINGDOMS

Game of Thrones *was first described to me, by someone familiar with the project from before its initial broadcast, as* "The Sopranos *meets* Lord of the Rings."

—JOHN LANCHESTER

The *Denham Tracts*, an anthology of British folklore written between 1892 and 1895, names all the supernatural beings once thought to have lived in the isles, among them satyrs, pans, fauns, hellwains, fire-drakes, spoorns, pixies, giants, Tom-pokers, Elf-fires, fiends, gallytrots, imps, Peg-powlers, pucks, ginges, trolls, silkies, cauld-lads, nacks, waiths, buckies, hell-hounds, boggleboes, hobgoblins, and something called "mum-pokers." Among the other strange creatures mentioned were hobbits. It was this collection that a professor of Old English named J.R.R. Tolkien stumbled upon while dreaming up his epic *The Lord of the Rings*. Tolkien's work would draw on the history and mythology of Anglo-Saxon England, which in turn came to hugely influence his intitial-sake, George R.R. Martin.

The origins of this folklore and the people who created it lie in the vast forests of Germany, from where the Angles and Saxons emerged in deepest history. As the Roman Empire fell into steep decline, beyond its frontiers great population changes were occurring, and what would become known as the *Völkerwanderung*—the movement of peoples—had begun. While the Franks conquered Gaul and the Visigoths Hispania, tribes to their north in Angeln, the "thin peninsula," which jutted out into the icy Baltic Sea, were put under pressure by land shortage. The Angles, along with neighboring tribes, the Saxons and Jutes, looked west.

The Angles had been mentioned by Tacitus as far back as the first century AD, but little was heard of them until their arrival in Britain; the Saxons were recorded as shaving their hairline to make their heads look bigger and drowning one in every ten prisoners they took as a sacrifice to a sea god.

Likewise, the Andals originated across the sea in the lands of the Axe, near to the Rhoyne and Rhoynar rivers, before conquering Westeros, their warriors carving a seven-pointed star on their bodies to show the religion they had imported. There was a war between the First Men and Andals, and some native kingdoms held out longer than others; the semi-mythical last king of the Rivers and Hills, Tristifer the Fourth, was killed in his hundredth battle fighting the Andals. The invaders went on to destroy the weirwood and defeat a combined army of Children and First Men, wiping out the former; however, the Children are still thought to haunt the hill at night. (Because of its conquest, the Dothraki called Westeros "Rhaesh Andahli," just as the French still call Germany "Allemagne," because of just one group who lived there, among many.)

The truth behind the Anglo-Saxon invasion is as clouded as the Andal equivalent. The bookish Hoster Blackwood explains: "No one knows when the Andals crossed the narrow sea. The True History says four thousand years have passed since then, but some maestars claim that it was only two."[1] Such confusion surrounds the arrival of the Angles, too, and although the medieval chronicler Henry of Huntingdon begins his history of the country with "in the year 449 after the incarnation of the Lord," when "the Angles and Saxons came to England,"[2] we cannot be remotely confident about that date, since the newcomers did not read or write. Indeed, they mostly avoided cities and Roman Britannia was left to ruin, its former settlements lived in only by ghosts; the people stayed away from old buildings, believing them to be haunted and to have been the work of superhuman goliaths. The Old English poem *The Ruin*, written in the eighth or ninth century, tells of a city, perhaps Bath, and calls the Roman buildings "the work of giants."

The conquerors of Britain lived under a warrior code in which men would pledge allegiance to another in return for food and protection; "lord" comes from *loafward*, literally "loaf-giver," someone who would provide shelter and sustenance for the men in his service. Living before the spread of castles, the focus of their society was the mead-hall, where a lord would entertain his sworn men and here tales were told and oaths sworn and much beer drunk.

These Germanic tribes had been working as soldiers in Roman Britain since at least the third century, but after 400 AD their numbers rapidly increased as they were hired to work as mercenaries protecting the region from Picts and Irish raiders.[3] Soon they overrun the east of the island and those remaining in the west the invaders called *Welsh*, "foreigner" or "dark stranger," although they still referred to them as "British" for many years aftewards. Michael Drayton's epic poem *The Miseries of Queen Margaret*, about the War of the Roses and published in 1627, still talked of the Welsh as "those of the British blood."

After the Saxons had captured the Severn estuary, the old tongue split off into Welsh in the west and Cornish in the south-west, but by the sixteenth century it was increasingly rare to hear in Cornwall "mees navidua cowzs sawzneck" (I speak no English).[4] The language died two centuries later.

The earlier Beaker People had largely replaced Britain's indigenous population, but now many Britons stayed behind as their countrymen fled west and to Britanny, and generation-by-generation more of these Britons would come to speak the more dominant language until eventually a tipping point came and theirs was forgotten— and so they had become Saxons too.

As one chronicler in Martin's world records, "the First Men were far more numerous than the Andals and could not simply be forced aside,"[5] and so the Andals took the wives of the conquered. This is what most likely happened in Britain after the fall of Rome, genetic studies showing that Englishmen carry a higher frequency of Anglo-Saxon ancestry on the male than on the female line. Some houses in the Vale at the time of *Game of Thrones* claim descent from the First Men, among them the Redforts and Royces, just as Anglo-Norman aristocrats like Roger Mortimer claimed a blood link to King Arthur, the legendary king of the Britons.

The Jutes ruled the kingdom of Kent, while the South, East, and West Saxon kingdoms became Sussex, Essex, and Wessex respectively, the latter centred around the southern counties of Hampshire, Wiltshire and Dorset, the latter originally called "Dorn". In the midlands the Angles had established a realm on the frontier with the Britons, called the "border" or Mercia; by the North Sea was East Anglia, a marshy, flat land resembling the Netherlands, between which people had always crossed; beyond that were the two most northerly kingdoms, Bernicia and Deira, which united to become Northumbria. And so later this era became known as the Heptarchy, literally "seven realms," although there were originally more than twelve and by the time any records were made there were just four left.[6]

As in Westeros, native resistance continued for some time and one warrior in particular is said to have fought many battles against the Saxons. The legend of King Arthur came to absorb much of the world it was told in, rather than the world it originally portrayed, and everything about it belongs in the high and later middle ages rather than the far grimmer and more primitive sixth century. The story really took off in the twelfth century in the French-speaking world and came to define how aristocratic men should behave.

The first mention of a heroic British warrior fighting off the Saxon onslaught comes from around the year 700, and it goes without saying that, at a time of universal illiteracy, the nearly two-century interval would make any historical accuracy impossible to verify. The tale of Arthur was most popularized by Geoffrey of Monmouth, but before that an oral tradition had been maintained in the Celtic lands of Wales, Cornwall, and Britanny, between which there would have been continual contact. The real-life "Camelot"—the word was not invented until much later—could have been anywhere from Cornwall to southern Scotland, Arthur's realm of "Lyonesse" being etymologically related to Lothian.

Lothian formed part of the "Old North," *Hen Ogledd*, a series of British kingdoms in what is now northern England and southern Scotland, among them Strathclyde, Rheged, and Gododdin, but which were conquered by the Anglian kingdoms of Deira and Bernicia. The kings of Northumbria had then established their strongholds at Bebbanburg*—later Bamburgh—Castle on the North Sea coast, an old fortress that had been used by Celtic warlords following the chaos of Rome's collapse. The Angles had taken the stronghold late in the sixth century, pushing the Britons further west during a centuries-long period of conflict.

In Westeros, the Andals did not conquer the North and likewise the Angles did not colonize all of England, since the hills made occupation harder in the more remote regions. Indeed, a large-scale DNA study published in 2015 showed that the Angles had not penetrated into the mountainous parts of Northumbria. The samples were taken from English people with four grandparents from one area and confirmed that, while Anglo-Saxon colonization had been heavy around the low-lying eastern part of

---

*It is also the home of Uhtred in the *Last Kingdom* book and television series.

Yorkshire, people in the mountainous Pennines carried mostly indigenous British genetic markers.[7]

And so, the first men and the old ways hung on in the less accessible regions. Until as late as the twentieth century farmers in the uplands of the West Riding of Yorkshire used a counting method called Yan Tan Tethera, which dated back to ancient pre-English languages once spoken there. Their word for four, *peddero*, is related to the Welsh *pedwar*, while *dix*, ten, is cognate with the Welsh *deg*. And while it took the Andals another thousand years to take the Iron Islands, much of England was only conquered by the Angles and Saxons much later; Cumbria and Devon, in the very far north and southwest respectively, held out until the ninth century, and not surprisingly the 2015 study showed the people in those parts to be genetically distinct from the rest of the English (beyond Devon, in the county of Cornwall, there was yet another, altogether different, set of genetic markers). Overall, the Anglo-Saxon contribution to the English genome is between 10-40 percent, which suggests a large invasion which, nonetheless, did not wipe out the natives.[8]

Arthur's Saxon enemies, Cerdic and his Cynric, are semi-historic but their British names hint at a native aristocracy who adopted Saxon identities or were at the very least mixed. Their kingdom, Wessex, had been formed along the Thames Valley, close to the Uffington White Horse, a figure drawn on the side of a hill in Berkshire and dating back to at least 800BC, before the arrival of the Celts. Nearby is Dragon Hill, a natural chalk slope with a flat surface where no grass would grow; according to local belief this was because dragon's blood had been spilled there. Later it became the spot where St George supposedly slew the beast; almost certainly it was the site for Iron Age rituals of some sort, probably involving something horrific. It was from these picturesque gently rolling hills and the prize farmland around the Thames that the fuure kings of England would emerge.

And yet, despite the absence of evidence for a real Arthur, the myth had a huge impact on medieval ideas of chivalry, romance, and heroism, and those of Westeros, even if in Martin's world it is a cynical idea turned on its head.

WINTERFYLLEÐ

This was a land of myth and monsters, as told in the eighth century Anglo-Saxon poem *Beowulf* about a hero pledged to kill the giant Grendel. *Beowulf* is set in Scandinavia, from where the Angles' ancestors had come, but it took its current form in the mid-eighth century and most likely was written down in Northumbria.[9] In many ways it is the archetypal story of a man overcoming a monster, one of the Seven Basic Plots, along with the Greek myth of Perseus, *Dracula*, and *Jaws*. But it is also a sort of lament for a disappearing past and a sad relection that, when all is done, glory is all for nothing.

This was a warrior society and men, even young children, were buried with their swords and shields, weapons which carried the *mana*, aura of those killed in battle. Although a ferocious fighter who battled a dragon, Beowulf was also "the gentlest of men, kindest and dearest to his people, and most eager for fame," but ultimately that fame is fleeting.

In the 1920s, J.R.R. Tolkien, having survived the Somme and horrified with much of what modernity could do, was a professor at Oxford where he was writing a new translation of *Beowulf*. As the world crept toward another catastrophic war, he penned his series of fantasy stories that in turn did much to influence Martin.[10] *The Hobbit*, written in 1937 soon after Tolkien's famous series of lectures on *Beowulf*, features a climatic battle against a dragon, while both Tolkien and Martin also drew on the Arthurian tradition. As one comparison of the two epics points out, fantasy writers have long "drawn upon Arthurian lore" from two medieval tales, *Sir Gawain and the Green Knight* and Sir Thomas Malory's *Le Morte d'Arthur*. "Whether mirroring, amplifying or spinning off from these earlier works, the great fantasy sagas created by Tolkien and Martin have a family resemblance because they've inherited the same narrative DNA."[11] Both modern epics tell of a threat of evil coming from outside; for Tolkien it came from the east and for Martin from the north.

Both Tolkien's and Martin's creations feature varging, or skinchanging, from the old English word *wearh*, meaning outlaw or man, and the Old Norse term *vargr*, meaning wolf. In Middle Earth, wargs are monstrous wolves ridden by orcs, while in Westeros wolves are on the side of men against the monsters. Similarly with *wights*; when the Christian gospel was brought to the northern people, an epic poem called the *Heliand* explained the Bible in terms Germanic people could understand, and so the biblical "Lead us not into temptation" became "Do not let foul wights seduce us to their will." *Wiht*, the old English word, simply meant any living creature, although in fantasy it came to mean in particular the undead or other similarly sinister beings.

Although epics celebrate the heroic virtues and that is what future generations remember, most Angles were not warriors, but farmers, eking out a tough living growing barley and other crops. After harvest time the food would be stored during the month of October, which the Anglo-Saxons called Winterfylleð, so called because it marked the first full moon of winter.[12] In other words, Winter is Coming. After that came *Blopmonap*, or Blood-month, when the animals were slaughtered for winter; this was followed by Ærra Gēola, "Before Yule," Yule being the midwinter pagan festival.

Like the Andals, the Angles were polytheists, although little is known of their religion except the gods Tiw, Woden, Thor, and Frigg, who left their names in days of the week. The Angles most likely believed in a variation of the Nordic Valhalla, an afterlife in which warriors would feast, fight, and fornicate in a drunken haze.

However, as in Westeros, the Angles were soon faced with a new and mysterious faith emerging from the east, which claimed there was just one god. As in Westeros, it was a religion espoused by foreign women. In the former imperial city, now a shadow of its former self and home to a few thousand people, there in the slave market Pope Gregory had seen two blond slave boys and inquired where they were from; told they were Angles, he famously punned *Non Angli sed Angeli*—not Angles but angels. A mission was sent and in 597 the king of Kent accepted Christianity, under the influence of his Frankish wife Bertha; within a few decades the north had also become Christian, too, largely thanks to Irish monks.

Paganism was eventually crushed, yet the descendants of Horsa and Cerdic had little reason to lament the loss of the old gods, for it was well known that the missionaries had brought with them the written word and with it the lost treasures of Rome. Within a relatively short time Northumbria, once a land of shadows at the very far edge of the world, had emerged into the light, in a flowering of culture that created such beautiful treasures as the Lindisfarne Gospel. The driver of this cultural renaissance was the monastic movement, the real-life *maesters* who had spread from continental Europe to Britain and formed the first centers of learning in the seven kingdoms.

The English, converted, now sent many missionaries across the cold sea to convert the lands where their ancestors had hailed from. In Frisia, the low-lying land by the banks of the great river Rhine, and in Saxony, they achived some success; further north, though, the people still worshipped the old gods. And beyond that, in the bitterly frozen north, there now emerged a terrifying race of people, the real-life Iron Born. Seeing the horror now inflicted on Britain, one monk recalled the terrible prophecy of the Book of Jermiah: "Out of the north an evil shall break forth on all inhabitants of the land."

15

THE DANCE OF DEATH

Death had lost its terror for Tyrion Lannister, but greyscale was another matter.

—A DANCE WITH DRAGONS

In August 1348, a ball of fire was seen over Paris; large and very bright, the star appeared during the evening in the west. In Italy the previous August, Florentine banker and chronicler Giovanni Villani observed a comet appearing in the Constellation of Taurus, called the Dark Comet or Negra. The comet, which resembled a great fire, was shaped like a sword and stayed in the sky until October.

The Italian *Nuova Cronica*—New Chronicle—at the time said the comet signified "the death of a powerful king," and indeed soon enough Louis IV, Holy Roman Emperor, died suddenly. The comet was, ominously, sixteen degrees from the head of the Gorgon Medusa represented by the star Algol, which was "widely regarded as the most malevolent star in the sky", strking terror into many. It was "horrible to look at, like . . . a sword . . . They say the comet is red. . . . It has a hypnotising appearance, with the tail of a dragon."[1] This "Pillar of Fire" was observed over the pope's home in Avignon too.

Shooting stars were often viewed as portents of ill-news, most famously in 1066 when Halley's Comet was spotted in the sky, months before the kingdom fell to invaders. And so *A Clash of Kings* starts with an ominous red asteroid in the sky, interpreted as a good omen by Joffrey and Edmure Tully, but taken as representing war by Aeron Greyjoy and the wildling Osha.

And in this case the comet did indeed herald terrible news. The 1340s had already seen a number of calamities, including earthquakes, storms, famines and floods, but what struck the known world that summer was a horror on a new level.

GREYSCALE

In Martin's world, a terrifying disease called greyscale afflicts people known as "Stone Men" because the illness causes their skin to become hard and dead. Usually these poor souls have to be exiled and live in the ruins of Old Valyria, where the affliction tends to drive them mad. Occasionally, with the help of the best doctors, or perhaps despite them, someone will survive greyscale, such as poor Shireen Baratheon, Stannis's daughter, who goes on to live a long and happy life (well, not quite). There was also once a great pestilence called greyplague, "a faster-acting, highly virulent version" of greyscale that in Oldtown killed three-quarters of the population. Lord Quentin Hightower ordered the city quarantined, all shipping was burned, and no one could enter or leave—as a result of which the Reach was saved from the outbreak.

Numerous disgusting diseases existed at the time, but the most obvious comparison to greyscale is leprosy, which was still widespread in fourteenth century Europe— perhaps one in two hundred in England had the illness—although by the following century it was in retreat. Leprosy was recorded as far back as Ancient Egypt, but only became common in Europe after Alexander's armies brought it back from India. During the early medieval period it became more common, and from the eleventh century laws were passed to keep sufferers away from the population. In 1179, the Third Lateran Council ordered that all lepers should be separated, reflecting the terror this disfiguring disease caused, even among churchmen. It could also take twenty years before the illness showed, which is partly why leprosy caused such panic.

When someone was infected with the disease, they would have a tribunal and be examined by surgeons, and if leprosy was confirmed then a week later they were taken to a church for "the separation," becoming attendees at their own funerals.

On the day, the unhappy man or woman, dressed in a shroud, was carried to the church on a litter by four priests singing the Catholic song for the dead, *Libera me*. Inside, the litter was set down at a safe distance from the congregation, and the service of the dead was read, similar to that of a funeral. The leper had to kneel down before the altar dressed in black clothes, where a priest would cast earth on the victim's feet with a spade and said, "Be thou dead to the World, but alive unto God."

Afterwards the priest would declare the victim forbidden to enter churches, bakeries or markets, or anywhere people might be found, to always wear leper's costumes, and to only speak to someone with the wind facing them. Singing the mournful psalm again, the clergy would carry the leper out of the church, through the streets, and out of town to the leper colony. He would be given a pair of castanets to warn others of his approach, a pair of gloves, and a bread basket, and his family would leave him to a sort of living death.

Since lepers were legally dead, all their possessions were given away, although if they were very unlucky—and in times of extreme stress—they might be burned to death. Such was the fear of lepers that, from 1310, barbers were placed at the gates of London to look out for sufferers trying to sneak in (barbers once performed lots of non-hair-related duties, such as surgery, which is why barbershops have red and white poles outside today, to commemorate the sticks patients used to grip during their ordeal).

Lepers had to live in colonies, of which there were two thousand in France at the time and an estimated 250 in England, as of 1230; the cleric Matthew Paris estimated there were nineteeh thousand leprosaria across Europe, although how he came to this figure is anyone's guess. Leper houses had very harsh conditions and there was even a leper riot, in Kingston, Surrey, in 1313; it was mainly against the futile treatments, which everyone knew didn't work, among them such outlandish ideas as blood-letting and purging, extreme diets, and eating leeks boiled with adders.

However, medieval attitudes to lepers were complex; although people were horrified and disgusted, and lepers were known as "the walking dead," many viewed them as being holy, because Jesus had cured sufferers and shown them special affection. This strange mixture of disgust and reverence influenced people's attitudes to the luckless real Stone Men.

Leprosy could affect all social classes, one of the most prominent being the Crusader leper king of Jerusalem, Baldwin IV, who ascended the throne at the age of thirteen in 1174. His teacher William of Tyre, later an archbishop, had discovered Baldwin and his friends one day playing a game in which they tried to injure each other by driving their fingernails into the opponent's arms; he noticed to his horror that Baldwin felt no pain, a symptom that meant only one thing. After becoming king, Baldwin's court was especially filled with scheming because everyone thought he would die soon; he would make it to twenty-four. Like Jaime Lannister, Baldwin's right hand was so badly affected that he learned to fight with his left.

However, by the time of the War of the Roses leprosy had been almost completely driven out of England, one of the reasons being that it was out-competed by other

similar diseases from which sufferers developed a cross-immunity, in particular tuber-
culosis, which remained a menace in Europe until the twentieth century. But it was
also because most of Europe's lepers had been killed by another, far more terrifying
disease.

THE GREAT MORTALITY

On June 23, 1348, a ship arrived in the port of Melcombe Regis on the south coast of
England, most likely from Calais in northern France. On board among the cargo of
that fateful vessel was the deadly *y pestis* bacterium, either in the rats onboard or
infected humans; within a year the realm of England had lost a third of its population
to the plague, the disease spreading across the country at a mile a day.

The Arabs called it "The Year of Annihilation." To Europeans it was the Big Death
or Great Mortality, the *huge mortalyte* in Middle English. Later in the sixteenth century it would become known as the Black Death, a term first used in Sweden in 1555.[2]
Never had humanity suffered such horrors and afterwards nothing was the same
again—the Church's power had slipped, the feudal system had gone into terminal
decline, and the mindset of Europeans changed forever, now far more morbid.

The continent of Europe, its population thinned by years of famine, had been hit
by another cold wet summer in 1335, followed by flooding in 1338 and 1342. There
were volcanoes in Italy, earthquakes in Austria, a tidal wave in Cyprus, and a swarm
of locusts in Poland. In the 1330s, there were huge upheavals faraway in China, millions dying in earthquakes and droughts. And then came the disease.

The *y pestis* bacteria that causes the bubonic plague lives on rodents in central
Asia, and is usually harmless to humans, but most likely climate change and human
population growth allowed it to jump species and become far deadlier. The bacteria
in its new deadly form was carried by X *cheopis*, the rat flea, "an extremely aggressive
insect" that "has been known to stick its mouth parts into the skin of a living caterpillar and suck out the caterpillar's bodily fluids and innards."[3]

The disease spread west, brought by trade and warfare, the two sides of the great
silk road from east to west. In Genoa's Crimean colony of Caffa, now Feodosiya, a
street brawl between Italian merchants and local Tartars had begun with insults, then
punches were thrown, after which knives were taken out and the fight escalated.
The Tartars gave an ultimatum to the Italians and an insulting response came
back—never a wise response—and so a siege began. However, soon the Tartars were

overcome with this unknown disease, dying first in the dozens and then hundreds and thousands. Fatally weakened they withdrew, but before doing so had some corpses put in catapults and, according to contemporary Gabriele de' Mussis, "lobbed into the city in hopes that the intolerable stench would kill everyone inside." Soon the disease was raging among the Italians, and the terrified inhabitants of Caffa climbed on board their ships and headed home, first arriving in Messina in Sicily. Only four of the eight Genoan galleys made it back home from the Black Sea—but that was enough to doom Italy.

For the infected, bad breath was the first, sickening sign; they would initially feel lightheaded and nauseous, then the vomiting would start, followed by pain in the groin and the appearance of the bubos, a lump the size of an apple, either on the neck, groin or armpit—*gavocciolo*, the Italians called them. By this stage the victim would be vomiting blood and a priest called to give the Last Rites. These terrifying lumps came to haunt the European imagination, made all the more disturbing by the strange deformities sufferers displayed; a limp for those who had the *gavocciolo* on the thigh, or a head stuck at an angle caused by a lump on the neck. The smell of disease in cities became overpowering.

Soon there was a feeling of the end times coming, the death of all mankind approaching; people in Messina witnessed a terrifying spectacle when the faithful gathered in church saw a black dog with a drawn sword in its paws, "gnashing his teeth and rushing upon them and breaking all the silver vessels and lamps and candlesticks on the altars and casting them hither and thither."[4] (Of course it's possible the dog had rabies, another widespread affliction.) Another story told of how a statue of the Blessed Virgin came alive on the way to Messina and refused to enter the city.

People across Italy perished in droves. One day "a man, wanting to make his will, died along with the notary, the priest who heard his confession, and the people summoned to witness his will, and they were all buried together on the following day."[5] In Venice, one dreadful day, a ship from the Black Sea arrived and moored close to the poet Petrarch's house in the Basin of St Mark. Soon, bodies were being shipped off on special boats, many on board still breathing, some dying of suffocation, and most of the oarsman catching the disease too.

During this summer of 1348, the boats, drapped in black to cover the corpses, went through the canals, with the cry "Dead bodies! Dead bodies!" ringing out every day. Ships thought to be infected were burned. Human interaction shrunk as taverns were closed, and the sale of wine was prohibited. The Venetian custom of poor families leaving the recently deceased outside the family home to get donations was banned.

As the disease spread across Italy, cities tried to prevent their neighbors from approaching, but it seemed impossible to stop. Orvieto's Council of Seven simply decided to ignore the coming plague in case it scared people; six of them died of the disease. In Pistoia in Tuscany "hardly a person was left alive," and some fifty years later the city's population was still less than a third of pre-plague levels. There will little the authorities could do to stop it, so in Ragusa the government ordered everyone to make a will.

In some cases, the disease led to a breakdown of social norms. In Venice criminals roamed the street because their jailors were all dead. In Florence survivors were terrorized by the *becchini*, gangs whose motto was "Those who live in fear die" and who drank and whored and robbed, threatening people with violence or rape unless they gave up their property. Others behaved like saints, the Florentine dead being gathered up by the *Compagnia della Misericordia*, a confraternity who wore red robes and hoods masking their face.

France was infected most likely via the southern port of Marseilles, and soon Avignon, the home of the pope, fell under the shadow of the plague. Every night cemeteries in the city were attacked by hungry pigs, the animals gathering in the dark and heading for that day's new batch of fresh bodies, their noses stuck into the newly-dug soil searching for fresh human meat. So many were dying that there weren't enough priests to give the Last Rites and so the pope consecrated the entire river Rhone; each morning corpses would pass by the town and its famous bridge, on their way to the Mediterranean. The disease soon raged in Paris where an estimated fifty thousand died before the plague had burned itself out; the living were thrown in with the dead, and the piles of corpses were seen to squirm.

Most likely the plague first arrived in Britain via Calais, now infested with sickness after an eleven-month siege by the English. In Bristol, "the plague raged to such a degree that the living were scarcely able to bury the dead . . . At this period the grass grew several inches high in High Street and Broad Street."[6] A writer in nearby Gloucester lamented: "Miserable, wild, distracted. The dregs of the people alone survive."[7] Oxford lost three mayors to the illness, and three Archbishops of Canterbury died in quick succession.

When someone fell sick, they went to a priest, and so naturally clerical casualty rates were high and religious institutions suffered especially shocking rates of death, some abbeys losing all their members. Some people behaved heroically and humanely during this disaster, but many fled and failed to look after dying relatives, something chroniclers lamented, although it is quite understandable.

There were grim, upsetting stories from the time. In Durham "a mad lonely peasant . . . in the years after the plague, wandered the villages and lanes of the region, calling out for his plague-dead wife and children. The man is said to have greatly upset the populace." Across the country there were mass graves in villages into which people would cart their loved ones, coughing to death themselves as they did so, knowing they'd be joining them soon enough. The black flag was flown from the church steeples of infected villages, as a warning.

At one point two hundred a day were dying of plague in London, which in 1348 was described as a "Nomanneslond," and a large field to the west was set aside as a mass burial site. Several hundred English villages were deserted altogether, although many were finished off by subsequent migration as desperate workers left for opportunities elsewhere.

Some people took decisive measures. A manorial aristocrat in Leicestershire burned and razed the village of Noseley when plague appeared; his descendents still live at Noseley Hall, so clearly it worked out for them. The city of Milan had a far smaller death toll than its neighbors after introducing the most stringent rules, so that when someone in a house became infected all the inhabitants were simply boarded up and left to starve. In a later outbreak the city of Dubrovnik, which lies on the Adriatic opposite Italy, insisted that all ships stay anchored for forty days, *quaranta*, so inventing the idea of quarantine.

Medical experts were baffled by the causes, and to make matters worse, and more confusing, there were two primary types of plague—bubonic and pneumonic—the first carried by fleas and the second by humans. There was also a third, less common form, septicaemic, that occurred when the blood was infected. The one thing all three had in common was that they caused an agonizing and horrific death, although the septicaemic variety had a fatality rate close to 100 percent. Plague can kill very quickly, with average survival time from first symptom to death being less than fifteen hours in some later outbreaks.[8]

It did not really occur to anyone that rats were responsible, as in the words of histo-rian Philip Ziegler: "Dead rats no doubt littered the streets and houses but this would hardly have seemed worthy of attention at a time when dead human beings were so much more conspicuous."[9] And yet this is still a source of confusion because some historians argue that a plague would have been preceded by numbers of dead rats so large even fourteenth century people would have found it worth noting. In fact, med-ical experts and historians today aren't entirely sure that the Black Death was *y pestis*, and a 2018 paper suggested that rats were not the culprits.[10]

Without any understanding of its causes, many people blamed the plague on con-spiracies by lepers or Jews or Muslims, or a combination of two or all of these groups. Rumors of enemies poisoning wells was as old as the plague of Athens, when Spartans were blamed for a disease no humans could possibly control, but in the fourteenth century there grew a belief that lepers, Jews, and the Muslim ruler of Granada were part of a cabal. Massacres started in Narbonne and Carcassonne where Jews were thrown in bonfires, and soon pogroms spread across France and Germany. In 1348, Pope Clement issued a Bull, or decree, "prohibiting the killing, looting, or forcible conversion of Jews without trial" but it made little impact.

As with times of warfare, people lived more for the day, were less fussy about mar-riage, and settled down to have children quicker. Jean de Venette, a French monk, observed that "Everywhere women conceived more readily than usual. None proved barren; on the contrary, there were pregnant women wherever you looked."[11] Crime also went up as people acted on impulse, and the exodus of aristocrats from plague-rid-den cities increased disorder. But life went on, grim though it was.

The modern consensus is that it killed between one-third and half of Europe, although small pockets in Bohemia, Poland, and to a lesser extent Flanders had rela-tively low fatality rates, while some regions suffered especially heavy losses; eastern Normandy saw a decline in population of between 70-80 percent from 1300 to 1400. Florence fell from 120,000 in 1330 to 37,000 after the outbreak, while most likely two-thirds of Venice was wiped out,[12] and fifty noble families erased forever. For centuries fishermen around the city stepped ashore on deserted islands made of the whitening bones of plague victims. Italy is supposed to have suffered the worst rates, with up to 60 percent dead on the peninsula, but across the continents of Asia and Europe the streets and fields were silent. For many, though, it felt like the end of the world was upon them.[13]

Plague was just one of many afflictions at the time. Smallpox, which killed uncontrollably until the discovery of vaccines in the eighteenth century, was also known as red plague; its 1440s epidemic killed more lives than a recent bubonic plague outbreak, and, in the 1460s, smallpox killed 20 percent of one English town in just twelve months. Then there was influenza, or the flu; the 1426-7 epidemic killed as much as seven percent of Europe's population. Typhus also swept through Aragon after Spanish troops returned from Cyprus where they had beaten the Moors. St Vitus Dance was another common problem, an autoimmune illness resulting from a virus, usually affecting children, and which caused involuntary spasmodic movements due to painful internal burning, resembling a sort of dance.

Plague eventually died out in Europe, the Marseilles outbreak of 1722 being the last; most likely the pestilence-carrying black rat was driven out by its cousin the brown rat, although the replacement of wooden houses with brick also made life less hospitable for the animal.

The tide turned against smallpox after Edward Jenner discovered a vaccine in the eighteenth century, having noticed that milkmaids infected with the related cowpox never suffered from the more serious illness (*vaccine* is from the Latin for cow). He tested his dangerous new treatment on the eight-year-old son of his gardener, but luckily for employer and employee he turned out to be right. Leprosy is now called Hansen's disease after Dr. Gerhard Hansen who, in the nineteenth century, isolated the bacterium which caused the illness; ironically, he discovered, the disease was not caused by contagion but by a bacterium, and is not that infectious, after all.

16

"CATTLE DIE, KINDRED DIE, WE OURSELVES SHALL DIE."

War was an ironman's proper trade. The Drowned God had made them to reave and rape, to carve out kingdoms and write their names in fire and blood and song.

—THEON GREYJOY

They came from the sea. Heathens! They plundered, and they murdered. Blood flew in the altar. Christians were trampled under foot like filth in the streets. Some of the brothers were carried off."[1] So wrote the Saxon chroniclers after the Lindsifarne monks were attacked by raiders from across the sea in 792.

The Anglo-Saxons were part of the culture of the German Ocean, as the sea that separated them from the "Saxons overseas" was called (it was not known as the North Sea until the eighteenth century). The Romans reached its southern limit but faced a storm which, the poet Albinovanus Pedo believed, was the work of the gods calling them from the edge of the world. The twelfth century Arab geographer Al Idrisi called it "the sea of perpetual gloom," where oceans clashed, resembling the abyss out of which the earth was created.

Beyond that world the Saxons knew little, only of travelers' tales at the court of the kings, of voyages by the fjords of Norway up to the Arctic Circle and its midnight sun; to the east there was the land of the mysterious Finns and their shamans, and beyond that the freezing, black world of "Great Sweden," as Russia was called; and then south to the Queen of Cities, Constantinople, a gilded, exotic metropolis that filled the imagination. To those even aware of them, the Saxons were considered to live at the end of the world. From "the western shores, where the sun sets . . . We know of no land beyond their islands, but only water," wrote a Muslim official in Syria, meeting some strangely dressed Anglo-Saxon pilgrims in 724. The exotic-looking Christians meant no harm and "they wish only to fulfil their religious law," the local dignatory concluded, letting them pass.[2]

Back in the sixth century, the Roman Jordanes had written about a frozen isle to the north of Germany called Scanza, surrounded by "many small islands" and "where wolves could pass when the sea was frozen. In winter the country was not only cruel to people but also to wild beasts. Due to the extreme cold there were no swarms of honey-making bees."[3] He described it as a "womb of nations," and home to numerous hungry tribes fiercer even than the Germans to the south. Now two centuries later they were more ravenous still, and in their desperation, had developed ships and navigational techniques that allowed them to cross the bitterly-cold ocean to their west, where there existed an island rich with plunder. There they were called *Denes* or heathens; since the nineteenth century we have known them through the Icelandic sagas as "raiders," or *Vikings*.

Like the Iron Islands, Scandinavia has few natural resources other than thin soil and salt water, and this absence of plowable land helped to create a pirate culture that glorified in raiding. As Balon Greyjoy says: "We are iron-born, we are not subjects; we are not slaves, we do not plough in the fields or toil in the mine. We take what is ours."

From the ninth century local warlords began to centralize power in Norway, Denmark, and Sweden, and these bitter struggles left the losers with little choice but to take to their ships, along with supporters and other adventurers. As many as 200,000 left this frigid region during the early medieval period, raiding, trading, and establishing colonies from Canada to Constantinople.

In Westeros, the Iron Born worship their own deity, the Drowned God, just as the Vikings were among the last people in Europe to accept Christianity. Like the Iron Islanders, with their rock wives and salt wives, they kept a second spouse, a *handfast* of lower status, often non-Scandinavian. And also like the Iron Born, the Vikings were slavers, and established Dublin as a trading port for that purpose, selling many unfortunates across the seas; such was the interdependency of the Eurasian continent during this period that the re-emergence of the Viking threat in the 860s had much to do with an African slave revolt in Baghdad in the preceding years that had led the Arab rulers to turn to Europeans instead.

The Iron Born have "slim, beautifully designed warships in which they strike at will along the coastline," while the Vikings had their longboats.[4] The Iron Born

despise trade and agriculture, the motto "we do not sow" showing that they considered raiding the only honorable activity. Such was their hostility to trading that Balon
tears Theon's neck-chain and shouts "that bauble around your neck, did you pay the
iron-price for it, or the gold?"[5] In this they were somewhat different from Vikings, who
were happy to become farmers or merchants when it was more profitable or expedient
than raiding. Later Vikings would settle down to work as peaceful farmers except that
they might still spend a few months of the year raiding, if it was profitable, such as
Svein Asleifarson of Orkney with his "spring trip" and "fall trip."

The Norsemen first appeared in England in 787 near Portland in the Kingdom of
Wessex, killing a local reeve on the shore. Six years later catastrophe arrived when "dire
portents appeared over Northumbria and sorely frightened the people"—immense
whirlwinds and flashes of lightning, and fiery dragons, were seen flying in the air. That
year Danes attacked the monks at Lindisfarne in Northumbria, on the spit of land
where St Aidan first knelt to pray when he founded his monastery in 635. To the Saxons
the terrifying heathens were killers sent by God as punishment, hailing from the frozen
north, the land of winter.

The "nexus of ancient Scandinavian culture"[6] was Uppsala, close to Stockholm,
where in the dark forests the Norsemen first emerged. It was here, near the hillfort of
Birka, that their god Odin dwelled, and hanged himself in order to gain the gift of
prophecy, spending nine days suspended in the tree. To the south at Roskilde, slightly
to the west of Copenhagen, the ancients lived by the banks of the now-dried up river
Lejre. This may even be the Heorot of legend, the hall of King Hrothgar that appears
in *Beowulf*. According to the tenth century chronicler Thietmar, here the ruler would
maintain his power with sacrificial rites; every nine years nine cocks, nine dogs, nine
horses, and nine men would be put to death. A German monk recalled similar scenes
at Uppsala.

While the Angles had gone through Christianization, with men now able to
acquire status as priests or monks rather than fighters, their cousins across the cold sea
had maintained a warrior culture in which a man's status was heavily dependent on
his ability to fight. Like the Iron Born, the Vikings also placed high value on virility,
so a man without a functioning penis was no man at all. A warrior buried at Repton
in Mercia who had been emasculated—a common atrocity after battle—had a boar's
tusk placed between his legs, most likely to ensure he was fully functional as a man
in the afterlife.

In their long ships, the Danish and Norwegian Vikings were experts at the rough open seas, and after a long absence they returned to England in the 830s. Then, in 865, a grand army led by the three sons of the mythical Ragnar Lothrbrok ("hairy trousers") arrived on the country's eastern shores. Ragnar, a Norsemen better known in the twenty-first century as the protagonist of the television show *Vikings*, may or may not have existed, but many of the stories attached to him are clearly untrue, unless he did actually die five times.

In the *Saga of Ragnar Hairy-Breeches* a beautiful princess called Thora is given a snake by her father, but unfortunately it grows up to become a dragon and soon is eating an ox a day and sitting on a hoard of gold which they've been forced to give it in appeasement. The father declares that whoever can kill the monster will be rewarded with Thora's hand in marriage, and so up steps Ragnar, son of the king of Denmark. He has some special trousers made which are coated in pitch, so that when the stabbed dragon dies and a huge tidal wave of poisonous blood floods everything around it his clothes protect him. Dragons feature regularly in Viking myth, and indeed their vessels were called "dragon ships" by the English, because of their shape, and because they often featured images of the creatures down the side.

In 865 Ragnar's son, Ivar the Boneless, captured the Northumbrian capital Eoforwic and established it as a permanent Danish kingdom, the town Danified as Jorvik, or York. Mercia and East Anglia were quickly conquered, the latter's king Edmund shot to death by arrows. This was at least more humane than with his Northumbrian counterpart, Aelle, who had his lungs ripped out while still alive, a notorious form of execution called the Blood Eagle. By the late 860s, all but one of the Anglo-Saxon kingdoms had been conquered. Then in 871, the Vikings invaded Wessex, and soon its inexperienced young king was hiding in marshland with only a small band of followers, desperately fending off the invaders. His name was Alfred, grandson of King Egbert and from the line of Cerdic, but as he was the youngest of King Ethelwulf's five sons Alfred had been groomed for the Church rather than for battle. After years of Danish pressure, Wessex's situation was desperate, and on Twelfth Night, January 6, 878, the last English king barely escaped with his life after defeat by the Vikings, fleeing with his army, or *fyrd*, to the Isle of Athelney in Somerset. During his darkest moments in these marshes it was said that dead saints visited the king.

But in an unlikely reversal of fortune, the young king then won a series of battles, starting with Edington in May 878. The two groups of soldiers would have stood in lines, round shields interlocked to protect them, both armies in triangle formation behind the front row. Insults were thrown and then men in the second and third lines threw their javelins at the enemy, after which the sound of shields clashing would have echoed alongside the screams, as men desperately stabbed at the foreigners with spears, so close to the enemy they could smell his breath. At the center was the king, even if he was king of only a few dozen men, surrounded on each side by his closest followers—for if he fell, they were doomed.

Battles in the ninth century would have had little in common with the grand spectacles of the late medieval period involving large and well-equipped armies. The soldiers owned no armor, and many wouldn't even have a sword, instead fighting the invaders with whatever was at hand on the farm—knives and staves and cudgels. Unlike the Norsemen, Alfred's *fyrd* was not made of soldiers but farmers and few would have had combat experience before the Great Heathen Army arrived. They fought not for coins but for their lord, their families, and their land.

And yet Alfred the scholar and his band of farmers drove the Danes out of Wessex and made peace with the Viking king, Guthrum, an agreement whereby the Norsemen would keep the east of the country and recognize Alfred's rule in Wessex and western Mercia. In 886, in the newly rebuilt city of London, Alfred was declared king of all the Anglo-Saxons not under Danish rule. He died in 899, succeeded by his son Edward, recognized as *fader* (father) and lord of all the island. Edward's illegitimate son, Athelstan, the product of his liaison with a shepherd's daughter, would then succeed him in 924 and, after a spectacular victory at Brunanburh against a Viking and Celtic army, he finally united the once-seven kingdoms of England.

One of the themes Martin borrowed from medieval Europe was that of the royal ward. In his world, fostering is an important aspect of kingship, and in real life the sons of princes would often be sent out to live with their father's lords. Ned Stark and Robert Baratheon grew up as wards of Jon Arryn, part of a web of aristocratic adoption networks that helped to build loyalty to the lord and bind leading families together. Sometimes, as with Theon Greyjoy, these wards were also hostages. Athelstan, though childless, fostered a number of royal princes, from as far away as Brittany, Scandinavia, and Ireland, although as with the Starks and the Greyjoys, there could be ambiguity about the difference between fostering and hostage-taking. Fostering was designed to build political bonds out of families who might need each other; it was sometimes within a family's interest to foster a child out to a powerful lord, but it also encouraged good behavior among potentially troublesome vassals.

In ancient Egypt, the sons of Nubian chiefs to the south were forcibly taken to be educated with their Egyptian masters, which would encourage them to learn Egyptian customs and an Egyptian worldview but also ensured their families behaved.[7] Likewise in ancient Rome, the sons of tribal leaders were often raised as hostages and given a Roman education; the Alemmani leader Serapio was named after the Greco-Roman god Serapis, following his father's time as a ward.[8]

Athelstan united the realm, although Anglo-Saxon kings were not content with the simple "King of England." Just as Westerosi monarchs are known as "King of the Andals and the Rhoynar and of the First Men, Lord of the Seven Kingdoms and Protector of the Realm," English rulers claimed lordship over all the peoples of the island, rather than just the territory. Athelstan's great-nephew King Eadred went by the title "Reiging over the governments of the kingdoms of the Anglo-Saxons, Northumbrians, Pagans and British." His successor Eadwig the Fair was "King by the Will of God, Emperor of the Anglo-Saxons and Northumbrians, governor of the pagans, commander of the British," by which he meant ruler of the English, the Vikings, and Welsh. After this, the standard title became the more prosaic "King of the English," with King John (1199-1216) the first to be called King of England.

REALMS OF ICE AND FIRE

The Norse deities were cruel, led by Odin, god of both battle and poetry, two activities seen as intimately linked in Viking eyes, since all their poetry was about fighting. Odin had one eye and two pet ravens, and was known for his wisdom, but also his skills and ruthlessness in battle. Among their other gods were Thor, the god of thunder, Loki, of chaos, and Freya, as well as Hodor, a blind son of Odin and Frigg who was tricked by Loki into killing his own brother with an arrow. In the *Havamal*, a collection of aphorisms and Icelandic poems written down in the thirteenth century, there feature a number of Viking mottos credited to the god Odin, literally "The Sayings of the High One." Among them is: "Cattle die, kindred die, we ourselves also die, but the fair fame never dies of him who has earned it."[9] Or as the Valyrian saying goes, *Valar morghulis*—all men must die.*

---

*Tweet that and it says below "translate from Swedish."

In Viking mythology, the world begins with *Ginnungagap*, the "yawning void," and the Icelandic poet Snorri "tells us of two realms of ice and fire, *Nifleheimr* and *Muspell*," from which eleven of twelve rivers flow "into the emptiness, mixing and condensing in the mist."[10] It ends with Ragnarok, where "everything will burn . . . whatever gods and humans may do. The outcome of our actions, our fate, is already decided and therefore does not matter. What is important is the manner of our conduct as we go to meet it."[11] For the Norsemen, winter was coming with *Fumbulvetr*, three intense winters which precede Ragnarok, signaling the end of the world. But then if you live in Scandinavia you're probably going to be conscious of the cold.

The religion of the Iron Born also borrows from Celtic and Norse folklore. Like the Druids, they baptized their babies in water to protect them from spirits and fairies; Ailill in the Irish epic *The Tain* was submerged in Druidic streams, just as the Welsh legendary hero Gwri was immersed in water (this long before Christianity arrived). The Celts may even have drowned people in sacrifice to their sea gods Manannan, Morgen, and Dylan, although since no one at the time could read or write it's likely to remain speculation. And whereas Celts would make oaths to "sea, stone and sky," the Iron Born call for blessings for salt, stone, and steel.

Just as in the Drowned God's halls heroes will feast while mermaids serve them, so in Valhalla divine female figures called "Choosers of the Slain," or Valkyries would serve mead and ale at a feast presided over by Odin, having first taken them to this afterlife. Odin lives in this Valhalla, "Hall of the Slain," with roofs made from warrior's shields, resting on rafters made of spears. In contrast Hel, goddess of death, rules over the other hall, where those who did not die in battle are sent—a considerably less enjoyable place.

· The other gods live in Asgard, which was connected to Midgard, that is earth, by Bifrost, the bridge of the rainbow. In the east was Utgard, the home of demons and trolls, while to the north was Jotunheimr, land of the Giants. But even on earth it was believed that Great Sweden—today's Russia—was filled with giants and "beasts and dragons of enormous size."[12] Being a land of endlessly barren frozen wasteland, men's dark imaginations would fill it with grumkins and snarks.

THE ARMY OF THE DEAD

Terrifying things came out of the north. Vikings believed in *draugr*, or walking dead, the deceased returning to life if there wasn't a proper burial, and always malovelent, even if the person had been good in life.[13] Although often guarding their burial mound, the *draugr* might also rise up and walk, attacking lifestock and people, ripping their bodies apart with their sheer brutal strength, and killing their victims so they, too, turn into *draugr*.

In the worst imaginings of the Norsemen,

> the armies of Hel march back from the grave. Every giant of fire and frost, all the trolls and underground things, all hasten to the Ragnarok to fight out their age-old enmity with the gods.[14]

In Norse mythology the *Naglfar*, or Nail Ship, was "made from the fingernails of the dead and crewed by all those who have ever drowned. We can picture a longship vast beyond imagining, muddy and rotten with weed, salt water pouring off its decks as it breaks the surface after the long rise from the bottom."[15] Because of their belief in the Nail Ship, Scandinavians were careful to trim the nails of a dying man or woman, so as not to aide the Army of the Dead.[16]

The most famous of these *wights* is Glam, from the fourteenth century *Grettis saga*, "a huge, grizzled, unsocial man, happy to take the job of shepherd at a farm high up in a lonely Icelandic valley where some inexplicable disappearances had already occurred."[17] Glam headed into a storm one evening, never to return and eventually his bloated corpse was found, blue and black, and then buried where it lay. Soon "it became apparent that he was walking again. Men fainted or lost their minds when they caught sight of him, and he started to ride on the farmhouse roof at night. His successor as shepherd was found with a broken neck and 'lamed in every limb.'"[18] Eventually a hero called Grettir cuts out his eyes but gazing into them he saw "the most terrifying thing that he'd ever seen in his life." Glam's head is cut off and burned, although Grettir afterward is cursed and becomes a shadow of his former self.

But all these dead will rise again for the final battle when the day comes, when cosmic wolves race across the sky in pursuit of the sun and frost giants and fire giants fight alongside Loki's hideous army of corpses, risen up from Hel.

Saxons and Norsemen alike believed in *alfar*, or elves and their dark cousins, *dvergar*, dwarves. Indeed "demons are so common in the North that they even perform menial tasks—like cleaning the stables," according to Olaus Magnus, a sixteenth century priest who wrote an influential book on Scandinavian folklore.[19] All northern peoples believed in helpful household spirits—in Germany they were the *Heinzelmannchen*, to the Scandinavians the *tomte*, while the Slavs called them *domovoi* and the Gaels the *gruagach*. To lowland Scots and northern English, they were *brunaidh*, or brownies, small, hobgoblin-like creatures who would help around the house in exchange for food but didn't like to be seen. The house elves in the Harry Potter franchise are based on brownies, while the junior section of the Girl Scouts is also named after them.

Then there were trolls, monstrous quasi-human figures who lived in mountains or caves and were usually hostile to humans. The origins of this myth are much debated, but one curious theory is that they represent lingering folk memories of a long-dead race of creatures who inhabited the north before the first men. Just as the Children of the Forest arrived before humans, so the Neanderthals had inhabited Europe before the appearance of their cousins, homo sapiens. Neanderthals ceased to exist around thirty-five thousand years ago, but it is possible that relic populations survived in more inhospitable pockets of the north. Trolls were often referred to in Scandianvian tales as "the old ones," and described as uglier versions of humans, but yet human-like, and in the 1970s Finnish paleontologist Björn Kurtén first suggested that trolls trace their origin to oral traditions relating to the long-dead Neanderthals.[20] (It was believed, until very recently, that Neanderthals were an entirely separate species, but it has since been confirmed that they could mate with homo sapiens, and thus Europeans and Asians today are about 2 percent Neanderthal).

The Vikings also practiced human sacrifice, a grizzly aspect of life in Westeros that was once all too common. There is evidence of live burial or ritual killing at a number of sites, such as Bollstanas and Birka in Sweden, and Oseberg in Norway. Women have also been found in the graves of Scandinavian warriors at Cernigov in Ukraine and the Isle of Man, possibly sacrificed because only by dying violently could they follow their masters to Valhalla. The tenth century Arab traveller Ibn Fadlan witnessed a horrific Viking Rus funeral in which a drugged slave girl was buried along with her master; the girl was gang raped by six Viking men, half-strangled, and then stabbed repeatedly, the Vikings banging their shields to drown out the sound of her screaming. However grim George R.R. Martin's imagination, far worse stuff happened in real life.

Ibn Fadlan was a native of Baghdad, then a city of 500,000 and the world's greatest center of learning, and was horrified by the blue-eyed barbarians, who rarely washed and openly copulated in public without shame. His chronicles later inspired the Michael Crichton novel *Eaters of the Dead* and the film adaptation *The Thirteenth Warrior*, about the Rus battling terrifying "mist-monsters" or "wendels," near-human creatures who may be relic populations of Neanderthals.

The Icelandic chronicler Snorri Sturluson's *Heimskringla* (Circle of the World) relates how one year the harvest failed in Sweden and so oxen were sacrificed in Uppsala. The following year it failed again so they sacrificed men. By the third year they got together and decided they would sacrifice their king, Domaldi, and so they reddened the sacrificial ring with royal blood. It seemed to work, and this is also what they do in Pentos if things go wrong.

SPEAR WIVES

The Free Folk have spear wives, women who take part in battle, and although the idea of Viking female warriors is a popular one and "shield-maidens" often appeared in sagas, convincing evidence of their existence is lacking.[21] Iron Born would not tolerate a female ruler, and the same was true of Vikings, whose leaders had to wield an axe or sword. Women did, however, have greater freedom in Scandinavian society than almost anywhere else, including the right to divorce and take half their husband's property.

Like the Free Folk, Scandinavians regularly stole wives, a common practice that survived long after Christianization. As Jon Snow says: "Amongst the free folk, when a man desires a woman, he steals her, and thus proves his strength, his cunning, and his courage."[22] Today the annual Wife-Carrying contest held in Sonkajarvi, Finland each June is a legacy of the tradition.

But the Iron Born also include some later Christian elements; the "god who died for us," as the islanders call him, sounds very Christian, as does their maxim "What is dead may never die, but rises again, harder and stronger."[23] Indeed, during the tenth century the Vikings had begun to adopt Christianity, and were sometimes quite devout, although often clinging on to elements of the old religion and the custom of having second wives survived for some time. It goes without saying that their behavior, also, hardly improved, and the most Christian of Viking kings, Canute the Great, mutilated and killed enemies and innocents alike.

These newly Christian Vikings made an unwelcome return during the reign of Ethelred the Unready, son of Edgar the Peaceful, *unready* meaning literally "badly advised" in Old English and a pun on his name, *ethel-red* or "well-advised." Medieval monarchs often had epithets, as they did in Westeros, where there was Baelor the Blessed or Joffrey the Ill-born. In Europe there were a number of monarchs called "the Bad" and several "the Blind," "the bold" and "the Brave" and numerous "the Conqueror," "the Fat," "the Good," "the Old" and dozens of "the Great." There were also four monarchs nicknamed "the Mad," among them Charles VI of France, the grandfather of England's own mad king.

Among the less common were Vasili II the Crosseyed of Muscovy, Constantine V the Dung-Named of Byzantium, Wilfred I the Hairy of Urgel in Spain, Henry IV the Impotent of Castile, Eric XI the Lisp and Lame of Sweden, Ivan I the Moneybags of Russia, Wenzel IV the Drunkard (king of Bohemia in the fourteenth century), Eric II the Priest Hater of Norway (he did not enjoy very good relations with the Church), and Ivaylo the Cabbage of Bulgaria. Worst of all was James II of Ireland, the "Be-shitten" or "shit-head," the term given to him by the Catholic Irish (*Seamus a Chaca*) after he was feebily defeated by his Protestant son-in-law William III.

Ethelred was unlucky as well as ill-advised, facing a formidable opponent in Sweyn of Denmark, known as "Forkbeard." Ethelred came to power in 978 after his half-brother Edward had been killed in a courtyard fight, possibly at the behest of Ethelred's mother Elfrida. Such was the horror associated with killing a king that afterwards a column of fire was reported over the wasteland where his body was left and when his brother was made king "a bloody cloud was seen many times in the likeness of flames; and it appeared most of all at midnight."[24]

It was an inauspicious start to a long and disastrous reign in which Ethelred tried to pay off the Vikings, such *Danegeld* becoming a byword for appeasement, although Alfred had at times had a similar policy. It failed and eventually Ethelred, in 1014, was driven out by Sweyn only for the Viking to unexpectedly die.

And so Ethelred returned, with the help of allied Norsemen who defended London from other Vikings. The bridge was torn down with the help of an absurdly strong nineteen-year-old Viking, Olaf Haraldsson, said to be so agile he could run along the oars of a longship being rowed at full speed. As was said of Balon Greyjoy: "At thirteen he could run a longship's oars and dance the finger dance as well as any man in the isles."[25] Ethelred lasted for two more years, after which Sweyn's son Canute took the crown from Ethelred's son Edmund Ironside.

Among Canute's first acts was to return some hostages his father had taken, minus their lips and ears, a habit continued throughout his brutal and effective reign. Mutilation was a common risk for anyone caught up with medieval kingship; just as Stannis rewards Davos by making him a knight but cuts off the first joints of all fingers on his left hand, so the Viking ruler of England mutilated anyone who displeased him or whose relatives did. But Canute also rewarded a loyal smuggler and pirate who aided his cause, a Sussex man called Godwin.

Later Canute feuded with his ally Thorkell, who he had arrested in 1021; it was resolved by swapping hostages, with Thorkell's son marrying Canute's niece Gunnhild, and Harthacnut, Canute's son by Ethelred's widow Emma, raised by Thorkell in Denmark as his ward.

Canute illustrates one area where the Vikings were very different to the Iron Born, who were "drab in their clothing and adornments." As one author put it "no Viking would have torn Theon's gold from him unless he intended to start a fight on the spot."[26] Indeed Canute, like most Vikings, covered himself in gold rings, broaches, and loudly-colored garments, proud of the wealth they had acquired from raiding. They also washed their hair regularly, an unusual habit at the time.

Canute was the first Viking leader to arrive on the European stage and had his daughter Gunhilda married off to the Holy Roman Emperor Henry; however, she was accused of adultery and to prove her innocence sought a champion who would fight on her behalf. Although the accuser was a giant, a gallant page boy promised to be her champion and killed the much bigger man—Gunhilda was cleared of the charge and refused to ever lie with her husband again. What happened to the brave champion we don't know; like Bronn of the Blackwater, men could make a name by fighting a renowned warrior in such a contest, but more often than not they would die.

Upon Canute's death in 1035 the crown of England was fought over by the sons of his English and Norman wives—Harold Harefoot, son of Elfgifu, and Hardicanute, son of Emma. The two men bitterly hated each other. However, both died within a few years, and the throne passed to Ethelred's son Edward "the Confessor."

Edward spent his reign in conflict with Canute's former regent, Godwin, Earl of Wessex, and his six sons, a division that would trigger a bigger catastrophe later on. Most likely the cause of the hatred was the fate of Edward's brother Alfred; during the reign of Canute and his sons, Edward and his brother had been exiled in Normandy, his mother Queen Emma's homeland, but after Canute's death Alfred had crossed the sea. There he was seized and blinded by Canute's son Harold Harefoot, but suspicion had always fallen on Godwin as an accessory.

Just as King Baelor the Blessed in Westeros put up the Great Sept of Baelor, so King Edward the Confessor built Westminster Abbey. Baelor was known for his piety, and for being frail and thin, just as Edward was unusually pale. Baelor forgave his brother's killers; Edward had to live with the man he blamed for the murder of Alfred, although whether he forgave is another matter. There was also the unhappy marriage, Baelor having his dissolved; Baelor also quarrelled with his hand, Viserys, while Edward fell out with his most powerful lord, Godwin.

Baelor is a sort of saint and is described as walking barefoot into a viper's nest to rescue his cousin Aemon, the snakes refusing to attack him. Scared of his own sexual desires, he locked his sister-wife Daena and his own sisters in the Maidenvault, and spent the days in prayer, leaving his uncle to run the realm as hand. (It is on the steps of the Great Sept that Ned Stark is executed). In real life, Edward's marriage was probably chaste, or at least did not produce issue, although it may have had something to do with the fact that his wife Edith was the daughter of Godwin. Whether he refused to consummate the marriage, or Edward's reputation for holiness extended to an aversion to sexual relations, we cannot know for sure. He never had any children out of wedlock, either, which was rare for kings of the era.

In 1053, Earl Godwin died suddenly at a feast in Westminster, possibly from choking to death on bread, or perhaps a stroke, and with the childless king growing old and sick, Godwin's eldest surviving son Harold effectively became heir apparent, though without Edward's public blessing. And yet the Godwins were themselves torn apart by feuds. Godwin's third son, Tostig, had been made Earl of Northumbria following the death of Earl Seward in 1055, who the previous year had defeated and killed the Scottish usurper Macbeth at the Battle of the Seven Sleepers near the Firth of Forth. Northumbria was an alien place to southern men, there were few passable roads between north and south, and the region was far more heavily Danish, especially the country around its largest city York. Tostig, despite his Danish name and Danish mother, was considered too southern by most of the magnates but the violence he displayed in maintaining the law, to both the guilty and innocent, also provoked hostility.

In October 1065 this led to an uprising in the north, led by two brothers from the old ruling house of Northumbria, Edwin and Morcar, who marched toward the

Thames. Harold acted as mediator, most likely agreeing to exile Tostig, making the brothers Earls of Northumbria and Mercia, and marrying their sister. As she was of the royal blood of Northumbria, this would give him a greater claim to the throne, which the lords of the north would support. Harold already had a *handfast*, in the Scandinavian manner, who was now put aside.

The final days of 1065 were marked by terrible storms. The noblemen of England came from all around the country to feast together at Westminster Abbey, which Edward had built, but it was clear that the king was gravely ill. Two monks by his bedside warned that England was cursed by God and would suffer evil spirits for a year and a day; on Twelfth night, January 5, the king died, and the following day Harold assumed the throne.

THE GREAT CITY

The Vikings—Danes and Norwegians—had most heavily settled on the rocky islands off the north and west of Britain, especially the Orkneys and Shetlands. According to the sagas it was the semi-legendary Norwegian king Harald Finehair who conquered Orkney with his famous ship, *Dragon*. The court poet of Haakon I, son of Harald Finehair, and known as Evyind "the plagiarist," had once composed an epitaph for his king that says much about their attitude to this fleeting life: "Wealth dies, kinsmen die, The land is laid waste, Since Hakon fared to the heathen gods, Many are thralls and slaves."[27] (Why he got the name "the plagiarist" we'll never know.)

Today the Shetlands retain a dialect with aspects of Norse, and DNA analysis suggests that the islanders are 30 percent Viking by blood, the highest rate in Britain, followed by their neighboring islanders, the Orcadians.[28] In contrast, mainland Scots overwhelmingly descend from the first men of the island, Picts as well as Gaels. The Vikings also inhabited the Hebrides, which in Gaelic is Innse Gall, "Isle of the Foreigner," and the Isle of Man, which remained Norwegian until 1266. Many of the islands retained their Viking culture for long into the modern age. In Uist in the Outer Hebribes in the 1870s, locals were heard by a visitor talking about how "nine days he hang pa de rutless tree," a clear reference to the old tradition about Odin, which had passed down in folklore almost a millennium after Christianization. Shetland still celebrates its Viking heritage on the last Tuesday of January with a festival called U-Helly-Aa, in which locals dress up as their ancestors. It used to involve dragging burning tar barrels through the streets of Lerwick (until this was banned in

1874, for obvious reasons). The Isle of Man, a sort of quasi-part of Britain, today has the oldest continuous parliament in the world, the Tynewald (from the Norse word for assembly—*thing*).[29]

The Vikings terrorized large swathes of western Europe and even reached as far as Islamic Spain, where the Muslims called them the *magus*, or fire-worshippers. They first hit Moorish Spain in 844 when some turned up the Guadalquivir river in 844 and attacked Seville. When they then attacked Cadiz, the Norsemen lost thirty ships and one thousand men at the hands of a strange flammable liquid they had never seen before. Clearly, al-Andalus was easily capable of driving away the barbarians; Rahman II ordered for ships to be built in Valencia, Lisbon, and Seville, and two fleets were established, and the fire-worshippers were driven out. Those they captured were converted to Islam, and a wall was built around Seville.

The Vikings covered huge distances, and reached as far as Iceland, a barren, treeless, volcano island which they colonized in the 870s, having discovered Irish monks living there. (Among its many lava caves are Grjótagjá, which is just below 50°C due to the nearby volcanic eruption and was used as a location for romantic scenes between Jon Snow and Ygritte.) The Vikings went further still, to Greenland, where, with pack ice reduced by global warming, a settlement of four thousand was eventually able to build a cathedral and two monasteries. The Vikings even reached mainland North America, going as far south as Newfoundland. But they also sailed east, beyond Finland and down the rivers of the east where they were called "the rowers," or *Rus*.

After travelling up the rivers that fed the Baltic Sea, these Rus would carry their boats across dry land until they found the south-flowing rivers that would bring them toward the warmer Black Sea. Sailing south, they established a statelet that would one day become the Grand Duchy of Kiev, from which the empire of Russia emerged. Finally, these tough wildenerness men arrived, astonished, to find themselves in Miklagard—the Great City. To others it was called the Basileuousa (Queen of Cities) or New Rome, but most of the world knew it as Constantinople.

17

THE BRETHREN
OF THE CROSS

Hypocrisy is a boil. Lancing a boil is never pleasant.

—The High Sparrow

Martin's world is different from ours, and not just because of the dragons. For all the comparisons between the Seven and Catholic Christianity, religion is mostly absent from public life. The High Septon does not attend the Small Council, there are no formal prayers at public events, and none of the characters regularly attend any religious service.[1]

Perhaps most significantly, the Faith is not especially associated with learning, reading, and writing, when in real life the Catholic Church *was* the education system in western Europe. It was almost entirely responsible for raising literacy from almost total non-existence during the post-Roman period to a considerable minority of the population in the fourteenth century, as many as 20 percent in the cities and 5 percent in the countryside.[2]

It was the monasteries that spearheaded these changes, where books were copied and written. Much of Ancient Greek learning had been preserved in the Arab world, but Latin survived largely through the monastic network, which began in Egypt in the fourth century and arrived in western Europe later. In monasteries brothers copied information for the next generation, laboriously, often painfully, with frozen quills in bleak northern cells. Without them what little of Roman writing survives— estimated at only 1 percent of what was put on paper—would have disappeared too.

Monks were the real-life maestars. As novelist Umberto Eco once put it, "A monastery without books is like a garden without herbs, a meadow without flowers, a tree without leaves." Yet none of the religious libraries could compete with the ancients—the Library of Alexandra had 500,000 scrolls in the third century BC, and one estimate has 700,000 volumes there two hundred years later. Even major libraries of the twelfth century had no more 500 or so manuscripts; this had improved somewhat over time, so that in 1338 the Sorbonne in Paris had 1,728 works for loan, although 300 of these were lost.

Many medieval libraries consisted of rows of chained books, which can still be seen in places such as Hereford Cathedral. However, books were often lent out—and never returned. Some feature curses threatening divine justice to anyone who fails to return them, while other lenders initiated contracts, a sensible precaution when books were hugely expensive.

However, monastic chronicles were in decline by the time of the War of the Roses, with increasing numbers of men choosing to go into secular professions instead; long before the Reformation, the Church was losing its monopoly over education and government.

In England among the most important of these real-life maestars was the Venerable Bede, a Northumbria monk born in 672 who, at the age of twelve, was sent to a monastery in Jarrow. Bede wrote *The Ecclesiastical History of the English Nation*, in 731, and was the first to refer to the people of the seven kingdoms as the *Anyclyn*, or English, although his most influential act was to popularize the idea of the dating system using BC and AD. If we imagine there is anyone who resembles Measter Aemon it would be Bede (Aemon also speaks with the north-east English accent of Bede's native land). There is also an echo of Beowulf when Sam says of Aemon: "No man was wiser, gentler or kinder. He was the blood of the dragon, but now his fire has gone out."[3]

Monasteries were tough places, and hungry mouths were often sent there at a young age by desperate parents. Orderic Vitalis was packed off to a monastery at the age of ten and was still bitter and angry when he wrote about it more than four decades later: "I did not see my father from the time he drove me into exile, like a hated stepson, for the love of the Creator." Anselm in the eleventh century described boys in the monastery "trembling under the master's rod." These young ones had to be silent and still at all times, and monks were even forbidden from smiling at novices. However, from the twelfth century monasteries began to refuse young children, just as the Church would not allow children to be betrothed, since they lacked the reason to make such choices.

Although Catholic priests were not fully celibate until the twelfth century, monks had been forbidden the sins of the flesh since the first monasteries and punishment for vow-breaking could be savage, in the Theon Greyjoy sense. A nun at Wilton Abbey in the south of England had become pregnant by a monk, and after he fled, her veil was torn off and she was whipped and imprisoned and put in prison on a diet of bread and water. However, they soon tricked her into revealing the whereabouts of the man responsible and once he was captured her fellow nuns, "eager to revenge the insult to virginity," asked the canons "if the young man might be sent to them for a little while."[4] There they forced the pregnant woman to castrate her lover and then the testicles were placed in her mouth. Ailred of Rievaulx commented approvingly on this somewhat excessive punishment: "See what zeal was burning in these champions of chastity, these persecutors of uncleanliness, who loved Christ above all things."[5]

Monasteries copied large amounts of information, and not just about religion. Bede wrote dozens of books, including works on science and history, and recorded what he had learned from travelers and stories from around the kingdom and beyond, to be recorded, copied, and used by later generations. He even speculated on such matters as how the moon affects the tides and the movement of the earth the seasons.

The number of monasteries grew especially in the twellfth century, by which stage European society was reaching take-off. Around this time some monasteries were gathering such a community of scholars that they attracted students and started teaching classes, informally and then formally. So the first universities were born in Bologna, Paris, and Oxford, founded in 1088, 1150, and 1167 respectively. Theologian and chaplain Robert de Sorbon had started off the library at the Paris university that bore his name, donating sixty-seven books; thirty years later it consisted of 1017 titles.

Life for students was grim and violent, and closer to the Night's Watch than *Brideshead Revisited*. At Paris, the most influential university of the medieval period, huge, fatal brawls between students and locals were common. In 1200, there was a fight after a group of German students smashed up a tavern and beat up the owner. The city's prevot (magistrate) raised a militia and attacked the Germans' hostel, but some Parisian students were killed too. Afterwards the scholars threatened to leave the city and as a result King Philippe Auguste issued the university's first charter and made the prevot endure a trial by ordeal. He survived but went into exile. In 1229, there were battles between students and locals in which as many as 320 were killed, their bodies thrown into the Seine.

Things were no better in Oxford, which experienced numerous disturbances lead- ing to hundreds of deaths, sometimes between students and locals and sometimes among students, usually between northerners and southerners. A riot in 1209 resulted in several fatalities and caused some academics to leave town and found a university at Cambridge instead. The most notorious incident occurred in 1355 when ninety- three died in a brawl between students and locals during the St. Scholastica Day riots. Each year afterwards on February 10 the city mayor and councillors had to walk bareheaded through the streets and pay the university a fine of one penny for each scholar killed—sixty-three in total. This procession lasted until 1825 when the mayor refused to take part, and a formal act of reconciliation was only made in 1955 when the mayor was given an honorary degree and the university vice-chancellor made a freeman of the city.

Perhaps the most notorious incident at Paris University concerned the scholar Abelard, who had begun a relationship with a young woman, which he had tried to keep secret. Unfortunately, his lover, Heloise, gave birth to a baby, Astralabe, and she was sent to Brittany in shame, although Abelard did the honorable thing, and lamented "in marrying, I was destroying myself."[6] Alas this was not enough for her family, and her uncle Fulbert was so angry that he had Abelard castrated by some of his thugs. This Reek-like crime was shocking in western Europe, where castration was unusual and considered alien. Some people did voluntarily cut themselves in the early days of the Church, since removal of male lust was viewed as a liberation, although the Church disapproved of such excessive behaviour.

As well as education, the Church also ran what we'd now call the civil service, until around 1400, when increasingly secular officials, especially lawyers, took over. Churchmen were, after all, the only people who could read. Indeed, schools were once exclusively for those in training for the priesthood, and so the first schools open to anyone prepared to pay a fee became known as "public schools" (which is why some private schools in England are still called that, confusingly).

As in Westeros, Archbishops of Canterbury and popes often found themselves in conflict with rulers, and even ended up murdered. Among those who died in the job, Archbishop Ælfheah was pelted to death with chicken bones by Vikings in 1012, and Archbishop Simon Sudbury had his head hacked off in 1381 during the Peasant's

Revolt. But the most famous case involved Thomas Becket, who died at the hands of Henry II's knights. Becket had not even been a priest when appointed as Archbishop; he was simply Henry's crony, a very worldly merchant's son famous for his ostentatious clothing. Yet once enthroned Becket became a genuine believer, like the High Sparrow, wearing hair shirts to emphasize his simplicity and holiness and condemning the seedy and squalid figures who lurked around the court. Most contentiously he refused to allow clerics to be tried in secular courts, a source of discontent not just for the king but the public who were outraged by a number of crimes committed by priests. This "Benefit of Clergy" clause allowed anyone literate employed by the Church to escape secular punishment—and only a very small proportion of criminals were caught in the first place.

Eventually Becket fled the country, but when he returned to Canterbury in 1170 and attacked the king from the pulpit on Christmas Day, Henry in Normandy erupted in fury with an expletive-laden outburst which four knights in attendance interpreted as a call to arrest the archbishop. The four men's argument with Beckett ended with one slicing off the top of the archbishop's head, and another blow slit his skull open, mixing brain and blood on to the cathedral floor. The murder was a great shock to Christendom, and Becket as a result won the argument over clerical freedom— although obviously at some cost. Spilling blood in church was considered especially evil, and even the worst kinds of criminals could not be forced out of particular churches as they were sanctuaries, just as embassies are today.

A true believer in simplicity and poverty, the archbishop had worn a hairshirt to the end, and when his body was stripped naked a chronicler reports that vermin "boiled over like water in a simmering cauldron" from his body.

LIGHT OUR FIRE AND PROTECT US FROM THE DARK

The Church itself could never live up to its own ideals, but then no human institution could be expected to. By the time of the crisis of the late middle ages, centuries of almost absolute power had inevitably left it more corrupt; this in turn would spur fanatical new groups, every bit as demented as the Sparrows.

In 1300, Pope Boniface had thrown a huge party where he turned up wearing Roman insignia, shouting "I am Caesar." His successor Benedict XI survived only nine months, poison being suspected, and his replacement Clement V was notorious for nepotism, making five members of his family cardinals (many cardinals appointed their bastard sons into positions, referring to them as nephews, or *nepos*). John XXII, who succeed Clement in 1316, was estimated to have a personal fortune of florins weighing ninety-six tons; during his reign he bought forty pieces of gold cloth from Damascus for 1,276 gold florins and spent more still on furs. He also had an ermined trimmed pillow, and the clothes of his entourage cost eight thousand florins a year (it is hard to calculate but one florin would be worth around $7,200 today, so certainly tens of millions of dollars). By the fourteenth century, various bribes could be paid to the Church, whether to legitimize children, to permit nuns to keep maids, to marry relatives or trade with Muslims; some popes also took cuts from usurers, such high-interest lending officially prohibited, and sold Church positions. Life in Avignon, where the papacy had moved to from Rome for political reasons, was pleasant enough, with fresh fish in abundance, sheep and cattle from the foothills of the Alps, and the finest vegetables from this lush region of France available to the rich—not to mention some of the finest vineyards on earth. The papal palace also featured a steam room, a zoo which was home to a bear and a lion, and countless rooms home to the expensively dressed relatives of the pontiff.

Such was the corruption that a number of churchmen became rich by illegally holding numerous parishes. Bogo de Clare, younger son of an earl, in 1291 held twenty-four parishes or parts of parishes as well as other church sinecures, earning him £2,200 a year, a fortune. He spent more every year on ginger than he paid a man to run one of his parishes, and a monk visiting another of his parishes found only "some dirty old sticks spattered with cow-dung" where the high altar should have been.[7]

There was also sexual corruption. In Flaxley Abbey in Gloucestershire in 1397, it was found that nine monks were sleeping with women, and the abbot was "doing" three, as the report put it. In Norwich in 1373, ten priests were accused of "incontinence," one involving two women, Beatrice and Juliana. He was fined five shillings. A priest in Devon in 1331 was found to be having affairs with three different women; at nearby Marychurch the priest was accused of embezzlement and going AWOL frequently. In the same period many priests were charged with drunkenness, others working as tradesman, usury, forging wills, selling the Sacrament, gossiping about what they heard in Confession and even black magic.[8]

People in the late medieval and early modern period began to take religion more seriously, whereas paradoxically in a previous, less-educated age it seemed to be worn lightly by many, some of whom might have maintained some traditional practices alongside Christianity. People used to regularly talk through church services, or even laugh and joke, while numerous chroniclers in the twelfth and thirteenth centuries lament that many people don't believe in anything. People also held numerous unorthodox beliefs, some of them relics from pagan times, while it took many centuries for the Church to enforce monogamy among aristocratic men. People now took religious discipline more seriously, whereas before it was just accepted that numerous clerics might have mistresses, drink heavily, or get into fights. The upside was a more restrained and less violent society; the downside was a more intolerant one.

In Westeros, Cersei reinstates the militant orders of the Faith, the Warrior's Sons and the Poor Fellows, but she soon finds that religious fanaticism in the city is out of control and they turn against her. In real life the late medieval period was one of growing zealotry.

Heretics had always been persecuted—that western Europe was 99 percent Catholic on the eve of the Reformation is testimony to that—but the Fourth Lateran Council of 1215 had ratcheted up intolerance toward deviant thinkers. There was also growing intolerance toward Jews, and numerous tracts written against them, in fact a whole literary genre called *Adversus Judaeos* ("Against the Jews") was created—among the popular works of the time were *An Answer to the Jews; On the Sabbath, against the Jews; Eight Orations Against the Jews; Demonstration Against the Jews; Homilies Against the Jews* and the somewhat strange-sounding *Rhythm Against the Jews.*

Jews were now seen as not just wrong about the Messiah being only a man, but actually wicked. They were now forced to wear distinctive clothing and suffered increasingly brutal laws passed against conversion, intermarriage, or even the employment by Jews of Christians.

THE SPARROW IS THE HUMBLEST AND MOST COMMON OF BIRDS.

In Westeros things change with the emergence of the Sparrows, who are outraged by the callousness of the war and the way the Small Folk are treated, in contrast to the luxury and corruption of the wealthy. According to the Barefoot septon: "the sparrow is the humblest and most common of birds, as we are the humblest and most common of men."[9] There are also the Begging Brothers, a mendicant order who reject materialism and wander from place to place. Eventually a Sparrow is appointed as High Septon, replacing a previous prelate murdered during rioting in the city, and they even take on the royal family.

There were movements toward poverty in the Church from the thirteenth century, most particularly the Franciscans, who became mendicant preachers, going from village to village speaking to crowds and living on what people gave them. Their founder, St Francis of Assisi, was an aristocrat's son who gave away all his possessions so he could more simply live the faith. The Church authorities considered him dangerous and he came close to being labeled a heretic; instead they co-opted him.

By the fourteenth century, there was growing anger at the often-grotesque wealth of churchmen, many of whom had lost their Christian idea of poverty, but the Black Death led to a whole new level of religious insanity, including disillusionment with the Church authorities, and scenes of open hostility and violence.

In *Game of Thrones*, the religious authorities are alarmed by the arrival of a militant group, and real-life movements did arise after the Black Death, the worst being the Brethren of the Cross, also known as the Flagellants. Flagellation had begun in Italy around 1260, but it had been adopted by the Germans who took it much further and to greater extremes—as they have a historical tendency to do with Italian ideas. The Italian Flagellants were also incorporated into the Church, as was often the case with potentially dangerous groups, but the German version was much more anarchic and anti-authority and developed its own organization and rituals. And they were utterly demented.

Flagellants formed a circle in which worshippers would strip to the waist and would then drop to the ground in different positions to represent their various sins—adulterers with their face to the ground, perjurers lying on one side holding up three fingers. They would then start beating themselves, rhythmically, using whips with iron spikes and needles attached, and "this part of the performance concluded with the Flagellant master passing among the fallen, lashing the sea of bleeding, sweating flesh beneath him with a scourge," a stick with three large spiky whips attached.[10]

"Each man tried to outdo his neighbor in pious suffering, literally whipping himself into a frenzy in which pain had no reality. Around them the townsfolk quaked, sobbed and groaned in sympathy, encouraging the Brethren to still greater excesses."[11]

It was recorded that "as members walked in a circle around the churchyard two abreast, each man would lash himself violently on his naked torso until it became 'swollen and blue.'"[12]

The movement soon became too crazed for its more moderate sympathizers, who began to drift away. Some of the Brethren claimed to have supernatural power and said they could heal the sick or raise the dead and that they had eaten and drunk with Christ or talked with the Virgin Mary. One believed that he used to be dead. The corpses of children were placed in the center of their circle, supposedly in the belief that they would rise again.

The Brethren would turn up in towns in huge numbers, and anyone who objected was accused of being a scorpion or antichrist; near Meissen two Dominican friars who tried to interrupt a meeting were attacked, and one killed. They were soon joined by bandits too, who saw an opportunity to rob or create havoc, and they almost certainly spread the plague wherever they went, and attacked Jews and priests.

Their popularity came amid a big rise in anticlerical hostility—in 1350 the cardinal-legate in Rome was booed by a crowd—and the authorities were so alarmed that Emperor Charles IV petitioned the pope to suppress them. The Flagellants were denounced by the Church leaders, and in 1350 many of the group were punished in Rome by being beaten publicly in front the High Altar of St Peter's—which couldn't have been a huge deterrent.

The movement spread across Germany and the Low Countries, although it fell flat in England. A group from Holland arrived in London in 1350 where their performance outside St Paul's cathedral was met by embarrassed, awkward silence. The group were deported.

However, the Brethren of the Cross soon vanished almost as quickly as they'd risen, although they were not the only wacky group to emerge after the Plague. There was also the Beghards, or Brethren of the Free Spirit, who claimed to be in a state of grace without benefit of priest or sacrament, and "spread not only doctrinal but civil disorder."[13] These free spirits believed "God to be in themselves, not in the Church, and considered themselves in a state of perfection without sin,"[14] which they argued allowed them to indulge in guilt-free sex with whoever they wanted and take anyone's elses property.[15] The Church, unsurprisingly, did not approve.

Other instances of mass hysteria reflected a society under strain. In 1374, the Rhineland was hit with the "dancing mania" following heavy spring floods. Circles were formed in streets and churches and people danced for hours, screaming and leaping and "crying that they saw visions of Christ or the Virgin or the heavens open-ing."[16] It would conclude with dancers falling to the ground and begging people to trample on them. St John's Dance, as it was also known, led to people suffering from hallucinations and jumping uncontrollably until they collapsed.

It spread to Holland, Flanders, and Germany, and everywhere featured a large proportion of women, especially the unmarried. The dancing may have been a prod-uct of social stress following the plague and other disasters, although it is possible it was the result of ergotism, a fungus that grows in rye bread: "Joining hands, the vic-tims dance in wild delirium until they fall exhausted, foaming at the mouth. This communal fit is treated either by swaddling the victims like babies, to prevent them from injuring themselves and others, or by exorcism."[17]

The dancing plague returned, once more, in Alsace in July 1518. It all began in Strasbourg when a Mrs. Troffea began dancing and within a week, thirty-four others had joined in. In total some four hundred people took to dancing for days without rest, the mania going on for a month during which up to fifteen people a day were dying from exhaustion, strokes, or heart attacks.

For all the unattractiveness of this fanaticism, the main difference between Mar-tin's world and ours is that they have a far more pre-Christian attitude, so that there is little sympathy for the poor or suffering. In medieval Europe there were almost unbridgeable class differences and the peasantry were despised, yet there was the paradox that the official religion taught people to venerate and love the poor, even if they often fell short of this ideal. Cersei and her ilk would have been far more at home in Rome than medieval Christendom.

The Sparrow is an unsympathetic figure, and yet he is the only one with a Christian sympathy for the downtrodden. As Ross Douthat of the *New York Times* put it:

The High Sparrow is a ghost of Christendom in G.R.R. Martin's otherwise more pagan/stoic vision of medieval Europe. On the show and the books, he's an apparently sincere man of the people, one of the few commoners to play a political role in Westeros. He champions equality before law, redistribution of wealth—ideas far closer to liberal values than anything his antagonists support.

His main foe is Cersei, a fascinating but objectively wicked character . . . The rest of his rivals, apart from (arguably) Daenerys, are largely indifferent to the common folk who die in their game of thrones.[18]

And yet audiences are moved to support Cersei in her battle with the fanatics.

The High Sparrow comes to a bloody end, during a scene that mirrors the Gunpowder Plot of 1605—had it been successful—when Catholic extremists attempted to blow up the Protestant James I in Parliament, after years in which the followers of the old religion had faced growing persecution. Had Guy Fawkes and his fellow conspirators been successful the explosion would have destroyed almost everything within two-thirds of a mile, causing hundreds of fatalities at least.[19] Before that, though, thousands would die as a result of increasing religious fanaticism.

18

THE DROWNED TOWN

The world is nothing but smoke and shadows.

—Motto of a Venetian house in Crete

Crossing the English Channel was "a dreaded undertaking" and "those who completed the ordeal would claim that the effort had impaired their health."[1] At the mercy of the tides, people might be stuck on a vessel for days on end, even for relatively local journeys. The trip across the Channel could take a few hours but also four or more days if the weather was bad. King John once spent eleven days trying to cross this sea, while a knight called Sir Herve de Leon endured over two weeks between Harfleur and Southampton during a storm and, as well as his horse being lost overboard, was so traumatized by the event "that he never had health thereafter."[2]

On the high seas, "the timbers grind against one another, as if the ship is trying to wrench itself apart," and storms were especially terrifying.[3] A Venetian captain called Peitro Casola recalled the occasion when his craft was hit by a tempest while taking pilgrims to the Middle East, where in the hold in the pitch black the passengers were thrown from side to side, feeling the ship "twisted by the fury of the sea," creaking "as if she would break up," after which water streamed through the hatches and the hold was overwhelmed by the sounds of screaming "as if all the souls tormented in hell were down there."[4] In comparison, Tyrion's experience of sea travel is positively luxurious.

Captain Casola recalled that "death was chasing us . . . the sea so agitated that every hope of life was abandoned by all . . . During the night such heavy waves struck the ship that they covered . . . the whole galley in general with water . . . the water came from the sky and from the sea; on every side there was water. Every man had 'Jesus' and the 'Miserere' constantly in his mouth, especially when those great waves washed over the galley with such force, that, for the moment, every man was expected to go to the bottom."[5]

Each ship carried a cook and a cat, to eat the rats, and a lodesman or pilot. However, it was not until the great Portuguese navigators of the fifteenth century that people had any great idea where they were going and "navigation was almost one of the black arts."[6] Even hugging the coastline was not a guarantee you'd know where you are, and a French ship going to Scotland would not dare go near the English shore, just as an English captain would not risk getting too close to France on the way to Aquitaine.

There were now regular journeys not just across the Channel to Calais, Bruges, or Harfleur but beyond, a thirty-day adventure sailing down the coast of Spain and through the Strait of Gibraltar toward the great Italian powerhouses of Genoa and Venice.

Italy was the first to revive after the collapse of the western Empire and by the tenth century there were merchants at fairs in Pavia on the river Po, selling "Russian ermine, purple cloth from Syria [and] silk from Constantinople."[7] Milan had grown beyond its old walls and already had a hundred towers around this time, its wealth built on its trade network. It also became the chief armorer of Europe, and "its smiths and armorers turned out swords, helmets, and chain mail for the knights of Italy, Provence, Germany, and even more distant lands."[8]

Between antiquity and 1200 AD no western city surpassed twenty thousand in population; by 1300 there were nine cities in Italy alone of more than fifty thousand; Paris had meanwhile increased from twenty to two hundred thousand in a century. By the time of the Black Death three Italian municipalities had more than a hundred thousand, among them Genoa, Pisa and, most magnicifent of all, the real-life Braavos.

The destruction caused by the Hun horseman following the fall of Rome had led a group of people to flee to a lagoon in the north-east of Italy to seek shelter. They came to live inside an archipelago of 118 islands protected from the Adriatic by a long sandbar called the Lido, and so hidden from prying eyes. The city of Venice, began as a refuge, grew to become the most important in the world, a great center of banking, trade and empire. But unlike other cities, Venice had no walls or gates, as it had lagoons and swamps to protect it.

Likewise, the Secret City, as Braavos is also called, was founded by slaves following a rebellion in the Jade Sea, the fugitives choosing their new home on the advice of a sage, but mainly beause the location was well hidden. Both cities were founded on a group of islands, and both were famous for their canals and bankers. Both are also sinking, and Braavos has an older section that has already fallen into the sea, the Drowned Town, while Venice is still sinking at a rate of 2mm a year, a result of sub-sidence and global warming. Both were a sea power, with Braavos led by a sealord and Venice by the *Doge* (duke). *Bravo* is Italian for bold, but it also meant hired killer, and Braavos is famously home to the Faceless Men death cult.

The Braavosi were originally a people "who were no people: scores of races, a hun-dred tongues, and hundreds of gods."[9] Although the different groups had nothing in common but their bondage, they spoke Valyrian as a common language for trade, a *lingua franca* (the original Mediterrean Lingua Franca was a pidgin spoken in the eastern Mediterrean, but "Frank" in that region applied to any westerner, not specifi-cally just the French, and the language was closest to northern Italian).

Just as Braavosi evolved from High Valyrian, the language of Venice, *Vèneto*, developed from Latin, although Veneto also borrowed from German, Croatian, and Spanish, ports always being subject to overseas influences. The highly-sexed English romantic poet Lord Byron called it "sweet bastard Latin" during his time there, where he claimed to have enjoyed the company of two hundred women in two hundred nights. Venetians had borrowed the phrase *sciao vostro* or *sciavo*, literally "[I am] your slave," from Croatian, which became the standard Italian *ciao. Lagoon, lido,* and *gondola* are also Venetian, the latter becoming gondolier; *arsenal*, another word, was brought into the European lexicon from Venice but originally comes from the Arabic *dar al sina'ah*, workshop.*

Later Tuscan began to dominate as the main literary language of Italy, with writers such as Dante, Petrarch, and Machiavelli writing in that dialect, and so becoming today's standard Italian; despite this some four million still speak the Venetian language.

Although Venice was a sea power, it was also the driving force behind the birth of banking, and almost all of Europe's bankers came from northern Italy, despite the Church's restrictions on lending with interest. Francesco Datini, merchant of Prato,

*Braavos is also famous for its arsenal.

went by the motto written on his ledger, "In the name of God and of profit."[10] Geno-ese banker Antonio Pesagno had brokered loans to Edward II, around twenty-five thousand pounds a year, while his son borrowed from the Florentines, much to their regret.

The Republic of Venice developed the most advanced banking system in the world; in 1156 it raised a public loan, the first since antiquity, and also passed the first banking laws in Europe, so that "sophisticated sea-loan and sea-exchange con-tracts spelled out obligations between ship-owners and merchants, and even offered insurance—mandatory in Venice beginning in 1253."[11] Contracts were called *com-menda* or *collegantia* and Venetians could be assured that it was worth the paper it was written on. Venice's first merchant bank dates to 1157, the industry partly devel-oped by Jewish moneylenders who had fled Spain and offered credit and insurance services. They couldn't buy property in Christian cities and so bought a bench, or *banco*, at the piazza.

Venice was uniquely blessed in having what sociologists now call high social cap-ital, levels of trust and social solidarity conducive to lending and joint ventures. On Venice's main island, across its Grand Canal, lies the Rialto Bridge where trading ventures were agreed upon by merchants, and investments raised, often in a very short space of time.

The goods on display at the Rialto were enough to astonish any visitor. There was English Cotswold wool and Russian fur being sold to Egypt, Syrian cotton to Germany, Chinese silk to Florence, sugar and Indian pepper going to England, tin, paper, fried fish, copper from Slovakia, "minerals, salt, wax, drugs, camphor, gum Arabic, myrrh, sandalwood, cinnamon, nutmeg, grapes, figs, pomegranates, fabrics (especially silk), hides, weapons, ivory, wool, ostrich and parrot feathers, pearls, iron, copper, gold dust, gold bars, silver bars, and Asian slaves," all passing through a trade route that linked the Middle East, Africa, and Europe, east and west.[12] However, their subsequent wealth and reputation for greed naturally made them enemies. Pope Pius II said Venetians were hardly better than fish, while to Syrian Arabs "Venetians" and "bastards" sounded conveniently identical.

In atmosphere it would not have been unlike Braavos, Venice being a city with "decaying palazzos, busy markets, lively brothels and wine-soaked taverns" while "the streets thronged with high-born ladies in strange headdresses, merchants hurrying to make their next deal, servants scurrying on errands in the fish and fruit markets and traders crying out their wares."[13]

The city was "opaque, secretive, and rife with transgressions and superstitions. Even those who had lived their entire lives in Venice became disorientated as they wandered down blind alleys that turned without warning from familiar to sinister. The whispers of conspiracy and the laughter of intimacy echoed through narrow passageways from invisible sources; behind dim windows, candles and torches flickered discreetly."[14] The evening mist would emerge from the canals and the city's seedy side would come to life, as prostitutes walked the Castello while plots were hatched inside its grand houses.

Braavos has no slavery and will not deal in slaves. This was not true of Venice, or its marine rival Genoa, which had more unfree men than any other city in Europe. Human cattle in Venice were sold young—boys in their teens, girls a bit older. Most slaves who turned up in Venice were shipped to the city as domestic servants where they could expect to be sexually abused as a matter of course. Others were sent to Crete to work on plantations, an even worse fate. Tartar slaves, horsemen from central Asia, were especially expensive, a third more than others, since it was believed that no Tartar ever betrayed a master—and the Tartars would not sell their own kind nor did they take kindly to those who did.

Some Christians were illegally sold to the Mamluk slave armies in Egypt, and Spanish traveller Pero Tafur recalled: "The seller makes the slaves strip to the skin, males as well as females, and they put on them a cloak of felt, and the price is named. Afterwards they throw off their coverings, and make them walk up and down to show whether they have any bodily defect . . . If a slave dies of the pestilence within sixty days, he will return the price paid."[15] However, in 1381 slavery was abolished in Venice altogether.

Venice was a republic ruled by 150 families, less than 1 percent of the population, and no new clans broke into the aristocracy after 1297; indeed, only twenty-seven families supplied half the members of its 480-man grand council. Their leader, the Doge, "was a mystical figure, rarely glimpsed by the public, who presided over Venice's longstanding, mystical relationship with the sea, often portrayed as a marriage."[16] The Doge's state boat, the *Bucintoro* or Golden Boat, was a luxurious, gilded vessel with two decks and covered with a crimson canopy, rowed by 168 men.

Just as Braavos held an annual Uncloaking festival to celebrate the city's decision to reveal itself to the world a century after its founders had fled slavery, so in Venice there was the carnival, famously depraved, in which orgies supposedly took place inside the walls of the city's great houses. Every spring the city also held a ceremony where the Doge tossed a gold ring into the Adriatic to symbolize the city's "marriage" to the sea, renewing these vows. The *Bucintoro* sailed past flying the city's flag, the banner of St Mark, a man at the prow dressed to symbolize justice, holding scales and a sword. As the flagship cruised out into the Adriatic so it was followed by a flotilla of ships, representing the city's power and accompanied by drums and pipes and cannon. The Archbishop faced the water and mouthed the words: "Grant, O Lord, that for us and all who sail thereon, the sea may be calm and quiet," at which point the Doge took out a golden ring from his finger and threw it into the sea, announcing "We wed thee, O Sea, in token of our true and perpetual dominion over thee."[17]

Likewise, in another free city, Pentos, where "each new year, the prince must deflower two maidens, the maid of the the sea and the maid of the fields. The ancient ritual—perhaps arising from the mysterious origins of pre-Valyrian Pentos—is meant to ensure the continued prosperity of Pentos on land and at sea."[18] However, if things go badly and there is famine or war, the king is sacrificed, which is why it's not an especially sought-after role.

Venice's marriage to the sea could be volatile, and few forgot the flooding of January 1106. The *sirocco*, the notorious wind that comes out of the Sahara and pushes hot air and sand onto southern Europe, had been blowing up, the atmosphere became sultry and there were signs of a coming storm. People noticed moisture on walls, the sea was said to groan, and then the storm broke and rain hammered the lagoon. The Adriatic rose, overwhelming the Lido and swamping the city; an island, the town of Malamocco, was entirely destroyed.

"Wherever water runs" a Venetian can be found selling and buying, so it was boasted, and soon this trade dominance developed into an empire, one the *Veneto* called the "Quarter and Half a Quarter of the Empire of Romania," by which they meant they ruled three-eighths of the Roman Empire. And yet this empire was not given to them freely by the many predators found in the sea. The Normans under Robert Guiscard fought them off coast of Albania, and the Venetians responding to their enemy's courage with primitive torpedoes and ramming logs, sinking and damaging many enemy vessels. Venice soon acquired a series of colonies, including Dubrovnik, which later became the independent Republic of Ragusa. Dubrovnik, a sea-state like Venice, later adopted many innovate ideas during its brief period of independence: it created a health service in 1301, with its first pharmacy opened in 1317 (still operating), and its first public almshouse in 1347; slave trading was abolished in 1417, and an orphanage created in 1438. This remarkable city contributed a huge amount to humanity considering its small size, and added to that proud record in the twenty-first century when it became the location for King's Landing. (Although some is shot in Malta, and Braavos is actually filmed in Spain, with Yunkai and Pentos shot in Morocco.)[19]

The growth of a shipping industry led to the invention of insurance as a way of spreading risk; the Thin Man in Braavos, whom Arya is sent to kill by the docks, has a stall selling shipping insurance. Marine shipping contracts were first developed in the fourteenth century in Venice, Genoa, and elsewhere in Italy, although they only really took off in the coffee shops of London in the seventeenth (insurance broker Lloyd's of London was originally a coffee house, where investors would meet and talk shipping news).

Italy was not the only place where proto-capitalism was flourishing. Just as Braavos is directly across the sea from Westeros, so over the North Sea from England were the Netherlands and the Hanse towns, the "free imperial cities" as they were called. This loosely confederated group of ports on the German Ocean were all mercantile hubs and exercised a fair amount of freedom, among them Lubeck, Hamburg, Bremen, Visby, and Danzig. Like the Free Cities, the Hanseatics were in forested regions by a shivering sea to the north, the Baltic and North Seas. Likewise, they all spoke related languages that descended from the same tongue, in this case German, Dutch, Danish, and Swedish.

Both Free and Free Imperial cities relied on trade more than arms and in Tywin Lannister's phrase, fought with coins. The Netherlands, in particular, would become the most important center of banking and trade in the seventeenth and eighteenth centuries. The "Easterlings," as English people called the Dutch and Flemish at the time, were viewed as being upright but also financially rapacious, a reputation that became only more entrenched as the Netherlands developed modern capitalism. As one author put it: "The functionaries of the Iron Bank of Braavos lack the dash of

Venetians; instead they share the austere canniness of the moneymen of the Low Countries."[20]

The Secret City is flanked by a gigantic statue, the Titan of Braavos, which is similar to the Collosus of Rhodes, a 100-ft high bronze statue of Helios the sun god which had been built in 304BC and was one of the seven wonders of the ancient world. Not for long, however, as it had collapsed a century later following an earthquake and been left to rot; eventually it was broken up and sold as scrap to a merchant from Edessa, who needed 900 camels to take it away. Although a great loss, there are similar enormous statues still in existence, such as the Guan Tu in Jingzhou which is 190ft tall and weighing 1,320 tonnes, the warlord primed for battle and carrying a sword.[21]

After 1200, Venice became involved in the Crusades, although criticized by the papacy for trading with Muslims. The empire was an immense undertaking, as it took twenty-five days sailing from Venice to Crete, the same as Bombay to London in 1900, and it took three months to get to Tata on the Black Sea. Nevertheless, there were regular trips from Venice to Alexandria, Beirut, and Constantinople; the Black Sea Venetian merchant convoys went to Alexandria in late August or early September and reached their destination to coincide with the arrival of goods going the other way. The strict timetable all depended on predictable delivery, without which profits would be hit hard. Many got rich, although for the rowers on board the galleys, life was less rewarding, an exhausting existence with food and water always in short supply.

By the late fourteenth century, Venice was shipping four hundred tons of pepper a year from Egypt and huge volumes of trade from the Levant, and some million pounds of spices were passing through the city each year. Yet they had acquired an acquisitive rival who sought to counter their trade domination.

Genoa, located on the north-west coast of Italy, was surrounded by trees with which to make ships, but no rich land. It had a sheltered port, and its climate was much more pleasant than the lagoon around Venice, which was prone to malaria. The two rivals were opposites in so many ways; the Venetians, forced by nature to work together to stop the lagoon silting up, created large communal enterprrises, while the Genoese were noted for their individualism. The Genoese were also far more innovative and at the forefront of new technology, including clocks and marine charts.

The two cities were almost continually at war during the late middle ages, and a major conflict erupted in 1294 over competition in the Black Sea, a rich source of grain which could only be accessed via Constantinople. Both cities had colonies in the city and, at some point, the Genoese sailors hurled the Venetian *bailo*, bailif, out of a window and killed a number of merchants. The Venetians reacted angrily and dispatched a captain, Malabrance "the cruel claw," to attack Galata, Genoa's colony opposite the Golden Horn.

In 1295, the Genoese sent 165 galleys and 35,000 men into the Mediterranean to destroy their rivals; but the Venetians changed course and reached home. Finally in 1298, the two fleets met off Curzola in the Adriatic, a battle in which 170 galleys were involved. It was the largest maritime battle the republics fought, and only twelve of ninety-five Venetian galleys returned home. During the course of the combat, Genoese admiral Lamba Doria's son Ottavio was struck by a Venetian arrow next to his father, but he refused everyone's pity and said "Throw my son overboard into the deep sea. What better resting place can we give him than this spot."[22] He continued fighting and won.

The Genoese captured eight thousand men, and the Venetian admiral Andrea Dandolo, in disgrace, "lashed himself to his flagship's mast and beat his head against it until he died of a fractured skull, thus depriving the Genoese of the satisfaction of executing him."[23] Yet so many Genoese died that when Admiral Doria stepped ashore at home there was only silence.

Among those taken was a commander called Marco Polo; as he talked in jail about his experiences, another prisoner, Rustichello da Pisa, saw a good story and began to write down Polo's tales.

The two powers fought another war in 1352, in Constantinople, in which a sea battle was fought in the dark. After Venice had finally crushed Genoa, the city instead submitted to its northern neighbor Milan, whose ruler sent the poet Petrarch to persuade the Venetians to make peace, warning them "the dice of fortune are ambiguous . . . For to hope for a bloodless victory over such an enemy, beware less it betoken a fatuous and fallacious confidence."[24] They ignored it, unwisely, as Genoa then rebuilt a new fleet and soon captured six thousand Venetian sailors.

In 1378, Genoa and Venice squared up for one final battle. The winter was exceptionally cold—snow fell hard, the frosts were biting, and the wind from the Hungarian steppes made life in Venice harsh. Command of the Venetian forces was given to

Carlo Zeno, a man who had led a quite extraordinary life. Orphaned as a child after his father was killed in battle, he grew up to become "a scholar, a musician, a priest, a gambler" as well as a soldier of fortune. On another he was left for dead after a Turkish siege, then wrapped in a shroud and put in a coffin; the nails were going in when signs of life were detected. He once climbed up the prison in Constantinople by rope in order to release Pope John V. People called him the Unconquered.

At the climatic Battle of Chiogga in 1380, Venice, under Carlo Zeno, finally crushed its enemy once and fall. Afterward Paduans, Hungarians, and mercenaries were separated from Genoese POWs by asking the prisoners to pronounce *capra*, goat, which the Genoese could only enunciate as *crapa*. Some four thousand were marched off to prison camps where many died, while the others, mere sellswords with whom they had no real fight, were freed.[25]

And yet both powers were in a sense doomed. The final defeat of the Crusades had ruined the market in the east and led the Genoese to explore other avenues of trade. In 1291, two brothers sailed out past the Straits of Gibraltar and into the Atlantic Ocean, hoping to find a passage to India. They were never seen again—but they were on the right track.

19

THE SMALL FOLK

That was the way of war. The smallfolk were slaughtered, while the high-born were held for ransom.

—TYRION LANNISTER

No Parliament met between April 1348 and February 1351, and so no tax-raising powers could be voted to restart the war, a small mercy the plague had brought. However, this would not put King Edward off all together, and even during the summer of 1350 he managed to hunt some Castilian ships where, when the cry "Ship ahoy" was heard, he ordered for helmets to be put on and wine to be drunk as they steered the enemy vessels in the manner of a "demented ten-year-old in the dodgems."[1] After this victory, Edward and Henry Percy celebrated by spending the night "in revelry with the ladies, conversing of arms and matters of love."[2]

The English won a second great victory, at Poitiers in 1356, when six thousand Englishmen under Edward III's young heir Edward of Woodstock, known in later centuries as the "Black Prince," beat a French force twice its size. Edward was the eldest of the king's five sons and had first seen battle at 16, alongside a father who was just 34. Now, ten years later, he led his men to victory. The French king Jean II, who had inherited the throne from his father Philippe, was taken captive, despite apparently having nineteen identically dressed doppelgangers on the field.[3] However, being an aristocratic hostage was not a fate worse than death, and as the great medieval historian A.L. Poole said: "For the higher ranks, war was, in part at least, a game governed by the strict code of chivalry; it was only the unfortunate peasantry and other non-combatants who suffered from the savage plundering of the routiers."[4]

For monarchs, imprisonment was always luxurious, and the king of France was transported to London and showered with golden leaves along his hours-long procession. Jean was dressed in black and rode a white horse alongside Prince Edward, and "past houses hung with captured shields and tapestries, over cobblestones strewn with rose petals, the procession moved through fantasies of pageantry that were the favorite art of the [fourteenth] century. In twelve gilded cages along the route, the goldsmiths of London had stationed twelve beautiful maidens, who scattered flowers of gold and silver filigree over the riders."[5] At a feast the English toasted and honored him as a great and brave king, with the Black Prince waiting on him at the table, an elaborate and ostentatious example of chivalry.

During his captivity in England, Jean lived in the Duke of Lancaster's palace of the Savoy west of London, the most sumptuous luxury home in the city, where his household accounts show money spent not just on horses and musical instrument but the cutting-edge technology of the time, a clock. He was much desired by London society and, in fact, so well-treated in England that in 1364 he died from overindulgence at parties; Jean was especially feted because he had voluntarily returned after his son had escaped English captivity, as a matter of honor.

A peace treaty in 1360 had failed to end the conflict, and the English instead courted the Castilians. In 1367, the Black Prince sent three diplomats to the Alcázar to talk with King Pedro the Cruel, on the same spot where Jaime Lannister meets the Dornish leader Prince Doran Martell. Nothing came of it. (Pedro is alleged to have murdered his wife Blanche de Bourbon, whom he deserted just three days after their wedding; for that event she had come with an outfit made of 11,784 squirrel skins, mostly imported from Scandinavia.)

After Lancaster's death, the Savoy Palace, along with his title, passed to his son-in-law, King Edward's third surviving son, John of Gaunt. Gaunt became very rich indeed, with a gross income of £12,000 as well as a pension from Castile worth £6,600 a year, which he acquired through his second marriage (to put those numbers in perspective, the average baron had an income of between £300 and £700). He also grew increasingly unpopular as his father's health deteriorated and he took a more active role in government.

While aristocrats lived gilded lives even in war, for the small folk there was no such comfort, and Norman poet Robert Wace remembered of another conflict:

What sorrow and what injury they did to the fine folk and the good land . . . burning houses and destroying towns, knights and villeins, clerics, monks and nuns they hunted, beat and murdered . . . you might see many lands devastated, women violated, men speared, babies disembowelled in their cradles, riches seized, flocks led off, towers brought low and towns burnt.[6]

Indeed, for the peasantry life was pretty awful even in peace time. Society was unforgiving and unsympathetic to the poor, illustrated by the words that stem from the medieval class system. "Generous" comes from *generosus*, and "gentle" from *gentilis*, two names for the upper class that have the same etymology as "genetic" and mean "born," but implying "high born"; the opposite was *Nativi*, the word for the poor, also meaning literally "born," but suggesting born unfree. In contrast, various words that originally applied to the medieval poor retain a derogatory air, among them ignoble, churlish, villain, and boor (from *gebor*, an Anglo-Saxon peasant).

It was generally believed that high-born people were of better and more moral stock. *The Owl and the Nightingale,* a poem of the time, recalled the belief that the low born were of inferior breeding:

> A wicked man
> from a foul brood
> who mingles with free men
> always knows his origins
> and that he comes from an addled egg
> even though he lies in a free nest.[7]

Peasants were generally despised, and most poems and tales depict them as credulous, greedy, and insolent. As Littlefinger puts it, "Most of them believe that if a woman eats rabbit while pregnant, her child will be born with long floppy ears."[8]

However, the class system was not quite as terrible as imagined by later eras. In one chilling moment, the dead-eyed psychopath Roose Bolton tells his even more awful son how he was conceived: "The moment that I set eyes on her I wanted her. Such was my due. The maesters will tell you that King Jaehaerys abolished the lord's right to the first night to appease his shrewish queen, but where the old gods rule, old customs linger."[9]

Droit de seigneur, alternatively "First Night," where lords took the virginity of peasant girls on the day of their wedding, is a powerfully horrific idea, appealing to our fears of sexual abuse and cuckoldry, and has appeared in historical drama. It's also a modern myth, only first mentioned in the sixteenth century and becoming popular among French Revolutionaries and Marxists to illustrate how wicked the aristocracy were—but it never happened. No doubt many low born women were raped by their lords, but it was never institutionalized or justified.[10]

Some nobles were indeed deeply unpleasant, but as the medieval era went on it became far harder—at least in England—for them to abuse those beneath them. Increasingly laws protected the poor, who also enjoyed more land rights and mobility; indeed, in England there is a great deal of evidence that even by this stage there was a free market in land.[11]

Varys is one of the few characters in Westeros who has risen far in the social order, from child-beggar and prostitute in Myr to a member of the small council. Lord Baelish inherited some land and a title, but he's from a new family, and is despised for it. One fourteenth century comparison is with Geoffrey Chaucer, whose father and grandfather were London wine merchants, his parents owning twenty-four shops; Chaucer as a very young man fought for Edward III in France, having an utterly miserable time, and then went into service for Edward's daughter-in-law Philippa, Countess of Ulster, later ending up head of customs and brother-in-law to John of Gaunt.[12] He rose so far that his son Thomas became Speaker of the House of Commons and his granddaughter Alice was a member of the higher aristocracy during the War of the Roses. Most people, of course, know Chaucer better as a poet who wrote bawdy stories, but that was something of a sideline.

Another example is the de la Pole family. William de la Pole was a Hull wool merchant who grew so rich that he was able to fund Edward III's war, in return for which he became Baron of the Exchequer; this laid the groundwork for his son Michael to rise even further, much to the annoyance of contemporaries of better breeding. Alice Chaucer later married another William de la Pole, so linking the two *nouveau riche* families, and by the end of the Cousin's War, the de la Poles had come close to winning the crown—instead failure meant destruction. They were looked down upon because bloodline was everything in the medieval period; indeed, people would sue over allegations they came from serf blood, and with good reason, as it could be used by predators to seize property.

In Westeros, small folk can rise up by becoming members of the City Watch or septons; they could also become knights, although rarely. In real life, it was unusual for villeins to go far, although not impossible, and the Church was the best avenue.

William of Wykeham was the son of a Hampshire freeman and rose to become Bishop of Winchester and also Chancellor of England, equivalent to the Hand in Westeros. He also founded Winchester College, the oldest public school in England, with its famous motto "Manners makyth man." Wykeham was fortunate to have received patronage from two wealthy men, and after becoming a chaplain acquired a reputation as a good administrator in the service of the king. Two centuries earlier, Robert Grosseteste was born into a humble Suffolk family in 1175 and rose to become Bishop of Lincoln; among other things, Grosseteste is generally thought of as having pioneered the scientific method.

However, the best means of social mobility was through warfare, a brutal sort of meritocracy, especially if a humble soldier could capture someone of value. William Callowe, an archer at Agincourt in 1415, ransomed a prisoner worth £100, equivalent to more than ten year's wages for someone of his station. John Hawkwood, the Free Companies leader who became the most feared man in Italy, may have been a humble tanner's son in Essex, although his origins remain mysterious.

In very rare cases someone might really go far. Bulgarian Tsar Ivaylo was supposedly a swine-herder to start with, but after leading a group of peasants in defeating an invasion from the Mongol Golden Horde he then took on the reigning tsar and killed him in battle, and so the Byzantines helped install him as a puppet. Against the odds, Ivaylo then defeated the Byzantines before ending up being thrown out by his own people and going to the Mongols for help. They beheaded him.

Only one pope rose from very humble origins, Silvester II, originally Gerbert of Aurilliac. He was the son of a mountain peasant from the Auvergne region of southern France and ended up tutor to the Holy Roman Emperor's children before ascending to the papacy, largely on account of his intellectual reputation. But his rise was so unusual that, rather than being celebrated, many suspected the devil must have played a role.

In Westeros, "most smallfolk are poor, illiterate, and live very provincial, humble, simple lives. They do not have surnames. They dress in raw wool and dull brown roughspun. They use roads which are crooked muddy tracks that do not appear on parchment maps."[13] Surnames become ubiquitous in England in the thirteenth century, so while in 1160 very few English tenants had them recorded, by 1260 all did. The main reason was the growth of the state and the increase in record-keeping and taxes, which required proper identification, especially at a time when people were very unimaginative about names.

In England many surnames relate to trade and location (West, for example) but in the Highlands of Scotland and in Ireland almost all surnames are patronymic, reflecting the importance of parental ancestry. The Welsh individually used extensive patronymics, so that the Lancastrian soldier Owen Tudor's full name was Owain ap Maredudd ap Tudur—Owain son of Maredudd son of Tudur (Theodore)—a common practice even in relatively recent times (people used to say "as long as a Welshman's pedigree").* Irish and Scottish Highland surname patterns are due to the survival of clans, which were long broken up in England—except in the far north. Before the growth of the state people relied on the protection of close-knit extended families, which usually practiced in-group marriage and placed great significance on a common ancestor, but as people came to depend on the law, such family ties weakened.

In England, the most common name was Smith, which accounts for just over 1 percent of English people today. This is unsurprising as blacksmiths were often admired or feared, "likely to be a dominant figure since at least the twelfth century, sometimes the leader of a gang, often rather a sinister fellow, recognizable by the lead rings in his ears,"[14] and often associated with supernatural practices. However, even in England seven of the ten most common surnames are originally patronymic, including Johnson, Davies, and Williams.

Village life was extremely tough, even in peacetime: skeletons from the period show widespread bone deformation, osteoarthritis, and other signs of continual grinding labor. The harvest was cut using an eighteen-inch sickle—the scythe didn't come about until the sixteenth century—and this involved gruelling, repetitive work, with people bent down from dawn to dusk with a threshing flail weighing twenty pounds, brought down on grain every five seconds for hours upon hours, day after day."[15]

Most people lived in fairly awful conditions. Shepherds and cowherds would sleep in the barn with their animals, usually the most valuable possession they owned. Thatched roofs were common, being the cheapest and most effective form of insulation, unless they became rotten with damp, or burned down, which they did very

---

*Gulf Arabs still have this practice, so that the notorious terrorist's full name was Osama ibn Mohammed ibn Awad ibn Laden.

easily; they were also home to numerous rodents or insects. In the High Medieval period most peasant houses were incredibly flimsy, with walls so thin that one poor man was killed while having breakfast, shot through the head by a stray arrow.[16] In fact, "house breaking" meant just that, and coroners' records describe wrongdoers smashing through the walls of buildings with agricultural instruments. A court in Elton in East Anglia punished a minor who hadn't received his inheritance and so "tore up and carried away" a house once belonging to his father.

Roughly half the population of England occupied the lowest position in society, serfs or *villeins*. Serfs were unfree peasants unable to move from their manor and subject to severe restrictions, although they were not slaves, being tied to the land almost as a fixture rather than by being owned by another human. Their lord could not arbitrarily kill them, for instance, as with a slave, and they could not be removed from their families, one of the cruelest aspects of slavery. (A serf in Scandinavia was called a *thrall*, as with the Iron Islands, from which we get the word enthralled.)

They were also subject to some punishing taxes and restrictions; if a villein's daughter had sex out of wedlock she or her father had to pay their lord a fine called a *leirwite* or *legerwite*. When they died various possessions were grabbed by their lord, including animals, any gold or silver and brass pots. The Church also installed a "mortuary fine" on top of this.

Crime was widespread, and rarely punished, although many of those in trouble with the law had committed rather pathetic offenses, as manorial court records illustrate. Edith Comber, maidservant to William son of Letitia, "carried away some of the lord's peas," while Alice, servant of Nicholas Miler, was fined for stealing hay and stubble.

The favorite rural past time was drinking, most of it done in taverns which were usually just the house of a villager who had recently brewed cheap beer. Horrific accidents were the norm. One Margery Golde died in Oxford in June 1279, burned to death after being "drunk beyond measure," having spent all day in a tavern, after which she stuck a candle into the wall above her bed, which was made of hay. William Bonefaunt, a skinner, was recorded as standing "drunk, naked, and alone at the top of a stair . . . for the purpose of relieving nature when by accident he fell headforemost to the ground and forthwith died." A goldsmith called John de Markeby was in 1339 "drunk and leaping about" at a friend's house when he accidentally stabbed himself with the knife he carried in his belt, bleeding to death that night.

Alcohol also inevitably lead to violence. In 1306, court records state that members of elite village families in Bedfordshire were involved in an enormous, drink-fuelled brawl in which John Ketel, "twice juror and twice ale taster . . . broke the head" of Nicholas, son of Richard Smith and badly beat Richard Benyt, "and moreover did hamsoken upon him"; John, son of Henry Smith, four times juror, "struck Robert Stekedec and drew blood from him," while his brother Henry Smith "pursued John [Smith] . . . with a knife in order that he might strike and wound him." And these were the county's intelligentsia.

WE'VE HAD VICIOUS KINGS, AND WE'VE HAD IDIOT KINGS.

And now, following the Plague, rural unrest was growing across Europe. In 1355, there was a new tax in France, set at 4 percent for the rich, 5 percent for the middle class, and 10 percent for the poor, further aggravating growing anger.

There had been revolts of the poor before. Back in the 1190s, London's downtrodden had been roused by a rabble-rouser called William Fitz Osbert, who called himself the "savior" of the poor and whose political career ended at Tyburn. There was the Pastoureaux revolt, or Shepherd's Crusade, which broke out in northeast France in 1251. Some sixty thousand people "wandered in bedraggled, penniless bands from village to village in the northern provinces, finally descending on Paris as a horde incremented by thieves, vagabonds, gypsies and tarts."[17] They at first received sympathy from much of the population, but inevitably it turned violent and priests, nobles, and Jews were attacked, and numerous buildings burned down. The Parisians tired of them and drove the rustics to Rouen, and then the king, returning home from crusade, massacred them all.

The Plague changed things, though, since everywhere there were differences in mortality between classes. In some areas twice as large a proportion of serfs died as of noblemen, and soon there was upward pressure on wages; the town of Coucy in France was among those that suffered "the fires of mischief" caused by a lack of laborers.

In the early summer of 1358, widespread discontent in the French countryside erupted into the Jacquerie, so called because Jacques Bonhomme was an insulting term for peasant, after the simple clothes they wore, the *jacques* (from where we get jacket). In Paris it was led by a demagogue called Etienne Marcel, who brought a mob of three thousand people to storm the Grande Salle. Marcel and his followers burst into the chamber of the king's son, the Dauphin, and shouted "We have business to do here," the crowd seizing a royal counsellor and hacking him to death on the spot. Another royal adviser fled but the rebels caught and killed him, dragging his bloodied corpse out and throwing it into the courtyard below in front of a screaming mob. The Dauphin, terrified, was saved by Marcel, who smuggled him out in disguise. Paris was overrun by rioters, criminals, and students.

The Dauphin's family were at Meaux just outside of the capital when a swarm of peasants numbering nine thousand arrived "with great will to do evil," threatening murder and rape; the Dauphin's wife, sister, and infant daughter, as well as three hundred ladies and their children were guarded by a small, increasingly nervous band of lords and knights and were now imperiled. The mayor and magistrates of the town had sworn to the Dauphin that they would allow no "dishonor" to his family, but they proved craven and opened the gates to the rebels, giving them bread, meat, and wine. Now the rustics poured into the city and filled the streets with "savage cries" while the ladies trembled in fear. Their fortress was connected to the city only by a bridge and a strip of land between the river and a canal; as with the women of any sacked city, they knew what their fate would be if the rebels overran the castle.

As the ladies prayed, at that very moment two southern knights were riding through the area, on their way back from travels, when they heard the commotion. Jean de Grailly, Captal de Buch, and Gaston Phoebus, Count of Foix, were on opposing sides in the war, the former loyal to the House of Plantagenet and the latter to the Valois claim. But they were also cousins and while the two houses were holding a truce they had gone on crusade in Prussia together to fight the pagans. They had no love for the Dauphin Charles, or his family, indeed for the northern *Franchimen*, as the Gascons and Occitans called them—but they could never allow noble ladies to be endangered by a mob in this way.

The two Guyenne knights hastened to the town along with 120 men, and when they saw the castle where the women cowered, they did not hesitate. Along with twenty-five knights in bright armor with "pennants of argents and azure displaying stars and liles and coucgant lions," the two men rode through the portcullis and fought the peasants in close-armed combat. The rebels were butchered—"killed like beasts"—and by the end of the day several thousand lay dead; just a few knights had been slain. Afterwards de Grailly and Phoebus burned down the town and the mayor was hanged, along with many other disloyal city folk, and they escorted the noble ladies back to safety.

Most of the violence was centered on Paris, and the area just north of it, but soon the tide turned, and the revolt was crushed by an especially sinister nobleman, Charles of Navarre, known as Charles the Bad. Indeed, he was so immersed in plots that when the peasants had stormed the royal palace one of Charles's men had been discovered close by with poison sewn in his clothing, apparently with orders to assassinate the Dauphin and his uncles. A second plan to kill him also had to be abandoned in 1359. When, in October 1360, the Dauphin was afflicted by an illness which caused all his hair and nails to fall out and he was left "dry as a stick," it was believed that Charles of Navarre had poisoned him with arsenic; he continued to suffer ill-health afterwards.

In England, rising wages led the authorities to enact hopeless laws aimed at restricting the "outrageous and excessive apparel of many people above their estate and degree, and to the great destruction of all the land."[18] Wages were fixed, and punishments doled out to anyone who left his land to find work elsewhere, but the law was widely ignored. The plague returned again in 1368, pushing up the cost of labor further, and in 1375 there was a bumper harvest and the price of food declined again; things had changed forever for the hierarchy, although many were unable or unwilling to accept it, least of all the now senile monarch.

The pinnacle of chivalry in his glory days, King Edward had grown weak and melancholy and for the people too the last years of his reign had been miserable ones. Over the hot summer of 1375, people lived in dread of the plague returning; the old king, a widower now losing control of his faculties, grew infirm and depressed and was seemingly under the spell of his grasping mistress.

Edward III finally died in 1377. only a day after a great feast at Windsor where he made his grandson Richard of Bordeaux a Knight of the Garter. A year before the king's death. his eldest son Edward went to the grave, and so the crown passed to Richard, the Black Prince's surviving son. A boy of only ten years was now on the throne.

So on June 21, 1377 the guildmasters of London rode into the Black Prince's former palace at Kennington, south of London, and swore their loyalty to the new king. There were many petitioners waiting to see the new monarch, among them John Wiltshire of London who requested that he confirm the right of he and his heirs to "hold a towel when our said king shall wash his hands before eating [breakfast] on the day of his coronation." The records were checked, and it was found that this was indeed his family right.

Edward III's funeral was the grandest affair anyone alive would have ever seen, his hearse escorted by four hundred torchbearers and carried through Westminster Abbey with twenty-four knights dressed in black. Behind the coffin stood King Edward's three surviving sons: John of Gaunt, Edmund of Langley, and Thomas of Woodstock. Along with their deceased siblings Edward and Lionel of Antwerp, the brothers had held a tight bond around a strong and unifying ruler—but over the next century their descendants would destroy each other in a war of unusual ferocity.

A few weeks later there came Richard's coronation, a brilliant display where "girls showered gold leaves on the king," and a boy dressed as an angel bowed to the monarch and offered him a crown.[19] But such was the size of the throng that came to the king that the boy almost fainted, until carried onto the shoulders of his adult mentor Simon Burley.

For the coronation a champion was appointed, to defend the new monarch.[20] During the banquet he would ride into the hall fully armored and bearing arms where he would challenge anyone to deny the king's right to the throne before throwing a gauntlet down. Richard's uncle Gaunt gave the champion's right to Sir John Dymoke, Lord of Scrivelsby in Lincolnshire, apparently the wish of the late king, and so it became theirs as a hereditary privilege. However, the champion turned up in his shining armor at the doors of Westminster Abbey too early and was only saved because Henry Percy, as marshal of the coronation, had placed himself by the door in case of trouble. Seeing the over-excited and possibly inebriated Sir John storm through, Percy stopped him, telling him to "take his ease, and rest awhile." Then, during the banquet, Dymoke barged in, saying that if anyone questioned Richard's right, he was "redy now till the laste houre of his brethe, with his bodie, to bete him like a false man and a traitor, on what other daie that shal be apoynted."[21] This tradition of throwing down the gauntlet has been maintained down the centuries, although it was once picked up—during the coronation of George III in 1760, by a woman who was worried "that so finely dressed a gentleman should lose his glove in so great a crowd." The Dymoke family maintained the right since, with the sole exception of the coronation of William IV in 1830 when the authorities tried to cut costs; although the direct line of the family died out in 1875, relations of the Dymokes still carry out the role today.

For two days in 1377, there was a public holiday in London while the city was cleaned and enormous statues of classical gods and bizarre creatures were placed on triumphal arches on the major roads, with musicians and jugglers at every corner. Richard's procession went from the Tower of London to Westminster and before him marched the serjeant at arms at the head of armed troops, followed by esquires in the livery of their patrons, the mayor of London, alderman and sheriffs, as well as Gascon and German mercenaries. The city's Goldsmith's Company had paid for a castle to be built out of which free wine flowed, while between the turrets was a golden angel holding a crown, who as the king passed by descended to hand it to the monarch. On each turret a girl scattered gilt leaves at the crowds.

After fifty years of rule by a great warrior monarch, at a time when life expectancy was barely half that, a boy sat on the throne. There was trouble ahead.

Richard's reign began with a series of military failures in the war against the French, and from the start it was ridden with factionalism. In Westeros, the realm is ruled by the Small Council, made up of a handful of men, among them the Hand, the Master of Coins, and the head of the Kingsguard; in real life the monarchs of England ruled with the help of the Royal Council, and with a boy on the throne they would wield more power than usual. Most powerful was Gaunt, who had in the last years of his father's reign been raised to Duke of Lancaster and was the most obvious man to rule in the king's name. And yet from the start Richard resented his uncle.

Royal finances were often perilous and for most of the late medieval period the crown was in dire levels of debt; those in charge were always looking at new ways of extracting money from subjects, and the declining population had aggravated their problems. Taxes had already gone up twenty-seven times in Edward's reign but desperate for money, the Council settled on the idea of a poll tax, levied not on land or wealth but on every member of a household who had reached adulthood; this was raised in 1377 and again in 1379, but when a third poll tax was issued in 1381, huge numbers of people simply disappeared off the register.

And so in April 1381, the authorities sent armed men into Essex to enforce the tax, and three parishes in the county erupted into violence. Soon the villages of Essex and Kent emptied as armed men formed mobs—killing royal officials, breaking into prisons, and freeing the inmates.[22] The uprising swelled to as many as fifty thousand men from the two counties marching on the capital. The Kentishmen reached the edge of

London on June 12, and the following day they were let in, whether from fear or sympathy it is not known. Among its leaders were Wat Tyler and a radical priest called John Ball, who said that "things cannot go right in England . . . until goods are held in common and there are no more villeins and gentlefolk, but we are all one and the same."[23] Ball said the Lords "are clad in velvet and camlet lined with squirrel and ermine, while we go dressed in coarse cloth. They have the wines, the spices, and the good bread: we have the rye, the husks, and the straw, and we drink water."[24] This was dangerous stuff, and Archbishop Sudbury of Canterbury accused Ball of preaching heresy.

What began with aims and some degree of organization descended into mob violence after the wine cellars of the city's grand houses were looted. Soon after, and inevitably, the mob turned on unpopular targets such as Gaunt's Savoy Palace, which they ransacked and burned, and foreigners, mostly Flemish immigrants.

A contemporary, John Gower, wrote of Tyler that "his voice gathered the madmen together, and with a cruel eagerness for slaughter he shouted in the ears of the rabble, 'Burn! Kill!'" Another, Thomas of Walsingham, described the "filthy" rustics with "uncouth and sordid hands" as "ribalds and whores of the devil." It did not help that most of the male population was legally armed and would have had either a long bow, sword, or dagger on hand, and many had experience using them; indeed, since the reign of Edward I earlier that century regular longbow practise had been mandatory.

The mob in a medieval city was a terrifying prospect, and this was made worse by the absence of any experienced leaders. Gaunt was in the North on his way to fight the Scots, where he fell out with Henry Percy, the first of his line to drop the French "de" from his name. Percy would become the first Earl of Northumberland and feature prominently in the unfolding tragedy, but his line was almost destroyed in the conflict. The two men did not get on, and when Gaunt arrived in Berwick, Percy's soldiers refused him entry without their lord's approval. "How cometh this to passe? Is there in Northumberland a greater sovereign than I am?" he asked. The men replied that they were following orders of the earl, "a principall and sovereigne of all the heads of Northumberland."[25] They knew no other king but the king in the North, whose name was Percy.

Back in London the boy-king, alongside his cousin, Gaunt's son Henry of Derby, cowered in the Tower on the eastern edge of the city when the mob stormed in, killing every nobleman they could find and ransacking the building. Henry, just fourteen, escaped only because an elderly soldier among the mob, who had previously been involved in the sack of the Savoy, now took pity and hid the boy. The Queen's mother was humiliated by being forced to kiss low born men but, while the mob was distracted with destroying her chambers, an aide ferried her out, perhaps saving her from rape. The Archbishop of Canterbury was not so lucky; he almost escaped until he was spotted by one woman in the crowd and was beheaded.

King Richard, just a few month's older than his cousin, agreed to meet the rebellion's leader, Wat Tyler, at Smithfield, outside the city. Tyler, a common laborer from Dartford,[26] was said to have started the revolt by killing a tax inspector who sexually assaulted his daughter. Now he raised his hands aggressively to the monarch, but the young king held his nerve, even when the Kentishman made a series of outrageous demands that "men should be free and of one condition."

The atmosphere was calmed by the king's calm demeanour, and the rebel leader then ordered for beers to be brought, but when one of the king's men muttered that he was "the biggest thief in Kent," Tyler drew his knife. The mayor, William Walworth, a former fishmonger, pulled out his own weapon and fatally stabbed Tyler.[27] The king placated the stunned mob and offered safe passage home and an end to the Poll Tax, but afterwards royal forces massacred hundreds of men as they made their journey back to Essex and Kent, while many more were executed in bloody reprisals. Tyler was finished off by the mayor's men while dying in the hospital; Ball was hanged at St Albans in the presence of the king. Fifteen rebels were executed in that town, to the north of London, drawn through the fields they had claimed and hanged from trees; some sympathizers had cut down the corpses for reburial, but the king ordered bailiffs to find them and make iron chains so that they could be re-suspended. The townsmen were ordered to rehang the putrefying corpses with their own hands.

Serfdom, an economically obsolete system, ended during the fifteenth century; labor services were relaxed manor-by-manor, and fines for refusing feudal services declined, although it's arguable that the revolt did not help. For Richard the violence left him with a lasting fear and dread of the London mob—although his real enemies were closer to home.

20
WILDFIRE

Why is it no one trusts the eunuch?

—Varys

R ome did not die. In the fifth century, while the West was overrun by Lombards, Vandals, Goths, Franks, and Saxons, in the East the Empire and people survived and thrived, and would continue for another thousand years, in a new city that was for many centuries the beating heart of Christendom. Its magnicifent churches would marvel blond-haired barbarians from the north, its greatest jewel being the Hagia Sophia. It is said that envoys of the Grand Prince of Kiev, upon entering the basilica, were moved to tears and could not tell whether they were on heaven or earth. Constantinople was the greatest city that was or ever will be.

Sick of the corruption in Rome, in the early fourth century the Emperor Constantine had sought a new capital. He chose a spot close to the Black Sea on the site of the old fishing village of Byzantium, founded in 658 BC by a semi-mythical Byzas and colonists from Megara, thirty miles west of Athens. The city was in a prime location, controlling the Bosporus waterway that led from the Black Sea to the Aegean, but it had never been able to grow because of the lack of available fresh water. Roman engineering was able to solve that problem and it grew to become the largest city in the world, initially called New Rome, but inevitably better known after its founder. At one point it would be home to more than a million people.

The city Constantine built was laid out "in a grid of colonnaded streets, flanked by public buildings with elegant columns, great squares, gardens and triumphal arches."[1] The streets were lined with statues and monuments from around the classical world, "a city of marble and porphyry, beaten gold and brilliant mosaics," and gigantic in comparison to anything in the west.[2] It had imperial palaces and churches "more numerous than days of the year," westerners observed, calling it "the city of the world's desire."[3]

The Queen of Cities had street lighting, sewers, drainage, hospitals, "orphanages, public baths, aqueducts, huge water cisterns, libraries and luxury shops," as well as seven palaces, among them the Triconchus roofed in gold.[4] It was the crossroads of Europe and Asia, between the Mediterranean and Black Seas, the Bosphorus bringing icy winds down from Russian steppes, clouding the city in winter with fog and snow. As Pierre Gilles, a French traveler of the fifteenth century, wrote of Constantinople: "with one key it opens and closes two worlds, two seas."[5]

Straddling Asia and Europe, it was the finest city the world had ever seen, but its position made it vulnerable to attack from numerous nomadic tribes, among them the Huns, Goths, Slavs, Gepids, Tartars, Avars, Turkic Bulgars, and the Pechenegs. They came down from the steppes of Asia, the forests of Russia, the Balkan mountains and the plains of Hungary. In 626, the city was attacked by Avars from the north while the Persians stormed the frontiers of the east; the Bulgars, another Turkic tribe, mounted sieges in the eighth, ninth, and tenth centuries; then there was Prince Igor the Russian, who came in 941, leaving a trail of devastation.

It was also engaged, in the seventh century, in a seemingly never-ending conflict with the Persian Empire. And almost unseen, a new threat emerged from the south, a nomadic tribe who emerged out of the desert with devastating momentum. The Arabs, united by a new religion brought to them by the prophet Muhammad, swiftly overran the ancient cities of Damascus, Alexandria, and Jerusalem, and even mighty Persia. In line with prophecy, they now had their sights on the mightiest of jewels—Constantinople. From 672, Arab ships secured the coast of Asia Minor and two years later they launched their attack on the Queen of Cities; against the onslaught of the most successful conquerors in history, its cause looked hopeless.

THE GREATEST CITY THAT EVER WAS OR WILL BE

Constantinople is obviously very similar to Qarth, one of the world's great ports and filled with rich merchants trading in silks, spices, and other exotic goods from further east.[6] Qarth's harbor was "a riot of color and clamour and strange smells. Winesinks, warehouses, and gaming dens lined the streets, cheek by jowl with cheap brothels and temples of peculiar gods. Cutpurses, cutthroats, Spellsellers, and moneychangers mingled with every crowd. The waterfront was one great marketplace."[7] In the show it looks like Petra, the desert city in Jordan, but in every other way it resembles Constantinople,[8] including its position on the Straits of Qarth connecting the Summer and Jade Seas.

Qarth's Spice King is very wealthy, despite his grandfather being only a humble pepper salesman, and in real life spices were extremely lucrative in the Mediterranean and silk road trade between Europe, the Near East, and China. The Spice King is part of the Thirteen, a sort of city elite made up of traders; another member, Xaro Xhoan Daxos, is a merchant prince and also fantastically rich, owning eighty-four ships; he allows Daenerys to stay at his absurdly enormous palace, which makes Magister Illyrio's manse in Pentos resemble "a swineherd's hove," and has gardens "full of fragrant lavender and mint, a marble bathing pool stocked with tiny golden fish, a scrying tower and warlock's maze" and floors made of green marble and walls drapped with silk.[9] While she is there he gives her perfume, monkeys, ancient scrolls from Valryia, a snake, a litter for her to be carried in, and two bullocks to pull it, as well as a thousand toy knights made of "jade and beryl and onyx and tourmaline, of amber and opal and amethyst," covered with shining armor made of gold and silver. The point is that Qarth is a very, very rich place.

As the odd-looking warlock Pyat Pree says to Daenerys: "Qarth is the greatest city that ever was or ever will be. It is the center of the world, the gate between north and south, the bridge between east and west, ancient beyond memory of man and so magnificent that Saathos the Wise put out his eyes after gazing upon Qarth for the first time, because he knew that all he saw thereafter should look squalid and ugly by comparison."[10]

Compare this with Fulcher of Chartres, a Frenchman who came to visit Constantinople in the eleventh century, and said:

> O what a splendid city, how stately, how fair, how many monasteries therein, how many palaces raised by sheer labour in its broadways and streets, how many works of art, marvellous to behold: it would be wearisome to tell of the abundance of all good things; of gold and silver, garments of manifold fashion and such sacred relics. Ships are at all times putting in at this port, so that there is nothing that men want that is not brought hither.[11]

It was a golden metropolis that, in the words of historian of John Julius Norwich, conjured in the western mind "visions of gold and malachite and porphyry, of stately and solemn ceremonial, of brocades heavy with rubies and emeralds, of sumptuous mosaics dimly glowing through halls cloudy with incense."[12]

Since the early medieval period Byzantium inspired a lurid fascination among jealous, impoverished Latin Christians. Nothing in their world could compete with the Emperor Theophilius's Triconchose, or Triple Shell, supported on pillars of porphyry and with huge slabs of colourful marble. Its silver doors opened to reveal a semi-circiular hall, lined with marble, in which the fountains flowed with wine. To the north was the Hall of the Pearl, "its white marble floor richly ornamented with mosaic, its roof resting on eight rose-pink marble columns."[13]

Close to this was the Kamiles, "in which six columns of green Thessalian marble led the eye up to a field of mosaics depicting a fruit harvest and on to a roof glittering with gold."[14] To the north was the Palace of the Magnaura, built by Constantine, and where Theophilus installed mechanical birds by the imperial throne, around which were lions built of gold; at a given signal the birds would burst into song and the lions roar, after which a golden organ would sound.

In the center of Constantinople there stood the "Million," marking the foundation of the city and consisting of four triumphal arches forming a square and supporting a rounded dome, above which stood a piece of the True Cross on which Jesus died.[15] The equally grand Serpent Column was brought by Constantine from Delphi where it had been erected in the Temple of Apollo by thirty-one Greek cities in gratitude for victory against the Persians at Plataea in 479 BC.

More important than all of New Rome's palaces were its walls, built of concrete, brick, and locally-quarried limestone. The first line was constructed in 413 under the Emperor Theodosius and was enough to put off Attila the Hun, "the scourge of God," when he attacked the city in 447. That year the wall collapsed after a severe earthquake while Attila was in nearby Thrace, and sixteen thousand of the city's citizens rebuilt the structure in record time, adding an outer wall with a series of towers and a brick-lined moat, the fosse. During its height the city was also protected by 192 towers, part of a defensive system that comprised five zones, each one a hundred feet high and two hundred feet apart, with sentinels scanning the horizon in all directions. The towers had chambers with siege engines capable of throwing rocks and the city's infamous secret weapon, Greek Fire.

No army arriving from the land could break the city walls, and many had tried. The Avars had brought their sophisticated stone-throwing machines. The Bulgar khan Krum tried performing human sacrifices to aide his hoped-for conquest, all to no avail. Even Rome's enemies suspected that God protected the city, and until the catastrophe of 1204, the walls were never scaled.

With its vast wealth, its palaces, its technology, and trade, the Great City awed a Latin world which had been plunged into darkness. It also disgusted them, becoming symbolic of duplicity; Italian bishop Liudprand of Cremona described Constantinople as "a city full of lies, tricks, perjury and greed, a city rapacious, avaricious and vainglorious."[16] For people from small towns and villages, such a large city with its court tensions and intrigues must have seemed poisonous—"Smoke, sweat, and shit. If you have a good nose you can smell the treachery too."[17] And perhaps nothing puzzled them more than its eunuchs.

A MAN MAY HAVE WITS, OR A BIT OF MEAT BETWEEN HIS LEGS, BUT NOT BOTH

Constantine had only established himself as undisputed ruler after having two rivals, Licinius and Martianus, killed, rather setting the tone for court politics in the city. Constantine also had his son Crispus arrested and then put to death by slow poison; a few days later he had his second wife Fausta suffocated by steaming in the bathhouse, or *calidaroim*.[18] Possibly she had falsely accused her stepson of trying to seduce her and when her husband realized the truth of her lies had her killed too; alternatively Crispus may have plotted the emperor's overthrow. Afterwards both their names were eradicated from all records and inscriptions, a common Roman practice called the *Damnatio memoriae*, or "condemnation of memory."

Constantine had legalized Christianity and eventually installed it as the official religion before converting on his deathbed when he could be fairly certain he wasn't going to be killing anyone else. He planned his own modest grave to be built alongside twelve sarcophagi, sacred pillars to represent the twelve Apostles, in the center of which would be his. Constantine, not a man lacking in self-confidence, had even adopted the title "Equal of the Apostles," which later emperors were to use.

He was succeeded by his second son Constantius, who lost little time in removing his rivals—first inventing a rumor that a scrap of parchment had been found in Constantine's fist accusing his two half-brothers of poisoning him. They were soon brutally murdered, along with another leading figure, Julius Constantius, who was butchered alongside his eldest son, and likewise another rival, Delmatiuys, with both his sons.

This became a running theme throughout the empire, with figures such as Emperor Zeno, who died before long "by homosexual excesses and venereal disease."[19] Zeno became obsessed with a prophecy that he would be overthrown by one of the thirty picked officials in his entourage, and so for no particular reason picked on one, Pelagius, a popular figure who was immediately arrested and strangled.*

Eunuchs were often at the forefront of these court feuds. Emperor Arcadius, ruling from 395 to 408, was a weak figure dominated by a courtier called Rufinus, who wished to marry his daughter to the emperor. However, he had a rival in the "Superintendent of the Sacred Bedchamber" (*Praepositus Sacre Cubiculi*), an elderly eunuch named Eutropius.

Eutropius had an egg-bald head and wrinkled yellow face, was not an impressive figure to look at, and had worked first as a male prostitute and then pimped out younger boys for powerful officials, before entering the Imperial Household. But "he was intelligent, unscrupulous and ambitious; he too wished to control the Emperor, and to that end he was determined to thwart his enemy in every way he could."[20] To stop his rival, Eutropius had arranged an imperial marriage between Arcadius and a Frankish girl called Eudoxia.

"Beautiful, worldly and ambitious," Eudoxia was rumored to have had enjoyed a number of lovers, one of whom may have been the father of her son, the Emperor Theodosius. She owed her position to the eunuch but had grown jealous of his influence over her husband and after four years, her marriage with Arcadius had descended into "mutual loathing." In 399, Eutropius ended up consul, much to the outrage of the aristocracy who could not bear to see the prestigious title taken by a former male prostitute and eunuch. Later that year his enemies engineered his arrest and he was exiled to Cyprus and then beheaded.

However, his rival Rufinus ended up cut down by his own troops, his body mutilated beyond recognition and his head put on a stick and paraded through the streets. The men who once fought for him chopped off his right hand and walked around the city, having it open and shut to passers-by, calling out "Give to the insatiable."

Constantinople was not the only city to employ eunuchs, who also appear at the courts of ancient Egypt, China, Japan, and the Umayyad Caliphate. Back in 210 BC, a eunuch called Zhao Gao had ruthlessly taken over the Chinese court after the death of the emperor Qin Shi Huangdi. Zhao Gao forged documents suggesting the old man had wished for all of Gao's court rivals to commit ritual suicide, before

---

*Zeno was obsessed with an early form of backgammon and is best remembered for having once landed the most unlucky hand in history, which was recorded and reconstructed in the 19th century.

maneuvring to have his own protégée installed as emperor, and then later having him assassinated. He was eventually murdered, too, rather inevitably. In ancient Greece a eunuch called Hermias had become tyrant of Assos, off the coast of Turkey, and offered his sister Pythias's hand in marriage to the philosopher Aristotle; he accepted, and they lived happily ever.

The Romans had used castration clamps, with which priests of the goddess Cybele would remove their own testicles in her honor. Some early Christians had gone in for self-mutilation, including the third century scholar and ascetic Origen, although he later regretted it—rather understandably. The Church was not keen and the council of Nicaea in 325 banned self-castration, although the Greek Orthodox church allowed castrated men to become priests and some rose high.

Eunuchs were highly prized, so that when in 949 the Italian king Berengar sent his emissary Liutprand to Byzantium, the latter brought four young eunuchs as a gift to the emperor, along with two silver gilt cauldrons and nine high quality armored breasplates. At the start of the tenth century an embassy from Tuscany to Baghdad brought the caliph some twenty Salvic eunuchs alongside beautiful slave girls, swords, shields and hunting dogs.[21]

Merchants brought slave boys and girls from across Europe to Constantinople and carried out castration on arrival. One Arabic author advised that if you took Slavic twins and castrated one he would become more skilful and "more lively in intelligence and conversation" than his brother, an interesting science experiment no longer available to academics today. Castration was belived to be good for the "Slavic mind" but supposedly had the opposite effect on black Africans. The Arabic word for eunuch—*siqlabi*—comes from their ethnic term for Slavs—*saqalibi*.[22]

The minority of eunuchs who had lost both testicles and penis, the *carzimasia*, were even more valuable, since the operation was very dangerous; the boy would only survive if covered with black pitch or hot sand immediately to cauterize the wound and stem the bleeding.

Castration of both kinds is common in Essos, and almost unknown in Westeros where, like in western Europe, the practice was considered immoral. Eunuchs were exotic, and carry a particular image in the modern mind, in the words of one historian "invariably a fat, sly, lazy, scheming, untrustworthy, cowardly, epicene and unmanly monstrosity", like Varys. But in fact "in Byzantine days, they often proved themselves to be highly intelligent, brave, hard working, and as open and honest as any other human being." [23] Also like Varys, a eunuch, without family to promote, was far more dedicated to the state itself rather than individual faction of family, and his position could not become hereditary. Indeed, eight official positions in Constantinople were reserved for eunuchs, one of which was the *parakoimomenos*, a highly-trusted official who slept across the door of the emperor's bedchamber.[24]

Eunuchs could become very powerful and influential, employed to guard the empress, and also as high officials in the state; Justinian II's tax-collectors included Stephen of Persia, "a huge and hideous eunuch never seen without a whip in his hand." They even became generals and high-ranking statesmen. With eunuchs so prized, many families willingly castrated a younger son in order to speed his career in the imperial service—although castration was also carried out as a punishment on the sons of disgraced emperors or rebels.

In the Known World, eunuchs comprise the most powerful of armies, the Unsullied, but in reality, they didn't make very effective fighters because of reduced testosterone, the hormone responsible for aggression in male mammals—something understood in medieval times, even if the exact medical reasons were unknown. Eunuchs could lead armies, however, among them perhaps the most celebrated of all Byzantine generals, Narses (478–573), who fought the Goths in Italy and was said to be good at strategy "for a eunuch." In fairness he did conquer Rome, although this was because he was good at logistics and administration, had self-discipline, and also didn't drink to self-destruction, as with many army leaders.

Among the most famous of Chinese admirals, the fifteenth-century Zheng He was a eunuch (and, incidentally, a Muslim); and in the tenth century the castrated Peter Phokas headed the Byzantine imperial guard under Emperor Nikephoros II. Phokas was possessed of almost superhuman strength, and when challenged to single combat threw a lance at the Russian leader, splitting his body in two.

A WALL OF RED-HOT STEEL, BLAZING WOOD, AND SWIRLING GREEN FLAME

And so, in 677, after three years of grueling siege, it appeared that the prophecy would be proven true and the Arabs would take Rûm (Rome), as they called the Byzantine capital. The Saracen ships brought heavy siege engines and huge catapults to break the walls, and thousands upon thousands of soldiers who had experienced only victory in their rapid conquest of the Near East. But then, as the enemy ships closed in on the city, the Romans unleashed their secret weapon, a hellish stream of liquid fire. The flames landed on the water's surface between the Arab ships, where to their horror they appeared to set fire to the sea. More flames shot out from the Roman towers, fire that seemed to shoot horizontally, and with the blaze came the deafening, terrifying noise, louder than thunder, and the smoke and gas. All around them the Arabs in their ships saw an inferno on the surface. The burning liquid shooting at them did not just engulf the water; it stuck to their ships, their masts and hulls, the wood burning like tinder and the flesh with it. The terrified crews were burned alive, screams filling the air as thousands died. The followers of the caliph Yazid had met a terrible fate, helpless against this bizarre, terrifying weapon, unlike anything they'd ever seen.

The Arabs had been introduced to Greek Fire.

Perhaps the most dangerous weapon in Westeros is wildfire, a flammable substance impervious to water that may have been developed by the Targaryens. It is used with devastating effect at the Battle of Blackwater, where thousands of Stannis's troops die, Davos recalling: "A flash of green caught his eye, ahead and off to port, and a nest of writhing emerald serpents rose burning and hissing from the stern of Queen Alysanne."[25]

The real wildfire would have been equally terrifying, and bizarre, and so effective it remained a state secret. "Greek Fire" was developed in 672 by chemists in Constantinople, a sort of Guild of Pyromancers, but it was probably originally brought to them by a Greek refugee from the Muslim invasion by the name of Kallinikos. He came from Syria with "a technique for projecting liquid fire through siphons," using the black petroleum found throughout the Near East, which is refered to as far as back as the fifth century BC, although its raw power was not realized until the modern age.

The core ingredient was crude oil from the Black Sea, mixed with wood resin, which made it adhersive. The Byzantines had found a way to heat this compound in sealed bronze containers, pressurizing it and then releasing the liquid through a nozzle and igniting it. It took great skill and engineering, especially onboard wooden boats, but then the Byzantines were Romans after all.

The French chronicler Jean de Joinville described facing Greek fire when it was used against Crusaders in 1249:

From the front as it darted towards us it appeared as large as a barrel of verjuice [highly acidic juice from unripe grapes], and the tail of fire that streamed behind it was as long as the shaft of a great lance. The noise it made in coming was like that of a thunderbolt falling from the skies; it seemed like a dragon flying through the air. The light this huge, flaming mass shed all around it was so bright that you could see right through the camp as clearly as if it were day.[26]

The weapon was brought aboard hundreds of flame-throwing *dromons*, or war vessels, either sprayed using a pump or put in boxes and catapulted at the enemy; unmanned fireboats were also used, if the wind was right.[27] In 2006, academic John Haldon published an account of an attempt to recreate it, photographs showing heated liquid coming from a narrow tube "with a loud roaring noise and a thick cloud of black smoke."[28] With a reconstructed siphon and oil from Crimea, flame was projected ten to fifteen meters and was "so intense that in a few seconds it completely burned a target boat."

After getting battered by Greek fire, the Arabs fell victim to a freak autumn storm on their return home. Not to be put off, they attacked again in 717, and this time did no better. In 814, the Bulgars were poised to attack Constantinople after defeating a Byzantine army, their leader Krum having had the Emperor Nicephorus's body exposed naked on a stake, before turning his skull into a drinking cup. As the Bulgar army approached, rumors spread throughout the city of the weapons these barbarians would bring, of gigantic battering rams. However, on April 13, Holy Thursday, as he was about to attack, Krum had a sudden seizure, blood poured out from his mouth, nose, and ears, and he dropped dead.

In the summer of 860, the people of the city endured another terrifying ordeal; on June 18, soon after the emperor had led a force on campaign against the Saracens, a fleet arrived from the Black Sea at the mouth of the Bospherous and headed toward the city, burning monasteries and pillaging towns, before arriving and casting their anchors by the Golden Horn. No one had even seen these people before, and the Patriarch asked who these "fierce and savage" warriors were, "ravaging the suburbs, destroying everything . . . thrusting their swords through everything, taking pity on nothing, sparing nothing."[29]

They were the Rus, the Vikings of the east, who, carrying their longships across the Great European Plain and down to the Black Sea, had come to a city so large it barely seemed to be of this earth. Urgent messengers were sent to Emperor Michael to alert him, but by the time he arrived the Rus had left, which many attributed to the intercession of the Virgin and her robe which had been carried shoulders-high around the city walls. Others said the Patriarch dipped the robe in the sea and a tempest destroyed the Russian fleet. The more prosaic explanation is that, finding the walls too difficult for their primitive technology to break into, they just gave up to pillage elsewhere.

It was part of a great adventure for the Norsemen in the east; Scandinavians' grave epitaphs back home in their runic alphabet boast of travels as far south as "Serkland," the land of the Muslims (Saracens), and they traveled so far that a semi-permanent Viking colony may have even been established as far away as the Persian Gulf.[30] They became a regular presence in the Queen of Cities, familiar but always feared. In Qarth, only a "few Dothraki" are permitted inside the city at one time, afraid of what large numbers might do; likewise, a maximum of fifty Rus were allowed into Constantinople at any one time in the tenth century. However, eventually they were incorporated into a guard for the emperor, called the Varangians, from the old Norse word for "pledged faith." (The imperial palace itself was protected by the *Vigla*, or Watch, and among the highest positions in Constantinople was the *droungarios tes Vigles*, commander of the Watch.)[31] Today in the Hagia Sophia, now a museum in Istanbul, one can see on the upper story graffiti left by these Vikings, the Norse name "Halfdan" being identifiable.

So the Byzantines had tamed the Rus, although at huge sacrifice to one individual. The barbarian leader, Vladimir, had in 988 arrived as part of a military treaty in which he would send a force of six thousand fully-equipped Varangians. In return, he asked for one thing only, Emperor Basil's sister Anna, prized even more for being *porphyrogenita*, "born in the purple" (i.e. when her father was ruler). Vladimir already had four wives and eight hundred concubines and ruled a people beyond the borders of civilization. When told of her fate, the princess wept bitter tears, accusing her family of selling her into slavery, and yet a young princess had little choice if her brother required her to marry a savage, especially a savage with an army behind him. The marriage agreement was honored—otherwise their new friends might soon become enemies. Reluctantly she went to the boat that would take her to the Rus city of Cherson, and the six thousand troops returned to Emperor Basil. The prince of Kiev was baptized and the Rus, who might have turned to Islam, fatefully adopted Christianity. Vladimir, despite his hundreds of concubines, became a saint on account of his work promoting Christianity; his Byzantine bride helped to build a number of churches, although she never bore him a child.

Soon afterward, one of the most sordid figures in Byzantine history appears, the "strange and sinister figure of John the Orphantorophus," a eunuch "who had risen, through his own intelligence and industry, from obscure and humble origins in Paphlagonia to be a highly influential member of the civil bureaucracy."[32] The eunuch had become director of the city's principle orphanage, and had four younger brothers, of whom the two eldest were eunuchs too. They were money-changers and forgers, but despite this were also charming and handsome; the youngest, Michael, was in 1033 brought by his brother to meet the Emperor Romanos and his consort Zoe in formal audience where Zoe instantly fell in love, as his eunuch brother had planned. An affair began, which Romanos remained oblivious to, even after his sister had warned him.

By this stage, among the most famous of all Varangians had turned up, the exiled half-brother of King Olaf of Norway. Olaf the Fat had become part of English folklore after pulling down London Bridge in 1014, and later he returned home and won praise from the Church as a great Christian ruler despite relentless fornication. Olaf's policy of Christianization, however, had been bitterly resisted by some noblemen and, in 1028, he was defeated and killed in battle by an alliance led by the Danish king Canute. The defeat put Olaf's fifteen-year-old half-brother Harald in mortal danger; he had been seriously wounded, but after escaping in the cold had come to the home of a peasant couple who took him in. Hunted in his native home, he had fled east and followed the Viking route down the rivers of Russia to Constantinople.

Harald Hardrada, "hard-ruler," as he was later known, grew into a 6'6" man-monster known as the Thunderbolt of the North. He was a brutal and enthusiastic fighter who took great pleasure in his acts of daring do, but was also an eccentric man who loved poetry almost as much as he loved fighting, which was a lot; he had one eyebrow higher than the other, blond hair, a long moustache, and huge hands and feet. (Likewise the Iron Born had a similar-sounding leader, Harwyn Hardhand, of whom it was said: "Tempered in the Disputed Lands, he proved to be as fierce afoot as he was at seat, routing every foe.")[33]

Harald became a noted warrior in Byzantium and there are many stories attached to his time there, and some of them may even be true. He battled with a lion in an arena after seducing a noblewoman, but heroically slew the animal, as he did with a giant serpent he encountered. He also left a trail of destruction across southern Italy fighting on behalf of the empire, an adventure he seemed to hugely enjoy.

Yet when Harald returned to court he was drawn into imperial intrigue. Zoe and her young lover Michael had begun to openly flaunt their adultery and soon her husband was found dead in the bath; indecently soon afterwards Michael was crowned emperor and the couple married that same day. And yet the new leader was cursed, and as his epilepsy grew more serious he withdrew into a monastery, refusing to see his wife. John the eunuch, unwilling to lose power, insisted that Zoe replace Michael IV with his nephew, Michael V, who she adopted as her son. It was not long before the two tired of each other, and in 1042 when the young emperor had his new "mother" banished from her court her supporters had him blinded, along with his surviving uncle Constantine. Harald, who had fallen out of favor with the young emperor, took both their eyes out.[34]

And yet the giant Viking soon found himself in trouble, for reasons that remain unclear, and was forced to flee. In the Battle of the Blackwater, Tyrion Lannister uses a giant chain to trap the fleet of Stannis, another historical tactic borrowed from the Byzantines. While Constantinople had depended on her walls, it was also protected by a great chain fixed across the Golden Horn that separated the city from the Genoan colony of Galata on the other side. Only one man is known to have broken the chain—Harald Hardrada, after breaking out of prison and taking Maria, a beautiful young relative of Zoe, who may or may not have been his lover.

Harald and a group of Varangians seized two galleys in the Golden Horn and sailed off determined to jump the chain, with Maria as their hostage. Sailing toward the chain, Harald ordered for the oarsmen to sail full speed while the crew ran to the back, tilting the ship up so that it leaped into the air, before quickly running forwards to lean it back. The Vikings sailed into the Black Sea and freed Maria on the banks of the Bospherus, to be safely escorted back to the Byzantine court; a second galley failed to repeat the trick and its men were lost.[35]

With Canute and his sons now dead, Harald finally made it home, where he edged his brother Olaf's son Magnus off the throne. But there was one last adventure waiting for Harald, for Magnus had long before made a pact with Canute's son Hardicanute, king of England, that whoever died first would leave the other his kingdom. Canute was dead, Hardicanute was dead, and now Magnus was dead, but the deal, in Harald's mind, was still binding, and England his by right. And then, at the beginning of 1066, King Edward was dead too—and so began the war of the three kings.

21
THE MAD KING

"Burn them all," he kept saying. "Burn them all."

—JAIME LANNISTER

With France's Charles V dying in 1380 there were now boys on the thrones of France as well as England, and both would end in tragedy, although for young Charles VI of France it would involve far greater suffering.

Under the rule of the boy-king's four uncles, France now brought the war to England, through its northern frontier, which proved rather a cultural shock. In Westeros, technology in the south is more advanced than the north, and even more so than beyond the Wall. The Wildlings cannot forge iron, but have amassed some weapons through trade or warfare. Only the Thenn, who live in an oasis of fertile land and are the most technologically advanced of the Free Folk, are able to mine tin and copper, the metals used to make bronze.[1]

When the Scots asked for help from the French in 1385, the dashing nobleman Admiral de Vienne sailed north with fifteen thousand men, including eighty knights, as well as fifty thousand gold francs and fifty suits of armor, and lances and shields for his nobles.

And yet the men from the lush Loire, Seine, and Rhone valleys had no idea just how impoverished Scotland was. "What kind of a country has the Admiral carried us to?" one Frenchman asked, calling it a place of "hard beds and ill nights."[2] The French were accustomed to "tapestried halls, goodly castles, and soft beds" and what they got were castles "bare and gloomy with primitive conditions and few comforts in a miserable climate. The damp stone huts of clan chieftains were worse, lacking windows or chimneys, filled with peat smoke and the smell of manure. Their inhabitants engaged in prolonged vendettas of organized cattle-raiding, wife-stealing, betrayal, and murder."[3] The Scots had no iron either, nor even leather for saddles, all of these having to be imported from the continent and they were stunned by the material wealth of their allies. "We never knewe what povertie meant tyll nowe," one Scotsman told the admiral.[4]

It was not long before there was a fight over supplies, after impoverished farmers had objected to foraging by French troops; over one hundred Frenchmen were killed in violence with local men over the course of a month. To further stretch the relationship, the French leader—defying all stereotypes—engaged in "guilty amour" with the king of Scotland's cousin, which angered the monarch so much that he wished to kill him.

It was also getting colder. In the 1380s, Normandy experienced very harsh winters with frequent snowfalls; in England the winter of 1385-6 was "wonderfully evil and hard."[5] The Scots and French under de Vienne burned their way through northern English villages, and a French chronicler recorded that his countrymen brought "murder, pillage and fire" to the north, "destroying all by sword or fire, mercilessly cutting the throats of peasants and anyone else they met, sparing no one on account of rank, age, or sex, not even the elderly or the infant at the breast."[6]

Jean le Bel, an eyewitness, wrote:

These Scottish men are right hardy and sore travailing in harness and in wars. For when they will enter in England, within a day and a night they will drive their whole host twenty-four mile, for they are all a-horseback . . . They take with them no purveyance of bread and wine, for their usage and soberness is such in time of war, that they will pass in the journey a great long time with flesh half sodden, without bread, and drink of the river water without wine.[7]

Facing them was Henry Percy, great-grandson of the man who had fallen in the catastrophic year of 1314, and now in charge of protecting the realm. And yet, while fighting along the border would continue for the next two decades, the French were soon out of the picture, faced with their own problems.

The young king Charles had insisted on marriage just four days after he met his betrothed, a fourteen-year-old German princess called Isabeau who arrived in a hugely expensive and luxurious carriage, wearing the priceless crown that the king had sent to her as a gift. Before the marriage, Isabeau, like any woman due to marry a king of France, was inspected naked by the ladies of the court to "determine if she were properly formed for bearing children." As the next decade would show, she was indeed properly formed to do so, although whether all those children in question were the king's is more of a mystery.

The wedding was a fabulous occasion, and after the feast the ladies of court put the couple to bed, the king "so much desir[ing] to find her in his bed." A chronicler reported that "they spent the night together in great delight, as you can well believe."[8] Alas a marriage rushed into in a fit of youthful passion would descend into contempt and hatred, and Charles's mind would fall apart, followed by his kingdom.

At Queen Isabeau's coronation she was upstaged by her sister-in-law, the Milanese Valentina Visconti, wife of the king's brother Louis d'Orléans. Her rival was escorted by 1,300 knights and wore a wedding robe featuring 2,500 pearls and "sprinkled with diamonds."[9] Valentina had had an unprecedented dowry of half a million gold francs, as well as part of Piedmont, the rich province of Italy between Lombardy and Provence. Before Valentina was set for France, Gian Galeazzo, Duke of Milan, left for Pavia, unable to face the departure of his dear daughter without weeping. Young women were "peace-weavers," their job to make alliances between rival lands—but this did not make it any less upsetting for the girls or their families.

And soon a darkness overcame the realm. In 1392, there was an assassination attempt on Charles's friend and adviser Olivier de Clisson, the son of the pirate Jeanne. De Clisson had switched sides in 1369, despite his own father's murder, after his squire was killed by the English. De Clisson swore never "to give quarter to any Englishman" after that, and the following day attacked an English fortress, taking fifteen captives; he ordered for the fifteen men to be released one by one, and as each prisoner walked through the door he chopped off their head with a huge axe.

De Clisson was a major figure in Brittany, one of the king's liegemen, and in response Charles now mounted an expedition to hunt down the would-be assassins. August 8 was an extremely hot day, dry and intense, the sun beating down on their skulls as they made their way west. Along the way a stranger in a smock stopped the royal party and warned them, "King, ride no further! Turn back, for you are betrayed!" Charles's attendant, thinking the man mad, beat him.

At midday the royal party left the forest and crossed the broad sandy plain under a boiling hot sun. Charles's uncles, the Dukes of Berry and Burgundy, were one hundred yards to his left. A chronicler wrote: "The sand was hot underfoot and the horses were sweating." The king was overdressed, wearing "a black velvet jerkin, which made him very hot, and a plain scarlet hat."[10] Behind him rode a page in a polished steel helmet followed by another with a lance. Distracted by the heat, the second page dropped his lance, the weapon falling and striking the helmet of the man in front of him.

Frossiart recorded:

> There was a loud clang of steel, and the King, who was so close that they were riding on his horse's heels, had a sudden start. His mind reeled, for his thoughts were still running on the words which the madman or the wise man had said to him in the forest, and he imagined that a great host of his enemies were coming to kill him. Under this delusion, his weakened mind caused him to run amok. He spurred his horse forward, then drew his sword and wheeled round on to his pages, no longer recognizing them or anyone else.[11]

Charles's uncles looked over and Burgundy shouted "Disaster has overtaken us. The king's gone out of his mind!" There was the sickening sound of steel cutting flesh as the tormented man, believing himself to be in battle, struck at the pages around him, shouting "traitors." By the time he was overpowered the mad king had killed five men, his brother Louis of Valois only surviving after running for his life.

Afterward, the frightened and confused young king was brought to Le Mans where a well-respected and learned ninety-two-year-old doctor, Guillaume de Harsigny, was dragged from his home and brought to him. He regained consciousness and was moved slowly and delicately to Paris. Later in the autumn he was well enough to make a pilgrimage of thanks to Notre Dame de Liesse, a church near Laon in Picardy.

But, in fact, it was only the beginning of the mad king's personal hell.

In January 1393 Charles, now recovered, attended a masked ball in Paris. The dance was held to honor the third marriage of the queen's lady-in-waiting, and such remarriages were often celebrated in a spirit of mockery and license, with masquerades and outlandish music.

It was common in late medieval Europe to dress up as "wild men" for parties, and records of such a tradition date back to at least the ninth century and are found in Celtic, Slavic, Germanic, and Latin folklore. It was believed that *lutins*, wild men, lived in remote mountain areas—in France the Pyrenees was said to be home to many—and they danced by firelight as part of fertility rituals or for supernatural purposes. This folklore may reflect the lingering survival of older indigenous groups driven into the mountains, and at harvest times people dressed as wild men and ran around until they were caught, after which an effigy of the wild man was burned, an obviously pagan ritual of unknown origin.

The fatal masquerade in Paris involved six young men, including the king and Yvain, bastard of the Count of Foix, disguised as woodland savages. They had linen cloth sewn onto the bodies and soaked in pitch to hold the hemp, giving them the hairy appearance of the *lutins*. Their face masks, meanwhile, concealed their identity.

The party had been thought up by the "cruelest and most insolent of men," Huguet de Guisay, a man of "wicked life" who "corrupted and schooled youth in debaucheries," and was a much-demanded figure at court. He was also a sadist. Holding the poor in contempt, he called them dogs and was known to force them to bark at the point of a sword. He even made his own servants lie on the ground while he stood on their backs and had them make the sounds of a hound, shouting "bark, dog!" as they screamed in pain.

That night the six anonymous mask-wearers arrived at the royal ball, imitating the howls of wolves and stunning and delighting their fellow guests. King Charles was flirting with and teasing his fifteen-year-old aunt the Duchesse de Berry when his brother Louis and another young dandy Philippe de Bar walked in, heavily intoxicated from another party.

Louis of Orléans, a "devoted servant of Venus" who liked the company of "dancers, flatterers, and people of loose life," was a risk taker and a show-off, and now entered the hall with torches, despite the guests having been forbidden to carry any flames during the dance. Some people later suggested that he wished to see who these mystery men were, or that he simply got a thrill out of the danger; others had darker explanations. A spark fell, a flame flickered up a leg, and first one man was on fire, then another. The queen, who alone knew that Charles was among the group, shrieked and fainted, and the room erupted with screams and cries of horror as the men burned in agony; guests tried to fight the flames, desperately tearing the fancy dress costumes from the burning flesh, many sustaining agonizing injuries themselves. But the tar was too flammable.

Charles was alive only because his quick-thinking young aunt threw her skirt over him, so shielding him from the sparks. Another wild man, the Sire de Nantouillet, saved himself by jumping into a large wine cooler filled with water. The others were not so

lucky; as the Monk of St Denis wrote, "four men were burned alive, their flaming genitals dropping to the floor . . . releasing a stream of blood."[12] The Count de Joigny burned
to death immediately, and Yvain de Foix and Aimery Poitiers both succumbed two days
afterward. Huguet de Guisay took another three days to die in agony, and as his coffin
was carried through the streets of Paris, the small folk shouted out "Bark, dog!"

The disaster became known as the *Bal des Ardents*, the Ball of the Burning Men.
The people of Paris were shocked but also disgusted, and now viewed their rulers as
incompetent and decadent, and even suspected Louis of attempting to kill his brother.
The king's nerves were broken, and he collapsed again later that year, and would
continue to do so repeatedly.

During his frequent periods of insanity, Charles foamed at the mouth, became
covered in sores, and would eat from the floor. He came to believe he was made of
glass and might shatter if anyone touched him. People thought his condition was
caused by wet or melancholic humor—black bile—but they also believed, probably
correctly, that he had inherited a weak constitution. Charles's mother Jeanne de
Bourbon had suffered a nervous breakdown too and while historical diagnosis is a
sketchy business, many today suggest he suffered from schizophrenia, which like all
mental illnesses is hereditary. Charles's grandfather Peter of Bourbon had also been
mentally unstable.

The king's servants at the Hotel St Pol, the royal residence in Paris, walled the palace
doors to stop him escaping, and he ran around wildly indoors. The mad king would
scream that he felt a thousand iron spikes were ripping into his flesh; he refused to bathe
and could be found covered in his own feces. His spirit "was covered by such heavy
shadows" that he could not remember who or what he was.[13] He didn't know he was
married, or that he was king, or even what his name was; he appeared particularly hostile to the royal coat of arms, which he tried to vandalize in a rage, and also to his wife,
from whom he ran in terror. When she talked to him he would scream "who is that
women the sight of whom torments me? Find out what she wants and free me from her
demands if you can, that she may follow me no more."[14] When the king saw the arms of
Bavaria—his wife's sigil—he made rude gestures. He didn't even know his own children, although he recognized brothers and uncles, but much to the queen's rage the
only person he would talk to was his brother's now-estranged wife, Valentina, who he
called "dear sister." Naturally many believed she had bewitched him with poison.

In 1399 alone, Charles suffered six serious attacks, while his wife entertained a series of lovers and amassed a fortune in treasure, jewels, and cash.

No doctor brought to the king made any positive difference. "An unkempt, evil-eyed charlatan and pseudo-mystic named Arnaut Guilhem" was given the task of treating the patient after claiming to possess a book given by God.[15] He insisted the madness was caused by sorcery, but even after he was removed others had similar ideas. Two monks, having failed to make any progress from magic chants and a liquid made from ground-down pearls, suggested cutting open his head. When the Duc d'Orléans refused their suggestion, they accused him of sorcery and so were tortured and—after admitting to being in league with Satan—put to death.

It was not unknown for monarchs in the middle ages to suffer from madness. Joanna of Castile and Ivan the Terrible of Russia were two of the most striking examples, while William of Hainault-Bavaria, cousin of John of Gaunt and the Black Prince, had been "a raving maniac confined in a castle for thirty years, most of the time with both hands and feet tied."[16] The mentally ill were rarely confined away, although large towns would have a "narrentum" or "fool's tower" and as far back as 872 the Islamic ruler of Egypt had established the first home for the mentally ill, in which music was used as therapy. London's Bethlehem hospital was founded in 1329 out of the priory of St Mary Bethlehem and from 1377 it took "distracted" patients who were chained to the wall by the leg or ankle and dunked in water and whipped if they got violent.[17] Until the eighteenth century, visitors could pay money to watch and laugh at them. Needless to say, not many recovered.

Among the other treatments, on top of rest and sleep, bleeding and potions made of metal were also used, as was exorcism, with patients having a cross shaved into their head or tied to the rood screen above the altar at church while Mass was said. Surprisingly, this didn't seem to help much, either. Since it was often seen as having spiritual origins, the mad were also frequently found on pilgrimage stops such as Mont Saint-Michel, Compostella, or the road to Rome, along with "the paralytics, the scrofulous, and the very numerous cripples."[18]

The dark insanity at the heart of French politics mirrored a mood of despair following the Black Death. The *Danse Macabre* was a new kind of poem that first appeared in 1376 and reflected the darkness that had overcome the European mind. It consisted of the dead, or death himself, speaking to people from various spectra of society, reminding them of their upcoming demise, a reflection of mortality known as the *memento mori*—"remember that you have to die."

The Danse appeared on numerous frescos and houses, reminding the traveler who passed by:

> Emperor, your sword won't help you out
> Sceptre and crown are worthless here
> I've taken you by the hand
> For you must come to my dance[19]

Tombs from the thirteenth and early fourteenth century showed the departed at their peak, often in a knight's outfit or as a beautiful young woman. Those from the fifteenth century show the effigies as skeletons, even with worms poking out of their eyes, to reinforce the message that horrible death was always close.

To make matters worse, a new pope was elected in 1378 and he also turned out to be insane. Urban VI, a Neopolitan from outside the Church hierarchy, had appeared to have undergone a complete change of character within weeks of his election, hurling insults at stunned cardinals during Church councils, and even physically lunging at one. He launched abusive tirades aimed at Joanna, the Queen of Naples, and soon some of the French Church leaders were expressing alarm—so he had six of his cardinals tortured while beneath the interogation chamber he muttered passages from his prayer book as the screams echoed out. This led to a schism with a second pope elected in Avignon, Clement, who was bad rather than mad, having had the whole town of Cesena massacred, an act so gruesome that it horrified even the English mercenaries he'd asked to carry it out.

Urban was eventually driven out of Naples by Joanna's successor, Charles, Duke of Durazzo—and with some mercenaries went on a rampage through Italy, dragging behind him the cardinals he had accused of conspiring against them, killing five en route. His rival Clement, "the Butcher of Cesana" died of a heart attack or apoplectic stroke in 1394, of "profound chagrin," after hearing of a proposed strike by academics, perhaps the most effective such action in academia's history. Urban had expired six years earlier, having moved to Perugia with his army, where he fell from a mule and died of his injuries—although poison, naturally, was suspected.

But then, of course, all men must die.

22
FIRE AND BLOOD

Aegon the Conqueror brought fire and blood to Westeros, but afterward he gave them peace, prosperity, and justice.

—DAENERYS TARGARYEN

The Valryians are physically distinctive people, with silver hair and purple eyes, so unusual-looking that it is thought they are "not entirely of the same blood as other men."[1] One maester thinks it most likely the result of some sort of selective breeding, so that they have developed distinctive traits, one of which is that they do not seem to get sick. At least, one might assume, they have developed resistance to the most common diseases that affect other people. This is not that odd an idea, indeed it has been observed throughout history, the most common example being smallpox. The disease had affected populations in the old world for many centuries before arriving in the Americas through the Spanish where it immediately proved devastating to the native inhabitants. Some 90 percent of the New World's indigenous people were wiped out by the illness, while most Europeans would recover, after centuries of outbreaks had left the surviving population relatively immune.

Even today, because of epidemics that took place in the first millennium AD, some 1 percent of northern Europeans are immune to the HIV virus and another 15 percent carry mutations that reduce their chances of infection from even the riskiest activities, with the highest proportion being among Swedes.[2]

When the Anglo-Saxons arrived in Britain in the fifth century, they might also have had greater immunity to the Justinian plague that was then rampaging through Europe, according to one theory. However, the people who conquered them, the inspiration for the Valryians, had an even stronger advantage, for just as Aegon conquered with dragons, so William the Bastard conquered with cavalry.

Among the restless, violent peoples that emerged out of the early medieval period, there were few more frightening than the Normans, who were descended from a group of Vikings who had settled the land around the Seine River after repeatedly menacing the Franks. They would play a major part in English history and inspire Martin's world too. In the author's own words, the story of Aegon the Conqueror, founder of the Valryian dynasty, is that of William, Duke of Normandy,[3] one of the greatest and most ferocious figures of this period, and who conquered a nation much larger than his own.

An enigmatic figure whose only friend was his bastard half-brother Orys Baratheon, Aegon is a great warrior who wears a shirt of black scales and is faithful to his spouse (even if he has two, so not really, you might say). The real-life Conqueror was not so different, a fearsome and ruthless leader in chain mail who grew up to trust no one except close kin, especially his half-brothers, and who never kept a mistress—so unusual for French aristocrats that some actually found it sinister.

By the Christmas of 1065, with his grand abbey almost complete, King Edward lay dying, in a state of delirium shouting about hideous curses that would ruin the kingdom; across the narrow sea to the south, William the Bastard, Duke of Normandy, was expecting to be named successor, although his claim was tenuous in the extreme. William was a great-nephew of King Edward, whose Norman mother Emma was the sister of William's grandfather, Duke Richard II. The Norman leader had convinced himself that Edward had promised him the throne, even though this was not within his power, since kings at the time were selected by the Saxon ruling council, the Witenagemot.

Duke William had been out hunting when a messenger gave him the unhappy news that the Witan had named Harold Godwinson as king, crowned on the same day as Edward's funeral. His rage knew no bounds, and soon the sounds of axes against trees could be heard across the duchy as he assembled a fleet. This was bold, for despite their own Viking ancestry, the Normans were not a seafaring people and the barons were scared of crossing this dangerous stretch of ocean.

William called a council, where with bullying and lying and the promise of riches, he proclaimed that he would become King of England. His success in doing so is testimony to his sheer force of will; appropriately, as his name, which would have been closer to the German Wilhelm than the French Guillaume, meant just that, "willful protector."

Today in the British Library in central London there is a codex, an A4-sized paper listing all the families that came over with the Conqueror, part of antiquarian Sir Robert Cotton's great collection amassed during the seventeenth century. It was once a matter of great importance to aristocratic houses to trace their line to that bloody Saturday in October 1066, when as many as fifteen thousand men fought on a sloping hill in Sussex.

Normandy was "a bloody crossroads of war since antiquity,"[4] viciously fought over by Celts, Romans, Franks, Vikings, and later the English. From the time of Clovis it had come under the sway of the Franks, who were the leading experts in cavalry warfare. But with Charlemagne's grandsons, the kingdom of the Franks had fallen into civil war, a bad time to have a family argument since Viking raids were intensifying in Britain and France. For many years they threatened the River Loire region before returning to England, but Alfred the Great's military success drove them back to France again; there the Norsemen had terrorized the northwest coast until, eventually, in 912 the king of the Franks granted them territory by the mouth of the Seine.

William's great-great-great-grandfather Hrolfr, literally "wolf" (from which we get the name Rolf) hailed from Norway. A man apparently so big that he couldn't fit on any horse and had to walk everywhere, Hrolfr was said to be descended from the Ynglings ("the fair-haired"), the oldest Scandinavian dynasty who could trace their mythical origins back to the earliest migrations. As part of the Frankish deal, Hrolfr accepted baptism and took the name Rollo, and within a short period the settlers had adopted the Latinate language of the Franks and became enthusiastic Christians.

The King of the Franks and "the duke of the pirates," as the Norse leaders were contemptuously called by their neighbors for many years afterwards, had a difficult relationship. The idea of bending the knee was especially repugnant to Vikings, who prided themselves on their freedom. The story goes that when Hrolfr/Rollo was due to kiss the feet of King Charles he refused because he "never lowered the nape of his neck to any king"; instead he ordered one of his men to do so, but the man, also a giant by all accounts, was similarly reluctant to bend down and so lifted the king up, upending him. This story is probably not entirely true but reflects an aversion to kneeling or other forms of submission.

This pirate colony was not expected to survive, and that it did had much to do with their mastery of horses. Medieval mounts were much bigger than the animals used by Greeks or Romans, and it was the Parthians (of modern-day Iran) and Byzantines who began the development of big warhorses. However northern France was where horse-breeding was intensified, and as this part of western Europe was so bitterly contested, so it saw an arms race of larger and more aggressive animals as cavalry became the most effective form of warfare. The Normans bred a warhorse called the *destrier*, and pioneered a new and terrifying tactic, the cavalry charge.

Cavalry was an aristocratic concern since metal was very expensive and a Frankish soldier on horseback would carry fifty pounds of iron, "at a time when a forge might only produce 10 lb of iron over a two or three-day smelting process."[5] Because of this, these destriers had to be strong, and breeding horses for war took effort and energy partly because horses found battle stressful and often bolted. The Normans developed armor to protect the mounts, but also bred animals that were temperamentally better suited for war; indeed, they could be trained to bite.

Orchestrated cavalry charges began with very small numbers of six or maybe eight men on horseback working in concert, but with the Franks and Normans that number grew into large-scale formations. The Normans also spearheaded new military technology, and innovations of this period included the conical helmet, the mail coat, and large, kite-shaped shields. These are what would become associated with the Normans in particular, although all Franks wore much the same thing, as did Saxons and Vikings, and at Hastings the two sides would have largely been distinguishable only by hairstyles—the Saxons having long locks and moustaches and the Normans crops and clean-shaven faces.

William was the illegitimate son of Normandy's Duke Robert and a low-born woman whose father may have been an embalmer of corpses.[6] Robert was said to have spied William's mother Herleva while she was out washing by the river in her home town of Falaise, a tale borrowed by Martin to explain how Lord Bolton first saw the mother of his psychotic bastard Ramsay Snow. Yet this tale was rather more romantic, and the spot where she washed can still be seen—if the story was even true.*

Herleva was certainly of modest background, and they were unmarried, but although a bastard, William was accepted as his father Duke Robert's heir—something that would have been unthinkable a century later. In the early medieval period, and

---

*Later the people who ran Falaise Castle would sell tickets to visit the room from which Robert spied the mother of the Conqueror. The room in question was only built during the reign of William's son, but that doesn't seem to have bothered anyone, and today the small town has a fountain sculpture celebrating the event. France has a lot of pretty towns in competition, so who can blame them?

especially among Vikings, bastards could inherit a throne or lordship if they were strong enough, but as the Church and established marriage became more ingrained, and the position of wives stronger, so the status of natural sons declined. William's grandson Robert of Gloucester was in 1135 the most suitable person to take the throne, but by now his illegitimacy ruled him out.

The future conqueror was close to his mother's relatives, but then his father's relations were mostly trying to kill him. When William was only seven, his father decided to go to the Holy Land, perhaps out of guilt for the death of his brother Duke Richard, who passed away in somewhat mysterious circumstances and may have been the victim of poisoning.

Duke Robert died on pilgrimage, leaving William highly vulnerable. His first protector, Count Gilbert, was murdered, as was his tutor Turold. Later, Osbern, head of the royal household, was stabbed to death by William of Montgomery in the young duke's bedchamber, while the boy looked on. Montgomery was himself later killed in the same fashion. That he survived to manhood, and then repeatedly defeated and in many cases destroyed rival magnates and relatives, was testimony to his strength and ruthlessness. The Normans under William had also defeated the armies of neighboring Flanders, Brittany, Anjou, and the kingdom of France itself, but he wanted more.

William claimed that Harold had sworn an oath to him when the Englishman was shipwrecked in northern France, which may be true, but if Harold did so then it's unlikely he had much choice. By sheer right of ancestry, the crown should have gone to Ethelred's great-grandson Edgar Atheling, but he was just a boy.

And England was also divided. The Godwin family were strong in their Wessex homeland, but the north was barely under their control, while Harold had also alienated his brother Tostig, who in a fury sailed around the North Sea looking for allies to help him attack his brother. Having been rejected by King Sweyn of Denmark, Tostig found an unlikely partner in Harald Hardrada, now king of Norway after his many years in Constantinople. Growing old, and having crushed all opposition at home, the Thunderbolt of the North gambled on one last great battle to seal his glorious reputation and ensure his name was sung of at firesides for years to come. An armada of three hundred ships set sail from Norway toward the Shetlands and down the coast of eastern Scotland, bringing more Vikings from the islands with them.

In Westeros, some members of the Targaryen family have prophetic dreams and likewise along the way Harald had a vision of meeting his brother Olaf, who warned of the disaster that awaited him. Yet he continued, for what would be the last ever great Viking adventure.

After landing in Northumbria, Harald's army crushed a small English force led by young Edwin and Morcar, now the earls of Northumbria and Mercia but still barely men. But Hardrada had woefully underestimated his enemy, for King Harold's army was already marching north at rapid speed. At the battle that followed at Stamford Bridge, Hardrada and Tostig were killed; King Harold, mercifully, allowed the surviving Scandinavians to go home, among them Hardrada's two sons, who many years later would return this act of mercy by giving sanctuary to one of Harold Godwinson's sons. Of more than three hundred Nordic ships that sailed across the ocean only twenty returned, and a chronicler writing sixty years later observed that there was still a mountain of bones by the site, now bleached by the sun and lying in a very different country. The Viking age was over.

Although Harold did not yet know it, the Normans had already set out into the sea, now that the wind had finally changed, along with mercenaries from across France and western Europe. Just as with the Dothraki, bringing horses across the water had been the major problem facing them, since the animals tended to panic in boats and cause them to capsize, but this they found an answer to. While in Sicily the Normans had picked up a technology used by the Byzantines, a sling-harness for carrying horses at sea—and now on their journey across this stormy water they brought three thousand with them.

The Normans arrived in Sussex, the Godwinson home, plundering the land and burning villages. Harold could have stayed in London and let the invaders run out of food, but he was tempted out, for as lord he could not stand by while the people of Sussex were mistreated. This was a foolish decision, but good lords could not allow their vassals to be violated with impunity, and so it was a common way of drawing them into fights.*

The climactic struggle of October 14 comprised between seven thousand and eight thousand on each side. It was unusual, since in medieval Europe rulers tried to avoid pitched battle as it was too risky, since everything could be lost in a couple of hours. The English had grabbed the higher ground, and so William choose to charge

---

*There is a similar situation in the invasion of Westeros by the Valyrians, where Aegon drew out one of the kings, Ardilac, who should have remained in his city but was drawn out by the mistreatment of his vassals.

uphill, which would to some extent neutralize the advantage of cavalry. This was fraught with danger, and yet time was against him, as more men would surely flock to Harold's cause, the Normans were in a hostile land, and the longer the wait the greater the risk of disease breaking out (until the reforms of Florence Nightingale in the Victorian era, disease almost always killed more soldiers than battle).

There are only three recorded accounts of the battle, highly stylized, but it most likely began at 9 a.m. and went on for most of the day. The invaders were in three formations, with Bretons on the left, French on the right, and Normans in the middle. William, according to one account, had three horses killed beneath him and, at one point, panic ran through the ranks as rumor spread that he was dead. The duke lifted his helmet so that his troops might see him, shouting at his men that if they panicked and fled they would all die. All day the Normans launched attacks while the English stood rooted to the spot, and with nightfall approaching the men would have been exhausted.

Harold had three thousand *housecarls*, battle-hardened soldiers whose two-handed axes were wielded with enormous force, but the Normans had the advantage of cavalry. The deadlock was broken by a ruse, the fake retreat, another innovation borrowed from the Byzantines. On the left the Bretons began to flee and, when the English followed them down the hill—most enemy casualties were taken during the rout when their backs were turned—their formation was broken. The Norman cavalry charged uphill with devastating effect and destroyed the English line.

The Normans also had an advantage in archery—the defenders only had a small number of bowmen—and this soon began to tell as increasing numbers of English soldiers were fatally hit, their lifeless bodies often still stuck in the close-packed shield wall. Harold's brothers Gyrth and Leofwine were killed and, at some point, the king himself was as well, either through a random arrow or cut down by a death squad of four knights. (He may also have been emasculated.) Afterward, the Normans went from town to town laying waste until London surrendered, supposedly after a traitor let the invaders through the Lud Gate, where the old gods had been worshipped a millennium before. William was crowned on Christmas Day at Westminster Abbey.

When his wife Matilda of Flanders was enthroned as Queen of England the following year, attendees would have been met by the sight of a champion arriving in the cathedral, a "great hulk of a man" called Marmion. This terrifying giant rode his horse into the middle of the hall, heavily armed, and shouted that "if any person denies that our most gracious sovereign, lord William, and his spouse Matilda, are not king and queen of England, he is a false-hearted traitor and a liar; and here I, as champion, do challenge him to single combat."[7] Surprisingly, no one took him up on the offer.

The Norman Conquest helped bring England closer to the mainstream of Europe, which was increasingly dominated by northern France. English names such as Ethelred, Athelstan, Tostig, or Leofwine were replaced by Carolignian ones, so called because they are associated with the Franks under Charles (Carolus) the Great. These were the names popular with the northern French aristocracy—the Frankish William, Henry, Robert, Richard, and Geoffrey, along with biblical or Greek names like John, James, Catherine, Margaret, and Thomas. And so, to give Westeros a medieval feel it features such names as Robert, Jon, Catelyn, Margaery, Joffrey, Willem, Tommen, Rickard, and Rickon (Dickon was a common nickname for Richard at the time).

In fact, across Europe from the eleventh to the fourteenth centuries, local names and local religious cults were replaced by a Europe-wide culture, one in particular dominated by the Franks. Some native traditions and naming patterns survived, and in England the only surviving English names were Edmund and Edward, which remained in fashion because of the cults attached to Edward the Confessor and St Edmund (Alfred would later have a revival after the popularity of Alfred the Great rose in the sixteenth century). Bran or Brandon, by contrast, is an Irish name meaning raven or crow, appropriately.

Indeed, numerous characters in Westeros have names with real life parallels in England. There is a knight in Westeros called Blount, from House Blount of the Crownlands, who owe their loyalty to the Baratheons; this archaic-sounding name is borrowed from a real warrior family who rose to prominence in the twelfth century and who feature throughout the medieval period. Robert Le Blount had sailed over with the Conqueror while a John Blount accepted Edward II's surrender and Walter Blount was killed in the War of the Roses in 1471, at the Battle of Barnet. The most famous Blount, however, is the singer-songwriter James, who simplified it to Blunt— and like his forefathers, he spent time in the military before becoming a professional musician.*

---

*As well as giving us "You're Beautiful," Blunt may have prevented World War III in 1999 when he apparently refused an order to attack an airport in Kosovo that the Russians had seized.

Tyrell, spelt Tirel, was the name of an aristocratic family who played a significant part in Anglo-Norman history, one of their number accidentally killing William's successor. Drogo, the name of the Dothraki leader, was also the name of one of Charles Martel's grandsons and various other figures in northern France.

William the Conqueror spent the twenty years following his invasion fighting rebels and rivals, and falling out with almost everyone around him, including his eldest son Robert, his wife Matilda, and his half-brother Odo.

Although a cleric, Odo had probably taken part at Hastings, waving a club, as churchmen were not allowed to shed blood. This we know because the entire story is immortalized in a famous embroidery made soon afterwards, known as the Bayeux Tapestry and rediscovered in the eighteenth century. It was most likely commissioned by Odo, or at least it is believed so because the Tapestry, unlike the written records, paints him in a heroic light. It was also made in Kent, the large county which had been given over in its entirety to the grasping churchman, who had become grotesquely rich under William, owning properties in over twenty counties.

Strangely the tapestry contains one of the few visual images of dwarves in the pre-modern period, a man called "Turold" who is seen in the court of Ponthieu, standing next to a Norman ambassador telling Ponthieu's Count Guy to hand over Harold Godwinson. Turold is one of only fifteen people named in the tapestry, although who he was and what his role was in the events remain a mystery. The first mention of dwarves is found in ancient Egypt, at the court of Khufu, who died in 2566BC, on a tomb close to the Great Pyramid belonging to a dwarf called Perni-ankhu. His job "was to entertain the king and members of the royal family, perhaps by dancing and singing: the ancient Egyptian equivalent of a medieval court jester."[8] Dwarves were also recorded in ancient Rome, and in the early medieval period they were often employed in courts: in the 1060s Bishop Gunter of Bamberg, now Regensberg in Bavaria, is known to have been accompanied by a dwarf called Askericus, while the twelfth century Count Henry II of Champagne, king of Jerusalem, had a dwarf called Scarlett "who, in a bizarre accident, perished with him as he tried to save his lord and master from falling absent-mindedly out of a window."[9]

In 1087 the Conqueror was back at war and attacked Mantes, in the rival duchy of Maine, besieged it and set it on fire, but the embers frightened his horse and, when it fell, William's fat stomach was ripped open, leaving him to spend five weeks dying in agony.

RED KEEP, WHITE TOWER

Soon after Christmas 1066, the conquerors began work on building their first castles. There had been such structures in England before the Normans, but only a dozen or so, mostly wooden and small—now they built hundreds, not just to protect themselves from the natives but from each other, becoming "the bones of the kingdom."[10] The most famous was the White Tower to the east of London, known as the Tower of London and the inspiration for the Red Keep.

Castles were another form of technology brought from the east. The old Germanic feasting halls where the likes of Beowulf were told around the hearth could be surrounded and set on fire, and while Alfred the Great had built burghs (fortresses for safety against Viking raids), these new brick-built constructions were far harder to attack. Early forms of castles were pioneered by the Byzantines in their sixth century campaigns in north Africa, featuring thick walls and high towers, one of which was designed to be the last refugee, a feature that would become the keep in later European models. The Muslims adopted Byzantine masonry fortification in Spain in the eighth and ninth centuries, and the Christians there later copied it.

But no area had more castles than western France, in particular the Loire Valley to the south of Normandy, where in 863 France's Charles the Bald first ordered that they be built against Scandinavian invaders; later they would be used in the struggles between the rival Normans, Angevins, and Poitievins.

In the typical high medieval castle, a keep was closely encircled by a high wall, called a chemise, with an entry gateway from where one climbed a revolving outside staircase up to the roof, from where one could walk across a platform toward the keep. They also featured drawbridges, usually raised by chain and so vertically facing the gate—or portcullis—adding an additional barrier for any invaders. And so any attacking enemy, were they able to penetrate this barrier, would then have to force their way up stairs and *then* walk across the bridge to reach the keep—at all times under fire.[11]

Castles came with slits called arrow loops or *meurtrieres*—murderesses—out of which crossbowmen would fire at the attackers, the holes splayed so that the archer could shoot at an angle while presenting enemy snipers with only a tiny target.[12] Boiling liquids or quicklime might also be poured out of these murder holes at the attacking army.

In the thirteenth century, castles were increasingly built on the sides of hills, with the inner bailey backed up against the higher ground to make it extra secure. Despite the best efforts of the master builders, all castles had vulnerable spots, the most obvious of which was the latrine, or *gardebrobe*, which required holes for disposing of waste. In Season Seven of the show the Unsullied take Casterely Rock through the toilets but such a thing did actually happen in 1204 when Philippe of France seized the prestigious Chateau Gaillard in Normandy from the English by sending his troops through the latrines.

The territory protected by a castle was called a *detroit*, or district, which comes from Latin *distringere*, to coerce, and anyone who controlled a castle was effectively independent. William's age was known as "feudal anarchy," because power rested largely with relatively small baronial warlords who held a castle. It was this period more than any other when powerful barons were able to inflict horror on their peasantry, Europe being far more violent in the eleventh century than the fourteenth or fifteenth.

The Normans are, in particular, associated with the concept of feudalism, although something similar existed already in England, and historians dislike the term. Feudalism denotes a hierarchy in which everyone was bound by some form of pledge to a more powerful man above him, with the king at the top. When people knelt before their lord to do homage they said "Lord, I become your man" and then received a kiss on the mouth. Often the lords would act as godfathers to the children of their vassals, swearing to guard the child from the Devil and protect them for seven years "from water, fire, horse's foot, and hound's tooth."

In return the lord would say to his underling "You are mine" or "you exist through me" and "You are my man and your duty is to do my will." From the eleventh century a knight had to swear: "I will not attack the Church, her lands or her stores; I will not attack priests or monks or their escorts, should they be unarmed themselves." Knights also "promised especial aid to noble women, widows and nuns travelling alone," and, since this system developed in France, "wine merchants."[13]

Under this system legitimate sons and nephews were generally sent to the household of a social superior, so that the sons of castellans—lords who owned castles— would live with the duke, while the castellans took in the sons of knights.[14] Afterward they might live with their adoptive father and marry one of his relatives. Even quite young children might be sent into the household of another, in order to strengthen bonds in a society low in trust, and this system lasted, in England at least, into the early modern era.

Feudalism brought duties and privileges, some of which were ceremonial; so for example a small landholder in Kent had the role of "holding the king's head in the boat" when he crossed the Channel in bad weather (although there is no mention of whether he had the honor of wiping up the sick, too).[15] More fiercely fought over were roles at the coronation, symbolizing a family's importance, which is why Piers Gaveston's hijacking of Edward's enthronement grievously insulted so many people.

William the Bastard's invasion most likely did not introduce feudalism, but it did bring a new elite, the Conquest seeing the largest exchange of land in English history; just eleven barons were given a quarter of England, another quarter of which went to the monarch with just 5 percent remaining in the hands of the natives. Naturally with baronial power came rivalries and jealousies that would dominate the next four centuries.

The Norman Conquest would also introduce, or encode, a system that we today call chivalry. The word comes from the French for horseman, *chevalier*, and describes a warrior code for knights (as they are called in English) that later came to encompass rules for war, especially the treatment of aristocratic prisoners. Although the Anglo-Saxons were in many ways more cultured than the Normans—they had a far more sophisticated native literature, for instance—their politics were also far more violent. Ethelred's court featured numerous murders and blindings, while William executed just one nobleman, the last to die this way in England for 250 years. William even abolished capital punishment, although his son reintroduced it.

The main rule of chivalry concerned the treatment of noble prisoners, but it later also encompassed ideas about the treatment of women and children. This code only began to collapse with Edward I and his son, culminating with the viciousness of the War of the Roses, where captured prisoners were routinely beheaded—while perversely ordinary soldiers were far better treated.

THE HILL TRIBES

Resistance to the Normans was most fierce in the north, which was harder to conquer and also more feud-ridden. Cospig, William's appointee in the north, had immediately used his new position to try to kill a rival, Osulf, but Osulf escaped and raised an army and a month later surprised Cospig, who ran for a local church. Osulf set fire to the building and so forced him out and killed him.

At the start of the decade the leading northern magnate had been Earl Siward of Northumbria, who when told his son had been killed in battle with the Scots at the Battle of the Seven Sleepers in 1054, asked if the wounds were on the front or back. When informed the former, he replied: "I rejoice, for I would not deem any other death worthy for myself or my son." Siward was said to have become Earl of Huntingdon after killing the previous holder of that title over a tiny infringement, the man brushing past him on a bridge.

Siward had died before the invasion but his surviving son Waltheof was involved in the 1069 uprising, which began with the massacre of a Norman garrison in Durham. Soon northern rebels were joined by Sweyn of Denmark, the people of the north seeing the Danes as their own blood. William headed north and crushed the uprising with great brutality, leaving at least one hundred thousand dead; one Norman knight even went home in disgust at the atrocities his people had committed. The half-Norman chronicler Orderic Vitalis wrote that William "commended that all crops and herds, chattels and food of every kind should be brought together and burned to ashes with consuming fire."[16] Afterward many peasants sold themselves into slavery or joined bands of outlaws, while the roads were littered with decaying bodies and wolves came down from the hills for the feast. The rebel leader Cospatric submitted in 1070 and William spared him, most likely on the advice of one of his minor barons, William de Percy, who had recently come over and was in the army that had headed north. Percy was put in charge of Topliffe, the post between two regions of north Yorkshire and Durham, and had to police the Wensleydale area, which was notorious for desperados and killers.

Rebellion also continued in the fenlands of eastern England. In Westeros the Crannogmen live in the southernmost part of the north: "Their homes are reed-thatched huts, built on stilts or on floating islands made of bundles of reeds, and they live by catching fish and frogs. From their fen fastnesses they can harass anyone who passes across the narrow causeway of the Neck."[17] Crannogs is a word in Irish and Scots Gaelic for an artificial island in a lake, which in northern Britain have been built since the Neolithic period. In Westeros, the Crannogmen take part in guerrilla warfare, their homeland hard to pacify, and in real life one of the most difficult parts of the realm to tame was East Anglia, marshy country in which outlaws often disappeared. In particular, the Isle of Ely was "impenetrably surrounded on all sides by meres and fens, accessible only in one place, where a very narrow track affords the scantiest of entries."[18] It could only be reached by boat, and it was here that the fen dwellers led by an outlaw called Hereward the Wake continued resistance for the longest.

Hereward had returned from the continent after 1066 to find Normans had occupied his estate, killed his brother and put his head on a spike outside.[19] After a protracted guerrilla campaign he was finally surrounded, perhaps betrayed by a monk who revealed the way to the fens—or the Normans used a witch. Hereward eventually fades into memory, his fate a mystery. Outlaws continued to live in this marshy country for many centuries, however, and only much later was the Fenland drained, and the region became prosperous due its trade links with the Netherlands. Later still it would become the heartland of Puritanism and would provide the vast bulk of colonists to New England.

As with the Valyrians and Andals, the invaders married native females, and by the 1170s it was observed that it was hard to tell the English and Normans apart. Yet the north did not recover for many centuries, and until the thirteenth century northerners "griev[ed] through want of a king of their own, and of the liberty they once enjoyed." The Norman domination of the conquered Saxons proved lasting as even in 1800, three-quarters of a millennia after Harold was fatefully struck down, people with Norman surnames were eight times as likely as the general population to be Members of Parliament.[20]

The rightful heir to the House of Wessex, Ethelred the Unready's great-grandson Edgar the Atheling, had been a mere boy in 1066, but had been a figurehead in the later northern rebellion. However, on the advice of his brother-in-law, the king of Scotland, he had finally submitted to William and eventually ended up commanding a fleet manned by the Varangian Guard. He died "penniless, unmarried and childless," but William's son Henry I would marry his niece Edith, so uniting the Norman and Saxon houses.

23
THE DEATH OF KINGS

Any man who must say "I am King" is no true king at all.

—Tywin Lannister

What later became known as the War of the Roses had its origins a century earlier in the reign of Richard II, an unstable and violent individual whose erratic, paranoid behavior was his undoing. By the time the war for the throne was over, three more kings had suffered violent deaths and most of the noblemen of England were corpses. *Game of Thrones* sometimes seems to go heavy on killing off characters, but the reality is that the fatality rates for England's aristocrats was very similar. Over a dozen princes died in the conflict and some fifty members of the higher aristocracy—around half of the total—were either killed in battle or executed. Among some families, such as the Percys and Beauforts, the casualty rate was extremely high: five generations of Percy heirs died violently, and four Percy brothers out of six died in battle within just four years. The Courtenay family suffered a similar rate. With the Beauforts, all four brothers of one generation died in the violence, and the legitimate line ceased to exist.

The powerful magnates fighting for the Houses of York or Lancaster could call on the services of men who would fight under their banner—a Falcon and Fetterlock for Richard of York, or the Sun in Splendour for his son Edward. As in Westeros, this was in part a battle between north and south, although in real life it was the Lancastrians who controlled much of the north and the Yorkists (despite the name) whose stronghold was London, close to the family seat of King's Langley Palace in Hertfordshire. On top of the main conflict between the Yorks and Lancasters, there were various other regional houses fighting over land and status. In the far north the Nevilles fought the Percys and in the south-west the Courtenays and Bonvilles battled for supremacy; some families, in particular the Nevilles, were also split between different branches, old disputes over land and titles that spilled over into bloodshed as war erupted in 1455.

The seeds of the conflict were sown in the year 1399 with a king whose thirst for revenge had alienated the leading noblemen of the realm. As he entered the city of London during those last weeks of the tumultuous fourteenth century, King Richard II would have been greeted by the intense smells of the people living there, of livestock, rotting vegetables, fish remains, and feces. The city was overcrowded and squalid, and even with the plague killing so many, it still contained over one hundred overpopulated parishes. Outside the walls the king would have seen the carcasses of animals lying in the street; within he would have been overpowered by the odor and sight of rubbish in the narrow alleys and cobbled streets, the stagnant water lying in buckets in the event of fire. Greeting newcomers on the junction of Watling Street, the main road from the north-west, and Tyburn Road, the major route to the west, was the Tyburn Tree, from where his grandfather had hanged Roger Mortimer.

In the capital, King Richard was jeered and pelted by the populace, and placed in the Tower of London, the fortress built by his ancestor William the Conqueror three centuries earlier. Now his cousin Henry Bolingbroke, heir to the Duke of Lancaster, arrived at that same place where as children in 1381 they had both hid from a murderous mob, now the head of a group of rebel magnates. A list of charges was read out, among them the murder of two leading magnates, Woodstock and Arundel. Soon four of Richard's associates were tied to horses and dragged through the city, before being beheaded.

The king knew his fate would be similar and was filled with anguish. No more is heard from the monarch, but Shakespeare would put into Richard II's mouth words that remain timeless:

> For God's sake, let us sit upon the ground
> And tell sad stories of the death of kings;
> How some have been deposed; some slain in war,
> Some haunted by the ghosts they have deposed;
> Some poison'd by their wives: some sleeping kill'd;
> All murder'd: for within the hollow crown
> That rounds the mortal temples of a king
> Keeps Death his court and there the antic sits (Act 3, Scene 2)

As always, Shakespeare's peerless prose captured an essential and eternal truth, for a recent study of 1,600 European monarchs from the year 600 onwards showed that one in seven died violently at the hands of rivals or in battle: "Calculated as a homicide rate per ruler-year, the risk of being killed amounts to 1,003 per 100,000, making 'monarch' the most dangerous occupation known in criminological research."[1]

In A Storm of Swords, Ser Barristan Selmy talks of Rhaegar Targaryen, son of the mad king Aerys: "He liked to sleep in the ruined hall, beneath the moon and stars, and whenever he came back he would bring a song. When you heard him play his high harp with the silver strings and sing of twilights and tears and the death of kings, you could not but feel that he was singing of himself and those he loved." Richard, too, would become a pitiful monster, and his death a tragedy.

The boy-ruler was a sort of mixture of Aerys and Joffrey. As with the Mad King, he had shown promise in his youth, but was driven half-mad by the various rebellions and machinations of his leading lords, his paranoia eventually becoming self-fulfilling. Aerys had arrested Brandon Stark and when his father came to negotiate for him, as agreed, had him arrested too, and executed both; likewise, Richard II had invited a rival to a banquet and had him put to death. And Richard, like Aerys, would end his life violently.

Like the other men of his family Richard was tall, at six feet, with a sharp nose and round face, but with his long blond hair and rosy cheeks he appeared quite feminine. As a boy, King Richard had no military experience and became "drunk on majesty," a brat and a "spiteful, vengeful king."[2] Just as Joffrey demanded that people "kneel before your king," so Richard, in love with his own divine power, would force subjects to kneel before him three times in the manner of an oriental despot. Eventually the leading barons were pushed too far, and yet to overthrow a monarch was a great and heinous act, and one that men dreaded to take for fear of what it might bring. And with good reason, for this was the start of a great tragedy.

Richard had been born in the English-controlled region of Gascony, the last king of England to have French as his first language, and as a young boy was taken to live at the palace at Kennington where his father lived out his last, sick years. Raised without any boys of his own age, the lonely prince grew to trust only his former tutor Sir Simon Burley, and his much older half-brothers John and Thomas Holland, as well as Robert de Vere, the Earl of Oxford, who had been raised in the royal household.

The Holland brothers had a sinister air and were later implicated in several brutal acts; John Holland had killed Ralph Stafford, the eighteen-year-old son of the Earl of Stafford, after an argument between their retainers. Richard, incensed, pledged to punish his brother but went back on his word and lost the backing of the Stafford clan. Such violence between retainers was common, even among the clergy; in 1384, when the Bishop of Exeter refused to let the Archbishop of Canterbury visit his diocese, three household esquires forced the archbishop's messenger to eat the wax seal of the letter he was carrying. Some of the archbishop's men later got revenge by seizing one of the bishop's entourage and making him eat his own shoes.

As a young man Richard had been given *De Regimini Principum*, written by the thirteenth century archbishop Giles of Rome, which proposed a new idea, that of the divine right of kings. Just as Joffrey believes it was "primitive" that lords had their own armies, so now this new theory of monarchical absolute power seemed the more modern idea. Once barons and lords had almost total control of the area around their castles, but with the development of sophisticated states capable of raising large amounts of money through taxation, and with large-scale archery and then gunpowder, kings now had the money and men to crush small warlords. Absolutism was the future—but for a young man it was a toxic and enticing idea.

Richard is the first English king of which we have a royal portrait—the first that resembles what we imagine of "Renaissance art"—and it is almost entirely gold, showing him carrying a gold sceptre and sat in a chair in front of a gold wall. He also commissioned the Wilton Diptych, which showed him beside St Edward, St Edmund, and St John, as well as the Virgin Mary. Richard was also the first king to use the royal "we," and to insist on being called "your majesty" rather than "my lord."

Even early in his reign the boy-king acted with impunity, and unwisely. He disobeyed his grandfather's will by taking land Edward had earmarked for three monasteries and giving to his friend Simon Burley. He rejected the bride chosen for him, one of the fantastically wealthy Duke of Milan's many daughters, and instead married Anne of Bohemia, the sister of the German Emperor, Wenzel the Drunkard (he liked a drink).

At the end of 1381, Roger Mortimer, the Earl of March, died during a scuffle with rebel chiefs in Ireland, continuing a family tradition of dying young and violently. Mortimer was the great-grandson of his namesake hanged at Tyburn, but Edward III had restored the family to the land soon after and his grandson had fought so well for the king that he had become a Knight of the Garter. Indeed, Roger Mortimer had married King Edward's granddaughter, so his two young children were heirs apparent to the crown. The king, rather than placing their land in safe trust, as was expected, gave it to his cronies—Burley, Robert de Vere, and Michael de la Pole.

Richard's chancellor, Lord Scrope, refused to play a part in such a theft, and the magnates forced the king to create a committee to run the Mortimer property instead, led by two of the most outspoken critics of the king's land grab: Thomas de Beauchamp, the Earl of Warwick, whose mother was a Mortimer; and the king's uncle Thomas of Woodstock, also related to the late Roger Mortimer's children. As with every aspect of the conflict that followed, people's loyalties were defined by their blood relationship. These two men would form the nucleus of the opposition to the king.

When Parliament met at Salisbury in November 1384, there was great anger among the leading men of the realm. Another of the king's critics, Richard Fitzalan, the Earl of Arundel, launched an attack on his behavior. Arundel was the grandson of Henry of Lancaster, and so through his mother was a kinsman of Richard's cousin Henry of Derby, known as Bolingbroke in Shakespeare's plays. Fitzalan was also the Admiral of the West and an ally of Thomas of Woodstock, both men opposed to the peace with France which Richard had pursued.

In Parliament, the king listened and after a pause exploded in a rage, stunning the ensembled noblemen as he threatened Arundel. Attempts by churchmen to reconcile the king and his enemies at Salisbury failed when rumor spread of a plot on the monarch's life, with his uncle John of Gaunt being behind it. Hearing allegations made against Gaunt, the burly, violent Thomas of Woodstock threatened anyone, even the king himself, who might harm his brother.

And indeed, Richard had in fact planned his uncle Gaunt's murder. Since the death of the old monarch, Gaunt had been in effect the ruler of the kingdom, and it was common when boy-kings ascended the throne for an uncle to take charge (just as Tyrion rules for Joffrey, and Charles's uncles in France). Yet Richard, still just seventeen, could not abide his father's brother, and increasingly felt threatened by him.

In February 1385, a meeting of the king's council descended into open shouting between Richard and his uncles Gaunt and Woodstock. That same night de Vere and another of the king's companions, the Earl of Mowbray, tried to have Gaunt arrested, but the royal uncle, watchful and paranoid, had slipped away. Ten days later, after a private row with his nephew, in which he told him to rule justly like a king, Gaunt escaped into the night, and onto his own territory in the north-west.

At the next meeting of the council, William Courtenay, the Archbishop of Canter-bury, criticized Richard's rule and the unlawful murder of enemies, and the king flew into a temper. Courtenay came from the most powerful family in the south-west, who held the earldom of Devon, and was not without allies. The meeting broke up in acrimony, with Woodstock trying to calm both sides. A reconciliation meeting on a barge on the Thames ended with the king lunging at the shaken archbishop, the hysterical monarch held back by his uncle Woodstock.

Medieval Europe was hostile to new men, the Littlefingers of this world, who inevitably had to be ruthless to get so far, and so there was disgust when in November 1385 Richard made parliament promote Michael de la Pole to Earl of Suffolk. De la Pole's father was a wool merchant and to his aristocratic detractors his low-born ances-try made him contemptible, and yet the following year Richard raised de Vere again to Duke of Ireland, without asking his leading lords.

In 1385 opportunity arose for the king when Gaunt sailed to Spain, having married Constance, daughter of the murdered King Pedro the Cruel, claiming the throne on behalf of his wife. Instead Richard fell into conflict with Gaunt's younger brother Thomas of Woodstock, two men who could not have been less suited, tempramen-tally. Whereas Richard was a complex bundle of neurosis and psychological com-plexes, his uncle was straightforward and popular, but also quick-tempered and indiscreet. The following year parliament rejected de la Pole's request for more money for the crown, and instead impeached him and put him in jail. Within weeks the king simply ignored them by having him freed.

Richard's list of opponents grew longer; in 1384, Thomas Mowbray, Earl of Norfolk and one of the king's allies, had married Elizabeth Fitzalan, the daughter of Arundel. A descendant of Edward I, Mowbray had fought in Scotland and held the title of Warden of the East March and, after his father had been killed on his way to the Holy Land, had become a ward of the king. Now he came under Arundel's sphere of influence.

Then in 1387 Richard turned on his enemies, Woodstock, Arundel, and Warwick, as well as two others, Scrope and Cobham. He forced Parliament to declare restric-tions on royal power illegal and made magistrates agree to the arrest of "traitors" in Parliament. When a magistrate objected to this blatantly illegal act, de Vere punched him in the face. And so Woodstock went to his seat of Gloucester in the south-west to raise men, while Warwick headed for his in the midlands; Arundel now strengthened

his defences, as did Mowbray. The other leading lord, Henry of Derby, wavered, seeking his father Gaunt's advice from Spain by letter, some 1,300 miles away from
Lancashire.

In real life there were no crows to deliver messages over long distances, although
homing pigeons had been used since the ancient Persians and both Greeks and
Romans employed them. King Sargon of Akkadia, modern-day Iraq, was known to use
pigeons in the twenty-third century BC, ordering that all messengers carry a bird and
if they were caught to release it so that the secret would not be captured and the pigeon
would fly back to the king. During the crusades, Richard the Lionheart's men captured a pigeon on its way to a besieged Muslim town telling them an army would arrive
in three days; a forged message was put in place telling them no help would come, and
they surrendered. However, their use was still more common in the Middle East at this
time and would not become so widespread in the west until the nineteenth century.
Although King's Landing is five hundred leagues from Winterfell—1,500 miles or the
distance between Boston and Miami—the longest recorded flight for a trained pigeon,
by the US Army Signal Corps, was an astonishing 2,300 miles.[3]

In November 1387, the three rebels, Woodstock, Arundel, and Warwick, swore an
oath to each other, so becoming the Lords Appellant, and calling for the impeachment of five men, among them de la Pole and de Vere.

On the 17th of that month Richard sat with his court in Westminster Hall, waiting
for the Appellants to come. Finally, the three lords, dressed in full armor, turned up to
greet the king; they linked arms, reiterating their demands. He agreed to them . . . and
then promptly went back on his word. Instead he sent de la Pole to Paris to seek help
from the King of France, but the hapless earl was recognized in Calais and arrested.
The favorite was sent back to King Richard, who allowed him to escape the country.

And now the Appellants had grown from three to five, with Mowbray and Derby
joining the rebellion. Gaunt's son was potentially the most dangerous enemy the king
could have had, ahead of Woodstock in the succession and the first fully-grown man
in line. Henry was the same age as Richard and from the age of nine had been sent to
live with him, although they were never close, and were opposites in temperament.
Derby was obsessed with jousting and war, considered among the best tournament
fighters in Europe, and had been on crusade. He was also tremendously wealthy,
even without his father's vast fortune, being married to the Duke of Hereford's
younger daughter Mary de Bohun, making him brother-in-law to his uncle Thomas.

Through his mother he also controlled Lancaster, a county palatinate possessing semi-independent powers.

De Vere had raised five thousand men in Cheshire, a county that had always been loyal to the sovereign, from where the monarch traditionally recruited soldiers for battle with the Welsh. The Cheshiremen, led by the brutal captain of Chester castle, Thomas Molyneux, followed de Vere toward London, but the Appellants had cut them off; instead the king's ally was forced to head for the river Thames through the Cotswolds, also known as the Vale of Evesham and one of the richest parts of the realm, its wealth founded in wool production.

And when the Cheshire men arrived in the town of Stowe, they found themselves surrounded by the armies of the five lords. Soon de Vere's men were trapped as Woodstock emerged from behind them, with Lancaster's army to his right. De Vere tried to rally his troops but, realizing that their nerve was about to waver, he fled, and slowly but with growing momentum the Cheshiremen began to run, too. Fighting to the last was Molyneux, who was caught by an old enemy, Thomas Mortimer, the illegitimate son of Roger. Mortimer, unlike most bastards, had been raised in his father's household and treated almost like a true-born son, and had come to work for his greatuncle, Woodstock. Molyneaux pleaded for his life, but Mortimer took off his opponent's helmet so he could stick a dagger into his eye.

The common soldiers from Cheshire surrendered, and after being stripped of their possessions they were allowed to go home. De Vere had made a remarkable escape through the mist—at one point an archer fired and almost killed him but he managed to find a bridge and ditch his expensive armor underneath. From there he rode back on his horse along the Thames toward London, bringing the disastrous news to his king.

And it was disastrous.

On New Year's Day 1388, the arrests of Richard's favorites began, along with their chamberlains, treasures, stewards, clerks, and sergeants-at-law. With the king helpless against his enemies, the Appellants and their men went through the Palace of Westminster, rounding up the servants of the five most wanted men and stripping their possessions, finding de Vere's bedroom at Westminster filled with treasures from his time at the heart of power.

Yet the Appellants were disunited about how to proceed. Whatever the king's faults, he was still king; Warwick, Mowbray, and Derby never considered removing the monarch, but Woodstock was tempted to grab the throne himself. Arundel supported him, but Mowbray and Derby, his senior in succession terms, opposed the idea, and so for now Richard survived.

But with the king powerless to prevent them, their revenge was brutal. De Vere, de la Pole and two others who had left the country were convicted *in absentia* of treason and sentenced to death. Now came the turn of Sir Simon Burley. He had done more than anyone to spread corruption in the court, but he was also popular, and Mowbray and Bolingbroke spoke in his defense, but were voted down, and even when Richard asked his uncle Edmund of York to plea for Burley's life the leading opponents could not be persuaded. After three months of the Merciless Parliament, all of Richard's friends had been dragged to their deaths or exiled. The king was totally alone.

De la Pole died in Paris in 1389; another favorite, Alexander Neville, expired in Louvain in Flanders three years later. Robert de Vere had also made it to Flanders, where in 1392 he was killed by a boar, a not uncommon form of death and one that finishes off Robert Baratheon, too. Boar-hunting, usually done with an *alaunt*, a now extinct breed of hound thought to be the ancestor of the bulldog, was dangerous. Gaston de la Foix wrote of boars in *Livre de la Chasse* that "I have seen them kill good knights, squires and servants," while Richard's nephew Edward of Norwich in his book *The Master of Game* observed: "The boar slayeth a man with one stroke, as with a knife. Some have seen him slit a man from knee up to breast and slay him all stark dead with one stroke."

In May 1389, Richard declared himself old enough to rule and announced that the past was put behind him; inside he was burning with hatred and planning his revenge. The paranoid king could trust only three people now—his Holland brothers and another old friend, John Montague. He became more tyrannical and eccentric, sitting in silence on his throne for hours on end, his crown upon his head, each person in the room forced to bend their knee whenever he looked their way. He spent lavishly, giving out largesse to supporters, and entertained hopes of becoming German emperor.

His wife Queen Anne died in 1394 and when Arundel arrived late at Westminster Abbey for her requiem, Richard seized a cane and hit him over the head, the earl falling down injured. As people looked on in horror, Richard repeatedly beat him until blood ran down the gutter, and he may have killed him were he not in church. Afterward Arundel spent several weeks in the Tower and was fined £40,000.

The moment now come, in July 1397 Arundel was invited to a dinner with the king, and unaware of what was happening, was arrested and sentenced to death. In September the king sent armed retainers to Pleshey Castle in Essex, home of Thomas of Woodstock, where he was awoken and arrested too. Parliament was called and surrounded by the king's three hundred Cheshire archers, their bows pulled back and aimed at the nervous members. John of Gaunt, now returned from Spain, was forced to take part in a show trial where Arundel was sentenced to death, while Warwick escaped execution after pathetic pleading, and was instead sent to the Isle of Man to live in poverty. When the time came to pass sentence on Woodstock it was announced that the royal uncle was already dead, of natural causes, although the king had certainly had him strangled with a towel.[4] Even his enemies' children were disinherited, their land distributed to Richard's supporters, and the king threatened that he would pardon everyone but fifty "unknown individuals."

In a letter to the count of Holland in the winter of 1397-1398, Richard justified his behavior in increasingly hysterical terms, stating that the children of traitors must be "forever shut off from reaching the height of any dignity or privilege, that posterity may learn what it is to offend the royal majesty, established at howsoever tender years." concluding "For he is a child of death who offends the king."[5] Then in March 1398 the heir to the throne, the young Roger Mortimer, was killed in Ireland aged just twenty-four—no one was in Richard's way now.

The Appellants who had opposed Burleigh's execution had been left out of his vengeance; at this point, however, these two men fell out. Mowbray had told Henry of Derby of a rumor he heard of a royally-approved plot to murder them for their previous rebellion: "We are about to be undone" he warned him. Derby, unnerved, had told his father, who then informed the king—and the two men accused each other of lying.

And so to resolve the dispute, Richard ordered that they settle it by the laws of chivalry—a joust.

24
A SONG OF HEROIC DEEDS

I don't fight in tournaments because when I fight a man for real, I don't want him to know what I can do.

—Ned Stark

The large-scale cavalry perfected by the Normans was difficult and took a great deal of coordination, skill, and courage—and most of all practice. So in the tenth century, there arose "tourneys" or tournaments, huge sporting events where knights could hone their skill in battle.

The popular idea of tournaments, and the kind we see in Westeros where the Knight of the Flowers fights the Mountain, is the late medieval version of the fifteenth century. By this point the sport was dressed up with romance and chivalry, with women in attendance giving out prizes (as well as the possibility of sexual rewards). However, earlier tourneys were far less decorous, and they were also extremely dangerous, scarcely less so than battle. Also called *behourd* in French, these events had originated in northern France, naturally the same place where horse-breeding and cavalry was most advanced, the first recorded tournament held near Tournai in 1095; the local lord, Count Henry III of Louvain, was killed in that event.

There were essentially two types of fights, the one-on-one joust and the melee. The joust came from the twelfth century game of *pas d'armes*—passage of arms—in which a knight would stand on a bridge or narrow pass and challenge anyone to pass him, assuming they were of the same rank. The melee in constrast often involved as many as a hundred knights on each side, attempting to take the opponent's base and capture them. *Tournament* meant literally "to whirl around," and that was often what happened as a knight was dragged from his horse and thrown onto the ground. Before a melee the knights had to decide whether they would fight a *l'outrance*, to the death, which meant using sharp weapons, or *a plaisance*, with restricted weapons, which was merely to score points. The battleaxe was not permitted in any tournaments.

One factor driving this sport was the peace movement of the eleventh century. The Church instituted something called the Truce of God, pressuring rival lords to agree not to attack each other for four days a week; it also decreed that violence was not permitted near a church, and so villages began to grow around these holy buildings. The religious authorities also ruled that certain people—clerics, women, and others—were exempt and were not to be harmed. Tournaments, therefore, partly developed as sort of toleration zones for violence, and although brutal, they were an accepted feature of life among the aristocracy; Henry III tried to ban them but only because he feared they would promote conspiracies.

Tournaments were staged regularly—there was at least one every fortnight somewhere in western Europe—and would attract huge numbers of entrants, there being an almost limitless supply of hungry, violent young knights. (In Westeros hedge knights are poor men not affiliated to any particular house, and in real life there were gradations of men-at-arms, from lowly bannerets to batchelors to knights.)

One reason for the growth of tourneys was the excess of otherwise unemployed aristocrats with little in the way of skill sets other than violence. It was these "free lances" who were often at the forefront of any army or colonizing force, across the British Isles, down into Iberia at the expense of the Muslims, and in Eastern Europe, Sicily, and the Middle East. The term "freelance" was coined by Walter Scott, the nineteenth century historical novelist also responsible for "War of the Roses," and would become applied to any trade in which people pursued their trade independent of any employer.

Many young aristocratic men died in these events, which had fatality rates that only early motor racing has in modern times come anything close to approaching. In Westeros at the great melee at Last Hearth in "170AC" some eighteen men died and another nine were maimed during a tournament, but real-life casualty figures were far worse. In 1241 in Germany some eighty knights were killed in one tournament, although many died from heatstroke caused by wearing armour on a very hot day. The previous year at a tourney in Dusseldorf around sixty knights were slaughtered, mostly hacked to death. Even the royal family of France lost members; in 1279 the king's brother Robert sustained terrible head injuries and was an invalid for life afterwards. Numerous high-ranking families lost members to the games, but this was a risk they were prepared to face, for as Varys says, these events "give the great a chance of glory and the lowly a respite from their woes."

Injuries were also common, and even a relatively minor one sustained at a tournament could kill if not treated. In Westeros the Hound pours boiling wine on a wound, a technique used by the ancient Greeks, and alcohol is still used today to clean wounds. However, by the middle ages medical technology had hardly improved in Europe, and there was little that could be done if an artery was struck or a wound became infected. Cauterisation had been introduced by this time, but the odds of survival were not fantastic. In this procedure red hot irons were applied to wounds to stop blood loss and infection; there was no anaesthetic, so people used alternatives such as a "concoction of lettuce juice, gall from a castrated boar, briony, opium, henbane, hemlock juice and vinegar," mixed with wine before given to the patient.[1] This wildly unsafe medicine was called *dwale*, pronounced "dwaluh" and the hemlock often killed the patient—although without it the victim might also die of shock. Opium is the real "milk of the poppy," coming from the *Papaver somniferum* plant, or opium poppy. Its use as a pain killer probably dates back to at least the Sumerians—its use on a clay tablet from 2100BC—and it was widely used in the Near East in the Middle Ages, although it only became common in Europe from about the sixteenth century. Opium is also, of course, addictive and chemically modified synthetic forms such as heroin far more so.

Other, more desperate methods, such as trepanning—drilling a hole in the head to release a build-up of blood—were even more likely to end badly. Although occasionally people got lucky; a body from England dating to 1100 was found to have been hit with a heavy, blunt object and to have survived trepanning. It healed at any rate, although what kind of quality of life he enjoyed afterwards we can't tell.

The Church soon grew hostile to the tourneys, refusing burial to those who died in them, although it abandoned this stance in 1316 when Pope John XXII concluded they were good training for crusaders. The Annals of Dunstable records that "tourneyers, their aiders and abettors, and those who carried merchandise or provisions to tournaments were ordered to be excommunicated, all together, regularly every Sunday."[2] That this had to be a regular proclamation each Sunday suggests that the Church ruling was widely ignored by the young. Fines were also issued for those organizing the events, with huge penalties of one hundred marks handed out—and yet "neither the sight of one's own blood, nor the cracking of one's teeth, nor the wordy moralizing of the clergy, nor the interference of royal administrators could check the 'beautiful horror' of the tournament."[3]

SIGILS

These games led to the development of heraldry, partly because men needed to know whom they were fighting during huge melees. Families began to adopt badges to identify themselves, and, in particular who their ancestors were (sigils as they're called in Westeros). Each symbol had a meaning and their place on a coat of arms a signifi-cance, and as rules developed men were employed to determine what went where. A coat of arms was a bold claim about one's right, and a dangerous one—Henry VIII had a relative executed for changing his coat of arms in a way that seemed to make claims on the throne.

Badges of sorts go back to antiquity, and boar-crested helmets are mentioned as early as *Beowulf*, while the *Song of Roland* tells of shields with "many cognizances" (badges). However, heraldry, a system with formal rules about who can display what, is first mentioned in England in 1140, the same year as the tournaments reached the country.

Heraldic badges usually carried messages about a man's ancestry, often including the animals their ancestors had displayed as their symbols—both Mowbray and Arun-del had lions on their arms. Warwick's was of a gold bar between six crosses, while Woodstock and Derby both displayed the quartered lions of England and fleur-de-lis of France, as their royal blood gave them a right to. Arms might be quartered to illus-trate an illustrious pedigree, and further subdivided if there were yet more prestigious ancestors, and so there was heraldry inflation as people attempted to fit more distin-guished forbearers onto their coats of arms. By the fifteenth century one knight rode into battle with a coat displaying thirty-two different coat-of-arms, all of which must have been impossible for anyone to make out anyway.[4]

Carrying a banner was a great privilege and losing it in battle was tremendously bad for morale. At Verneuil in 1424, a Norman soldier jumped into the thick of the French forces in order to take back King Henry's banner, possibly turning the tide of the battle.

Tournaments had great symbolism. During the reign of Henry II, a story was told of a melee between Normans and Bretons in which Henry's father Count Geoffrey of Anjou fought for the Celts, the story deliberately aimed at linking Henry with the land of King Arthur. After the melee ended without victory, the two sides nominated a champion for single combat, the Normans choosing an enormous English warrior, with Geoffrey representing the Bretons; Geoffrey unhorsed his giant opponent before cutting off his head.

The legend of King Arthur went hand in hand with the growth of this world. Arthur was seen as the pinnacle of chivalry, and of particular fascination to people in more advanced regions like France and southern England, who were drawn to the more mystical, misty Brittany, Cornwall, and Wales. It was a fantasy world, a sort of Wild West and Hobbiton roled into one, and poets and their patrons were obsessed by the legends preserved in oral Celtic poetry. And so from the time of Edward I, tournaments would often re-enact scenes from the life of King Arthur, Roger Mortimer being among the most obsessed with dressing up like the hero of Camelot.

The Arthur legend instructed knights on how to behave, but also affirmed that they were good men in a world riddled with evil. As Thomas Malory's *Le Morte d'Arthur* put it, being a knight meant being bound "never to do outrageously, nor murder and always to flee treason, also by no means to be cruel, but to give mercy unto him that asketh mercy . . . and always to do ladies, damsels, and gentlewomen succour upon pain of death."

The Arthur story was hugely anachronistic, implanting a high medieval idea of chivalry onto the earlier dark ages, not to mention much later technology and fashion. Likewise, Samwell Tarley says the same of stories about knights who supposedly lived hundreds of years before knights could even have existed, but then implanting more recent mores and codes onto a distant past is almost a universal human cultural habit.

The tournament summed up what it meant to be a knight, but of course there were other motivations for young men. Modern screen depictions of jousting almost invariably feature heavily-bosomed damsels in attendance, and toward the later medieval period this was indeed a feature. Knights fought for their ladies, or just as often other people's ladies. Chrétien de Troyes's late twelfth century romance *Erec et Enide* tells the story of a man called Erec who vows to take part in the tournament to honor Enide, whom he loves, even though she's wearing an old, tattered dress. Erec beats the mighty Yder and gives him a serious injury, and the hero wins his heroine after acquiring a sparrowhawk as a prize: "That day she had won much honor, joy and dignity. Her heart was full of gladness for her bird and for her lord: her joy could not have been greater." It also features a dwarf who "has insulted the queen by striking her damsel," disabilities and disfigurements being associated with evil and even witchcraft.[5]

Chretein was a sort of prototype of the romantic novelist and also created the character of Lancelot. He was a court poet for the count of Champagne, a job that involved
praising the patron and his ancestors and giving "spiritually edifying" stories revolving around the saints. By the period he was writing in, the 1160s, *courtoisie* (courtesy)
and *fin'amor* (courtly love), *chevalerie (chivalry)* and *clergie (*learnedness) had come to
be held as ideals among the French-speaking aristocracy of France and England, and
later Germany. Old Celtic tales of Arthur, Tristan and others were used to emphasises
these ideals, but also explored the gap between fantasy and reality.[6]

French court poets chose from three subject areas: the history of France, British
legends such as Arthur, and Greco-Roman mythology—also known as the Matter of
France, the Matter of Britain, and the Matter of Rome—the former celebrating the
courage of Charlemagne and his knights, a type of epic poem called the *chansons de
geste,* the "song of heroic deeds." Chretien's other works, such as *Lancelot, the Knight
of the Cart,* and *Perceval, the Story of the Grail,* all follow a similar theme, singing of
knights performing deeds of daring do, and this culture influenced the games, which
were still at this time brutal. Tournaments became a chance to show off in front of
women, and so became somewhat less violent, since women tended to be less
impressed by men gouging each other's eyes out than other men were.

Druerie—love—was an incentive to *chevalerie,* as the romantic poems of the time
emphasized. The French poem *Lai du Lecheoir,* the Lay (Poem) of the Lecher, features eight ladies in a Breton court, "wise and learned," discussing why knights fight
in tournaments. Why do they like gallantry? Why do they refrain from doing evil?
Why do they dress in new clothes? The answer, they conclude, is *con*—or the "solaces
of the lower part."[7]

These romantic ideals changed the nature of the tournaments, which by the late
medieval period were less brutal, although by the standards of modern sports still very
dangerous. It was during this era when heavily armed knights would charge at each
other with a barrier separating them—an innovation introduced in the fourteenth
century—and women in attendance giving out prizes afterwards, with knights winning favor with ladies by dedicating their victory to them.*

---

*And so the mad king Aerys angers his wife by naming Lyanna Stark as his "Queen of Love and Beauty"
after a tournament.

And yet, despite all the romance, the reality of knighthood was that it was underpinned by violence and a sword with pretty ribbons would still kill you. One tale, *Yvain*, had a description of a fight between two men: "never were there two knights so intent upon each other's death . . . At last my lord Yvain crushed the helmet of the knight . . . Beneath his kerchief his head was split to the very brains."

And the thirteenth-century romance *Havelok the Dane* illustrates the violence of knighthood:

> He broke their arms, he broke their knees,
> He broke their shanks, he broke their thighs.
> He made the blood come running down
> To the feet right from the crown;
> For there was not a head he spared.[8]

And yet beneath the squalid violence the ideal did matter to some. No doubt many knights did live up to the romanticized code of honor, as epitomized by Brienne of Tarth, serving Renley and his Rainbow Guard despite the taunts and setbacks. Indeed, there was one such knight in particular, a man famed for heroic deeds and loyalty to those he served even in the face of daunting odds, who ended up having a huge impact on all our lives. His story begins during a horrific civil war known as the Anarchy.

25

THE CURSE OF THE KINGSLAYER

The north is a place for warriors, not knights.

—JAIME LANNISTER

The Norman monarchs had prevented great magnates from holding large amounts of adjoining territory so that they did not develop a regional power-base, the exceptions being the marches and the borders with Scotland and Wales, where the barons had to be strong to protect the realm. Just as the Starks are Wardens of the North in Westeros, so leading families in medieval England held military positions in which they enforced the monarch's law on the northern border but with some degree of autonomy. And yet it was these marcher lords in the north and west who would always provide the greatest threat; for Edward II it was the lord of the West, Roger Mortimer; for the king-killer Henry of Lancaster it would be the lords of the North.*

Wales was mountainous and hard to conquer, but its people showed no interest in threatening their neighbors; in contrast only three English monarchs between 1040 and 1745 did not endure invasion from Scotland, or invaded them in turn.[1] And so the North had a military system much more like Anglo-Saxon England, which had a *fyrd* or militia of men ready to be called up to defend the realm; many northern men would also have had axes and swords for use, even if they were not trained soldiers.

Life in the North was tough, and the Percy land in Cumberland was described in 1570 as "consyst[ing] most in wast grounds and ys very cold hard and barren for the wynter."[2] It "bredyth tall men and hard of nature, whose habitaciouns are most in the

---

*The title marquess comes from "march," or border.

valleys and dales . . . they have but little tillage, by reason whereof they lyve hardly at ease, which makyth them tall of personage and hable of endure hardnes when necessute requyryth."[3] When Ned Stark arrives in King's Landing, he's asked whether he wants to wear something "more appropriate," his clothes appearing rough and coarse to southern eyes. At the time, northern aristocrats in London really would have looked far poorer and less elegant, the region further away from the sophisticated courtly centers of France and northern Italy. Likewise, in Westeros "Northern fighters use the older style of interlinked chain mail . . . rather than the heavy and limiting plate armour of the southern knights, or they may wear leather breastplates."[4] Northern horses were also cheaper, so that only seven out of 304 Percy horses were worth more than £15, compared to a quarter of the southern Earl of Salisbury's. Percy's own mount was valued at between £20 and £25 while Salisbury had mere knights riding £50 horses.[5]

Much of the poverty was down to sheer geography, the North being rockier, with poorer farm land, and further away from the rich markets of the continent. In the 1440s the future Pope Pius II, Aeneas Piccolomini, was journeying through the borderland in Northumberland on his way to Scotland, close to "a river, flowing from its source on a high mountain, which determines the boundary between the two countries." The Italian ate with a local priest and witnessed the immense poverty of the region, so alien to his native Tuscany.

"Afterwards, all the men and women of the village came running as if to some unusual spectacle, and just as we wonder at Ethiopians or Indians, so they stared in astonishment at Aeneas,"[6] he wrote, describing himself in the third person. He produced bread and wine, which the local people had never even seen, and "the feast went on until the second hour after sunset, when the priest, host and all the men and boys together left Aeneas and hurried out, explaining that they were fleeing to a tower a safe distance away. This they did, they said, out of fear of the Scots, who often crossed the river when the tide was low and came marauding at night." They left the women to their fate, the Italian was surprised to learn, as they didn't consider rape a crime, or presumably at least less of an ordeal than the murder the men might face. "After much of the night had passed, two girls led Aeneas, who was heavy with sleep, into a chamber strewn with straw. They would sleep with him, such was the custom in their part of the world, if they were asked," but he had other things on his mind. When he arrived back in Newcastle "there for the first time he felt he was returning to a recognizable world and a habitable country again. For Scotland, and the part of England which borders it, has nothing in common with the country in which we live, being as it is rough, uncultivated and inaccessible to winter sun."

The North had by the turn of the century become ever more militarized. In the 1390s, there were seventy-nine fortress towers in Northumberland between Alnwick and Berwick, which also acted as shelters for villagers. However, as they could fit many men and also forty cattle in the basement, raiding clans often used the pele towers as bases.

Despite the hostility, the northern English also had a great deal in common with the Scots, divided by a wall and border but sharing a comman culture. The two sides of the wall spoke the same language, albeit diverging dialects, and such were the simularties in speech that battles often involved what today would be called friendly fire; when the two sides fought in the dark at Otterburn in 1388, with Percy's son Harry Hotspur leading the fight against a Scottish force led by James Douglas, a large number of Englishmen were killed by their own side. Because of the cultural similarities between the two people, spying was also routine; a John Hardyng worked as a spy for the Earl of Northumberland in Scotland from 1418, and was there for several years, still alive despite numerous beatings by suspicious locals.

The Northumbrians had never been happy with southern rule, and there had been uprisings ever since English unification; back in the tenth century northern men had risen up and declared "that their country has been wont to have a king of its own and to be tributary to none of the south Angles."[7] English kings rarely spent much time in the north; Edward the Confessor never went once, and Richard the Lionheart only got as far as Nottingham in the midlands. Without kings of their own, naturally the Percys came to win men's loyalty more than any southern ruler.

But just as the Starks have their rivals in the Boltons, so the Percys were threatened by the Nevilles. They also had a number of smaller but no less proud houses whose dignity had to be appeasaed; in Westeros there were the Karstarks, Flints, Tallharts, Glovers, and Hornwords, while in real life there were the Cliffords, Dacres, de Ros, and the Scropes of Bolton.[8]

The North has warring hillside tribes often beyond the reach of any law, groups such as the Clans of the Mountains of the Moon who are descendants of First Men who did not submit; they are almost like wildlings, with practices of bride-stealing in common. Again, this has a real life parallel, for the border regions of England and

Scotland were long populated by clannish "reiver" families who often lived outside of the law.

Among these notorious border clans were the Scotts, Burns, and Irvines north of the Tweed and the Fenwicks, Millburns, Charltons, and Musgraves on the English side. Some clans were found on both, such as the Halls, Grahams, and Nixons, although in reality the border meant little to border people. Among the most notorious were the Armstrongs who, when the law caught up with them, "melted away on their hardy ponies into the hospitable boggy scrubland."[9]*

These families lived beyond the control of either London or Edinburgh, the pacifying effect of the rule of law being non-existent, and so border folk still relied on the protection of their clans; this honor culture perpetuated cycles of violence that spanned and stained generations.

The border people had a culture unique in England that was clannish, stubborn, and exceptionally violent. There were northern ballads a plenty, such as "The Battle of Otterburn" and "Chevy chase" which portrayed a society of personal vendettas and close family networks. The former recalled that:

> The Percy and Montgomery met,
> That either of other were fain;
> They swapped swords, and they twa swat,
> And aye the blood ran down between.[10]

The reivers maintained cousin marriage and blood feuds long after a strong centralized state had stamped these practices out elsewhere. Many of these clans were outlaws and some were lawmen; others were both or either depending on circumstances.

But even noble families would still thieve or murder when it suited them. The Dacres of Cumberland, who had been sheriffs since at least the thirteenth century and Wardens of the Middle March later, were widely suspected of engaging in law-breaking, but they weren't the only ones. Raiding and violence was so common on the border that there sprung a tradition whereby truces were arranged in return for

---

*In 1972, Langholm in the Scottish borders, ancestral home of the Armstrong clan, invited a certain Neil to visit. He accepted, much to their surprise, and upon visiting told them "I consider this, now, my home town." Safe to say he had traveled further than any border man.

"blackmail," a tribute to border chiefs. The word, which may come either from the Scottish Gaelic *blathaich*, rent, or more likely from the Middle English *male*, tribute, in the nineteenth century came to mean any sort of extortion.

The thinly-populated area of the western march from Carlisle to Langholm was known as the Debatable Land, so unsure were people what country they were in, who owned the land, and whose law held sway. This region, with its majestic lakes, is among the most poetic and beautiful on the island, but it has also historically been a place of grinding poverty. (Likewise, the North of Westeros has its "Disputed lands.")

The border family vendettas were notorious, among them those involving the Johnson clan and their habit of "adorning their houses with the flayed skins of their enemies the Maxwells in a blood feud that continued for many generations."[11] The border folk also long maintained their unique beliefs and superstitions, often to do with witches, who could be detected by the howling of dogs or a warm current of air.

Large numbers of reiver families later migrated to Ulster and then onto the American colonies, playing a leading role in the founding of the United States, Scots-Irish settlers being the most ardently pro-independence group during the American Revolution. They also shaped, in particular, the mountain culture of the Appalachians, "hillbilly" just being border slang for "hill folk." Many historians and sociologists view the persisitently higher rates of violence among southern whites compared to northerners as being related to the honor culture of the borders, which encouraged a readiness to commit violence, and to become engaged in blood feuds rather than resort to law.[12] The clannishness of families such as the Hatfields and McCoys, who conducted a famous feud on the West Virginia-Kentucky border over three decades in the late nineteenth century, is cited as an example. Even today this region has clear cultural differences to the rest of the United States, with surveys of cultural attitudes showing far higher support for using violence in situations other Americans think inappropriate, and strong support for the military.

THE BLOOD OF THE KING

The joust between Henry of Derby and Thomas de Mowbray, arranged for September 1398, attracted people from across western Europe, and for the event Derby commissioned armor from Milan and Mowbray all the way from Bohemia. It was to be the greatest event of the age, and yet at the last minute the king stopped proceedings and ordered both men banished from the kingdom, Mowbray for five years and Derby for ten—or whenever his father died. Mowbray left for Venice and Derby for Paris, where the regent Louis, Duke of Orléans, allowed him to settle under heavy guard. Orléans had his own plans to establish a kingdom in northern Italy and thought Henry would be useful as a destabilizing influence on the English crown in the meantime. The following February, Gaunt passed away, and Richard told the king of France in a letter that he felt "a sense of joy" about his uncle's death. And now the king had all of his cousin's lands confiscated, before embarking for Ireland to bring retribution for the killing of Mortimer.

Orléans was supposed to keep a close guard on Derby but he now purposefully let him escape and the new Duke of Lancaster landed in Yorkshire, on a spot called Ravenspur, to reclaim his land—or so he claimed. This was Percy country.

Henry Percy had in 1377 become the first Earl of Northumberland and three years later was put in charge of raising troops in the North; he was also briefly, in 1383, Marshal of England, a role that originally entailed being in charge of the king's horses but evolved to have a wider scope over royal ceremonies. Percy was also Admiral of the Northern Seas, in charge of the realm's eastern coastal defenses until it was merged with the position of Admiral of the West in 1412 to become Lord Admiral of England. But the House of Percy felt increasingly threatened by the House of Neville, who had grown in power under the new king.

The Percy and Neville clans had once been friendly, at least until the mid fourteenth century, when both northern magnates engaged in protecting the frontier. And yet the edge to their rivalry was to turn bitter as the Nevilles expanded at the expense of their rivals. In 1382, Percy was commissioned as joint guardian of both marches alongside Ralph Neville, but soon afterwards the two northerners fell out, most likely because Neville was too close to Gaunt, whom Percy disliked. Despite this Percy had married Neville's sister. Then in 1382, Gaunt humiliated Percy, putting his rival in charge of the east and west marches, so that Neville territory now surrounded them. However, it was Ralph Neville's elevation to Earl of Westmorland in 1397, putting him on par with the far older, more established family, that lit up the enmity between Percy and King Richard.

And so when Henry of Derby arrived in Percy country the Earl of Northumberland should—and could—have stopped him. He let him pass.

As he headed south, Henry amassed followers and soon realized he could take the crown. Indeed, he had to take the crown or die. Richard was isolated, and when he landed in Wales on July 24, he found that the realm had turned to his rival. Even the Cheshire archers had deserted him. Richard fled to Conwy Castle, sending John Montacute, the Earl of Salisbury and one of the last men loyal to him, to raise a Welsh army.

Montacute's grandfather William had been Edward III's closest compainion and had captured Mortimer with him. As a young man the grandson had fought against the pagan Slavs in Prussia alongside Derby, and the latter's eldest son Henry of Monmouth was entrusted to him after the boy's mother had died; but despite this he now stood by the king even as his support faded. And yet Montacute could raise only one hundred men, and now even the king's uncle Edmund, Duke of York, who had been placed in charge of the capital, came over to Derby.

It was Percy who lured Richard out of the castle, telling him that his cousin had sworn on the sacraments that he would remain king if only he restored the duchy of Lancaster to his cousin; instead Richard was seized and taken to Chester, and soon the last of his followers abandoned him. On the way down to London, King Richard had tried to escape out a window of the carriage, but to no avail; his fate was sealed. Richard swore revenge against the Percy house and that its head would suffer "bitter death."

Political instability and violence was a feature of late medieval England and now Richard was on his way back to the city he once ruled as a prisoner of Henry of Lancaster, his fate all too clear—for a king who lost his crown soon enough lost his head. It was a huge and dangerous step to usurp a man chosen by God to be king, but Henry now called on parliament to proclaim him ruler "with their hearts as well as their mouths"; adding, with false modesty, and that if they didn't "it would not be any great surprise to me."

Warwick was allowed back from the Isle of Man. The king had wished to be reconciled with Mowbray, but it was too late—he had died of plague in September. Having been captured, Richard refused to give up his crown to his cousin, and so placed it on the ground, symbolically abdicating to God. After a plot to free Richard led by Montacute, numerous supporters were beheaded, Montacute included, and the former king died a few months later. His cause of death was officially declared to be hunger strike, but few believed it.

In the words of historian Nigel Saul: "A dangerous new element of instability had been introduced into politics,"[13] and many more men would die before the fighting for the throne was done.

At the coronation, Percy bore King Henry's sword, the weapon he'd worn on arriving in England, while Sir Thomas Dymoke, the son of Richard II's champion Sir John, continued the family tradition. The king had commissioned a new royal crown and had himself anointed with special oil but, it was noticed, lice emerged from his hair. When the archbishop gave Henry a ceremonial coin representing his kingship the king-killer dropped it, and it rolled away never to be seen again. It was a sign from God.

King Henry, by overthrowing and most likely murdering the anointed king, had committed something monstrous in many people's eyes. As in Westeros, where Jaime Lannister is tarnished with the name Kingslayer, the killing of a monarch was a crime of supreme depravity in medieval Europe. His reign was cursed with ill-health and with rebellions in the north and west, numerous assassination plots and increasingly bizarre attempts to put ever-less-convincing Richard impersonators on the crown. Henry's life would fall apart, and his line would come to a tragic and bloody end.

Percy had been rewarded for his part in the overthrow, made Constable of England and Lord of Man, while the earl's eldest son Harry "Hotspur" became justiciar of north Wales, responsible for enforcing English law in that region. Northumberland's brother Thomas, Earl of Worcester, was made steward of the royal household, while the Percy family were also well paid for their part in the coup, a total of £4,900, while his rival Westmoreland received just £146.

But they were discontent, nonetheless. Percy's heir, known as Hotspur for the speed in which he once launched into the Scottish lines, was widely feted for his great fighting abilities, but he was also impetuous and proud. It was not unusual at the time for people to witness extreme violence even at an early age, and Hotspur had first been on a battlefield at the age of nine, where he would have seen men slashed to death. Knighted at twelve alongside the future Richard II and Henry IV, he was in Ireland on campaign at sixteen and two years later on crusade in Prussia before becoming Warden of the East March at twenty. The following year he went with King Richard on campaign in Scotland.

The border remained volalite, and liable to explode. From 1377 there had been ongoing war between the Percy and Douglas clans. At Otterburn in 1388, Hotspur had attacked the Scots at night under a full moon, having chased James Douglas around the north, partly in order to get back Hotspur's standard which the Earl of Douglas had taken in a previous skirmish. Although the Scots won, and captured Hotspur, Douglas was mortally wounded.

In 1402. the Percys fought the Douglas clan again, at Homildon Hill, this time facing Archibald Douglas, a grandson of Black Douglas who had inherited the title despite his father being a bastard. Only five Englishmen died in the battle—while five hundred Scots perished just from drowning while trying to ford the Tweed. Douglas lost an eye and was captured, but this began a disastrous series of events for England's leading houses.

King Henry insulted both Percy and Douglas by insisting that the prisoner be transferred to London. According to border law, unwritten but no less real for that, prisoners should have dignified treatment and were allowed cross-border visits on the honor system, in which they had to give their word to return, the custom called *parole* ("word" in French). Prison in the south would have been a much more traumatic prospect, a land alien to people from both sides of the border.

And King Henry faced an even bigger problem in the west. A Welsh gentleman by the name of Owain Glyndŵr had begun a rebellion largely motivated against local magnate Lord Grey of Rythin; the two had an old grudge, and Grey had previously got Glyndŵr listed as a traitor after purposely losing his military summons. Glyndŵr was descended from the ancient Princes of Powys, the hilly, landlocked region of Wales facing Mercia (it literally means countryside, related to the words "pagan" or French pays), and now he raised enough support in the hills to have himself proclaimed Prince of Wales. In 1402, Glyndŵr won a great victory at Bryn Glas against a larger English army led by Edmund Mortimer, a great-grandson of Edward III and one of the leading border lords. Mortimer was also the brother of the late Roger, and although Roger had left a son (also confusingly called Edmund), certainly Edmund Mortimer's claim to the throne was better than that of Henry, Earl of Derby.

Mortimer's own Welsh troops had now changed sides and the captured English baron was led away into captivity. Yet there he fell in love with and married the Welsh leader's daughter Catrin and joined Glyndŵr in rebellion, upset that the king had refused to pay the ransom, another miscalculation by Henry. The web of aristocratic family ties dictated the allegiances people followed in conflicts, and as Mortimer's sister was married to Hotspur, so Percy edged closer to the western rebels.

Finally, in July 1403, Hotspur marched south, recruiting Cheshire archers to his side. The plan was to capture the king's heir Prince Henry in Shrewsbury, but the monarch reacted quickly and reached the border town with fourteen thousand troops. At the ensuing slaughter young Henry was hit in the face with an arrow but survived after undergoing agonizing treatment. Hotspur was not so lucky; he lifted his visor and then a steel-tipped arrow went through his eye-socket, killing him instantly. Douglas survived but lost a testicle. Eventually the Scotsman was released, in 1407, signing a statement proclaiming his loyalty to Henry, and then went back to raiding immediately.

It was the first time two large armies had fought in England since 1066, and up to five thousand lives were lost—but it would not be the last. After the battle Percy's brother Thomas, Earl of Worcester, was captured, hanged, and quartered. Hotspur's corpse was dug up, salted, and put on show in the Shrewsbury pillory, after which his head and intestines were displayed in the north as a warning.

And yet the northerners remained loyal to the Percys, always. Sir William Clifford, Hotspur's captain, held Berwick castle in his name and was put in charge of his ten-year-old son, another Henry. He refused to hand over Berwick to the king unless the dead lord's lands were returned to his boy.

Earl Percy himself went into alliance with Glyndŵr and Mortimer in 1405, an agreement in which they would split the country three ways, with Percy king of the North. Another of Edward III's descendents, Edmund of York's son Edward of Norwich, was also implicated in the plot against the king, denounced by his own sister, and sent to the Tower where he took to translating a treatise on hunting, *The Master of Game*.

Then in May 1405 Archbishop Scrope of York gathered eight thousand armed men in York to protest about tax and the treatment of clergy, and to support his cousin Northumberland. Ralph Neville, Earl of Westmorland, faced down the rebels and when Henry reached the city he had Scrope executed, being made to ride a mule backwards on his way to his death.

Over 1407-8, Europe was hit by the "Great Frost and Ice," the coldest winter in a century, and clerks and monks could not write records because the ink froze in their jars "every second word." Under these harsh conditions of snow and ice, early in the new year Percy raised an army in the north under the banner of Richard II; in doing so he followed his son to the grave.

King Henry had been chasing Percy north when he found that he could not stop without screaming in pain. He then woke up after a nightmare crying "Traitors! ye have thrown fire over me"; he was burning up, a mysterious illness that no physician could understand, and which today remains a mystery, perhaps gangrenous ergotism, a sort of fungal infection, or leprosy.

Percy was now dead and soon Edmund Mortimer was, too, after a siege. The Welsh rebels submitted, their support from France drying up in 1411 when feuding between two factions at the French court exploded into full-on civil war. Although the English had ground out victory in Wales by drowning prisoners and starving the small folk, Glyndŵr disappeared into the mist.

And yet although his enemies were now dust, the king-killer could find no joy. Three years to the day after Scrope was killed he suffered a stroke and could not speak without much difficulty; he spent his last years in agony, his body covered with red pustules and crying out as if on fire. All sorts of stories abounded around the kingdom and beyond about his mysterious illness, which left him screaming in pain, and sometimes, he wondered, if he was dead already, and in hell. He died in 1413, now aged beyond his years, convinced he was suffering divine punishment for the killing of his cousin the king.

As for his rival, the head of Henry, first Earl of Northumberland, now greeted visitors passing over London bridge, his arms and legs thrown into sacks and sent to the four corners of the North. The family was defeated.

26
"I HAVE OTHER SONS"

A bastard had to learn to notice things, to read the truth that people hid behind their eyes.

—Jon Snow

In the year 1152, a five-year-old boy was taken up to a wooden construction outside Newbury Castle in Berkshire. In the distance his father looked on as a noose was placed around the child's neck, emotionless as he awaited the coming execution.

The infant's name was William and his father John Fitzgilbert was a major baron in the region, once the heartland of the kingdom of Wessex. Thirteen years earlier the realm had descended into war between two claimants to the throne, the Empress Matilda and her cousin Stephen of Blois, both grandchildren of William the Conqueror. The Anarchy, as the civil war became known, was an exceptionally unpleasant conflict that produced a number of cartoon villains who make Ramsay Bolton look like Gandhi.

Fitzgilbert, who held the title of Marshal of the Horses, was a Norman nobleman ruthless and violent even by the standards of the day. His father Gilbert had been marshal to Henry I, the same role Henry Percy would briefly hold centuries later, and the son had inherited that honor upon Gilbert's death in 1129. When King Henry I died in 1135 and war erupted Fitzgilbert sided with Henry's daughter Matilda, but her rival Stephen's forces captured Fitzgilbert's castle and King Stephen had tried to win the baron's loyalty by making him hand over his fourth and youngest son William as hostage. In return, Fitzgilbert was allowed back to Newbury castle on the condition that he did not rearm. Yet John Fitzgilbert "had no time for the idea of peace" and so put his "child's life in danger, because the king [soon] realized that he had been tricked."[1]

John Fitzgilbert, or "le Marechal" (marshal) as he was also known, was mentioned in chronicles as "a scion of hell and the root of all evil." He bore a horrific scar on his face dating back to 1141 when he had barricaded himself in Wherwell Abbey and Stephen's men had set fire to it; le Marechal climbed the bell tower to escape but in the engulfing inferno some burning metal fell on his face, "with horrible consequences."[2]

But now le Marechal watched impassively as the conquerer's grandson mulled over his options over how to respond to this slight. The reality was that King Stephen had no choice, and one of his knights now stepped forward and advised him "to hang the child." The war had been burning for over thirteen years by now and many such atrocities had taken place, and one more innocent death would make no difference; and yet, as subsequent history was to show, *this* one would.

Le Marechal refused to hand over the castle, and a chronicle recalled, *Il dist ken e li chaleit de l'enfant, quer encore aveit les enclumes e les marteals dunt forgereit de plus beals*: "He said that he did not care about the child, since he still had the anvils and hammers to produce even finer ones."[3] The line is of course borrowed by Walder Frey when Catelyn Stark threatens to kill one of his children: "I'll sire another." Enraged, Stephen ordered that young William be taken to the gallows to be hanged in front of his father.

In Westeros, women have not been allowed to rule since the Dance of the Dragons, a civil war in which many of the Targaryens died. The conflict started when the king passed away and his eldest daughter by his first wife and his son by his second both claimed the crown. Instead it was agreed that a woman's son must rule in her place and so the second Rhaenys Targaryen becomes known as the "queen who never was." (Later she dies fighting a battle on dragonback—which is where fantasy diverges from reality, obviously…and unfortunately.)

Something like this really happened in England, which for twenty years was crippled by feuding warlords as William the Conqueror's heirs fought over the country. The conflict allowed local strong men in castles to take total control of surrounding land and to rule like kings, often extremely cruelly, and during the Anarchy the dungeons of barons' castles were filled with "both men and women put in prison for their gold and silver, and tortured with pains unspeakable."[4] The casual brutality inflicted on the small folk in Westeros is far more true to life to England's twelfth century civil war than its fifteenth century equivalent, where the poor largely escaped the horror.

This earlier dynastic conflict also inspired the backstory for King Joffrey and his unfortunate demise (unfortunate for him at least).

The Conqueror had three surviving sons from his marriage to Matilda of Flanders, all of them stocky and barrel-chested like their father. He hated his eldest, Robert, whom he tormented about his height, calling him Curthose, "Stubby Legs" or "Short Arse"; so bad was their relationship that in 1079 Short Arse almost killed his father in battle. Yet when he died on campaign in Maine the king had left him Normandy, bound by an older oath, while middle son William Rufus inherited England; his youngest Henry received just five thousand pounds in coins.

It was Rufus who built Westminster Hall, the grand building which, along with the White Tower of the Tower of London, serves as the inspiration for the Red Keep.[5] Westminster Hall, which at 240ft was the longest in medieval Europe for some time, is still part of the Houses of Parliament today, having survived various fights and fires, and has seen the trials of Thomas More, Guy Fawkes, and Charles I, among others; it is still used to host foreign dignitaries such as Pope Benedict XVI in the twenty-first century.

William II was not a successful ruler; a drunk who had little respect for clergy, he was accused by his clerical enemies of holding homosexual orgies and presiding over an effeminate court. From the start of his reign he was almost immediately in conflict with his brother Robert, until the war was postponed when Robert was drawn into the crusades; William could not attack his brother's lands while he was fighting a holy war without being excommunicated by the pope. With Robert away, he had more time to indulge in his passions, among them hunting—until August 2, 1100 when disaster struck.

Rufus was out in the New Forest in Hampshire with Walter Tirel, a Norman lord considered one of the best shots in the realm. On the eve of their hunt, William had been presented with six arrows and, taking four for himself, he handed the remaining two to Tirel, telling him, "Bon archer, bonnes fleches" ("To the good archer, the good arrows"). On the day of the hunt, king and lord became separated and Tirel took aim at a passing stag; it missed and instead hit the monarch in the chest, puncturing his lung. William tried to pull out the arrow shaft, but this only worsened the injury. Tirel, in a panic, fled to France.

Hunting is a dangerous sport, and one that has been killing aristocrats for centuries. The Conqueror's second son Richard also died hunting in the New Forest, while

Robert Curthose's bastard, another Richard, was likewise killed in a chase just months before Rufus, accidentally shot by a companion. The Norman lifestyle was not risk-averse, and young men were encouraged to take part in dangerous—to our minds idiotically dangerous—activities, and numerous other aristocrats died in similar fashion. Indeed, this fondness for risky sports involving horses and weapons is something the English aristocracy has inherited from their French-speaking ancestors. In total, thirteen British MPs have been killed in hunting accidents down the years, the most recent being in 1935, and another two have died from shooting, including Sir William Payne-Gallwey who accidentally shot himself in 1881 after tripping on a turnip.[6]

And yet of course there was also the distinct possibility that Rufus's death was not an accident. William's younger brother Henry was at the time not far from Winchester, home of the Treasury until it was moved to Westminster the following century, and he claimed the throne immediately. He then had the killer quietly sent to France and let off. It was extremely fortunate timing for Henry; in 1099 the crusaders had conquered Jerusalem after three gruesome years fighting in the desert and his eldest brother Robert was on his way back, now a hero of Christendom.

Among those who had joined the crusade was Edmund Ironside's grandson Edgar the Atheling, by the laws of succession the rightful king of England. Edgar's sister Margaret had joined a number of Anglo-Saxon aristocrats in moving north across the border, where she had married King Malcolm III. Their daughter Edith was later proposed to by William Rufus, but after nothing came of this Henry married her instead, changing her name to the Norman-sounding Matilda. They had two surviving children, on top of his estimated twenty-two to twenty-five illegitimate children, by "six or eight" different mistresses, a royal record to date (and probably unlikely to be bettered any time soon).

Unlike his boorish brothers Henry had learned to read, reflected in his nickname, *beauclerc*, "good scholar," but he was also a brutal and ruthless leader and those who upset him soon knew about it. Over the twelve days of Christmas in 1124, he had the men who minted coins across the kingdom rounded up and their rights hands and testicles all removed, for debasing the currency by mixing it with inferior metal. He once blinded a Norman minstrel who sang a song critical of him.

Henry defeated his brother in battle and late in 1120 also finally defeated Robert's son William Clito, confirming his supremacy over Normandy and England. And so, in November the royal party was on its way back across the Channel and had gathered at Barfleur on the Norman coast waiting to sail. On board the White Ship was King Henry's only legitimate son William, along with 200 leading young aristocrats, including two of Henry's illegitimate children, 140 knights, eighteen noble women, and "virtually all the aristocracy of the county of Mortain" in western Normandy. And yet in the immediate thrill of victory their cups had overflown with wine, even the crew piloting the ship. In fact a small number of passengers were so concerned by the amount drunk that they disembarked, among them Henry's nephew Stephen.

The revellers dared the captain to catch up with the royal ship ahead, this despite it already being dark, and at the very tail end of the sailing season, a dangerous period for crossing this stretch of water. Before it even left the harbor the boat hit some rocks, and the laughter turned to screams as the damaged ship rapidly filled with water. Most were drowned below decks, and even those who escaped this coffin were dragged down by their fine silk clothing, but young William was pulled onto a life-boat, only to go back for his half-sister Matilda; they both died. Only one man—a butcher who was on board collecting money—managed to hang on to a raft until morning and survived.

Drowning at sea was sadly common, especially in the English Channel, one of the most dangerous stretches of water in the world. In March 1170, for example, four hundred courtiers, including the king's doctor, died on their way from Normandy to England.[7] If the Norman barons were once scared to cross the water, the deaths of so many of their progeny showed the wisdom of that fear.

King Henry ruled for another fifteen unhappy years, remarrying after his wife passed away although unable to produce any more children. He had only one legiti-mate heir, Matilda, and asked his barons to swear an oath promising to support her when he died, and despite Matilda's sex there was a crush before him as the leading men battled to be first to give their fealty; at the very front was his sister's son Stephen of Blois.

A monarch was expected to lead in battle and it was not until the mid-fifteenth century that one failed to carry out this duty, the mad king Henry VI. And a woman could not do so. Although most people had different views about women's abilities than we do today, a major reason for opposition was physiognomy, in that military leaders had to wield heavy swords and female body strength is on average just over half that of men's. From the mid-sixteenth century, and the use of gunpowder and regiments, such ideas about a royal military leader become obsolete, while monarchs were expected to be more than axe-wielding killers, but instead to be civilized, and cunning too.

A handful of women found themselves rulers during this period, but they were rarely happy events. Alfonso VI's daughter Urraca tried governing Leon and Castile for seventeen years from 1109, a hugely difficult reign. Her nickname was "the Reckless"; unfortunately, her abusive marriage led to open civil war in the country, and she faced numerous rebellions. She also had an affair with a courtier, leading to an illegitimate child, which helped confirm the idea that she was unfit as a ruler. That her contemporary Henry of England had twenty-two bastards would not have stood as an excuse.

Neither the Franks nor the Vikings, the two dominant cultures of northern France, had any history of queens regnant; besides which, under Anglo-Saxon custom the previous king's child did not automatically inherit the throne, but rather the new monarch was chosen by the leading men out of a pool of people considered throne-worthy—*atheling*. Of the five kings before William the Conqueror, none was the rightful successor by blood.

And Henry had many nephews, his favorite being Stephen of Blois, his sister Adela's youngest son. Stephen had two older brothers, Theobald, Count of Champagne, who was also Count of Blois, the family's ancestral home, and the eldest William the Simple, who may have had mental deficiencies and is never considered by chroniclers to be a candidate. Stephen was by the accounts affable and friendly, and one author likens him to the "charming, popular Renly,"[8] who also has an older brother who precedes him.

Indeed, the new king had many admirable qualities which nonetheless made him unsuitable to take the throne. He was "a mild, good humored, easy-going man, who never punished anybody," says the *Anglo-Saxon Chronicle*, which was not meant as a compliment, as he allowed his continental mercenaries to plunder the land. After an uprising in the west country was crushed Stephen pardoned its leaders, which to modern eyes seems the moderate, forgiving course, but in the twelfth century was just seen as weakness.

Matilda was considered arrogant, at a time when men found women rulers difficult. As historian Helen Castor wrote, "The risk these queens ran was that their power would be perceived as a perversion of 'good' womanhood, a distillation of all that was to be feared in the unstable depths of female nature."[9] The ancients talked of "man-hearted" women like Clytemnestra who murdered her husband Agamemnon, while the medievals called them "viragos," and women who would today be celebrated as empowered were instead feared and hated.

Matilda was also to some extent a foreigner, having been the child-bride of Emperor Heinrich and so more German than Norman. After Heinrich had died, she further cemented her unpopularity with the Norman elite by marrying Geoffrey of Anjou, scion of a neighboring county whom the Normans viewed as vicious barbarians, and who was barely half her age. Three sons followed in quick succession, the second labor almost killing her.

And so despite his promises, within days of Henry's death Stephen had seized the throne, having his brother Henry, Bishop of Winchester, anoint him king. The war burned slowly at first but, once ignited, erupted into all-out conflagration in 1139 when Stephen went to arrest three bishops, administrators during Henry's reign; that year Matilda, calling herself "Lady of the English," finally landed in Arundel in Sussex. Kidnappings, robberies, and murders rocketed, and local barons took the opportunity to lock people up and demand money from them, so that dungeons across the land were filled. The *Anglo-Saxon Chronicle* later lamented that "Never did a country endure more misery. If the ground was tilled the earth bore no corn, for the land was ruined by such doings; and men said openly that Christ and his saints slept. . . . we suffered nineteen years for our sins."

NOT ALL BASTARDS NEED BE DWARVES

Matilda was aided by her half-brother Robert of Gloucester, one of the most influential bastards of the era. Robert had been very close to his father and was there at his death. Matilda was also consistently supported by another of her father's illegitimate children, Reginald. Numerous real-life bastards played important roles in history, and at this time the division between legitimacy and illegitimacy was not as stark as it later would be. Royal bastards, in particular, were privileged and even got to have special coats of arms marked with a "baton sinister," a strip that runs from the bottom left. (*Sinister* is "left" in Latin. It got its current meaning from a common belief that left-handed people were "touched by the devil.")

Although Henry I's total is probably a record, Henry II had up to a dozen bastards, among them Geoffrey Plantagenet, who became Archbishop of York. Another, William Longsword, would lead his half-brother King John's ill-fated attempt to win back

Normandy in 1214. King John had five, but much later Charles II had at least fifteen, and of twenty-six English dukes today, five directly descend from Charles II's illegitimate children (among Charles's descendants are Princess Diana, Camilla Parker-Bowles, various prime ministers, and Kit Harington and Rose Leslie, better known as Jon Snow and Ygritte).[10] Robert of Gloucester himself had at least four bastards.

Another of Henry I's illegitimate daughters became the duchess of Brittany and the countess of Perche, and such children could even be included in a marriage alliance. "Bastard," though an insult, did not always signify contempt. Richard III referred to his "dear bastard" son in an affectionate way, while the greatest jouster of the 1460s was the Grand Bastard of Burgundy, son of the Duke of Burgundy, as with the Bastard of Orléans during the Hundred Years' War.

The Church's increasingly strict rules about legitimacy were partly designed toward protecting high-born wives, who were keen to have their own children inherit the land rather than their husband's other offspring. As Jon Snow knows, life for a bastard could be cruel. In Westeros, they could be legitimized only by the king, a prize offered to Snow and taken by Ramsay Bolton; in real life, the four illegitimate children of John of Gaunt by his mistress Katherine Swynford were later legitimized by Parliament and became the House of Beaufort, although their mother had by this stage married their father. And the act legitimizing them specifically said they could not inherit the throne; generally speaking, though, instances of bastards becoming legitimized heirs were very rare, since the wife's family would strongly oppose it.

Problems arose when the position of wife and mistress were confused. Lord Tytos, the father of Tywin Lannister, was widowed and gave his mistress not just gifts and honors but power too, even asking her views on the running of Lannister affairs; soon she was in charge of Lannisport. The unnamed woman, a lowborn daughter of a candlemaker, even took to wearing Tywin's mother's jewels. But after Tytos's death from a heart attack, Tywin had her expelled from Casterley Rock and confiscated her jewelery, before making her walk naked around the city "like a common whore."

Edward III was widowed after Philippa of Hainault died in 1369, by which stage he had already made Alice Perrers his mistress, the girl just fifteen when the elderly king had first taken her. The notoriously greedy Perrers, a former lady-in-waiting to the queen, came to rule over the increasingly doddery old king during a period of economic turmoil and as he became more elderly he further fell under the spell of his mistress, whom he lavished with cash, jewels, gold dresses, and fifty manors.

Although Perrers was high born, the chronicler Thomas Walsingham described her as a "shameless, impudent harlot" and stated that "she was not attractive or beautiful, but compensated for these defects by her seductive voice."[11] Walsingham believed that she employed a friar who was also a sort of warlock to make wax images of her and Edward together, with magic herbs, in order to gain power over him; whether this is true we can only guess, although the king was highly susceptible to more obvious, less supernatural female charms. She gave him three bastards, a son born before his wife even died, and two daughters. Perrers's downfall came in 1376, by which time the king was senile, when Parliament finally had her tried for corruption and banished, inventing a new device to bring one of her ministers down, called impeachment (since abandoned in England but still used in the United States).

Similarly Edward's grandson Henry IV was also widowed after his wife Mary de Bohun had borne him four sons and a daughter; she died giving birth to their youngest, Philippa. Henry took a second wife, Joan of Navarre, but after the king's death his heir Henry V arrested his stepmother on charges of sorcery and employing a necromancer, a magician who communicates with the dead, and she was imprisoned in Leeds Castle. Although a religious fanatic, the king's motives were certainly to some extent financial, as Joan's personal fortune of six thousand pounds was enormous.

THE DANCE OF THE DRAGON

Most of the fighting during the Anarchy took place in the Thames valley, the rich swathe of land between London and the west country, and mostly concerned the taking of castles, often by stealth or cunning, but sometimes through sheer brutality.

In 1139, when Stephen wished to capture Devizes castle from its lady-owner, yet another Matilda, he took captive her lover Bishop Roger of Salisbury and their son, former chancellor Roger the Poor; he brought Bishop Roger in chains and had gallows built outside and threatened to hang the younger Roger before the walls. A rope was put around the former chancellor's neck and he was led to the gallows, at which point his mother immediately surrendered, shouting "I gave him birth, and it can never be right for me to cause his destruction."[12] Afterwards Bishop Roger was a broken man and retired from affairs; the younger Roger went into exile and was ruined, thus his enduring nickname.

On another occasion, Stephen captured Shrewsbury castile and hanged the entire garrison of ninety-three men and its commander, Arnulf de Hesdin—that he was still considered unduly merciful tells us something about the time.

Stephen also approached Malmesbury, the castle controlled by a mercenary captain, Robert fitz Hubert, "a man of great cruelty and unequalled in wickedness and crime."[13] Fitz Hubert boasted that he once roasted alive eighty monks in a church and "would do so again," according to William of Malmesbury, who also claimed he smeared prisoners with honey and left them in the midday sun to be attacked by insects. This time, though, fitz Hubert surrendered to the royal army on the advice of a relative.

Later, fitz Hubert attacked John Le Marechal and tried to force his submission, but Le Marechal captured him instead, demanded he hand over Devizes and when he refused, simply hanged him. Some barons changed sides to suit whoever was winning; one, Ranulf, Earl of Chester, switched sides seven times during the conflict. He was the son-in-law of Robert of Gloucester, his wife, of course, being yet another Matilda.

In 1141, the major battle of the Anarchy took place at Lincoln when Stephen laid siege to the city's castle; however Ranulf (then on Matilda's side) had escaped to Chester and appealed to Robert of Gloucester and together they marched east "with a dreadful and unendurable mass of Welsh." During the battle Stephen at first fought with a sword, with his "terrible arm," but after intense fighting his weapon broke and someone passed him a battle axe. He continued to struggle "like a lion, grinding his teeth and foaming at the mouth like a boar" until eventually he was captured "by the just judgement of God"; up to five hundred men drowned trying to cross the river to escape, more than the amount that died in the actual battle.

Stephen was later released in return for Robert of Gloucester, and so Matilda missed her chance to win the war. Soon afterwards London's leaders turned against her and she was forced to flee from the enraged city folk.

IF YOU THINK THIS HAS A HAPPY ENDING, YOU HAVEN'T BEEN PAYING ATTENTION.

The common people of Westeros are often faced with the horror of rampaging armies, with the burning of farms and killing of cattle, as well as the rape and murder that went with it, unable to attract the ransom money that protected aristocrats. As in Westeros so in England during the Anarchy, which saw a number of extremely cruel noblemen, "irresponsible and undisciplined desperadoes," in the words of the noted historian A.L. Poole.[14] Among them were Thomas de Marle, who Benedictine Abbot Guibert called "the wickedest man of his generation." He turned up at convents and stole nuns, tortured men by hanging them from their testicles until they were torn off, personally cut the throat of thirty townspeople in one rebellion, and turned his castles into "a nest of dragons and a cave of thieves."[15] He was eventually excommunicated, and an anathema was read out against him every week in his local parish, but later he died in his bed, leaving a generous amount of money to the Church.

Henry of Huntingdon says that during the Anarchy many lords put their peasants in prison and used

> indescribable torture to extort gold and silver . . . They were hung by the thumbs or by the head, and chains were hung on their feet. Knotted ropes were put round their heads and twisted till they penetrated to the brains. They put them in prisons where there were adders and snakes and toads, and killed them like that. Some they put in a torture chamber, that is in a chest which was short, narrow and not deep, and they put sharp stones in and pressed the man in it so that he had all his limbs broken.[16]

Chains were "fastened to a beam, and they used to put a sharp iron around a man's throat and neck so that he could not sit or lie or sleep in any direction."[17]

One known victim was a skinner from Pontefract in Yorkshire, tortured in order to get money, then kept with his hands chained behind his back and legs in wooden stocks at Selby Castle. Another, a little boy, was left as a hostage by his father and kept in fetters, while a woman was kept as surety for her husband owing six pounds and when he was only able to send nine pence, the knight who held her captive threatened to cut off her breasts and left her chained outside at night half-naked in winter. One victim was suspended by his feet and hands with mail-coats used to weigh him down and held above smoky fires and plunged beneath icy waters in winter. A squire called Martin was so tortured by two knights over the alleged theft of fifteen marks that he seized a pair of scissors from a seamstress and stabbed himself in the heart.

The launch of the Second Crusade in 1147 had eased the fighting somewhat; Matilda fled from Oxford two years later, escaping by rope from an open window and crossing the frozen river; she and her four companions were camouflaged in white against the snow. She never returned to England, and by now most of her supporters were dead, including her brother Robert. However, the war was continued by her son Henry Fitzempress who, in 1153, only seventeen or eighteen, attacked Malmesbury castle, having earlier tried to attack Stephen when barely out of his teens.

That year Stephen approached Wallingford, his son Eustace alongside him, where they engaged the enemy. "Eustace was already showing abilities as a knight though his beard had hardly begun to grow,"[18] but Stephen was thrown three times from his horse during the skirmish and was shaken by the ordeal. He was showing weariness, and that year the two sides had finally begun to negotiate; Stephen and Henry met, where "both complained bitterly of the disloyalty of their nobles,"[19] and it was suggested that Stephen would remain king but adopt Henry as his heir. Stephen controlled most of England and Henry the continental possessions, but the Anglo-Norman aristocracy would not accept a partition, so a compromise had to be reached; and from Stephen's point of view anything could happen—indeed Henry was seriously ill that year.

For Stephen's young heir it must have appeared a surrender and betrayal, and the Anarchy provided the inspiration for one of the most famous scenes in Martin's series. When the barons sued for peace with Henry Fitzempress, the notorious Eustace ravaged East Anglia; he arrived at the abbey of Bury St Edmunds, wrecked the lands when it refused his extortion, and then dined in its refectory, where he choked to death. As Martin told *Entertainment Weekly*: "I based it a little on the death of Eustace, the son of King Stephen of England . . . Eustace choked to death at a feast. People are still debating a thousand of years later: Did he choke to death or was he poisoned? Because by removing Eustace, it brought about a peace that ended the English civil war."[20]

Although the whereabouts and circumstances of Eustace's death remain a mystery, the *Peterborough Chronicle* recorded "He was an evil man and did more harm than good wherever he went; he spoiled the lands and laid thereon heavy taxes."[21] Or as Olenna Tyrell might put it, "he really was a cunt, wasn't he?"

On the day of Eustace's death, young Henry Fitzempress's wife Eleanor of Aquitaine gave birth to their first child, a boy. The game had shifted undeniably in Matilda's favor, while his heir's death seemed to destroy Stephen's will to fight, and now sick with a stomach ailment that would kill him within a year he formalized the treaty and agreed to pass the throne to Henry. After all this time Matilda's line would win, and the House of Plantagenet would rule for over three centuries.

As for five-year-old William, son of the Marshal—the king, pitying the innocent young boy, could not go through with his threat and took him into his care. The monarch, despite the pressure, had drawn back from committing such an appalling act, and Stephen and William were later seen that day playing at knights and laughing together. Although "such tender heartedness in a monarch was almost as little admired as John Marshal's brutality,"[22] Stephen did the realm a great favor. The boy would live to be an old man, William Marshal serving three kings and becoming the most famous knight in history, the embodiment of chivalry, and eventually regent of England (and the model for Ser Barristan Selmy). Most importantly to us, he also played a central part in saving and enshrining that most famous and important of legal agreements, Magna Carta.

27
A GOLDEN CROWN

Laughing. Drinking. Boasting. Those were the things he was best at.
Those, and fighting.

—Stannis on Robert Baratheon

C harles's insanity had by now driven France into two factions, one led by his pleasure-loving brother Louis de Valois, Duke of Orléans, and the other by a cousin—Philippe the Bold, Duke of Burgundy. After years of simmering tensions, the conflict escalated on November 23, 1407 when fifteen masked men in the pay of Duke Philippe and his son Jean "the Fearless" had attacked Louis of Orléans in Paris, stabbing him to death. After Louis's eldest son, Charles, forged an alliance with his father-in-law Bernard, Count of Armagnac, the two factions became known as the Burgundians and Armagnacs.

It so happened that England was now ruled by a religious fanatic who was also a military genius. Henry V was the virtual opposite of his Shakespearean character—humorless, ruthless, and religiously devout—and yet he was an inspiring leader who people followed. With his pudding bowl haircut, he resembled a monk more than a king, and in the first eight years of his reign had no physical contact with women. Already possessing great military experience when he came to the throne, as a young man Henry had learned the dirty trade of war in Wales where he had his own canon called "The Messenger" which he used to keep order in that rebellious land. He had also taken part in a skirmish in France, between the two factions, and acquired a taste for bloodshed there; his father, the sick old king, was opposed to any further involvement in France, leading to a fall out, and although father and son were eventually reconciled, the prematurely old man was already fading.

As monarch, Henry V faced the same dynastic uncertainty as his predecessor and two years into his reign there was yet another conspiracy—there had been at least six against the previous king—this one called the Southampton Plot. The aim was to overthrow Henry and have him replaced with Edmund Mortimer, son of the unfortunate Roger who had died in 1398, and nephew of the Edmund Mortimer who had joined Glyndŵr and Percy. The conspiracy involved a group of men entangled by marriage; the ringleader was Thomas Grey, who sat on the King's Council, and whose son was betrothed to the daughter of Richard, Earl of Cambridge, another conspirator. Cambridge, the son of Edward III's youngest son Edmund of York, was a cousin of the king and also the widower of Mortimer's sister Anne.

Edmund Mortimer had been born into dynastic conflict, on both sides of the family. His maternal uncle Thomas Holland, Duke of Surrey, had been killed in 1400 trying to free Richard II from prison, but the nephew had no such stomach for treason and now informed King Henry of the plot. All the conspirators were executed, but Mortimer received little reward for his loyalty. Two years later he was given a papal dispensation to marry a "fit woman," Anne Stafford, who was also his second cousin, but this angered King Henry who refused to give back his cousin's lands, even when he reached adulthood; he died without children in 1425.

Richard, Earl of Cambridge had left one son, four-year-old Richard, who would one day launch the rebellion against the mad king—the son of the man who killed his father.

That same year Henry V reignited the war with France, a country now perilously weak due to internal strife. Charles had appointed his son the Dauphin as Duke of Aquitaine in 1402, a slight to King Henry, and even though the Gascons remained loyal to the English crown; the House of Valois was determined to insult the House of Lancaster, whom they openly declared to be illegitimate. The conflict was also made more likely by the inability of the Church to meditate, overwhelmed by its own problems. In an attempt to end the Great Schism in which two men claimed to be popes, in 1409 a Church council met in Pisa; their solution was to depose the Avignon pope Benedict XIII *and* the Roman pope Gregory XII and instead elect a new, neutral pontiff, Alexander V. However, neither of the other men accepted this and so there were now three popes walking around.

Upon ascending the throne, Henry V signed a treaty with the Armagnac faction, who recognized his lordship over the regions of Poitou, Angouleme, and Perigord. However, in 1415 he also insisted on Normandy, Maine, Anjou, Brittany, and Touraine, the lands that had constituted the empire of his ancestor Henry II some two and a half centuries prior. When it was refused, as it inevitably would be, he prepared an invasion. In October 1415, Henry won a spectacular victory at Agincourt, destroying a French force perhaps six times as large as his own. Once again, the archers proved decisive, overwhelming the disorganized French cavalry who were bogged down in muck, many crushed to death under a pile of bodies, some even drowning in mud. The king was almost struck with an axe during the fighting, but according to one story was saved by Edward of York, brother of Cambridge, the man he had recently beheaded. Agincourt was perhaps the most spectacular military victory in the country's history, the English casualties totalling only 120 dead, against as many as 10,000 Frenchmen.[1]

These figures include the execution of several hundred French prisoners, ordered by the king himself as he feared attack from the rear, a sordid but perhaps necessary act that broke the rules of war. The highest-ranking English casualty of the day was Edward of York, who most likely died of a heart attack in his armor, but because of his gallantry his young nephew Richard was allowed to inherit his title.

Henry, after a terrible journey back at sea, eventually returned home to glory where in London wine flowed from the city's water pipes, a recent innovation, as the country celebrated a God-given victory. But away from the revelling the reality of the fighting, where so many men suffocated below the piles of bodies, or had their throats cut by Welsh mountain men, was horror. And what followed was even worse. Throughout 1417 the English besieged Caen in Normandy and, when the city fell on September 4, there was appalling violence, with rape, looting, and slaughter.

Then in 1418-1419 came Rouen, downstream on the river Seine, where the English king deliberately starved the inhabitants, refusing to allow several thousand hungry civilians to pass the lines, instead letting them die in the ditch between besiegers and besieged. Henry hanged prisoners in front of the city walls, and when he took the city its survivors were described as looking like the skeletons of funeral effigies. Afterward, Henry took part in an extended religious ceremony and gave a meal to every citizen who had defied him all that time. Several more cities in Normandy suffered the same fate, with prisoners hanged and civilians starved relentlessly. The country was once again overrun by *routiers*, or "rutters," groups of armed soldiers-cum-bandits, although King Henry at least placed some limits on the amount his troops could rob from the French, and he made efforts to prevent his troops from drinking, aware of what this could bring.

Despite the horror in Normandy, France's leading aristocrats hated each other too much to do anything. On September 10, 1419, Jean the Fearless, the Duke of Burgundy and leader of one faction, walked onto a bridge over the River Yonne for a meeting with the Dauphin Charles when the barriers closed behind him and on a pre-arranged signal he was cut down by Armagnac men. After this murder by trickery there could be no peace between the two French factions now, and Jean's successor Philippe now allied formally with Henry, offering him the crown. At Troyes on May 21, 1420 a peace was made, providing for marriage between Henry and Catherine, the daughter of the Mad King Charles, to the exclusion of her brother, the Dauphin. The poor king did not even know who Henry was, this man who had come to destroy his land and deny his son his patrimony.

And so Catherine Valois watched in December 1420 as her brother was formally disinherited, and on February 1 she set sail for England to prepare for her coronation. Here eels, prawns, shrimp, trout, and salmon were served, meat being prohibited during Lent, and for the honeymoon Henry took her to the siege of nearby Sens where he romantically ordered for musicians to play for her every evening as night fell around the starving city. Meanwhile Henry went to recuperate in English-controlled Paris, now witnessing a bitterly cold winter, the coldest anyone could remember. As the corpses multiplied, wolves were seen swimming across the river to feed on the human meat and desperate men turned houses into firewood.

The fanatical English king had brought horror to northern France, but his feats would become immortalized in Shakespeare's *Henry V*, part of the Henriad series that also told the stories of Richard II, and Henry IV. The play *Henry IV*, in particular, invented the character of Young Hal, a prince who was riotous and boozy and fun, great drama that had little relation to real life. Among those it inspired were George R.R. Martin, who based Robert Baratheon partly on one of Shakespeare's characters, Falstaff—the later King Robert, as Jon Snow puts it, "a fat man, red-faced under his beard, sweating through his silks" who "walked like a man half in his cups."[2]

Falstaff is a comic figure who nonetheless expresses some hard truths, perhaps more cutting because he is a drunk and a coward. He spends his time with thieves and rascals in the Boar's Head Inn in Eastcheap, a real tavern in the city of London at the time of Shakespeare, although perhaps not yet during the life of King Henry. Falstaff was based on the real historical figure Sir John Oldcastle, a friend of Henry V who was imprisoned because of his heretical beliefs. Oldcastle had fought with

Henry IV against Owain Glyndŵr and become a member of Parliament and later High Sheriff of Herefordshire. His third marriage, to Joan of Cobham, a wealthy three-time widow, had also brought him numerous manors across the country and from 1409 he was styled as Lord Cobham.

However, by 1410 Oldcastle had accepted Lollardy. The Lollards were a heretical group who arose after the Black Death and were attacked because they used to "make and write books" and "wickedly instruct and inform people." Led by John Wycliffe, an Oxford theologian, the Lollards believed that the Catholic Church needed to return to the scriptures rather than follow the hierarchy in Rome. Members of the sect began translating parts of the bible—at the time forbidden—and Wycliffe had himself transcribed large parts of it. They called themselves Wycliffites, the name Lollards being an insult, either from their habit of mumbling or a generic term for an uneducated person who could speak English but not French or Latin. Although tolerated at first, after the Peasants' Revolt in 1381 and the threat of Wycliffe's increasingly radical ideas, these aristocratic supporters melted away.

Lollards had also condemned luxury and believed that the Church had become corrupt. They had a point, of course, but there was also something fanatical in their beliefs that alarmed many people and offered the promise of future violence. After the Brethren of the Cross had imploded, the Lollards were one of several new groups that contained the zealotry of the Sparrows or the Faith Militant, especially its desire for a return to early religious simplicity. The phrase Faith Militant is borrowed from Church Militant—*Ecclesia Militans*—which is less confrontational than it sounds, but rather a concept whereby Christians are divided between three different groups: those still struggling on earth, the Church Militant; the Church Triumphant, that is those already in heaven; and the Church Penitent, those in purgatory. The phrase denotes the concept that to be a good Christian is a struggle, similar to the inner *jihad* of Islam, which also carries unfortunate connotations to most people.

Another heretical group, the Hussites of Bohemia, launched an armed rebellion starting with the 1419 "Defenstration of Prague," wherein they threw their Catholic rulers out of windows. Defenstration is a particular Czech tradition, this being only the first of three such events in their history where the leaders there were thrown out of windows.

Faced with growing religious discontent, the authorities across Europe were becoming less tolerant. In 1401, Parliament had passed *De Haeretico Comburendo*

(On Burning Heretics), which introduced burning at the stake for the first time; in 1410, tailor John Badby became the first layman executed for heresy. Oldcastle was charged with the crime in 1413 but was initially saved by his friendship with the new king; the zealously Catholic Henry, even as he escalated the persecution, tried to persuade his old friend to recant, but to no effect.

Nothing could be done to persuade him, so the king asked for forty days respite, during which time Oldcastle escaped, and now on the run plotted to overthrow Henry, arrest the royal family, and replace the system of government so that the monarch was restrained by the leading knights, a plan considerably ahead of its time. He was captured on the Welsh borders in November 1417 and the following month in St Giles's Field he was hanged and roasted in chains as he swung from a gibbet, promising to rise on the third day (he didn't).

It is believed that Shakespeare had originally called his character Oldcastle but that the Oldcastle family of his time had objected to the louche portrayal of their ancestor. Oldcastle's Tudor descendent Henry Brook, eleventh Baron Cobham, was a powerful man, holding the title of Lord Warden of the Cinque Ports (like his ancestor, he'd end up in jail for plotting against the king, in this case James I). To make matters more complicated, the character of Falstaff was also partly based on Brook or Brook's father William, the tenth baron, who was a common figure of satire in the period and also appeared in a Ben Jonson play. And by the time the Henriad was being made, Henry Brook was father-in-law to secretary-of-state Robert Cecil, the second most powerful person in England, so Shakespeare was forced to change it. Instead it became Falstaff, after Sir John Fastolf, another soldier of the time who had fought in the Hundred Years War, but who was in every way unlike the Shakespearean fool; indeed he was a cunning and tough old soldier known for his bravery.[3] And Shakespeare's play contains puns on the name "old castle" which would only make sense if it was written with that name in mind.

Henry and Catherine's marriage was soon blessed with a son, christened Henry and destined to be king of England and France. The messianic king was now avidly studying maps of Palestine and reading about the Crusades; still only thirty-five, he had conquered vast amounts of territory, founded a dynasty to rule both England and France, and, with three brothers beside him, seemed unassailable.

And yet fortune's wheel was always turning, and the biggest killer of the war was neither the longbow nor the sword, but the bloody flux, as dysentery was called. Now in May 1422, on campaign in Meaux, the king contracted the illness. Lingering in bed, it soon became clear to his followers that he would not make it, and he died in August, followed a month later by the King of France.

After the king's death his brother John, Duke of Bedford, was declared regent with particular focus on the war in France while youngest Humphrey, Duke of Gloucester, became lord protector and guardian to his nephew, the infant Henry VI. (The second oldest brother, Thomas, had been killed months before Henry.) And yet from the start of Henry's long and tragic reign there was bitter factionalism; Gloucester had hoped to become regent but in the inevitable power struggle this was denied him by his many enemies, chief among them his uncle, Henry Beaufort, bishop of Winchester.

Resistance to English rule continued in France. In 1424, the disinherited Charles of France, son of the last king and referred to by the English as "he who calls himself the dauphin," raised an army—a mixture of French, Scottish, Spanish, and Lombards, the latter the most feared soldiers in Europe largely on account of their Milan-made armor and their powerful horses. However in 1424 the English won yet another great victory, at Verneuil. They were led by Thomas Montagu, Earl of Salisbury, at thirty-six one of the most famous soldiers in Christendom. Despite the absence of their king, the English still had the advantage in warfare with their archers. Although plate armor could now withstand the most advanced arrow fire, the sheer volume of missiles caused soldiers to cluster in the center and disrupt their formation. As the French began to flee from the field their Scots allies found themselves outnumbered two to one, and since they had rejected quarter before the battle they had to fight to the death, the carnage ending with not one Scot left alive. Among the seven thousand French and Scots troops killed were the earls of Buchan and the veteran Archibald Douglas, having lost an eye and then a testicle and finally his life at the hands of the English.

By late 1428 the English were outside Orléans, south of Paris on the river Loire and a crucial junction offering control of France's largest river; the English controlled the west and the Burgundians the north and if the Duke of Bedford's forces could take the city then all French resistance would collapse. Bedford was opposed to besieging Orléans, thinking it could not be taken, but was persuaded otherwise by military commander Thomas Montagu. Montagu's father had been executed for plotting against Henry IV, but the young earl had had most of his father's lands returned before joining Henry V in his campaign in 1415. He was one of the most respected soldiers of the war, as well as being immensely wealthy.

A lengthy siege followed, now led by William de la Pole, the thirty-two-year-old Earl of Suffolk and grandson of Richard II's crony. By the end of October, after prolonged and vicious fighting, the besiegers had captured part of the bridge and the city looked doomed.

So the English were completely unprepared for what happened next. Late in February in Chinon, where the neurotic pretender Charles was holed up, now in desperate trouble, six armed men arrived with a curious looking young girl, dressed as a boy, with hair cut short and a fierce determination in her eyes. To the French she was a savior, a virgin who would liberate them from her occupation; to her enemies she was a witch who could only be cleansed with fire. They called her "the Maid," but she is better known today as Joan of Arc.

28

"I AM A KNIGHT, I SHALL DIE A KNIGHT"

I've burned away my years fighting for terrible kings . . . a man of honor
keeps his vows—even if he's serving a drunk or a lunatic.

—SER BARRISTAN SELMY

Childhood was short, and adolescence is a modern idea. Children were married at twelve and were ready to join the world of men and women. At that age John Marshal's fourth son William had been sent away from his Wiltshire home to live with relatives in Normandy, which must have dented an otherwise loving father-son bond. William trained as a knight first under his mother's cousin, William de Tancareville, and then her brother Patrick of Salisbury, a rival landowner to John Marshal who was also a star of tournaments. William Marshal would grow up in Chateauroux in Berry, a lawless part of central France desired both by the House of Capet and the Plantagenets, but controlled by a troublesome family, the Lusignans of Poitou.

Earl Patrick had gone into service with Eleanor, Queen of England, but in 1168 was killed by the Lusignans, and the twenty-one-year-old Marshal found himself without a patron or income. Being a younger son, William had no money and so instead he made his living as a professional jouster, earning a fortune by taking the armor of his defeated opponents. At a tournament at Eu in Normandy in 1178 or 1179 Marshal seized ten victims; over a ten-year period, he and a partner captured 103 knights, earning a huge fortune, and so his fame spread. Indeed, Marshal even employed a servant called Henry Norreis whose job it was to go around proclaiming his celebrity, a sort of medieval PR man.

Over the course of his career Marshal became a heroic benchmark of knighthood, the man others compared themselves to, just as people in Westeros talk of Arthur

Dayne, the Sword of the Morning, or Ser Barristan Selmy, "Barristan the Bold," the "greatest knight in Westerosi history."

But he was lucky to have such a patron in Queen Eleanor, who found employment for him in the service of her eldest son Henry, eight years his junior; the two became as close as brothers, even as Henry went to war with his real family. Eleanor was the most impressive woman of the period—a schemer, and later a politician-grandmother— but in her youth she was the most desired lady in Christendom. After presenting King Henry with eight children she moved onto to become a patron of the arts and a diplomat well into her seventies.* Eleanor was the ultimate mother-politician, indeed grandmother-politician, respected across Europe as a tough and powerful figure; but she was also a poisoner, most likely eliminating Rosamund, her husband's mistress.[1] She also had a monster of a son who she defended, however murderous and cowardly his behavior.

To the north of Iberia and to the south of the Frankish heartland the region of Aquitaine long retained a distinctive culture, as well as its own language. It was also the home of courtly love and romance. Like the Reach, its people were "brave, gallant and susceptible to the charms of women," and proud of their region's great fertility and its wine. Aquitaine is supplied by two giant rivers flowing into the Atlantic to the west, the Loire at its northern frontier and the Gironde further south, on the banks of which are vineyards producing the most expensive wine on earth.

The language of the south, the *lenga d'oc* or Occitan, so called because southern- ers said *oc* where northerners say *oui*, is distinctive enough even to an untrained English speaker. A study by linguist Mario Pei in 1949 comparing the degrees to which Romance languages differed from Latin found that Italian was 12 percent different to Latin and Occitan just 25 percent, while for French the figure is 44 per- cent. (Sardinian was the closest to Latin.) This division between the north and south of France remained pronounced until recently.

The south of France had come under the domination of the north, but the cultural influences flowed the other way, too, particularly the romantic tradition of Aquitaine expressed through its poems.

Duke Guilhèm (William) IX of Aquitaine (1071–1127) was "one of the most courtly men in the world and one of the greatest deceivers of women. He was a fine

---

*In this case very similar to Olenna Tyrell, the elderly matriarch.

knight at arms, liberal in his attentions to ladies, and an accomplished composer and singer of songs. For a long time, he roved the world, bent on the deception of ladies'"[2] Like the Moors of Spain, the men of Aquitaine wrote love poetry, Guilhèm's including one about pretending to be deaf-mute so he could visit the wives of "lords Guarin and Bernard."

Guilhèm's granddaughter Eleanor was in turn married to the two most powerful men in western Europe, King Louis of France and then the much younger Henry of England. By doing so she helped introduce the *troubador* tradition to both countries.

Eleanor and Louis's marriage proved explosive, and only got worse after he took her on crusade where, it was rumored, she began a romance with her dashing uncle Ramon. By the time the royal couple were journeying back to Europe she was already threatening him with annulment. Despite their two daughters—who could not inherit the throne—the Church agreed to dissolve their marriage, and on her way back home she agreed to a match with the Empress Matilda's son Henry—at nineteen, a whole decade her junior.*

As disastrous as her first marriage was, her second was arguably worse. Henry II was a highly intelligent man but renowned for his temper, appetite, and lust; his reign was marred by conflict, first with the Archbishop of Canterbury, Thomas Becket, and later with his four surviving legitimate sons Henry, Richard, Geoffrey, and John, who spent a turbulent decade and a half fighting their father and each other. The true-born sons were encouraged in this rebellion by their mother, who was imprisoned by her husband for sixteen years; after Henry's death in 1189 Eleanor enjoyed huge political power in her old age. Henry was also close to one of his bastard sons, Geoffrey of York, who remained loyal to his father even as his other sons rebelled.

During Henry II's reign the first proper legal records began, the birth of a civil service, and later the government would settle permanently in Westminster; yet throughout this period, and for much longer, the court was mobile, travelling from one part of the kingdom to another, much to the dread of the people, for just as in Westeros royal entourages always brought misery with them.

---

*Eleanor's daughter Marie of Champagne would later commission *Lancelot, the Knight of the Cart* by Chretien of Troyes. This poem was the first to mention the love affair between Lancelot and Lady Guinevere.

Accounts from one castle from June 1293 record the arrival of the king's nephews: "There came to dinner John of Brabant, with 30 horses and 24 valets, and the two sons of the Lord Edmund, and they stay at our expenses in all things in hay, oats and wages." Four days later it only reports, sadly, *Morantur*—they remain. A few days later and the record laments: "They remain until now, and this is an onerous day."[3]

Edward I made 2,891 journeys during his reign, a move every four days, and his son made 1,458.[4] The king would travel with a great entourage in tow, which included not just the Lord High Steward and Lord Great Chamberlain but also such characters as the Keepers of the Cups and of the Dishes, the Master Steward of the Larder, Usher of the Spithouse, Chamberlain of the Candles, Keeper of the Gazehounds, Cat Hunters and Wolf Catchers and Keepers of the Tents, as well as bakers, butlers, grooms, and servants. As the king approached a castle, men were sent ahead to remove unwelcome elements, including prostitutes and "laundresses and gamesters," petitioners, and people with lawsuits.

The House of Anjou fought amongst themselves relentlessly. Henry's younger brother Geoffrey had tried to abduct Eleanor after her divorce from Louis VII and three years later he rebelled against his brother once again; in the end Henry paid his brother £1,500 a year to submit, but luckily, he died soon after. Now Henry and Eleanor's eldest, Henry, had grown frustrated with his lack of power, and in 1172 father and son fell out publicaly and, to the old king's surprise and horror, young Henry took up arms against him. Escaping with his knights, young Henry offered his men the opportunity to head back to the old king; some did so, but Marshal was one of those who continued to ride with Henry, both men putting their futures in danger as traitors. The rebellion may have been encouraged by Eleanor.

Now Richard and his brother Geoffrey began to make trouble. Richard, although lacking his elder brother's glamor, had a ruthless streak and a military genius than even in his mid-teens was taking shape. The two boys, aged just sixteen and fifteen, rose in armed rebellion against their father in 1178, supported by Eleanor and the Scots, who rolled across the border; Henry's bastard son Geoffrey went north to fight off the invaders, and the Scots king was captured near Alnwick. "My other sons are the real bastards," the king told Geoffrey afterward.

Although the rebellion was defeated and Eleanor imprisoned, the following decade war broke out again; father and son were close to peace when the young Henry caught a fever while plundering a shrine in southwest France in 1183. Surrounded by his retinue of knights, including William Marshal, Henry died holding a ring his father had sent him as a token of forgiveness. For Marshal it was a devastating loss, but he also now found himself in a precarious position, a rebel against the rightful king. Before he had died Henry had entrusted his friend to go on crusade for the sake of his soul; Marshal approached the old king and, swearing homage, asked his leave to carry out his son's final wishes. Impressed by the young knight's devotion and honor, King Henry granted Marshal permission to travel to Palestine, assuring the young knight he would find a place for him on his return.

Eleanor's son Geoffrey followed his brother to the grave three years later, trampled to death during a tournament, yet another victim of the sport. The king's woes did not end there though, for his attempts to persuade his heir Richard to hand Aquitaine to his brother John provoked another rebellion. With his mother, Richard joined forces with the young King Philippe of France against the king in a war far more bitter than anything that came before.

The two sides agreed to peace talks at Le Mans, where Richard and Philippe were shocked by the enfeebled state of the old king, who resembled an elderly man although only in his early fifties. Henry was feverish and shivering with cold; Philippe offered him a blanket which the old king refused. In front of everyone Henry and his son embraced, and the old king whispered in his ear: "God spare me long enough to take revenge on you." Between the two armies, in no man's land, Richard—not wearing any armor—stumbled across Marshal, and the knight charged straight at him. Richard screamed "By God's legs, Marshall, do not kill me! That would be wrong, I am unarmed!" At the last moment Marshal instead plunged his lance into Richard's horse, spitting out "let the devil kill you, for I won't."

The peace of Le Mans was a trick. A few miles back from the meeting point Richard and Philippe were preparing for an assault on their enemy as he made his way back. The king's health was waning, and it was clear to all around him that soon power would reside with Richard; Henry's supporters began to melt away, and the old man was left with a shrinking band of knights to protect him. But Marshal stood firm.

The two sides met again in the summer, when Henry demanded that his son show him a list of those now in rebellion; as he was read the first name he replied that he needed to hear no more, for at the top of the list was his youngest and favorite son, John. Broken-hearted, Henry surrendered to Philip in July 1189 and expired two days later from a brain haemorrhage. The only son to stay by the king at his deathbed was his bastard Geoffrey.

Henry's son became Richard I, called "the Lionheart" on account of his courage, and one of his first acts was to call for William Marshal. In his final months the old king had rewarded Marshal for his loyalty with the hand of Isabel de Clare; she was the daughter of Richard de Clare—or "Strongbow," the Anglo-Norman warlord who had conquered Ireland—and his Irish wife, and Isabel came with most of south Wales and eastern Ireland.

Many men in that position would have hanged Marshal on the spot but Richard forgave him, as well as all who stood loyal to his father. He sent Marshal to England to maintain order there and free his mother. The new king also allowed the marriage to go ahead and Marshal, now in his mid-forties, headed to London to claim his sixteen-year-old bride, all of a sudden one of the largest landowners in the west.

Richard's friendship with King Philippe, however, turned into a bitter rivalry. The Lionheart spent most of his reign on crusade, where after a brilliant series of victories he fell out with Philippe and Leopold of Austria. This feud led to Richard being held captive in Germany, in exchange for which English taxpayers had to raise a "king's ransom" or thirty-four tons of gold, the equivalent of four years' national expenditure.

During his imprisonment, Richard's brother John revolted against his rule, in alliance with Philippe of France, but when the king arrived back in March 1194, he forgave his brother, left almost immediately to return to fighting. However, in 1199, in Limousin, southwest France, a cook armed with a crossbow took aim at Richrd during the siege of a small castle. The king stood posing to mock the sniper, a young boy who was using a saucepan as a shield. Despite wearing no armor himself, Richard applauded his first shot; the boy fired again and hit the king in the left shoulder; fatally, as it turned out.

Even the smallest of wounds in battle could prove to be lethal before the medical breakthroughs of the nineteenth century, and gangrene, or green rot, claimed a large number of lives; in the Lionheart's case the wound was not that serious, but the removal of the arrow was botched. Having spent his entire adult life in battle, he would have seen the rot take many men and knew his fate.

The peasant claimed that Richard had killed his father and two brothers, but as a last act of chivalry, the dying king pardoned him and asked that he be released after his death. Afterwards, however, Richard's chief mercenary Mercadier, had the boy flayed alive.

"TRULY A LITTLE SHIT"

In *Game of Thrones*, the minstrel Marillion writes a bawdy ballad about Robert, the boar, and "the lion in the kings' bed," a reference to Jaime's cuckolding of the king, and so Joffrey has one of his men rip out the man's tongue.[5] Although Henry I did actually have a minstrel blinded for singing a critical song, the king who most matches Joffrey's cruelty, cowardice, and lack of political sense is Richard's brother John, who inherited the throne upon his brother's sudden death; on one occasion he punished a pathetic old "rustic" who had prophesized his downfall by having him and his son torn to pieces by horses.

One of the few known events of John's childhood involves the game of chess, which had been brought to Christian Europe by the eleventh century, most likely via Spain. Chess was, surprisingly, quite a violent pastime, in that there are numerous recorded incidents of brutal fights breaking out over the game, which then featured very heavy pieces that would hurt if used as a weapon. During one game, Bauduin, illegitimate son of a nobleman called Ogier, "is said to have received such a violent blow with a rook" from another player "that both his eyes flew out of his head."[6] The chronicler Alexander Neckam recorded that during chess matches "insults are frequently uttered and the game does not maintain the dignity of a serious occupation but degenerates into a brawl." Among the advice Neckam offered to aristocrats was: "If you lose money playing at dice or chess, do not let anger plant savage rage in your heart." It was wisdom John did not heed. As a child he had been playing chess with a Fulk FitzWarin during which he "took the chess board and struck Fulk a great blow with it," very seriously injuring him.[7]

John was violent and a letch, merciless and cruel, and broke every promise he made. Two leading barons accused him of sexual crimes against a wife and daughter respectively, while he even tried to seduce the wife of his half-brother while he rotted in a French jail.

He was also a drunk and kept a vast stock of wine to fit out his fifty castles. In 1201, King John's stock of wine at Southampton featured 105 tuns of Poitevin wine, 143 tuns of Angevin wine, and 150 tuns from Le Blanc in Indre. But then this was not unusual at the time, since most people would have drunk several pints of beer a day and, if they were wealthy, wine too. Court rolls—which appeared fully in Henry II's time—invariably mention alcohol in many crimes and accidents. And Richard fitz Neal, a churchman in the service of Henry, wrote that crime in England was generally explained by "the drunkenness, which is inborn in the inhabitants."[8]

A contemporary, Geoffrey de Vinsauf, who despite his name was English, wrote of "that drinker, England" (Anglia potatrix).[9] Indeed, local government since Saxon times had entirely revolved around beer sessions, with each parish having a guild-house (a drinking house) where decisions were made. The common assembly house was identified as "an assembly of drinkers," and this might not have been an entirely terrible thing, since there is some research linking alcohol and high levels of trust in a society.[10] In medieval Paris, where the English comprised one-third of all students, they were famous for heavy drinking; described as "most discerning . . . outstanding for their manners, elegant in speech and in appearance, strong in intelligence and wise in their advice" and yet having three failings, women, "Weisheil" and "Drincheil" the latter two being toasts.[11]

Alcohol consumption in Europe fell considerably from the seventeenth century, with the advent of coffee, tea, and better access to clean water, and aside from events such as London's gin epidemic, the overall trend has been downward.[12]

John had deserted his first wife to take twelve-year-old Isabella of Angouleme, which came as a surprise to her fiancé Hugh de Lusignan. The wronged man appealed to his lord, Philippe of France, who demanded that John appear before him; when he failed to show up Philippe declared his lands in France, including all of Normandy, Brittany, and Anjou, forfeited. At the same time John's nephew Arthur, his brother's posthumous son, went to war with him.

And so, in 1200 Eleanor found herself, alongside notorious mercenary captain Mercadier—the flayer—besieging her own grandson Arthur in western France. She was now seventy-six, but in the ensuing peace treaty, in which King Philippe's twelve-year-old son Louis was to marry one of her granddaughters, she went to Castile to choose one for him. It was a one-thousand-mile round trip across snow drifts and the sometimes impassible Pyrenees mountains and when she arrived she chose the younger, Blancha, who came back with her to be married in cold, far-away Paris; Louis and Blancha would become the great-grandparents of the Iron King, Phillipe the Fair.

Arthur demanded the crown of England, and so John traveled to Normandy, where he invited his nephew around for talks in his castle and then beat him to death.

Philippe Auguste used John's appalling behaviour as a pretext to annex Normandy, whose people were sickened by John's mercenary troops. Not that the French king was much better, as King Philippe "cleansed the city with fire and the sword," and as always, war was merciless for the small folk. In 1204, Philippe's army swept across Normandy, driving the Plantagenets out entirely. John lost Chateau Gillard when the invaders used latrines to sneak into the building, after some two thousand people had been thrown out of the castle and left to starve, unable to pass the French lines. Later attempts by John to retake Normandy ended only in failure and increased taxes and trouble among the noblemen.

But although increasingly hostile to the monarch, the barons also fought among themselves. All major lords had their own private armies, composed of bannermen sworn to service, and their disputes often spilled over into violence. Those leading barons in John's time each had a retinue of knights, varying in size between ten and one hundred, who themselves had squires tied to them and below them yeomen and villeins. During the Anarchy many barons had begun a tradition of private peace treaties, which even involved effectively pretending to fight when their overlords demanded their service. They limited the number of knights they brought while also pledging to return any captured booty, making the whole thing a charade. During Henry II's reign, the Earls of Leicester and Chester, neighbors constantly squabbling over land, agreed to give each other fifteen days' notice of any war.

The king was getting more deranged as the years passed by. All kings held the children of enemies as hostages, and if things went wrong they sometimes suffered appalling fates, but the Plantagenets took it to excess. In 1165 King Henry had ordered hostages from Wales to be blinded and castrated, with the women having their noses and ears cut off. John went further by taking as prisoner twenty-eight boys aged around twelve, the sons of Welsh leaders, and then having them all hanged.

In Westeros, Ramsay Snow marries Lady Hornwood in order to gain her home but then leaves her to starve to death in a cell in a tower; she chews off her own fingers before dying. In real life, Marshal's main rivals as landowners on the Welsh borders were the de Briouzes, William de Briouze being a loyal follower of John during his Normandy campaign. The de Briouze family had been powerful magnates for at least four generations, and its head a ruthless figure himself typical of the Anglo-Norman warrior caste. His great-grandfather, another William de Briouze (or de Braoise), had fought at Hastings and been rewarded with land in Sussex, Surrey, and Berkshire, and his son and grandson had expanded their territory across the south-east, the latter in the service of Henry II. The current William de Briouze, the Fourth Lord of Bramber, had been born during the Anarchy and become a major proprietor in the border area. In one notorious incident in 1175, de Briouze had invited three Welsh princes and a number of lords to a feast at Abergavenny Castle to mark the end of the year and toast peace. De Briouze blamed one of them, Seisyll ap Dyfnwal, for the death of his uncle, and had not forgotten nor forgiven; thus at the end of the night when the order was given his men murdered all the Welshmen. Later de Briouze hunted down ap Dyfnwal's seven-year-old son and killed him.

King John had been generous with William de Briouze, giving him estates in Wales, including the Lordship of Gower in the south of the country and Glamorgan Castle; he also received land in Limerick. And yet the king had grown increasingly suspicious of him, perhaps because de Briouze knew too much about the circumstances of Arthur's unnatural death.

Whatever the reason, the king demanded that William de Briouze pay the crown the debts of £3,500 which he had racked up. The baron was unable to do so, so the king requested that he hand over his eldest son, also William; the baron refused, and fled to Ireland in 1210. Unfortunately, that year John's men captured his wife and the younger William, and when Matilda de Briouze blurted out that they knew about Arthur's murder, she and her nineteen-year-old son were taken prisoner and starved to death in Corfe Castle in Dorset, the stronghold where John spent much of his reign. A chronicle described the scene: "On the eleventh day the mother was found dead between her son's legs, still upright but leaning back against her son's chest as a dead woman. The son, who was also dead, sat upright, leaning against the wall as a dead man. So desperate was the mother that she had eaten her son's cheeks."[13] The father died soon after, of grief. The line continued, however, for the younger William had already fathered four sons, who were raised in secret by a loyal Welsh retainer.

The king had also demanded that Marshal hand over his eldest son William, which he felt forced to do, before heading to his estates in Ireland to keep away from the unstable king, who openly threatened him.

By 1212 John was isolated—excommunicated by the Church for refusing the Pope's choice of Archbishop of Canterbury, and detested by the barons, as well as the common people. John's attempt to win back Normandy in 1214 led to disaster at the Battle of Bouvines on July 27, taking place in intense heat with men "fighting half-blinded by the sweat cascading down inside their helmets, with a heavy dust kicked up by the thousands of horses."[14] During the course of the battle the Count of Flanders laid his lands on the king of France "but he drew back at the last moment, stunned by the horror of what he was about to do and by fear of committing a mortal sin if he tried to kill the man who was not only his natural lord, but was also placed under God's especial protection (by virtue of the unction of coronation)."[15] The English commander, William Longsword, was clubbed on the head by the bishop of Beauvais and taken prisoner.

John's disastrous defeat, on top of his cruel behavior, led a group of mostly northern barons to renounce homage and fealty. They even refused to rise to their feet when the king entered the room—a great and deliberate insult in a world in which every relationship was about fealty. They were led by two lords, Eustache de Vesci and Robert Fitzwalter, whose womenfolk had both suffered sexual injury at his hands; among the other rebels was Richard Percy, head of that rising northern family.

The "Northerners," as the rebels were informally called, raised an army in the spring and headed to Northampton, and civil war was only averted when Archbishop of Canterbury Stephen Langton brought the two sides together at Runnymede on June 15, drawing up a series of sixty-three clauses by which the sovereign would agree to rule; it later became known as the Great Charter of Liberties, or Magna Carta, to distinguish it from another charter about forests.[16]

There are a number of differences between Martin's world and ours, one of the main ones being the way in which kings rule without any sort of assembly (which probably makes for a better narrative). After Magna Carta was issued, however, rulers were always constrained by law and the reign of John's son saw the first meetings to be informally known as Parliament; under his grandson Edward Longshanks, knights first sat in Parliament, establishing what was then called simply the Commons—later the House of Commons. This was not the case in much of the world, but in most European countries similar bodies also developed at some point later; the Hungarian Diet was in use since at least the 1290s, and the first Swedish Riksdag met in 1435, although the world's oldest parliament is the Icelandic Althing, which dates to 930. However, MPs played little part in the everyday running of the realm, which was done by the "king's council" or "secret council."

True to form, King John reneged on the deal, claiming it was signed under duress, and civil war broke out. The barons had invited over Prince Louis of France, who claimed the throne though his marriage to Henry II's granddaughter Blancha. While Louis occupied London, John died of dysentery in Newark, Nottinghamshire, most likely caused by his gluttony.

Louis soon controlled most of the south-east, including London, and the fate of John's son Henry, just nine, looked bleak. At least two-thirds of the barons were actively with the invader, and the House of Plantagenet would have fallen were it not for one man—William Marshal, now almost seventy.

Before dying, John had entrusted Marshal with the kingdom and asked him to take care of his son. Marshal, despite the odds being stacked against the boy, swore to do so and while others around him thought of deserting young Henry, he ordered that he be summoned to him and on the road near Gloucester they met. Marshal lifted him up and then vowed to see Henry as king even if he had to carry the boy king "on his shoulders" from island to island: Henry was crowned at Gloucester Cathedral and from their base in the south-west the loyalists launched an attack on the invaders as they besieged Lincoln. There Marshal led the fighting with such enthusiasm that he had to be restrained from charging into battle without his armor.

The loyalists won and soon after at the Battle of Sandwich Louis's French force was beaten by an English fleet half the size but "aggressive and well skilled in naval warfare." The crossbowmen and archers were lethally effective and quicklime was thrown into the eyes of French sailors, blinding them.

The battle seemed to have turned, but in order to bring back many of the rebels to Henry's cause, some of whom were unhappy with French involvement, Marshal reissued Magna Carta in 1216 and oversaw its definitive edition the following year; previously an unsuccessful peace treaty, Magna Carta therefore become enshrined in English law as a protection against such evils as being imprisoned "without lawful judgment."[17] He ruled as regent until his death in 1219.

And yet his house did not last long, with all five of his sons dying young, and without heir, supposedly the result of a curse issued by an Irish priest. William's son Gilbert Marshal was killed in a tournament; he was showing off his horsemanship skills when his bridle broke and he fell from the saddle and, catching a foot in the stirrup, was dragged across a field to his death. Afterwards there was a big brawl in which one of Gilbert's retainers was slain and several on both sides injured. Likewise, Geoffrey de Mandeville, one of the leading opponents of King John who brought about Magna Carta, was killed in 1216 in a tournament, when "the knights attacked each other with spears and lances, galloping their horses towards each other."[18]

Ironically, like any nun-ravisher who later joins the Church, William Marshal ended up banning tournaments which were seen as "a danger to the kingdom and spoliation of the poor." Tourneys were finally killed off for good when Henri II of France was fatally wounded after being splintered in the eye during one event in 1559.

Marshal's fame might not have outlived his lifetime but luckily, in February 1861, a French scholar by the name of Paul Meyer was browsing through the index of Sotheby's auction house in Covent Garden when his curiosity was piqued by something listed as a "Norman-French chronicle on English Affairs (in Verse)" written "by an Anglo-Norman scribe." What it turned out to be was a biographical poem about Marshal's life, written soon after his death, which otherwise had been forgotten and may have remained so; Meyer failed to buy it and spent the next twenty years tracking it down, succeeding eventually, and so saving the greatest of knight's tales.[19]

29
THE WITCH

When the sun rises in the west, sets in the east, when the seas go dry and the mountains blow in the wind like leaves.

—MIRRI MAZ DUUR

Female military leaders were rare. Female military leaders who dressed as men were even rarer. At the Battle of Roosebeke in November 29, 1382 against the French, Flemish leader Philip van Artevelde had been trampled to death by his own soldiers alongside his banner-bearer, one "Big Margot," although not much else is known of her.

Women in combat were not unknown, especially as battle evolved to rely less on brute strength, and there were female commanders. After the Bohemian Hussite rebellion, some 156 women were taken prisoner, and a fifteenth century German chronicle depicts a woman handgunner and two halberdiers, a halberd being a long, two-handed pole. There was even an order of knighthood for females, the Catalonian Order of the Hatchet, established to honor the women who defended the town of Tortosa in 1149. The Muslims had besieged the Spanish city and the men considered surrendering, "which the women hearing of, to prevent the disaster threatening their city, themselves, and children, put on men's clothes, and by a resolute sally, forced the Moors to raise the siege."[1]

In England, some sixty-eight women were appointed to the Order of the Garter from 1358, although they weren't "companions," and the custom was abandoned in 1488, the next one being in 1901.[2] Females were not allowed to become full companions until 1987. Women who achieved damehood might have inheritance rights over their husband's wealth or the privilege to attend certain assemblies.

The Hundred Years' War had already seen Joanna of Flanders, who rallied Breton forces for her husband Jean Montfort. When the town of Hennebont was besieged by pro-French forces,

> the countess of Montfort was seen in full armor, mounted on a swift horse and riding through the town, street by street, urging the people to defend the town well. She made the women of the town, ladies and others, dismantle the carriageways and carry the stones to the battlements for throwing at their enemies. And she had bombards and pots full of quick lime brought to keep the enemy busy."[3]

In Westeros Lady Maege Mormont of Bear Island, brother of Lord Commander Jeor (who doesn't like her much) is described fighting in "full armor and brandishing arms,"[4] while her young daughter is equally belligerent. The crusades also empowered many aristocratic women who were left in charge of protecting the home while the men were off fighting. Much further back there was also Artemisia, queen of Halicarnassus who appears in Heredotus; she fought in the Persian Wars, for the Persians, and personally commanded the five ships she sent to the Battle of Salamis in 480 BC.*

Female warriors brandishing swords are even more common in fables. The Amazons were legendary ancient women fighters who cut off their right breasts and wore trousers, and the Greek hero Achilles fell in love with their Queen Penthesilea just as he killed her, which is unfortunate timing to say the least. Later romantic fiction was full of female knights like Brienne of Tarth. There was Britomart, a virgin knight who appears in Edmund Spenser's *The Faerie Queene* in the Elizabethan area, and her forerunner, Bradamante, in the Italian epics *Orlando Innamorato* and *Orlando Furioso*. Both women are in love with noble-born knights, and Britomart actually rescues hers from an enchantress.[5]

However female warriors were so unusual that when one now emerged, during France's darkest hour, no one entirely knew how to respond. Jehanne d'Arc was just seventeen and illiterate when she first appeared on the scene; the "Pucelle" or Maid came from Domremy in Lorraine, north-east France, and had been receiving divine voices

---

*She appears in the sequel to the film *300*.

since the age of thirteen, convinced that they were from God and not the Devil because they appeared on her right shoulder. Despite her youth, sex, and social station she nevertheless inspired men to fight for her, and was feared as a witch by her enemies.

Joan of Arc was "called by angels" to devote her life to the Dauphin Charles, son of the mad king, who until then had retreated into apathy and defeatism. Joan was a highly unusual figure, devoted to the man she saw as the rightful king, an almost sexless woman who wore armor and fought fiercely.[6] She faced sexual mockery throughout, from the time that one of the Dauphin's soldiers upon her arrival suggested she needed a good seeing to. She also faced the far more terrifying prospect of rape.

Convinced of the messages she was hearing, the young girl had smuggled herself to the court of the Dauphin at Chinon, where Charles's men had interrogated her and, persuaded by her sheer force of will, allowed her to help in the now desperate struggle on the Loire. The girl rode to Orléans on a white horse, with an army of several thousand soldiers and some priests, carrying a sword that some believed had once belonged to Charles Martel. Partly inspired by her supreme confidence, the French relieved Orléans and the English retreated up the Loire, dumping their cannons and heavy weapons in their haste to escape the resurgent resistance. On October 27, Salisbury was wounded by debris from stone cannonball fire across the river; when his attendants found him there was a bleeding, gaping hole where half his face had been. He died eight days later.

For the Maid it was the start of an extraordinary career of conquest, against the odds. It helped that there were numerous prophecies in the French countryside about a virgin who would be the country's savior, while long before Geoffrey of Monmouth had predicted in his *History of the Kings of Britain* that "a virgin ascends the backs of the archers, and hides the flower of her virginity."

Joan attracted devotion from her troops, who described how they strangely felt no desire for her, despite her sex and youth; the Duke of Alençon said he had seen her breasts which were beautiful but left him unaroused. Joan's hose and breeches, tightly knotted with cords onto her doublet, allowed her to ride a horse more easily but also provided some protection against rape. She was now supported by a growing number of men who became convinced by her message; among them was Etinne de Vignolles, better known as La Hire, or "hedgehog," one of the few men who really believed in her throughout the war and fought with her at Orléans. Almost everyone would recognize his image as he ended up being commemorated as the Jack of Hearts in traditional card games.

And on June 18, 1429 at the Battle at Patay, the French destroyed an English force, with Fastolf the only captain to survive. The following month Charles entered Reims and was crowned at the ancient coronation spot where kings of France had been ordained by God for close to a thousand years. Standing beside him was Joan, the simple peasant girl, as well as another supporter of hers, Gilles de Rais, one of the leading knights of the kingdom who had been appointed Marshal of France. After the ceremony the Maid knelt at Charles's feet and wept, "Noble king, God's will is done."

Now an attempt by the English to crown the young Henry VI in Paris ended in disaster when the organizers cooked food so bad even the city's poor and sick, traditionally given leftovers at coronations, complained about the quality.

And yet Joan had made a lot of enemies and her messianic character unnerved many. With her victories against the English, she now wrote an open letter to the Hussites of far-off Bohemia, warning them that if they did not submit to the Pope: "I shall destroy your empty and abominable superstition, and strop you of either your heresy or your lives."[7] Many of the French, even those bitterly opposed to the English, also viewed her as a heretic and, worse, a witch.

And so Joan of Arc, like Daenerys, went into the fire—except that in real life, alas, people don't come out.

After a couple of military failures the Maid was captured by the Burgundians on May 23, 1430 and sold to the English, who handed her over to the Church authorities to be put on trial. Her central crime was heresy but her non-conformity to traditional gender roles also made her something unnatural and frightening to many, and the court heard that Joan had "disgracefully put on the clothing of the male sex, a shocking and vile monstrosity."[8] She was accused of seventy different offenses, put in a grim prison with just bread and water and told she must recant. This ordeal went for a total of ten months.

The bishop who tried to persuade her was dressed "in fur-lined episcopal robes, a man of about sixty, old enough to be her grandfather, smilingly kindly, chillingly" and said that he came in friendship.[9] When she returned to face the court again, she was a "thinner, paler, and quieter" girl and her head had also now been shaved.

At the end of the trial, after being brought to a scaffold and told she would be burned there and then unless she submitted, she confessed her crimes and recanted her error, so she could be welcomed back and live the rest of her days in prison, eating the "bread of sorrow and drinking the water of affliction as she wept for her sins."[10] However just four days later, on May 28, she renounced her previous recantation and again donned men's clothing, frightened of being raped by the guards. She was duly convicted and was consumed by the fire on May 31 in Rouen, and afterwards her charred corpse was left on display so that the townspeople might know that she was just a woman. She was nineteen. With this murder John Tressart, secretary to Henry VI in France, reflected: "We are lost, we have burnt a saint."[11]

Charles VII, as he was now styled, had made no attempt to rescue his young supporter, who was deeply unpopular and unlamented in passing. Her later transformation into national saviour was a result of continuing devotion from the peasantry, despite official hostility, and the work of two influential figures.

Christine de Pizan was one of the most significant female writers of the medieval period. Born in 1364 in Italy, she served as court writer to Louis of Orléans and later Philippe of Burgundy, composing prose and poetry we well as offering marriage advice. She wrote forty-one books in total, having been widowed at a young age and needing to support her children as well as her mother and niece, among them *The Book of the City of Ladies*, set in a hypothetical city in which women's views are taken seriously. The year before her death in 1430 her last work was a poem about Joan of Arc, which helped crystalise continual sympathy for the Maid among France's downtrodden.

Joan's memory was also much helped by Gilles de Rais, who having retired from politics devoted much of his time to his great passion, theater. French and English theater had its origin in religious mystery plays, first acted as far back as the eleventh century in monasteries, although by the this point plays were performed by troupes, moving from town to town and performing both secular and religious dramas. Theater at the time was, by later standards, very vulgar and also featured graphic scenes of violence, although by the period that the first theater houses appeared in Shakespeare's time it had become considerably cleaner.

De Rais was obsessed with theater, and almost ruined his entire family with a hugely expensive play he wrote and produced on the Siege of Orléans, which appeared in 1435 and glorified Joan, now dead four years. The performance required 140 speaking parts and 500 extras, and 600 costumes were made for the spectacular, which were worn once and then disposed of, to be made again for the next show. He also provided spectators with unlimited supplies of food and drink, and unsurprisingly this venture virtually bankrupted him; so bad was his theater obsession that his family took legal action to stop him spending any more money.

And yet the real world contains more horror even than George R.R. Martin's rich and fertile imagination. During the 1430s, a number of children had disappeared in de Rais's native Machecoul on the southern edge of Britanny. One was a furrier's apprentice who had been sent to the famous knight with a message but had never returned, having been kidnapped on the way back—or so de Rais had said.

Later, in 1440, the famous knight had gotten into an argument with a local priest in a church and tempers had become so inflamed that he had tried to grab the cleric. Local churchmen began to look into his activities and, searching his chateau, found something they were not expecting—bodies. Several bodies. As the secular authorities were called into investigate, the horror mounted, and de Rais confessed to his crimes. History's first known serial killer, de Rais may have killed as many as 140 victims in total, aged between six and eighteen, the majority boys, and he was executed later that year. He became immortalized by the French folktale, *Bluebeard*, which was first published in Paris in 1697.

And yet only thirty years after Joan's death, public opinion had shifted so much that a new trial was ordered of her original trial, where it was now ruled that she was inspired by God. She had become a national hero, and later a saint.

CIRCE

For her enemies, however, Joan was that ancient terror, a witch, a feature of European folklore since as far back as *The Odyssey* where a sorcesses called Circe turned men into animals and exerted a hold over them.

"Magic was an integral part of the later medieval mind," wrote the great French historian Georges Duby, and all European societies had a fear of witches. The Vikings were obsessed with them, often vengeful females whose sexual advances had been refused. Their *Kveldridur*, sometimes called "night-riders" or "darkness riders," might also appear as supernatural creatures, or wolves. Nordic witches might use *henblane*, or stinking nightshade, a poisonous plant that could be rubbed into the skin and which caused dizziness and cramps, and irritation in the throat, but also contained a narcotic called skopolamin which brought about hallucinations and in particular the illusion of being able to fly. It was also believed to be an aphrodisiac, witches often having a sexual hold, both arousing and repulsive at once.

Many females unfortunate enough to be accused of witchcraft were merely "cunning women" who had some knowledge of herbal medicine, some of it effective and some of it junk. Others had put faith in cranks for less than laudable reasons, such as the Parisian woman who in 1390 had employed the magical powers of another lady to render the lover who spurned her impotent. Both women were sent to the stake. In reality, unlike in Westeros, it was not the alleged witches doing the burning, but the poor unlucky women accused of witchcraft being burned; in Europe the vast majority of people killed as witches were female, the exception being parts of Scandinavia, where there was a particular cultural horror at men doing magic, something seen as effeminate.

In the fourteenth century, the Church had become increasingly interested in sorcery, and a bull issued in 1320 by Pope John XXII ordered that magic books be burned, but despite this, prosecutions for sorcery and demonology only took off toward the end of the century. The 1366 Council of Chartres had also ordered an anathema to be pronounced against sorcerers each Sunday at parish churches.

This fear only paradoxically took off in the early modern period, especially after the invention of printing was able to widen it, since this new technology made it easier to disseminate lies and half-truths. The papacy appointed new commissions dealing with witchcraft in 1494 and again in 1521 and 1522. In Geneva over 1515-6, some five hundred people were burned to death as witches, or for heresy aggravated by witchcraft. In Como in Lombardy, some one thousand supposed witches were killed just in one year, 1524.

Before 1420, most cases of witchcraft involved specifically the use of supernatural powers to harm enemies, or *maleficium*, but increasingly allegations involved sexual wrongoings, some curious hysteria having overtaken European civilization. The victims were accused of copulating with Satan, who took the form of a black cat or goat with flaming eyes or a "gigantic man with black skin, a huge phallus, and eyes like burning coals."[12]

Fires went up across Europe as the witchcraft craze reached its peak from 1560 to 1630, and it even crossed into the New World, most infamously at Salem. Conventional estimates put the total number of European witch-burning victims at around fifty thousand.

Frenchman Nicholas Remy, a magistrate, Latin poet and historian, and a cultured renaissance man, recalled before his death in 1616 that he had sent three thousand people to their deaths. The witch craze in Germany was even more savage. Dietrich Flade, vice-governor of Trier and rector of the Rhineland city's university, proposed reducing the scale of witch hunting and tried to get convicted witches banished instead of burned to death. Soon, and inevitably, a witch hunter accused *him* of being a witch, because why else would someone oppose a witch-hunt? Accused witches were found to implicate him, the poor, desperate women promised the chance of an easier death if they helped.[13] Flade was arrested, strangled, and burned, a lesson for all of us—in the face of an irrational, violent mob bent on injustice, keep your head down.

30
THE SWORD IN THE DARKNESS

Night gathers, and now my watch begins. It shall not end until my death.
I shall take no wife, hold no lands, father no children. I shall wear no
crowns and win no glory . . .

—NIGHT'S WATCH OATH

The Temple church in the Holborn district of central London is all that remains of a huge complex once owned by an international order of knights tasked with defending civilization from its enemies. The Knights Templar were an elite band of brothers formed to protect Christian pilgrims on the way to the Holy Land, but they grew to control much of the region and became hugely rich until the failures of the crusade led their enemies at home to crush them.

Like the Watch, members of the Knights Templar referred to each other as brothers and were sworn to abstain from taking wives, indeed to avoid all physical contact with women, even relatives.[1] Templars were expected to swear oaths of poverty, piety, and obedience, and their lives were every bit as tough as the Crows, although stationed in the blazing heat of the Middle East rather than the freezing cold of the north.

The organization grew out of the First Crusade (1095-1099), the background to which was increasing religious intolerance in the Middle East, and in the West a growing population with large numbers of young knights trained in violence and with nothing else to do. The Muslim conquerors of the Levant had initially been quite tolerant, but in 1004 the Fatimid caliph al-Hakin, ruler of North Africa, Palestine, and southern Syria, launched a fanatical anti-Christian campaign. Property was confiscated, crosses were burned, and churches were set on fire, or forcibly converted into mosques. There were also increasing numbers of pilgrims from western Europe visiting the Holy Land, and who were often threatened by bandits and murderers; in 1064, during the most infamous incident, a large German pilgrimage came under attack from locals in Palestine.

Western Europe's population had begun to grow from 900 AD, an explosion that left large numbers of younger sons with little to do, and one way that incessesant violence could be reduced was by turning it outwards. The trigger for war came with the movement of Seljuk Turks into Anatolia in the eleventh century, much to the alarm of the Byzantines. Despite the tension between eastern and western Christianity—the two church leaders in Constantinople and Rome had mutually excommunicated each other briefly in 1053, leading to the schism between Orthodox and Catholic Christianity—when the Emperor appealed to the Pope for help there was widespread enthusiasm.

And so, in 1093 Pope Urban II made an impassioned appeal in the south of France, calling on western Christians to take up arms to liberate the Holy Land from the infidel. Villages emptied of men as Christians sought adventure in what were called "armed pilgrimages" at the time, but which were from the thirteenth century called "crusades," from the Latin for "cross."

It wasn't quite the adventure they hoped for, and only one in three of those who had left western Europe with the main army were alive two years later. In the desert of Syria in 1098-99, the crusaders were in such dire straits that some impoverished Flemings ate the Turks they had killed.

Jerusalem finally fell the following July, after which the crusaders massacred most if not all of the city's Muslims and Jews, and afterward, one of the crusade's leaders, Godfrey of Bouillon, was elected as king; however, he thought the title blasphemous so he preferred the somewhat more modest Protector of the Holy Sepulchre. Godfrey was widely celebrated for his nobility and chivalry; on one occasion, after capturing the wife of a Muslim prince, he sent her back to her husband when he learned that she was pregnant. However, he lasted barely a year in the job before succumbing to one of the various illnesses westerners died of in the Middle East. Or perhaps poison.

"LOVE IS THE DEATH OF DUTY."

The Knights Templar was founded twenty years later by the aging French knight Hugh de Payens, who had intended to retire to a monastery but was persuaded to instead create an order to protect Christian pilgrims. Along with eight other knights they became founding members of The Poor Fellow Soldiers of Christ.[2]

The Poor Fellows is also the name of an order in Westeros, who are sworn to the Faith of the Seven and also known as the Stars because of the seven-pointed star on their badge. They were mostly small folk, but there was also the Noble and Puissant Order of the Warrior's Sons, a more aristocratic band of knights who wore uncomfortable hairshirts, just as many pious medieval Europeans like Thomas Becket did. (Members of both orders accompany Cersai during her Walk of Atonement.) But the most obvious resemblance is between the Night's Watch and the Templars.

Godfrey's successor Baldwin, who had fewer qualms about going by the title King of Jerusalem, allowed the group to use the city's al-Asqa mosque, known as Templum Salomonis—the Temple of Solomon—and so they became commonly known as the Knights Templar. The knights had to "defend pilgrims against brigands and rapists" according to James of Vitry, a chronicler of the era, and also observe "poverty, chastity and obedience according to the rules of the ordinary priests."[3] De Payens had intended to become a monk and in every way, except their use of weapons, that is what the Templars were. They were particularly influenced by the Cistercians, a rather stern order set up by the charismatic twelfth century Churchman St Bernard of Clairvaux.

St Bernard and Hugh de Payens came up with the Rule for the Knights Templar, based on the Benedictine laws, and St Bernard warned:

> We believe it to be a dangerous thing for any religious to look too much upon the face of woman. For this reason none of you may presume to kiss a woman, be it widow, young girl, mother, sister, aunt or any other; and henceforth the Knighthood of Jesus Christ should avoid at all costs the embraces of women, by which men have perished many times, so that they may remain eternally before the face of God with a pure conscience and sure life.[4]

Or as Master Aemon put it: "Love is the death of duty."

Just as the Night's Watch have rangers, builders, and stewards, the Templars had three divisions: knights, sergeants, and chaplains. Only about one in ten of the twenty thousand or so Templars were actually knights, and only they wore its white surcoat, while the sergeants, often local Syrian Christians, dressed in black or brown. The Sergeants, like the Stewards on the wall, provide logistical support—the ratio of one soldier on the front line to ten personnel in support is not unlike a modern army—while Master Aemon has a role similar to that of chaplin.

White was only worn, according to St Bernard, "so that those who have abandoned the life of darkness will recognise each other as being reconciled to their creator by the sign of their white habits; which signifies purity and complete chastity."[5] (In Westeros the Kingsguard are also known as the White Cloaks.)

Templars lived harsh lives; they slept four hours a night, attended Mass seven times a day, and fasted three times a week. The Knights rose at 4 a.m. for Matins, or morning prayer, and then from 6 a.m. attended services and trained and groomed horses. They were not even allowed to wear fur or pointed shoes and shoe-laces "for it is manifest and well known that these abominable things belong to pagans."[6] In their conversation they were to avoid "idle words and wicked bursts of laughter"[7] nor could they talk about their previous acts of courage or sexual conquests.

They also had to cut their hair short, while also sporting beards—they couldn't shave—although the strictest rules concerned behavior in battle. According to an anonymous pilgrim of the time: "Should any of them for any reason turn his back to the enemy, or come forth alive [from a defeat], or bear arms against the Christians, he is severely punished; the white mantle with the red cross, which is the sign of his knighthood, is taken away with ignominy, he is cast from the society of brethren, and eats his food on the floor" like a dog.[8] Other punishments for wrongdoing included whipping and being placed in irons[9] the same sanctions monks faced for breaking their code. Like the Kingsguard in Westeros, they were forbidden from fathering children, taking a wife, or owning land.[10]

The Templars were not the only order at the time; there were the Knights Hospitaller (also known as the Knights of Rhodes or Malta), as well as the Teutonic Knights, who had started as a German breakaway from the Hospitallers. Then, like with the Night's Watch, the Teutonic Knights switched missions, going off to fight Mongols in Hungary and then launching a crusade to Christianize pagans in Prussia and the Baltic Sea. This brutal campaign took two hundred years, and the chronicles of the Knights detail the savagery of the Prussians, seen as people beyond civilization, and who would "roast captured brethren alive in their armor, like chestnuts, before the shrine of a local god."[11] During the fighting in Livonia—today's Latvia—crusaders established another military order, the Sword Brothers, to pursue the crusade, who were often promised the land of the pagans they were to conquer. For most members of sworn orders, however, there was little in the way of material gain; heavenly reward and earthly prestige was enough.

To start with, or at least in theory, anyone could become a Templar, although acquiring the training would have put it beyond the reach of any poor man. However, by the mid-twelfth century a Templar had to be the son of a knight or descended from one, and so this is where it diverges from fiction, where the brothers on the wall are better characterized as "Raper, raper, horse thief, ninth-born son, raper, thief, thief AND raper."[12] People like that joined the common infantry.

One attraction of the Night's Watch, and they are thin on the ground, is that once a man takes the black then the slate is wiped clean, which is why it's filled with criminals, as well as men just unlucky enough to be poor, or to have fallen out with their families. And so, while the Templars were often high-born, they did also attract people who hoped their sins would be forgiven. This had the effect of drawing in some dubious individuals to the Holy Land—the knights who murdered Thomas Beckett in 1170 did fourteen years service in the Templars. As with the later French Foreign Legion, there are also recorded cases of people joining because of romantic disappointment.

THE WATCHERS ON THE WALL

The Templars were prestigious figures, but they paid with their blood. Six of twenty-three Grand Masters died in battle or captivity; at least twenty thousand brothers were killed either fighting or in captivity after refusing to renounce their faith.

And soon the war between Christians and Muslims was reignited, in what later became known as the Second Crusade (1147–1149), and which ended with a stalemate and growing hatred and tension between various Christian groups. Then, in 1187, fresh attacks by the Muslims led to the reconquest of Jerusalem, sparking renewed warfare; weeks before that disaster, at the Battle of Cresson, some 130 Knights Templar rode into battle against 7,000 Muslim horsemen, three of them riding out again, and afterwards the heads of the Templars were fixed to polls outside the city. The horsemen were Mamelukes, a terrifying army of captured slaves raised to be killers.

The Third Crusade featured the two most charismatic leaders of the long holy war, Saladin and Richard the Lionheart. The latter was blessed "with the figure of a Greek god, he was tall, immensely strong, fair-haired and so handsome that he fascinated

both his friends and his enemies" and yet also "a man of some psychological instability, tending to fly from one emotional extreme to the other."[13] (In the Ridley Scott
film, *Kingdom of Heaven*, Richard is played by Scottish actor Iain Glen, aka Jorah
Mormont.)

Saladin was famed for his great chivalry; on one occasion while attacking a crusader fortress he ordered his men not to bombard one corner of the castle where a
wedding was taking place. He also sent fruit to his opponent Richard while he was
recovering from a fever to enable him to get well so they could fight again. But both
men were ruthless at times; Richard executed 2,700 Muslims in Jerusalem in one
notorious incident, which Islamic sources claim included women and children. The
massacre had a military rationale, since guarding his prisoners would have tied up his
army as Saladin's forces approached, but it was certainly unforgiving. On one occasion Saladin had 230 Templars "decapitated by the ecstatic sufis"[14] who had begged
the Muslim leader to let them kill the Christian knights; he also executed Hospitallers
in cold blood and ordered the crucifixion of Shia opponents in Egypt. Likewise,
throughout the crusades Christians were still at war with other Christians and Muslims continued fighting other Muslims. So much had the eastern and western Christians now fallen out that when Saladin captured Jerusalem in 1187, the Byzantine
emperor Isaac Angelos sent a message of congratulations.

Constantinople at the time was home to a large number of western Christians,
Venetians, Genoans, and Pisans, but in 1182 there was a pogrom of these Italians in
the city, of whom there had been eighty thousand. There was growing hostility to the
"Latins," who had been showed preferential treatment by the previous emperor, and
"men, women and children, the old and the young, the healthy and the sick, were all
attacked and many slaughtered, their houses and churches burned."[15] And so in 1204,
in the most squalid incident of the whole crusades, the western Christians sacked
Constantinople, capital of the empire they had once claimed to protect. In the ensuing destruction the Latins slaughtered vast numbers and stole priceless relics, while a
prostitute sat on the seat of the patriarch at the Hagia Sophia cathedral. One western
abbot found the store of relics at the Church of Christ the Pantocrator and, after
threatening to kill a Greek priest if he didn't tell him their location, ran off laughing,
taking them back to the ship, never to be returned.

Like the Watch, which began to fight the undead but evolved to keep out Wildlings,
the Templars also changed the nature of their service, from protectors of the faithful

to a sort of armed bank, the order growing rich through patronage and support across western Christendom. Visiting pilgrims in any large city could deposit their wealth with the nearest Templar house upon arrival and receive notes of credit, so that the money could be safely taken out from another, like a modern bank. Although the Catholic Church officially prohibited lending at interest, there were plenty of ways to get around it, such as calling it "expenses" or "administration" or charging below a 12 percent maximum.[16] Sometimes they didn't gain from money-lending but did so for reasons of prestige or to be owed favors.

One of the crusade leaders, Fulk V, count of Anjou and grandfather of Henry II, had on his return home granted the order an annual income in his county which other leaders soon followed. Hugh de Payen arrived in France in 1127 and was given land, and the following summer he was received with great honor in England by Henry I, who also gave the new order gold and silver. He established the first Templar house in London, by the northern end of Chancery Lane, just west of the city, and this became the start of a network of buildings, the last surviving part of which is the Temple Church, its rotunda style in tribute to the Church of the Holy Sepulchre in Jerusalem.

The Templars and Hospitallers also grew wealthy through the slave trade, as large numbers of captured soldiers, kidnap victims, or the children of impoverished parents passed through the port of Ayas (now Yumurtalık, in south-east Turkey). Most of the slaves were Turkish, Greek, Russian, or Circassian (an ethnic group from the Caucasus Mountains south of Russia) and the strongest males went to Egypt where they became the Mamelukes, a slave army renowned for their invincibility.

These boys, sold to Ayyubid Sultans in Egypt and raised to be soldiers there, became legendary and notorious for their bravery. Without a family they had no loyalties to any faction within a highly fractious society and thus were utterly ruthless; when they captured Acre from the Christians in 1291, there were mass beheadings afterwards, while the Mameluke leader Baybars murdered one thousand prisoners after the fall of Saphet in 1266. By this time the Mameluks had grown so powerful that they had also killed the Sultan in Egypt, ending the line of Saladin, and taking over instead.

Already the crusades were getting complicated with Muslims fighting Muslims. In 1244, there was an attack by a joint crusader-Muslim Syrian force against Egypt at the instigation of Walter of Brienne. His ally, the Muslim al-Mansur Ibraham of

Damascus, advised against the attack, and wisely; the Egyptians held them and a huge mass of Khwarezmian horsemen from central Asia attacked the flank. The Damascenes ran off and the Latins were slaughtered, with five thousand killed and eight hundred prisoners taken to Egypt, among them the Grand Master, Armand of Perigord. The Templars lost as many as three hundred knights that day, and only thirty-three survived, along with twenty-six Hospitallers and three Teutonic Knights.

Jerusalem was lost to the Turks in 1244, and the Templars endured another disaster six years later at the Battle of Mansurah, with 280 brothers dying and only two living to tell the tale.

The crusaders were in desperate trouble. However soon after, in 1249, they heard rumors of an approaching army from beyond Persia, and to the Christians it was clear that this finally was the great Christian leader from the East they had long heard of, the fabled Prester John, coming to their rescue. As one priest in Egypt said, breathlessly, the "king of the two Indies was hastening to the aid of the Christians, bringing with him most ferocious peoples who will devour the sacrilegious Saracens like beasts."[17]

But it was not Prester John—it was something far, far worse.

31

A MARRIAGE OF
FIRE AND MILK

*Every time a new Targaryen is born, the gods toss the coin in the air and
the world holds its breath to see how it will land.*

—Sir Barristan Selmy

T he world got colder. From 1430 there was an intensification of the worsening
weather in Europe as the continent entered deeper into the Little Ice Age;
although no one knew it, a period of reduced solar activity called the Spörer
Minimum was taking place and volcanic eruptions lowered the temperature even further.[1] A reduction in the growing season led to three successive crop failures in Europe,
the years 1437-9 being the worst harvests in a century, aggravated by two rainy summers;
the suffering was compounded by another bout of the plague hitting the continent.

The war in France was now going badly for the English, and the nature of conflict
was changing. Weaponry developed at a rapid pace—Gonnes, or canons, are mentioned in an account of the 1333 siege of Berwick and were also used at Calais in
1346, but they were now vastly more lethal. Continual warfare, as with 1914-45, was
helping to spur huge advances in technology.

The new French king, Charles VII, was weak in body and highly neurotic, and
yet from 1438 the French had managed to impose order on their army.[2] Charles
had them properly equipped, paid, and organized into twenty companies, a fifteen
thousand-strong professional army, and from 1445 Charles also established an elite
royal bodyguard of one hundred Scotsmen, Europe's first since the Praetorian guard
of ancient Rome. (Although it's also argued that Philippe Auguste, so worried
Lionheart would have him assassinated, had created the first bodyguard or
gendarmes—men at arms.)

For the English there followed a series of disasters. In 1435 the alliance with Burgundy fell apart as the two factions in France finally agreed to a peace treaty; in September that year Bedford died in Rouen, leaving behind a vast collection of books, tapestries, and treasures of various sorts, and with it England's hopes of ever retaining France. The French took Paris in the spring of 1436.

The war also continued to hemorrage money out of the English treasury, which groaned under the cost, with crown debts doubling in fifteen years so that, by 1450, they were over eleven times the country's annual revenue. And all of this was happening under the rule of a listless, mentally unstable king.

All mental illness is to some extent hereditary, and schizophrenia is no different, with up to 79 percent of the diseases's risk factors being genetic, the rest being a product of childhood environment.[3] Even to have one grandparent with the disease raises the chance of developing it five-fold, and whatever illness Charles VI suffered from, it was most likely inherited by his grandson Henry VI of England. Indeed, Henry's mother Catherine of Valois also exhibited similar symptoms before her untimely death at thirty-five.[4]

The sort of madness exhibited by an Aerys or a Nero has a certain glamor—violent, spectacular, and dramatic. The reality for Henry, as with many sufferers of mental illness, was a gradual withdrawal from the world, lethargy, and internal terror. His insanity was quite the opposite of the Mad King of fiction, and yet for the kingdom it was just as disastrous; as the world around him grew ever more violent, this gentle and pathetic man remained in childish innocence until the encircling political turmoil reached his own chamber.

Henry was born with an almost impossible burden, king of two warring realms before he could even walk or talk, one of them won by a charismatic, conquering father he could not possibly match. His childhood was the business of state, and yet he remained a boy all his life.

Henry VI, observers noted, had a weak chin and protruding lower lip and arms without muscle. He would, at times, agree to every proposal placed before him, tractable and obedient to everyone else's desires; at others, he was obstinate and would not take sound advice. He hated conflict of any sort, and with no initiative and no desire to make war, the king was helpless as his father's hard-won French territories were reclaimed.

Every king since the Norman Conquest had seen battle, but poor Henry was disgusted by the sight of a decayed corpse and objected to the impaling of executed prisoners as cruel. He also had a fear of nudity, and according to his teacher and biographer John Blackman, one Christmas "a certain great lord brought before him a dance or show of young ladies with bared bosoms" and the king "very angrily averted his eyes, turned his back on them and went out to his chamber."[5] Even the Pope commented that he was "more timorous than a woman."[6]

He was in many ways a saintly figure, so that when one intruder tried to behead him with a dagger, inflicting a wound so serious he thought he had succeeded, the king simply forgave him. And yet as Henry grew up it became clear there was something wrong with him that went beyond mere gentleness. Schizophrenia usually manifests between the ages of fifteen and twenty-five, and[7] a portrait of the young king "shows the staring, vacant expression characteristic of the disease,' while he ticked many other diagnostic boxes, among them inability to feel joy, great sensitivity to disagreement, strange emotional responses and inability to consider consequences of decisions."[8] Later, after a particularly shocking military setback, he slipped into a catatonic state, "taken and smitten with a frenzy and his wit and reason withdrawn," after which "he retreated into his world of mysticism and visions, probably happier than he had been for years."[9]

As the crown collapsed around the mad king, the realm's barons became more divided, their hatreds and struggles over prized inheritances unrestrained by royal power. The weak monarch bought them off with land and titles, turning lords into earls and earls into dukes, and so only raising their monstrous sense of self-importance. The great lords and their "affinities," mostly veterans with experience of killing, menaced rivals in land disputes, simmering violence escalating as more men returned home from defeat in France. At heart the conflict was about blood, brothers against cousins and families locked in marriage alliances joined in mutual destruction of rivals. They fought for themselves, their brothers, and their children, or to settle scores; but most of all to avenge fathers.

The period between 1440–1480 was known as the Great Slump. There was a decline in the supply of gold and silver and a fall in food production caused by the ever-colder weather. Land was also much reduced in value after the Black Death, and aristocrats found themselves competing against a gentry class of merchants, lawyers, and smaller landowners. The large number of offspring produced by Edward III— twenty-four grandchildren and at least sixty-nine great-grandchildren—also meant too many nobles with too few positions to fit their dignity.[10]

As in Westeros, the Realm was ruled by a King's Council, which included members of the monarch's own family, and was often (if not usually) beset by bitter rivalries. Although the monarch resided in Westminster, much of the time this story was based around the Tower of London, the city's fortress, palace, and prison.

Henry's youth was dominated by the bitter conflict between his uncle Humphrey, Duke of Gloucester, and his great-uncle Henry Beaufort, a hatred which only grew more bitter as the war turned against England. John of Gaunt had had four bastards by his mistress Katherine Swynford, but after Gaunt and Katherine married, Parliament and the Pope had declared the children legitimate, and they became the House of Beaufort. Henry IV had insisted on a clause stating that they were barred from the succession, and neither could any of their heirs claim the throne through their Beaufort line.

The eldest, John Beaufort, was given the title of Earl of Somerset and the middle son Henry rose to become Bishop of Winchester. Henry IV had made his half-brother Lord Chancellor back in 1403, but Henry Beaufort repaid the favor by siding with the king's son, the future Henry V, against him. Beaufort was now very wealthy and had financed the crown with loans for a war he supported. As he once said, in the duplicitous language of politicians down the years: "Let us make war so that we may have peace, for peace is the purpose of war."[11] He also had at least one illegitimate daughter, despite his office.

The conflict between Beaufort and his nephew had escalated back in 1425 when Humphrey had led a foolhardy military adventure in Hainault in pursuit of his wife Jacqueline's claim there; these disputed lands were now occupied by Jacqueline's first husband John of Brabant, who was supported by the Duke of Burgundy, an ally of England. The war, which went badly, endangered England's alliance with the Duke of Burgundy, Brabant's ally, and led to anti-Flemish rioting in London. Beaufort was forced to bring order to the capital with an army in late 1425.

Beaufort used his position to further the interests of his family and, in 1442, he convinced the council and Parliament to authorize his nephew John Beaufort, Duke of Somerset, to lead an expedition to Maine, in order to join up English territory in Normandy and Gascony. It was a complete disaster, and also angered the young lieutenant of France, Richard of York, who felt that his authority was undermined. Soon after his return Somerset died, possibly at his own hand, and Cardinal Beaufort now effectively retired.

King Henry had promised John Beaufort that, were he to die, then his widow should have the right to decide whom their infant daughter Margaret Beaufort should marry. However, he broke his word almost immediately and gave her wardship to his close friend William de le Pole, Earl of Suffolk, who betrothed her to his two-year-old son John. But then Henry was easily swayed by his inner circle: Suffolk; two senior clergymen, Adam Moleyn and William Ayscough; and James Fiennes, a soldier and sheriff who he appointed Lord High Treasurer (i.e. Master of Coin). Within a few months, in one brutal year of Henry's reign, all four men would be hacked to death by uncontrollable mobs.

SHAME! SHAME! SHAME!

Gloucester had meanwhile become another victim of witchcraft, or at least men's belief in it. Back in 1428 the arrogant duke had cast aside his wife Jacqueline of Hainault, having failed to acquire her land, and had the marriage annulled so that he could marry Eleanor Cobham, one of her ladies in waiting. The marriage had not been blessed with children and Cobham was known to have consulted what in southern England were then called "cunning women"—one Margery Jourdemayne, known as "the Witch of Eye Next Westminster."

She was not the only one; certainly Beaufort's nephew Edmund, who succeded as Duke of Somerset after his brother's suicide, had consulted Jourdemayne on his future, and had been told he would be killed in a castle, although if he only fought in the open he could avoid this grizzly fate, which Beaufort determined to do.

However, in 1441 Cobham was discovered to have been consulting with Jourdemayne over another matter, the prediction of the king's death, an incredibly serious crime. The Witch of Eye Next Westminster had even supposedly devised a wax image of the king so 'that by their devilish incantations and sorcery they intended to bring out of life, little and little, the King's person, as they little and little consumed that image."[12]

In July Cobham was tried as a witch and in November forced to walk the streets of London while carrying a candle for three days, as if she were a common prostitute, this being the common method of public shaming for harlots. She was forcibly divorced and made to live in various isolated castles on the Isle of Man and then the island of Anglesey. She was lucky; her co-conspirators were all executed. Jourdemayne was burned to death in Smithfield.

Humphrey of Gloucester had, in his combat with his uncle, failed to notice the rise of William de la Pole, who helped to ingratiate himself with King Henry and slowly sucked power away from the council which had ruled in his childhood and toward Henry's court. He became a deadly enemy of Humphrey.

While Katherine Swynford had got her hands into Gaunt and founded the Beaufort dynasty, her sister Philippa de Roet had married Geoffrey Chaucer, one of a handful of poets who emerged in the late fourteenth century when the English language had reasserted itself after three centuries of Anglo-Norman domination. Chaucer's *Canterbury Tales* are considered the most famous works in Middle English, the heavily French-influenced language that evolved from Anglo-Saxon (or Old English).

His son Thomas Chaucer had been one of Humphrey's many enemies, while Thomas's daughter Alice had become the second wife of the very wealthy Earl of Salisbury, which gave her large swathes of land in wealthy Berkshire and Oxfordshire. After the Earl's death she married de la Pole. They had a sort of pre-nuptial agreement, Alice being so much richer than her new husband; yet, quite unusually, it did become a love match.

William de la Pole, nicknamed Jackanapes, had been a leading commander in the war and Lord High Admiral from 1447. His grandfather Michael had been Richard II's close friend, but his father, also Michael, had sided with Henry IV and inherited the title of Earl of Suffolk; he married well and Jackanapes's mother Katherine de Stafford was related to the Mortimer and Beauchamp families.

Born in 1396, Suffolk had been injured at the siege of Harfleur in 1415 where his father had died of dysentery; later that same year his elder brother Michael had been killed at Agincourt, and Suffolk spent many long gruelling years fighting in France. In 1429, he had led the English retreat along the Loire, chased by six thousand French soldiers, Joan of Arc, and the Duke of Alençon before being captured, taken to Orléans, imprisoned, and ransomed for twenty-thousand pounds, a crippling amount at least seven times his annual income. He finally returned to England in 1431, where he became an ally of Cardinal Beaufort.

In 1432, Suffolk had been appointed to the royal council and later he was raised from Earl to Duke. Hard-working and diligent, he served on embassies and fought in Normandy, alongside a young Richard of York, and from 1433 became steward of the royal household, which gave him intimate access to the king. He was also the largest landowner in East Anglia and in this region his aggressive behavior toward neighboring estates had won him many enemies.

And so, with a vacuum in the leadership and the war going badly, Suffolk had taken the initiative by finding Henry a French princess who would bring peace to his realms and stability to his dynasty. He left for France in 1444.

The king of England, whatever his personal weaknesses, was a great catch and among the women considered as a match was Isabelle, Lady of the Four-Valleys, daughter of the Count of Armagnac, but her father was scared off by the king of France. Isabelle thereafter started a relationship with her brother Jean V, Count of Armagnac, and they had three children together, the only prominent case of full incest at the time (as far as historians know). Offending both popes and kings with this and various other reasons, Jean was eventually exiled and his marriage dissolved, the children declared bastards. Eventually allowed back, he wed again—to a woman who wasn't his sister—but died while his wife was eight months pregnant and she was forced to drink a poison that caused her to give birth to a still-born baby.

Instead attention turned to a fourteen-year-old girl with impeccable lineage, Margaret of Anjou.

TEARS AREN'T A WOMAN'S ONLY WEAPON.

The War of the Roses was dominated by two figures, a man and woman who would inspire two of the main characters in Westeros, Margaret of Anjou and Richard of York.

While the kingdom may have had a weakling on the throne, offended by nudity and dressed in a hair shirt, the queen who would share his bed was anything but. Formidable, beautiful, cunning, and ruthless, Margaret of Anjou was feared by her enemy Edward of York more "than all the princes of the House of Lancaster combined," according to one chronicler.[13] A correspondent of John Paston wrote: "The Quene is a grete and stronge labourid woman, for she spareth noo peyne to sue hire thinges to an intent and conclusion to hir power."[14] Arrogant and haughty, she kept a great household, with five female attendants and ten "little damsels."

Christine de Pizan wrote that "it is the duty of every princess and high-born lady . . . to excel in goodness, wisdom, manners, temperament and conduct, so that she can serve as an example on which other ladies and all other women can model their behaviour." The wise queen must also learn to cope with the failings of the men around her; their drunkenness, their vanity, lechery, and violence. De Pizan advised ladies with husbands who "conduct themselves abominably" to "bear all this and to dissemble" for responding harshly will gain them nothing.[15] She also insisted that a high-born woman requires knowledge of law, accounting, warfare, and various other important matters for the kingdom, adding: "The lady who lives on her estates must be wise and must have the courage of a man . . . She must know the laws of warfare so that she can command her men and defend her lands if they are attacked." Inevitably it was a task too much for Margaret, despite her best efforts.

Margaret's curse was to be stuck with a weak husband and to be a strong woman at a time when such people were called "viragos," an insulting term for masculine women. Like Cersei, Margaret wanted to take a man's role in government and to be respected for being better suited to it.

Born in Lorraine in north-eastern France, Margaret was the eldest of ten children to Isabella, Duchess of Lorraine, and "Good King" Rene. She was of solid blue blood, descended from King Jean II, as well as being the niece of Marie, the Queen of France. Margaret's father was in theory the Duke of Lorraine through his wife, as well as King of Naples, Sicily and Jerusalem as well as Duke of Anjou, Count of Provence, Duke of Bar, Count of Piedmont and king of Hungary. None of these titles amounted to anything in reality, and Rene endured a lifetime of military defeats during ill-thought-out adventures trying to claim them.

Many noble women led their estates and acted as regents for young sons because their men were away, or incompetent. Margaret's family was no different, and she learned at the feet of her grandmother Yolande de Aragon. Yolande had married Duke Louis of Anjou, from a branch of the French royal family who had controlled Sicily for many years, but after her husband's premature death she ruled in his place. Later when her son was away fighting for his various titles, she took his place at home too. The formidable Yolande played a prominent role in defeating the English in Maine and Anjou, alongside Joan of Arc, and became something of a surrogate mother to Dauphin Charles. Yolande also organized a network of mistresses for high-ranking men within the royal court and came to play a leading political role as a result. Margaret had lived with her grandmother for four years and it was here that she learned the art of ruling.

She endured much suffering. When Margaret's father was captured by the Bur-gundians, after yet another failed expedition, he was only released in exchange for two of his sons sent as hostages; one of them, sixteen-year-old Louis, then died in captivity from pneumonia.

Margaret was dark-haired and described as "handsome" rather than classically beautiful, although Chastellain, a Flemish chronicler of the time, said she was "a very fair lady, altogether well worth the looking at."[16] It was Suffolk who arranged the marriage and it was Suffolk who stood in for the king when he took the fourteen-year-old's hands at Tours cathedral in the prescence of King Charles in 1444.

Several months later she was brought over to England in a storm, setting foot in Hampshire, and after time spent at the many royal palaces along the Thames, the king took her to London where her new subjects declared her the savior of the two kingdoms. And yet Margaret and Henry's union was described as "marriage of fire and milk."[17] Like her predecessor Isabella condemned as a "she-wolf of France," she was tasked with an insurmountable burden in bringing order to a realm disintegrating under an unfit king. Dutch historian Johan Huizinga lamented that Margaret was "married at 16 to an imbecile bigot"[18] and while in later centuries Henry VI was regarded as a saint he was undoubatbly "pious, ineffectual and periodically deranged."[19] Even if he was not a bad man, the country could not tolerate a mad king.

The marriage was cursed, at any rate, being part of a peace treaty in which the English agreed to hand over Maine in 1448, viewed as a humiliation. Though it had been Henry's initiative, Suffolk was blamed.

Humphrey, now a fringe figure, had not even been invited to the 1445 peace negotiations, but such was the unpopularity of the treaty that when it became public knowledge his subsequent reputation as a martyr and hero was born even before his death. For then, in February 1447, Suffolk had arranged for his enemy to be arrested on trumped-up charges of treason, only for Humphrey to be found only five days later, dead, most likely from a stroke. Cardinal Beaufort expired just two months later.

Humphrey's career had ended in failure, and all the achievements of his brother Henry V would crumble to dust. His great legacy was his library, which on his death he donated to the university of Oxford—becoming "Humfrey's Library," the oldest reading room at the Bodleian Library.

32
A CLASH OF STEEL

The gods know the truth of my innocence. I will have their verdict, not the judgment of men. I demand trial by combat.

—TYRION LANNISTER

At Christmas 1386, a dramatic duel was fought between two Norman noblemen, Jean de Carrouges and Jacques Le Gris. Held in the center of Paris and watched in hushed silence by the great and the good, the contest became one of the most famous and brutal examples of the medieval system of justice—trial by combat.

The two men had once been friends, but earlier that year de Carrouges had accused Le Gris of raping his wife Marguerite, who had subsequently become pregnant. Only one person in the crowd that day could know for certain which of the men was telling the truth, but one thing was sure—one of them was going to die, for whomever lost the duel was deemed guilty in the eyes of God. The two men fought for more than their lives and honor, however, for if de Carrouges lost the fight then his wife Marguerite, watching from the sides, would be deemed a false witness and so would suffer the fate reserved for women accused of such a heinous crime—burning to death.

Jean de Carrouges was much older than his wife, and older men are always in fear of being cuckolded. He was a brave and ferocious warrior but also a difficult man, and he was suspected of being abusive to Marguerite—and at the very least it was a marriage lacking in love and compassion. He was also from a grand, more established family but now losing out to his newly risen rival, and the former friends fell into a dispute over land.

De Carrouges descended from a semi-mythical Count Ralph, who had fallen in love with a sorceress and met her for illicit love near a fountain in a forest—until his wife turned up one night with a dagger. The following day he was found dead and she escaped suspicion despite having a red mark on her face; soon she gave birth to their son, a boy called Karle who, the day he turned seven, developed the same red stain on the very spot. He became known as Karle le Rouge and for seven generations the family bore the red mark as their insignia, noted warriors who fought for the kings of France.

After his first wife and son had died, de Carrouges left for Scotland to fight the English and on his return married the young Marguerite de Thibouville, from a noble family that had nonetheless become disgraced after siding with the House of Plantagenet. Her inheritance brought him into conflict with his former friend Le Gris, who had also become the subject of his jealousy because of the favor the king had bestowed on him. The dispute relating to de Thibouville land had escalated into a lawsuit, but at a feast in 1384 they had resolved their argument, and the older man introduced Le Gris to his wife, whom he asked to kiss on the lips.

Le Gris, a tough soldier with an eye for the ladies, had grown wealthy while his neighbor was up beyond the wall. He was a big man, strong and intimidating, and in the bitter winter of 1386, while de Carrouges was in Paris, his rival arrived at his castle where he forced himself on Marguerite—or so she told her husband. De Carrouges, denied a trial by the local lord, journeyed to the capital to appeal to the king, but instead of demanding a criminal trial offered a duel instead.

Duelling was now rare, increasingly seen as a relic from a former age, but the king loved the idea, and Le Gris accepted. The accused claimed that at the time of the rape he was with a squire called Jean Beloteau, who unfortunately at this time was arrested while in Paris—for a different rape. Le Gris could have used benefit of clergy to avoid punishment, yet he wanted to win back his reputation, and the disputed land, too, and Paris's Parlement* too agreed to the duel, which was set for November 27, 1386 at the Abbey of Saint-Martin-des-Champ.

Trial by battle was something of an aristocratic luxury, and to the low born torture was the favored method of justice (not favored by them, obviously). Le Gris's servant Adam Louvel, who was accused of assisting in the rape, was "put to the question" to test if he was telling the truth, as were Marguerite's minions.

Such was the excitement around the duel that King Charles even delayed the event so that he could be back in time. The day before the trial his young son died but

---

*Unlike the Parliament of London, Paris's Parlement was a law court, not a law-making body.

instead of mourning, the king—six years before his first mental breakdown—ordered for parties to be held, with the combat a centerpiece of the festivities. Marguerite de Carrouge had also given birth to a son shortly before the battle, although whether a true-born de Carrouges or a bastard conceived of rape she could not know.

On the day of the fight thousands of people arrived at the Abbey before dawn, in a state of great excitement, including children, who were regularly taken to watch executions, whether it be "burnings, beheadings, hangings, drownings, live burials, and other cruel punishments."[1]

All except for one figure, alone and dressed in black—Marguerite. If it went wrong for her then she would be taken straight to Montfaucon, the grizzly place of execution at the northern edge of Paris, and "a city of the dead unto itself." This grim hillside was the "the notorious destination of murderers, thieves, and other condemned felons" recognizable to all by its giant forty feet high gallows with heavy crossbars large enough to fit eighty corpses: "Here live criminals with ropes already around their necks were forced up a ladder and hanged," while beside them the corpses of those who had endured drawing and quartering were beheaded.[2]

De Carrouges had been weak with a fever in the preceding weeks, and the sickness reappeared that very morning. His opponent was much bigger, and had a better horse and weapons, and armor. The accuser would have to depend on skill and speed if he was to kill the larger man who had raped his wife.

De Carrouges walked out first, repeating the charges against Le Gris, who was then knighted so that the men might be of equal standing when they fought. This was done with three taps on the shoulder with the flat of the sword: "In the name of God, of Saint Michael, and Saint George, I make thee a knight; be valiant, courteous and loyal."

This was a battle for honor, and for God's favor, and men fighting duels were banned from using any sort of charms or spells or other occult tricks, on pain of death. This was not a game, and between them there was no tilt-fence, as there was now in a joust; both men carried a longsword, axe, and a long dagger, and were protected by heavy plate armor.

Before combat began, de Carrouges went over to his wife. "Lady on your evidence I am about to hazard my life in combat with Jacques Le Gris," he told her. "You know whether my cause is just and true."

"My lord, it is so, and you can fight with confidence, for the cause is just," she replied. They then kissed.

Silence now descended, and it was decreed that anyone who interfered by entering the arena would be executed and anyone who dared even to "speak, gesture, cough, spit" would lose a hand or property.[3] Instead people would watch these deadly fights in total silence, "scarcely able to breathe."

Before a duel, the two combatants would join their left hands to show that their bond was one of hostility, as opposed to handshakes of peace made on the right. Mounting their horses, each fighter was a mountain of muscle, bone, and armor, and "the combined weight of horse, man, armor, and lance put nearly a ton of galloping momentum" behind a charge.[4] At high speed a lance could go clean through shield and armor and into soft flesh.

The two men launched at each other, in their first clash both hitting the other square on the shield with their lances, both almost knocked to the ground. De Carrouges and Le Gris were each back on their horses but managed to hold their grip and returned for a second charge. This time both men tipped their lances higher, aiming for the head, in almost perfect symmetry gathering speed as they headed straight for each other. They crashed, steel against steel so hard the crowd could see sparks, but both men remained on their horses, their strong frames taking the blows.

A third charge came, and the two opponents struck at each other "with great violence" so that both of their steel lance-tips smashed into the other man's shield once again. This time the lances were shattered and pieces of splinter flew in all directions.

They locked axes several times, tired and worn out. Then Le Gris took a two-handed swing at his enemy, missing but instead driving the sharp axe into his horses' neck, blood pouring out of the screaming animal, blood on the sand. De Carrouges managed to scramble clear, in turn maiming his enemy's horse, disembowelling it but losing his axe in the process; he drew his sword. Both men paused to catch their breath.

The two enemies stabbed and thrust at each other, exhausted under the weight of the metal and the stress, both their bodies pumping adrenaline and their hearts racing.

There was sunlight on metal and de Carrouges was blinded for a split-second; he slipped and his enemy caught him in the right thigh. Blood shot out and streamed down his leg and a low groan came from the crowd. Leg wounds were extremely dangerous, and even if an artery was not ruptured—which would have been fatal—it was now a race against time before blood loss overcame him, fighting with sixty pounds of armor against a mountain of muscle. In the background his wife sank against the railing behind her.

"THERE'S NO JUSTICE IN THE WORLD. NOT UNLESS WE MAKE IT."

As the medieval historian Georges Duby wrote: "God lays a cruel burden on those he arms with the sword of justice."[5] It was not much fun for those at the other end of the sword, either, as the prisons of Paris were places where "ears were cut off, tongues ripped out, eyes gouged from their sockets" and "the genitalia of wives who had betrayed their husbands were cauterized with white-hot tongs."[6]

Men were put to death by hanging and women by whipping, although burning was especially used against females. In France, homicide, treason, and rape were all punished by dragging the culprit through the streets and then hanging them. Arson and theft were also punishable by hanging, and sodomy with burning at the stake, while currency forgers were thrown into boiling water. Suicide was a crime, so the bodies of suicides were hanged, too. And yet people convicted of even quite serious assault usually escaped with a fine, this sort of regular everyday violence being seen as less of a threat. In contrast, a Parisian called Jean Hardi was burned at the stake for having sexual relations with a Jewish woman.

Justice was brutal everywhere; Venetians were notorioius for their love of money, so stealing from the city's treasury was punished by amputation of the right hand followed by hanging outside the treasury building. A man who let an outlaw or enemy of the city escape lost a hand and both eyes. Insulting the honor of Venice resulted in the tongue being cut out and perpetual banishment.

Punishments often fitted the crime. In 1382 Roger Clerk of London, who had "pretended to cure ailments with spurious charms, was sentenced to ride through the city with urinals hanging from his neck."[7] In Chester anyone brewing bad beer could be "put in the shit-seat," the *cathedra stercoris*, a chair in which the buttocks were publicaly exposed to mockery. By the fifteenth century, the stocks were commonly used in England and France; although they have a somewhat comic air to modern eyes they were often lethal, as stones might crack someone's skull, or they could suffocate.

Animals, too, were tried and condemned. A sow that killed an infant in the Rue Saint-Martin was hanged, and a pig that damaged a child's face was sentenced to death by burning. A horse who killed a man and then escaped was "convicted of murder in absentia and hanged in effigy."[8]

Justice systems had developed to end the cycle of feuding which otherwise plagued Europe in the early medieval period. In the north of England, a culture of blood feuds survived much longer than further south and in places like the Highlands longer still. Justice in Anglo-Saxon England was extracted through blood money, *Wergild* in old English ("man money"—the word *were* still survives in werewolf). This was the value of a man's life, and the amount his family had to be compensated if he was killed or injured, depending on social status, race, and sex (Welshmen, women, and peasants were worth less). This is a system still practiced by the hill tribes of the Mountains of the Moon, who retain archaic cultural practises as well as Anglo-Saxon sounding names like Ulf and Dolf.

Under Alfred the Great the state began to take a fine too, and in the case of accidental death the object that caused the accident was ruled to be a gift to God—*deodand*, the money going to the king. Later, under the Normans and Angevins, the state took on responsibility for finding murderers, which was previously a private matter, although the vast majority of killers escaped.

Vengeance was a common theme in honor culures like Westeros or medieval Europe, often passed through stories and songs, although people recognized the downsides. At one point Ellaria Sand wonders: "Oberyn wanted vengeance for Elia. Now the three of you want vengeance for him . . . If you should die, must El and Obella seek vengeance for you? Is this how it goes, round and round forever? I ask again, where does it end?"[9]

Just as *The Rains of Castamere* recalls old scores settled, so in real life the Icelandic *Njals* saga told of a fifty-year-old vendetta, and that was relatively brief for feuds at the time, which could go on for several generations. Today such vendettas still exist only in very unusually clannish parts of Europe, worst affected being Albania, which has had twelve thousand feuds in the past twenty-five years.[10] That they are illegal seems to make not the slightest difference to this ancient custom.

As states emerged, so more efficient if not fairer methods of justice also developed. In England, trial by ordeal had evolved in Saxon times, invoking the Almighty to decide who was guilty. A suspect might have to hold two hot irons and walk nine paces, and then have his hands bandaged; if they had not healed after a week he was hanged. Defendants might also suffer trial by drowning, to see if they were rejected by the water, or having their hand plunged into boiling water; the only exemptions were priests, who could choose "trial by morsel," which involved eating a certain amount of food in a given time—understandably a rather more popular option. Women were also prevented from trial by cold water on account of modesty, and there was criticism of "priests who peer eagerly with shameless eyes at the women who have stripped before they enter the water."[11]

Not everyone was convinced. Frederick II, Holy Roman Emperor and King of Sicily, and one of the great early skeptics who was suspected of atheism, wrote that the ordeal "is not in accord with nature and does not lead to truth . . . How could a man believe that the natural heat of glowing iron will become cool or cold without an adequate cause . . . or that because of a seared conscience the element of cold water will refuse to accept the accused?"

By the late Middle Ages local lords no longer had the power of life and death they once enjoyed during the period of the Anarchy. One definition of a lord was the possession of a gallows, giving them jurisdiction over lawbreakers,[12] and in the early thirteenth century there were sixty-five private gallows in Devon alone, which would not have had more than fifty thousand people.[13] Increasingly, though, the royal government exercised the sole right to take life.

Trial by torture was the more enlightened form of punishment used on the continent. In Germany, people lived in fear of *die verfuchte Jungfer*, the dreaded old maid, which "embraced the condemned with metal arms, crushed him in a spiked hug, and then opened, letting him fall, a mass of gore, bleeding from a hundred stab wounds, all bones broken, to die slowly in an underground hole of revolving knives and sharp spears."[14]

Another popular form, however, was trial by battle, alternatively known as the Judgment of God. Duelling is an ancient way of solving an argument—*The Iliad* describes two warriors fighting a duel over Helen of Troy—and the Vikings held such combats on islands where a circle of stones was laid out to mark the arena. Indeed, a man could claim another's land and even his wife by challenging him to a duel.

In the earlier Middle Ages, anyone could resort to judicial combat and public duels took place among peasants and town folk as well as nobles. But as class and status was marked out in every sphere in life, knights fought with swords and lances, while peasants used staves with iron heads. In civil duels, principals could hire champions to fight in their place, but in criminal duels two parties had to fight in person, since the penalty meant death, although women, the elderly, or the infirm could get a champion, a professional fighter to battle on their behalf; if they were poor their husbands would have to make do. In Westeros, Tyrion opts for trial by combat, finding a champion first in Bron and then in Oberyn Martell; Margaery opts for ecclesiastical court hearing. Neither is exactly fair.

These fights could be just as vicious as portrayed on the screen. In a duel in Flanders in 1127, "the two exhausted combatants finally threw down their weapons and fell to wrestling on the ground and punching each other with their iron gauntlets, until one reached under the other's armor and tore away his testicles, killing him on the spot."[15]

They could also be absurd, such as in 1372 outside Notre-Dame in Paris when a man fought a duel with a dog. This took place after one of the king's favorites had been found murdered on his estate outside the capital. It was a mystery but the deceased's pet, a giant greyhound, growled and barked every time it saw one Richard Macaire. He was known to have been jealous of the dead man and the king ordered for a duel to be held—Macaire got a club while the dog had a large barrel open at both ends where it could hide; waiting cautiously, the animal suddenly jumped at the man's throat, dragging him down until he surrendered. Afterwards he confessed and was hanged.[16]

Yet these events were in decline. In England, Henry II had established in 1166 a public prosecution service and a central court of justice at Westminster, and helped to create the jury system, which had its origins in Saxon traditions whereby a man could bring character witnesses. An accused was called to "be at your law twelve-handed," requiring him to find eleven "oath helpers"; the idea was that twelve men swearing on holy relics couldn't *all* be lying, but they were in essence simply character witnesses, judging the accused on previous behaviour (the opposite of today's jury system). These men were supposed to arrive at the "truthful answer"—*verdict* in French.

Trial by battle was therefore something of a relic by that point, although not entirely finished. Two nobles fought a duel in 1430 at Arras, and, in 1455, two burghers battled with clubs before a crowd at Valenciennes, and, in 1482, France's very last duel took place at Nancy. Combat survived in England even later and, in 1583, a duel to the death was fought in Ireland with Queen Elizabeth's approval.

Trial by combat was an accepted part of the justice system but as it faded, replaced by either trial by jury or torture, it evolved into the illegal practice of dueling, a highly ritualized practice that continued the judicial traditions, including a drawn sword as an appeal to duel, or throwing down of gloves—*jeter le gage*. Dueling remained as an aristocratic past time for many centuries, costing many lives needlessly, and Europeans often took up arms over the stupidest of reasons if they felt their honor was insulted. In one case, two Italian men fought a duel over the respective merits of the poets Tasso and Ariosto, during which one of them was mortally wounded; as he lay dying, the man admitted he'd never even read the poet he was supposedly championing (and presumably he never would now). The craze faded in the nineteenth century, increasingly clamped down on by the authorities and viewed with social disapproval, and, in England especially, mockery.[17]

"YOU RAPED HER, YOU MURDERED HER. YOU KILLED HER CHILDREN."

De Carrouges was now in mortal danger, and had Le Gris kept the knife in the wound it would have been fatal—but believing his opponent to be beaten, he took it out. And yet he was not finished: gathering the last of his fading strength, the aging warrior gave it one last push, seizing his mortal enemy Le Gris with his left hand, ferociously grabbing his helmet and dragging him down to the ground.

De Carrouges jumped on Le Gris, desperately trying to stab through the steel before he lost too much blood and faded away. His sword blunted, he used his dagger handle to smash open the face plate and tore it off, now demanding his enemy admit his guilt. Le Gris, pinned to the ground, cried out that he was innocent and de Carrouges thrust his dagger into his neck. Le Gris's throat gurgled, his body shuddered and then he went still. Exhausted, de Carrouges turned toward a figure in the crowd, bleeding and exhausted, and walked over to kiss his wife.

33

THE STALLION WHO MOUNTS THE WORLD

The Dothraki follow only the strong.

—JORAH MORMONT

In 1237, three riders appeared outside the city of Ryazan, 120 miles south of Moscow. To the gathered townspeople the figure at the front, a woman, shouted "One-tenth of everything! Of horses, of men, of everything! One tenth!" The cityfolk replied no, and the horsemen rode off. A few months later it awoke to the deafening thunder of horses; hundreds and thousands of horses.

"To the east, a black band of horsemen is hurtling across the horizon toward Ryazan under a dawn sky . . . the morning streets fill with slashing, cutting horsemen. People scream, body parts fly, pools of blood form in the fresh snow. Plumes of black smoke rise into a vermillion sky."[1] The city folk were slaughtered, men, women and children alike. The Mongols had arrived.

In Essos there live "dark-haired, copper-skinned riders, organized in bands of male warriors called khalasars, each with a khal at their head," living a nomadic life on horseback and preying on nearby towns and lives.[2] They are the Dothraki, so famed for their devastating fighting skills that the "Dothraki Sea is ringed with ruined cities ravaged by the horselords, and their reputations terrify those in their path."[3] These cities sometimes pay tribute to the Dothraki but also buy their poor wretched captives off them. The horsemen prey on the peaceful Lhazareen, "Lamb-men," who tend flocks east of the Steppes until the Dothraki turn up and destroy their town, enslaving and raping.

These people live in yurts and eat a diet almost entirely comprising of meat, including goat, duck, dog and, most of all, horse. Horses are their lifeblood, so central to their culture that even their name for themselves in their own language, "Dothraki," literally means "riders."

Viserys Targaryen describes the Dothraki as savages and certainly they aren't urbane: "Excessive drinking, feasting on roasted meats, public sex, ululation, howling rather than music, and loud and blatant boasting; these are the hallmarks of Dothraki celebration."[4] As Jorah Mormont says in the very first episode, when the young Daenerys sits awkwardly in her chair while watching the event descend into a bloody orgy: "A Dothraki wedding without at least three deaths is considered a dull affair."

Nomadic horsemen have been a menace to settled people since the dawn of history. For the ancient Greeks, the Scythians, hard-drinking barbarians from what is now the Ukraine, were seen as the antithesis to everything civilized—living outside of cities and dressing barbarically in trousers, they even drank their wine straight, whereas the Greeks diluted it with water. The Scythians were difficult to deal with, as Persia's Cyrus the Great found out when he tried to conquer them: "His head was then carried around in a skin filled with blood . . . so that the thirst for power that had inspired him could now be quenched."[5]

Perhaps the most terrifying nomads of the ancient world were the Huns, who came from central Asia during the last, chaotic years of the Roman Empire. The Huns were so devoted to the horseman's life that they even slept in the saddle. Everything about them seemed bestial to the settled Romans, including their tunics made from field mice stitched together and their habit of warming meat by putting it between their thighs and their horses. The Huns also looked strange, and later skeletal examinations reveal that they carried out cranial deformation of the young, sticking bandanges around the skull and so causing the head to grow pointed. (In Essos there are a nomadic group even further East than the Dothraki called the Jogos Nhai, who also do this.)[6]

The Huns were led by the terrifying Attila, who remains one of the most famous names in history, mostly because of the large-scale devastation he caused. Just as Khal Drogo had married the Westerosi Daenerys Targaryen in a bizarre wedding between civilized princess and savage, as her brother calls him, the Hunnish leader Attila had been promised the hand of Honoria, sister of the Emperor Valentinian III; or at least that's how Attila interpreted it when he was sent a wedding ring in 450AD along with a call for military help. He asked for the western empire as a dowry and got half of

Gaul. Later Valentinian denied him his bride and so Attila invaded Italy and left a trail of misery there, even threatening Rome itself.

Like Khal Drogo, Attila would lay cities to waste, but also like Drogo he would die a mundane death that did not live up to expectations, succumbing to a nosebleed at a feast while drunk and choking on his own blood.[7] Attila's body was encased in three coffins, one of gold, one silver, and one iron, covered first with the spoils of war and then earth, and afterwards everyone involved in the burial ceremony was put to death so that it remained a secret—and to this day the tomb has never been found.

Various other nomadic peoples emerged out of the steppes down the centuries. There was the Oghuz tribe, encountered by the widely-travelled Arab writer Ibn Fadlan, who estimated that they owned ten thousand horses and ten times that many sheep. "They live in felt tents, pitching them first in one place and then in another," he wrote. "They live in poverty, like wandering asses. They do not worship God, nor do they have any recourse to reason . . . They do not wash after polluting themselves with excrement or urine . . . [and] have no contact with water, especially in winter." One night the wife of one of the Oghuz men in attendance, the Arab recalled with horror, "as we were talking, she bared her private parts and scratched while we stared at her. We covered our faces with our hands and each said: 'I seek forgiveness from God.'" The husband found the visitors' prudishness amusing.[8]

Then there were the Xiongnu, who controlled grasslands to the north of China, and were described by a contemporary as "barbaric, willing to eat raw meat and drink blood" and truly a people who "have been abandoned by heaven."[9] On the other hand, the Khazars of the Caucasus mountains were so effective against Muslim invaders that in the eighth century the Byzantines sought marriage alliances with them. They eventually became Jewish, unusually. The Khazar *khagan* had twenty-five wives, according to Ibn Fadlan; each was a member of a different tribe and the daughter of its ruler, and these smaller groups recognized the overlordship of the Khazars.

Yet all nomads paled into insignificance besides the dreaded Mongols.[10]

THE WOMB OF THE WORLD

One westerner wrote of the Mongols: "They [are] like beasts . . . They live on wild roots and on meat pounded tender under the saddle . . . are ignorant of the use of the plow and of fixed habitation . . . If you inquire . . . whence they come and where they were born, they cannot tell you."[11]

Until their unexpected rise to world power, the Mongols were one of five tribal confederations living in the Mongolian plateau, fractious groups whom the Chinese emperors had encouraged to fight each other, which they were happy to do. The Mongols wore the "skins of dogs and mice," and one contemporary described them as "living like animals, guided neither by faith nor by law, simply wandering from one place to another, like wild animals grazing." It was said that "they regarded robbery and violence, immorality and debauchery as deeds of manliness and excellence."[12]

However, during the thirteenth century the steppes enjoyed unusually mild and wet conditions, allowing for a huge increase in the number of horses that could be fed. And it was at this time that a highly effective and highly dangerous leader united them; Temujin, or "blacksmith," was born in 1162 "clutching in his right hand a clot of blood the size of a knuckle-bone," according to Mongol tradition, which was interpreted as meaning he would have great glories ahead. That he certainly did.

Temujin, descended from a warrior called Boerte Chino, "grayish white wolf," was orphaned at age nine after some rivals poisoned his father. As he grew into a man, he recruited a band of allies called *nokjor*, a word denoting one who renounced allegiance to tribe or faction and instead followed a unifying leader. In 1206, Temujin, having defeated rival clan leaders, assumed the title of Cinggis, or Genghis Khan—universal ruler, from the Turkic word *tengiz*, "the ocean" or "strong."[13] From then until his death in 1227, he created the largest contiguous empire in history, stretching from the Caspian to the Pacific—the real-life Stallion who Mounts the World, the long-prophesized Dothraki lord who will conquer the entire globe.

Along the way the Mongols left a trail of bodies, the 13th century Persian historian Juvani calling their empire a "a peace of smoking ruins." In 1219, the invaders arrived in what is now Iran, where they "came, they sapped, they burned, they slew, they plundered and they departed."[14] It was said that "they killed women, men, children, ripped open the bodies of the pregnant and slaughtered the unborn."* In the city of Nishapur, the corpses were piled up to form a series of enormous pyramids to serve as

---

*Robert Baratheon foresaw the Dothraki in Westeros, in Season 1, Episode 5: "They go from town to town, looting and burning, killing every man who can't hide behind a stone wall, stealing all our crops and livestock, enslaving all our women and children."

a warning. One high-ranking official, Inalchuq, Governor of Otrar (in modern Kazakhstan) was executed on the orders of Genghis Khan in 1219 by having molten gold poured into his eyes and ears. The following year the Khan brought one hundred thousand Mongols to flatten the city of Bamiyan in Bactria; afterwards it was known as the Screaming City or Silent City.

Genghis Khan died in 1227, but his empire was inherited first by sons and then by grandsons who continued in a similar vein. Not long after, the Mongols arrived in Kiev and set fire to a church with the occupants inside; in 1241, they flooded into central Europe where, on April 9, an army led by the King of Poland and Duke of Silesia was devastated, the duke's head being paraded on a lance along with nine sacks filled with the ears of the European dead. Two days later the Hungarians were crushed. Panic gripped the continent, but luckily, though, the khan died soon after and the Mongols fell into internal squabbling. However, the Tartars, one tribe of the Mongols, took over Russia from the thirteenth to fifteenth centuries, and such was their importance in the founding of that great empire that a third of the old Russian aristocracy had Tartar names.[15]

To Europeans these people were exotic in the extreme: "They did not eat vegetables, drank fermented mare's milk and emptied their bowels without a single thought for those they were talking to—and in public, no further away from where one was standing than 'one could toss a bean.'"[16] Mongols also never washed and, since they were always around animals, to Westerners they smelled terrible.

THE DESERT OF DEATH

It was a three thousand-mile trek across the steppe and the arid desert of Mongolia, the real-life Dothraki sea, and unsurprisingly very few Europeans had made the journey. In the 1250s, Flemish missionary and explorer William of Rubruck had visited Mongolia where he described Tartar women as "astonishingly fat" with "hideously painted faces" and the men as having "monstrously oversized heads."[17] They were all very dirty and didn't wash, he added. Another traveler, Johannes de Plano Carpini, had gone in 1245, the first Westerner since 900 AD to travel east of Baghdad and return safely.

Carpini travelled from Kiev, recently sacked by the Mongols, and while in the region he described hailstorms so bad that 160 men drowned when the ice melted; he witnessed extremes of heat and cold, winds and drought that were alien to a Westerner.

Carpini learned that the Mongols didn't have cities but lived in tents; he observed that they were friendly to each although they had drunken binges after consuming fermented mare's milk. Mongols didn't like exchange but were very keen on receiving gifts (just like the Dothraki).

They worshipped the moon, which they called "the great emperor" and had religious ceremonies where men and animals were purified after passing between two fires while the women stood on the sides, pouring water on the men and chanting. Carpini went to Sira Orda, the court of the great khan by the Mongol capital Karakorum, now in Mongolia; there he learned that the emperor's mother had power "to execute justice" in his absence, just like in Essos where the dosh khaleen, the old widows of khals, are the effective rulers.

Europeans had begun to learn more about the East through two travelers, the Englishman John de Mandeville and Marco Polo, a Venetian. Polo spent twenty years with his father and uncle travelling to the court of Kublai Khan, encountering many strange sites and cultures. Along the way he visited the oasis town of Khotan on the edge of Taklimakan Desert in western China. Taklimakan means "Desert of Death" or "Place of No Return," hardly surprising when temperatures varied by 68 degrees Fahrenheit over a day.

He visited Malabar in India, where the king had five hundred wives. In India Polo also saw that faithful followers of a ruler "throw themselves into the fire together with the king of their free will, and are burnt with the king to bear him company in the other world." This practise of *sati*—where women burned in the funeral pyre of their husband—continued until the British empire suppressed it six centuries later.

He found yogis who had to apply to a religious position by first being tempted by women, who touched their 'members', and who failed if they were 'moved'. He also found Tebets, a Tibetan tribe who used to eat their parents when they died, a practice noted by Herodotus almost two thousand years earlier.

And the Mongol society he described on his return to Italy was strange in the extreme.

Mongols lived in portable villages, each family in a mobile home made of wood and felt called a *ger*, which they disassembled and carried on wagons when they moved. Their food was not to everyone's tastes: "They feed on flesh and on milk and on game, and also they eat little animals like rabbits, which are called 'Pharoah's rats.'" They also ate horses, camels, cows and dogs, drinking the milk of horses and camels too; if they couldn't bring milk with them on their travels they'd kill their horses as they went, or sometimes live off its blood by pricking its veins and drinking straight from it. They also kept dried mares' milk, which was eaten like a paste, which is probably as enjoyable as it sounds.

The Mongols drank koumiss, fermented mare's milk, which has a strong, sour taste, and when Marco Polo agreed to try the stuff his hosts pulled his ears back to ensure he swallowed it, which gives some indication of how flavorsome it was.

Mongol warriors, the Chinese observed, could survive for long periods without food or even water and were prepared to endure extreme hardships. Compared to Chinese soldiers they were also much stronger and healthier, living primarily on meat, milk, and other dairy products, rather than the grain which was a staple diet for settled peasants, low in protein and vitamins and leaving them weak boned and vulnerable to disease.

Genghis's grandson Kublai Khan became the fifth emperor in 1260, and under Kublai the Mongol rulers lived ever more lavishly in their northern or "upper capital," as they called it—Xanadu. There "the rich men and nobles wear cloth of gold and cloth of silk and under the outer garments rich furs of sable and ermine."[18] The Khan's special costume, bearing a total of 156,000 gems, went on display once a year at the court. Here two "great men like giants" guarded the doors of the feasting room, and people walking in could not touch the actual threshold and if they did they would be beaten (unless they were drunk, in which case it was excused).

In the Mongol-controlled Chinese city of Hangchow, Polo was dazzled: a "hundred miles around and guarded by twelve great gates, the city had blue-water canals, fire brigades, hospitals, and fine broad streets lined with house upon whose doors were listed the names of every occupant."[19] The city had twelve thousand bridges and "the most beautiful women in the world." In his palace there the Khan was served his meals by five singing virgins. Kublai Khan, his soldiers displaying his banner of a sun and moon, had come to own such extravagances as an albino herd of white horses, ten thousand or more in number, plus albino cows, from which only the Great Khan and his family were allowed to drink the milk. Albino animals were often prestigious to own which is why a white elephant was often given as a very grand—but very expensive to maintain—gift, and so gave its name to any dear but essentially useless project.

Each of the khan's four wives had an entourage of up to ten thousand people, Polo claimed: "Whenever he wishes to lie with any one of these four women, he makes her come to his room, and sometimes he goes to the room of his wife." On top of this he had "many other concubines." Every other year the Great Khan sent his messengers out to find the 500 most attractive females in his empire. Once assembled, the young women would appear before a group of judges and marked according to their "hair, the face, and the eyebrows, the mouth, the lips, and the other limbs—that they may be harmoniously and propionate to the body," and only those valued at twenty carats gold reached the presence of the Khan. After that, one of the older women in the khan's entourage would lie with the young woman in bed "to know if she has good breath and sweet, and is clean, and sleeps quietly without snoring, and has no unpleasant scent anywhere, and to know if she is a virgin'"—and implicitly rather more. Kublai Khan had twenty-two sons by his four wives and twenty-five sons by concubines; Polo did not mention how many daughters, but presumably this was not very important.

Even the Khan's minister Ahmad had forty concubines on top of his four wives, although rising high meant falling hard—after Ahmad's disgrace his four sons were executed. It was later learned that the minister owned a pair of tanned human skins and his eunuchs revealed that he made strange mutterings as if praying to something, presumably a demon.

Each Mongol man, Polo noted, "can take as many wives as he likes, up to a hundred if he has the power to maintain them," and they also had no taboo about marrying relatives.

Polygamy was the norm among all horsemen, and contributed to their relentless violence, an idea explored by a Royal Society paper, *The Puzzle of Monogamous Marriage*. Polygamy ensured that low-status men had little prospect of ever finding a mate and so "will heavily discount the future and more readily engage in risky status-elevating and sex-seeking behaviors," bringing increased levels of murder, rape, theft, kidnapping, and sexual slavery.[20] This absence of available women explains why nomads were driven to conquer settled people. In contrast the spread of monogamy in Europe, imposed by churchmen with the encouragement of rulers, was motivated by a desire to suppress internal violence.[21]

But the strong men who ruled these societies enjoyed huge Darwinian advantages. Ata-Malek Juvaini, a Persian historian who died in 1283, wrote that "of the issue of the race and lineage of Genghis Khan, there are now living in the comfort of wealth and affluence more than 20,000. More than this I will not say . . . lest the readers of this history should accuse the writer of exaggeration and hyperbole and ask how from the loins of one man there could spring in so short a time so great a progeny." But he was not exaggerating—one of the few well-known facts about Genghis Khan is that today one in twelve Asian men carry a Y chromosome originating in Mongolia, most likely the fruit of his over-active loins.

The Mongols had some customs that seem very odd to us. Marrying children is strange to modern mores, but it was the norm in medieval Europe; however, the Mongols went further by marrying dead children. After the "wedding" between two recently-deceased children a necromancer or shaman would burn all the documents relating to the marriage, with smoke announcing the union of the spirits of the dead. Then there was a feast, and later they made images of the newlyweds, placed on a horse-drawn cart with flowers and paraded them around before they were burned with prayers for a happy marriage in the other world. The two families exchanged gifts and kept in touch, just like with any in-laws.

No one can shed blood in Vaes Dothrak, but as Viserys discovers that does not mean you're necessarily safe. Likewise, the Mongols disliked shedding blood when they executed people, although this was nothing to do with any compassion—it was just a sort of tradition.

Indeed Mongol justice was strict. In 1252 Mongke, the fourth khan, punished seventy officers he believed to be plotting against him, forcing stones into their mouths, a common Mongol punishment. Kublai Khan had one minister, Sanga, a member of the Uighur ethnic group in central Asia, put to death by having his mouth filled with excrement. Ogul Gaimish, a princess who refused to declare her loyalty to Mongke, had her hands and legs sewn into a leather bag; he accused her and her mother of trying to kill him by magic spells, and so had them rolled up in rugs and drowned and her two chief counsellors also put to death. Under Mongol tradition, captives were killed if they failed the "measure of the lynch-pin," that is if they were taller than the pin at the end of the axle of the cartwheels. Men usually failed this test, while those who passed, mostly women and children, instead went off to slavery.

The Mongols were the unconquerable land force of their age but were inexperi-enced at sea. And yet Kublai Khan could not be "universal emperor," in his mind, while across the sea the island of Japan remained unconquered; he tried twice to remedy this, in 1274 and 1281, and failed twice. On this second occasion, a Mongol army tens of thousands strong carried in as many as four thousand ships could not defeat the Japanese, who like their island counterparts at the other end of the super-continent were aided by the weather, in this case a typhoon they called the "divine wind," or *kamikaze*.

Polo spent many years at Kublai Khan's court but eventually found an excuse to leave, and it was only after he was captured by the Genoese that his stories were widely circulated.

Polo's account sold only one-fifth as many copies as John Mandeville's tales of the east, but then he had the narrative advantage of having totally made it up—or at least some of his account was certainly invented and Mandeville was not his real name. In contrast, Polo was widely disbelieved at the time and mocked as a fantasist; local children shouted *Il Milione* at him, his nickname being Mr Million, as in a million lies. It was only in the nineteenth century, when academics painstakingly went through old court records from China and matched them with Polo's accounts, that it was accepted he was telling the truth.*

"EIGHTEEN TIMES THE HORSELORDS CHARGED"

The Mongols were brutally effective at warfare, employing giant slingshots and cata-pults to hurl stones, flaming naphtha (a sort of napalm) or dead corpses. Carpini wrote: "Sometimes they even take the fat of the people they kill and, melting it, throw it onto the houses, and wherever the fire falls on this fat is almost inextinguishable"—unless doused with wine.[22]

One of their tricks was to feign retreat and lure the opposition to a cliff where they were surrounded, and then overwhelm them with arrow fire, their ammunition some-times tipped with poison. Even their civil wars were dramatic and cinematic, such as in 1266 when Kublai went to war with one of his own men, Kaidu, a fight that involved two hundred thousand horsemen. Kublai Khan said he would have put Kaidu "to an evil death," wrapped in carpet and trampled by horses, had it not been for relatives intervening.

Mongols almost always won in hand-to-hand combat, and while they were famously brave and adept at horsemanship they also developed sophisticated weaponry too. The

---

Likewise A World of Ice and Fire described how in Westeros there is also *The True Account of Addam of Duskendale's Journeys*, a merchant's description of going through Essos, although 'spends most of its time finding ways to remind readers that the warrior women walk about bare-breasted and decorate their cheeks and nipples with ruby studs and iron rings'.

nomads had a different version of chain mail to the European type, and also carried hooks that could grab chain mail, while their boots had upturned toes to create air pockets to protect from frostbite. Mongol armor also had a mirror over the heart because they believed these could deflect evil forces, even spears.

At one point, Jorah talks to a young Dothraki man about the relative merits of curly and straight swords, and whether to wear "steel dresses" as he calls chainmail. Dothrakis have swords called *arakhs*, and as Jorah says: "for a man on horseback a curved blade is a good thing, easier to handle."[23] The Mongols indeed fought with curved *scimitars*, which were easier to use on horseback than straight European weapons, which were only later used by the Arabs, with whom Westerners now associate them.

In 1258, the Khan Mingke attacked Baghdad, then the jewel of the Muslim world and a city with twenty-seven thousand public baths. The Caliph Musta'sim had warned the Mongols that if he died "the whole universe will fall into chaos, the sun will hide its face, rain will no longer fall, and plants will cease to grow."[24] The Mongols weren't convinced, and launched a small attack, followed by a fake retreat, trapping the caliph's men. The city was soon captured and thousands of people massacred, its inhabitants dragged through the streets and slain. The caliph was wrapped in a carpet and trodden to death by horses, and his family was murdered, except a daughter who went into the harem. Baghdad lost 90 percent of its population to death or exile, its canals were destroyed, and the city never recovered; indeed, it marked the end of the Islamic Golden Age.

The Assassins now sent envoys to Europe, proposing a joint war against the Mongols, but too late; the horsemen destroyed the Assassins in 1256, and four years later they took took Aleppo, and a crusader leader sent a ship to Europe with the warning: "A horrible annihilation will swiftly be visited upon the world."[25]

In the Battle of Qohor, three thousand Unsullied face fifty thousand Dothraki, and while only six hundred of the eunuchs survive afterwards the triumphant Dothraki cut off their braids and throw them in front of the Unsullied in tribute to their bravery. The two real life models for these groups, the Malmuks and Mongols, did now face each other in battle, at Ayn Jalut in Galilee in September 1260. Setting aside their differences, the Malmuks had been given permission by the Christians to move north from Egypt where they faced the common enemy; they were victorious and afterward expelled the Mongols from Syria.

And in 1268, the Malmuk Sultan Baybars, nicknamed the Father of Conquest and famous for his brutality, had finally cornered the Christians in Antioch. He promised the Templars they could go but "when the gates were opened, Baybars grabbed all the women and children and sold them into slavery and decapitated all the knights and other men."[26] That same year Baybars took Safed, in what is now Israel, where, after defeating the Christians, he had the heads of decapitated Templars placed in a circle around the castle. Crusaders now controlled just a fortress on the edge of Acre; there the sworn brothers under marshal Peter of Sevrey held out while galleys evacuated Frankish civilians to Cyprus; a peaceful exit was agreed upon until the Mameluks began manhandling Christian women and children and so fighting broke out. On May 28, the fortress fell, and all the remaining Templars were killed.

When the Crusaders were forced out of the Levant, the Knights Hospitallers went to the island of Rhodes, and then the peninsula of Halicarnassus, the port of Tripoli, and eventually the island of Malta; as the Knights of Malta, they became famous as a defensive force against the Ottoman Empire and the Barbary Pirates.

The Templars, in contrast, were destroyed, but they had a lively afterlife. In Westeros, there is a Book of Brothers that records the doings of the Kingsguard, and in real life the Templars kept records in Cyprus. However, when the Turks captured the island they were largely destroyed, and as a result junk history has filled the void. In 1843, a book called *Historical Notice of the Order* first linked the order with the freemasons, who in reality only date back to the eighteenth century, and a genre of conspiracy theory was born.

34

THE SMELL OF
BLOOD AND ROSES

*I'll match him son for son, and I'll still have nineteen and a half left when
all of his are dead!*

—WALDER FREY

J ust as the Starks had their northern rivals, the Boltons, so the Percys had the
upstart Nevilles. In 1415, while King Henry V was fighting at Agincourt, the
northern baron Ralph Neville was defeating a much larger Scots force at
Yeavering, close to the border. It marked yet another personal victory for this prolific
head of an ascendent family, who had risen to become Earl of Westmorland, Warden
of the West March, and the most powerful lord of the north.

Ralph Neville had an enormous number of children, at least twenty-two by two
wives, and went to enormous lengths to get them all good matches. His first wife,
Margaret Stafford, descended from the Mortimer clan, produced eight children; his
second, John of Gaunt's daughter Joan Beaufort, gave him another fourteen, nine of
them sons.

Neville was able to advance his children through ruthless matchmaking, or "mat-
rimonial larceny" in the words of one historian.[1] Richard, his eldest son by his second
marriage, married Alice Montacute, who as daughter of the Earl of Salisbury passed
on to her husband her father's great wealth and title. His younger brothers William,
George, and Edward became respectively through marriage barons of Fauconberg,
Latimer, and Bergavenny. Many of Ralph Neville's daughters married well, too, to the
dukes of York and Norfolk and the earls of Stafford and Northumberland, so that most
of the participants in the War of the Roses were descended from him as a result. Only

one of his children did not marry, seventh son Robert, who thanks to his father's connections became Bishop of Salisbury aged just twelve in 1427.

Ralph Neville's second wife Joan was considerably more well-connected than his
first, and after her daughter Eleanor Neville had been married to the son of Harry
Hotspur, she had used her influence to have the Percys restored to their titles and land
in 1416. In theory, the two families should have been joined in alliance, as they had
once been when fighting the Scots, but it did not turn out that way.

Richard Neville's match to the Salisbury heiress was the most lucrative of all, especially after Thomas Montagu's face was blown off at Orléans. Joan and Ralph's eldest
son also inherited from his father large estates across Yorkshire and Westmorland, as
well as Essex in the south, and on top of this the wardenship of West March, giving
him control of much of the border too. Yet there was a sting in the tail. Much of the
fighting in this conflict involved disputes over inheritance, and Neville's second wife
had used her hold over her husband to favor her children at the expense of those from
the first marriage. As a result, the two branches of the House of Neville fell into
increased hostility.

Joan had also used her influence in the royal council to marry her youngest child,
Cecily, to the most expensive and most eligble child bachelor in the realm.

Richard, Duke of York, was a second cousin of Henry V and great-grandson of
Edward III through two different lines. His mother having died giving birth to him,
Richard of York was only three when his father was executed, and spent the next eight
years in the custody of Robert Waterton at the behest of Henry V. Waterton had been
one of the men involved in the murder of Richard II and had a very sinister air, and
these formative years must have done much to form his cold character. Although
King Henry eventually gave York his ancestral lands on account of his uncle's sacrifice at Agincourt, in 1423 the royal council sold York's wardship for three thousand
marks (some $1.5 million in today's money) to the Nevilles.

The House of York, despite the name, had their base in the English midlands, at
Fotheringhay Castle in Northamptonshire, "a mass of stone battlements and towers
rising, in the shape of a fetterlock, the family badge,[2] protected by a river and moat.

Northamptonshire is on the border of the major dialect regions of England, the
small village of Watford traditionally the point at which the South ends. It lies on the
linguistic fault line, or "isogloss," of the three main dialect divisions in English, and
to the south and east is the region around London where Received Pronouncation, or

the Queen's English, later developed; here people pronounce bath as barrth, while to the north and west the word was spoken as baaath. (Today, "north of Watford" is used to denote northern England, and in particular England beyond London, although confusingly Watford is also the name of a large town just north of the capital).

Fotheringhay Castle had been built in 1100 by Simon de Senlis, a Norman baron who had married the daughter of William the Conqueror's niece Judith. The castle had fallen into disrepair in the fourteenth century before being handed to Edward III's fourth surviving son Edmund of Langley, who was made Duke of York for taking part in an "ineffectual invasion of Scotland."[3] Langley had rebuilt the castle, which by this stage had been surrounded by a large keep nicknamed the Fetterlock because it resembled a type of latch used for horses. Langley had little interest in politics, was regarded as dim-witted and so had been handed rather minor duties, among them Master of the Royal Mews and Falcons. And so, the emblem of the House of York from 1402 onwards was the Falcon and Fetterlock, and which his grandson Richard of York wore with pride. It was here at Fotheringhay, at the Church of St Mary and All Saints, that the family crypt held their ancestors, as well as the memorial to Edward of Norwich, killed at Agincourt.

Richard of York was just thirteen when, as an orphan, he became attached to the Neville family. The following year Ralph died, his children's inheritance all secure. Soon after this York's childless maternal uncle Edmund Mortimer, Earl of March, who some had hoped to make king in 1415, also passed away, without issue, leaving York yet more wealth and another major title. Aged just twenty-four, York replaced Bedford as regent of France, despite very little experience, and although he had a number of successes the English position in France was unsustainable, the army and crown too stretched in terms of money and men. Richard and Cecily did not have children for another fifteen years, by which time she was twenty-four, a relatively late time to begin a family—yet they went on to have thirteen boys and girls.

During his time in Normandy York had fallen out with one of the Beauforts, John, Duke of Somerset, who had been favored by the king with positions and men and could offer only military failure in his attempt to relieve Gascony. Despite Beaufort's suicide in 1444, the feud with York was inherited by his brother Edmund; this deadly rivaly would intensify as the king's mental condition became more apparent.

York's first son, Henry, had died in infancy but was followed soon after by another, born in Rouen in 1441 and christened Edward; York's friend Baron Scales, a marshal of Normandy, stood as godfather. Another five of their children would die in infancy, but many more of their descendants would perish in fratricidal fighting over the next seventy years. There were later question marks over the legitimacy of Edward, born in Normandy at a time when York was often away from his wife and when she was alone and vulnerable, mourning the death of her first son. York was a distant figure and it was later said that a tall archer called Blaybourne may have comforted Cecily, and York was apparently cold toward Edward compared to his second son Edmund; and yet it was spoken of only by political rivals, and certainly Cecily Neville was also famed for her piety. Aristocratic women could always expect their name to be blackened.

Although York was married to a Neville his natural allies should have been the Percys, now hereditary enemies of the House of Lancaster. Despite losing land after their rebellion, the Percys still owned much of Northumberland as well as territory in Cumberland, Yorkshire, and Lancashire, while the Nevilles held most of County Durham and a slice of Yorkshire.

The Percys and the Nevilles were not the only families heading into conflict. A great feud in the south-west between the Courtenays and Bonvilles had accelerated after Henry VI had handed the stewardship of the duchy of Cornwall to two men at the same time. The Courtenay family had a private army of eight hundred horsemen and four thousand foot soldiers. The Beauforts were also a power in the south-west, while in East Anglia the de la Pole family had developed a rivalry with the Mowbrays, Dukes of Norfolk.

Elsewhere there was the Holland family, descended from Richard II's violent half-brother; one of their number, John Holland was in January 1444 made Duke of Exeter. Then there were the Staffords, descended from Richard II's uncle Thomas of Woodstock; in 1444 Humphrey Stafford, its most senior member, became Duke of Buckingham and in 1447 he joined the leading ranks of the dukes.

These conflicts were further worsened by disaster abroad. Provoked by piracy from English sailors, in July 1449 Charles VII renewed hostilities and invaded Normandy; Rouen fell to the French in October and Edmund, Duke of Somerset, fled under safe conduct from the French, agreeing to pay for his safe passage, an unchivalrous act in many people's eyes. York was furious, but as he was already proving himself to be an irritant to the king's circle at court, he had been sent away to Ireland as lieutenant in 1447.

War was changing. Chateau Gaillard, Richard the Lionheart's great Norman fortress captured by the French through its latrines, had held off the armies of Henry V
for a year in 1419. In 1449, when the English possessed it once again, the French
simply battered it to the ground with artillery and it was never rebuilt. New and far
more destructive technology was now in men's hands and the devastating results
would soon be seen by all.

After the Normandy disaster London was flooded with refugees, English and
French, collaborators who could never return home, and numerous former soldiers,
which led to an alarming rise in crime. The crown was now hopelessly in debt, by
almost £400,000, and unable to reimburse the House of York, Richard having spent
£20,000 of his own money funding the conflict. War was hugely expensive, and the
realm could not afford it while it was being ruled by a clique of the king's corrupt
friends—or at least that is what York felt.

In January 1450, violence exploded around the country. Soldiers in Portsmouth
rioted and murdered Bishop Adam Moleyns, who for fifteen years had been an ambassador and clerk of the privy council, and a close friend of the king. Now came the turn
of Suffolk, blamed for the hated peace treaty and even blamed for Humphrey's death.
On February 7, the Commons had him formally impeached of "high, great, heinious
and horrible treasons" and accused of inviting the French to invade England. It was
only through the king's intervention that this was reduced to a lesser charge and a
reduced sentence of banishment for five years. Chased out of London by an angry
mob, Suffolk went to Ipswich and set sail for Calais, swearing as he left that he was
innocent; however, as his boat reached the Channel they were intercepted by a ship,
the Nicholas of the Tower, and Suffolk was crudely beheaded by the crew.

Suffolk's death looked like piracy, yet the Nicholas belonged to the royal fleet.
Among his many roles Suffolk had been in charge of the Court of Admiralty, having
replaced John Holland, second Duke of Exeter in 1447. Holland was the son of
Richard II's half-brother John Holland, who had seduced and impregnated his wealthy
cousin Elizabeth, forcing the dissolution of her previous marriage. Brutal violence
ran in the family, as did venality, and the role of Lord Admiral was well known to offer
great opportunities for enrichment, bribery, and theft, "which made him, in practice, pirate-in-chief."[4] John's son Henry, the third duke, had been Constable at
the Tower of London and was so famous for his cruelty that the rack there was
nicknamed the "Duke of Exeter's Daughter." Exeter was also, since 1447, York's

son-in-law, married to his eldest child Anne, and Suffolk's political downfall had been led by Lord Cromwell, also one of York's men. And so, Suffolk's death was at least good fortune for young Henry Holland, who afterwards was made Lord Admiral.

In April 1450, the English were driven out of Normandy and the following month the county of Kent erupted into rebellion, spurred by a fear of French invasion, rumors of conscription, and the loss of trade caused by the collapse of the wine trade.

By June 6, while Parliament was in Leicester, armed men were assembling around the Kentish town of Ashford, and had elected as their captain one Jack Cade, who claimed to be a cousin of the Duke of York, although he was probably a low born Sussex man and little is known of him. By June 11, the rebels were at Blackheath, and Buckingham's kinsmen, William and Sir Humphrey Stafford, were sent with four hundred men to crush the Kentishmen. They were both killed, and their army destroyed.

On June 19, rioting erupted in London and the king allowed for the unpopular James Fiennes, also known as Lord Saye, to be arrested as a traitor and put in the Tower, despite their friendship. Violence further erupted across the country; another of the king's close friends, Bishop Aiscough, was chased by a mob in Wiltshire, his crime being to have married the king and Margaret of Anjou, and the mob caught up with him in Dorset where he was hacked to death.

The king, unnerved by rioting and by a lightening strike on his palace at Eltham, ran off to Leicester, along with his council, while the queen remained in Greenwich, just outside London; on the way to the safety of the midlands, a madman was arrested for trying to whip the ground in front of the king's horse, screaming that York should take charge. His nerves began to fray.

The rebellion descended into further carnage. At Guildhall, Cade set up a court for traitors, with twenty prisoners beheaded, among them James Fiennes; Fiennes's son-in-law William Crowmer was then hacked to death, and the two heads were made to kiss.

From Greenwich the Queen had advised the rebels to take offers of pardon and head home, which some did. The others were driven out of London and Cade was chased down to Lewes in Sussex and fatally wounded. His followers met with bloody retribution, the villages of Kent filled with the hanging corpses of rebels. Unnerved by the behaviour of the mob and the chaos his friend's discontent was causing, York's ally Lord Scales went over to Somerset's party, the proto-Lancastrians.

ROSES RED AND WHITE

Into this power vacuum Richard of York returned from Ireland in September, marching on Westminster with five thousand men in a show of force, amidst rumors he would be arrested. He sent the king two open letters complaining that he had been treated like a criminal, and despite attempts to delay York, he arrived in London on the twenty-seventh, where the king listened to his complaints but did not act on his implied demands that he wanted Somerset removed.

In London, tension between supporters and opponents of York led to punches been thrown in Parliament, but by November York had left London for his estates in the Midlands and Edmund Beaufort, Duke of Somerset, was back from Normandy. Somerset had been put in charge of breaking the resistance in Kent and then made constable, the highest military post in the country. He had also received a vast sum from the council in compensation for the loss of Maine, while York got nothing.

After the War of the Roses, Henry VII symbolized the end of the conflict by having a new emblem intertwining the red rose of the House of Lancaster and the white rose of the House of York, that of his wife, Richard's granddaughter Elizabeth. Although it later became known as the Quarrel of the Warring Roses and later War of the Two Roses, the House of York's symbol of the white rose and Lancaster's of red were rarely used.

"The War of the Roses" was first used either by Sir Walter Scott or another nineteenth century writer, Lady Maria Callcott, but the idea of the war being associated with these flowers went back to the fifteenth century, if not the exact wording.[5] However, it was powerfully represented by a scene in which William Shakespeare portrayed the point of breakdown. Here, in *Henry VI*, Somerset and York are depicted in the gardens of the Temple Church in Holborn where various noblemen pick red and white roses to show which side they are on.

Although this event didn't happen, roses have long had associations with blood, death, and lust. As far back as the fourteenth century, Florentine writer Giovanni Boccaccio used red and white roses in his collection of stories, *Decameron*, to symbolize love and death, while a white rose appears in Botticelli's famous artwork *The Birth of Venus* for the same reason. Likewise, in Westeros, Eddard Starks recalls his sister's deathbed screams and the falling of rose petals in a dream; he talks of the room where his sister died smelling of "blood and roses." Or as famous Dutch twentieth century historian Johan Huizinga wrote of the late medieval period: "So violent and motley was life that it bore the mixed smell of blood and roses."[6]

On December 1, 1450 a Yorkist mob tried to kill Somerset at Blackfriars, west of the city. Richard rode in the following day and restored order, but his reputation was damaged by the blatant thuggery and lawlessness of his supporters. Somerset was placed in protective custody in the Tower while York was in charge of the city, but he had to be released early in the new year.

Richard then used a client to petition Parliament in May 1451 demanding that he be made heir presumptive and sent letters to the towns of southern England calling on them to march to the capital and remove Somerset. In revenge, in June Somerset had Yorkists such as Thomas Young put in the Tower and then the following month another of his allies, William Oldhall, was locked up; several men from Standon, a Hertfordshire manor held by Oldhall were also taken away, and when Oldhall fled to sanctuary the Earls of Salisbury, Wiltshire, and Worcester broke in and dragged him out.

It came to a head in February 1452 when York marched on London, hoping to be added to the royal council; Somerset brought the king and his army to meet him, as well as the dukes of Exeter, Buckingham, and Norfolk. The royal force was camped at Blackheath, south-east of the capital with the Yorkists at Dartford a few miles downstream, and one of their boats equipped with cannon. But it was a trap, and the *Great Chronicle of London* recalled that York was taken "lyke a prisoner" until rumors—that his son Edward, Earl of March, was approaching with ten thousand men—forced Somerset to release him. Although Edward was now just ten, and it would have been extremely unlikely he had raised an army, it was possible that York's followers had gathered a force and put his son at the front as a figurehead.

Two weeks later at St Paul's, York was forced to swear a humiliating oath of allegiance to the crown, made to kneel before the king. York was excluded from government, going back to his estates near Ludlow, marcher territory he had inherited through his mother's Mortimer family. However, Somerset's forces then arrived in the town and so York fled east to Fotheringhay; many of York's tenants were convicted of treason and then told afterwards that they had been pardoned, "a demeaning trick to play on men who had no choice but to obey their lord's summons, and done to demonstrate York's powerlessness."[7] A partisan record states that when Somerset went to Ludlow in July 1452, York's tenants of "divers of the duke of York's townships . . . compelled to come naked with choking cords about their necks in the direst frost and snow" before being told they were to live.

Late in 1452, Edmund and Jasper Tudor, the king's half-brothers, were raised from commoners to earls, and Edmund was given the Honor of Richmond, a very prestigious title dating back to the Conquest. This move angered Richard Neville, Earl of Salisbury, who had been granted the profits from this honor for decades with the promise of eventual hereditary right. The Neville family had until this point loyally supported the king; now a crack had appeared.

Since she had shown herself a capable ruler during the Cade rebellion, Margaret of Anjou took over the role previously carried out by Suffolk advising the king. However, she had so far failed to carry out the most important function of a queen— providing the king with an heir—until the spring of 1453 when it was announced that she was with child.

And yet more disaster was to befall the realm, for in August that year Henry sunk into a catatonic depression, the king "indispost sodenly was take and smyten wt a ffransy and his wit and reson wt drawen."[8] The reason, as John Paston wrote, was that Henry had received a "sudden and thoughtless fright" upon news from France.

The war that begun as a medieval conflict of arrows had ended with the modern horrors of cannons and handguns. Body armor and castle walls were made obsolete by gunpowder and large, organized armies led by centralized monarchies. At the Battle of Castillon in July 1453, large French guns completely annihilated the English army—each shot killing six men in one explosive blast—and when reinforcements arrived they suffered the same fate. The English held out for an hour until the Bretons smashed into their right flank, causing further devastation. Their commander John Talbot was trapped under a horse; he was wearing a crimson satin robe and was recognized by an archer, Michel Perunin, who opened up his chest with an axe. Afterwards Talbot was only identified by his teeth. His son was killed with him and English rule in France was over, finally and forever.

This year often marks the end of the Middle Ages, but not primarily because it was the end of this long war. For several weeks earlier there had come to London the most shocking news possible from the other side of the continent, the greatest catastrophe to ever hit Christendom.

35

THE ROCK THAT BESTRIDES THE CONTINENTS

Some of them don't think Dothraki should breed with foreigners. They don't think the blood should be diluted. They are stupid old women. They don't realize that we have always diluted our blood.

—DOTHRAKI HIGH PRIESTESS

The Emperor in Constantinople had first known of the Turks back in the sixth century when ambassadors were sent to the nomads seeking an alliance against Persia. The horsemen had emerged from Altai in central Asia, close to what is now Mongolia, and their language still reflects these deep Asiatic origins, so that the Inuit and Turks have the same word for bear, *ayi* or *ayl*.[1] Indeed they were first referenced by the far-off Chinese way back in the second century BC, the Turks being just the name of a dominant tribe among many such nomads. "Turk" literally means "strong man" and, as with Mongols and Tartars, the name was applied to numerous groups; the leader of the Hungarians, once also a nomadic group before settling by the Danube, was called "Prince of the Turks," *Tourkias archon* by the Byzantines.[2]

Along with the Mongols, the Turks became the other great horsemen of the Middle Ages, although their trajectory was very different, driving them first to become an empire across three continents, then the leaders of the Islamic world and later a secular European republic. And the historical allusions obviously sting, as the Turkish military in 2014 banned officers from watching *Game of Thrones* because it supposedly insulted Turks by basing the nomadic Dothraki on their ancestors.[3]

According to historian Roger Crowley, "Like their cousins the Mongols, the Turkic peoples lived in the saddle between the great earth and the greater sky and they worshipped both through intermediary shamans. Restless, mobile and tribal, they lived by herding flocks and raiding their neighbors."[4] They were very effective, for in the words of Ibn Khaldun, nomadic people "have no gates and walls. They always carry weapons. They watch carefully all sides of the road. They take hurried naps only . . . when they are in the saddle. They pay attention to every faint barking and noise. Fortitude has become a character quality of theirs, and courage their nature."[5]

The Turks were riders, and in their saddles they lived on *pastirma*, thin slices of dried beef which became *pastrami* in Italian and later English. Another old Turkish word, *ordu*, or military, became "horde" and also "Urdu," the language of Pakistan. The horses they bred in the Pamir mountain range on what is now the Afghan/Tajik border possessed great strength, and the Chinese said they were "sired by dragons." More remarkably these animals were noted for "sweating blood," this effect caused most likely by parasites which bit at their skin; the Chinese desired these Ferghana horses so much that an army once marched several thousand miles to acquire the famous mounts.

The first Byzantine-Turkish alliance fell apart when, against renewed Persian counter attacks, the emperor had a sort of nervous breakdown, much to the Turks' fury; two years later their ambassador rejected another coalition and put ten fingers in his mouth, saying angrily, "as there are now ten fingers in my mouth, so you Romans have used many tongues.[6]

In 737, the Arabs defeated the Turks and soon after their leader Sulu was murdered by a rival over a dispute following a game of backgammon, yet their advance into the Middle East continued. The Turks were originally followers of shamanism and brought their druids with them; their emblems were a peregrine and a hawk, *tugrul* and *cagri*. However, as the Caliph of Baghdad recruited them into his armies as military slaves, so by the tenth century Islam had taken hold, although for many years they held onto some aspects of their indigenous religion.

The Seljuk Turks, one branch of the group, first appear in the late tenth century in Transoxania in central Asia, where they were still brigands. They were known to rarely waste an arrow and fought ferociously on horseback and, by 1045, under their leader Tughrul Bey, had established control over the Abbasid Caliphate in Baghdad and Tughrul was proclaimed "Sultan and King of East and West."[7] In 1055, the Turks entered Baghdad, where Tugrul Bey married the caliph's daughter in a Turkish-style wedding, a clash of cultures which French historian Jean-Paul Roux likened to "marrying an African chief to a Habsburg to the sound of tom-toms."[8]

These nomads swept into Asia Minor in the eleventh century; the Christian kingdoms of the Caucasus mountains appealed to the Byzantines, and, in 1071, Emperor Romanus Diogenes marched east to fight them; the ensuing battle of Mazikert proved a catastrophic defeat for the Christians, the Turks establishing rule over most of today's Anatolia. Their leader Alp Arslan, whose "moustaches were said to have been so long that they had to be tied behind his back when he went hunting," made Emperor Romanus kiss the ground before him, and then put his foot on the victim's neck.[9] After being helped to his feet by his conqueror, the Emperor had to hand over four provinces, ten million gold pieces and one of his daughters.

Afterward, Constantinople fell into dismal decline, and never recovered after the sack of 1204. As well as stealing many of its holiest relics, the crusaders had taken away many of the city's most skilled craftsmen, too, further hastening its decline. But although horsemen without a civilization to match the Romans, the Turks were far more open to adaptation and adoption than any of their enemies. Greek was spoken at their newly established court at Erdine and numerous Arabic and Farsi words were absorbed into their language (later it imported huge numbers of French words, too). They were also open minded about military matters, and in the fourteenth century developed a more modern form of warfare than the western Europeans, who were "still fighting pre-gunpowder wars, in which heavy cavalry, imprisoned in armour, charged off pretentiously after quarrelling leaders had windbagged away as to who would lead," in historian Norman Stone's words.[10] As they absorbed so they expanded, overwhelming Anatolia before spreading into Europe, surrounding the increasingly meager remnants of the "Roman Empire."

In the fourteenth century, having conquered most of Greece, the Turks set up the first paid professional army in Europe since the fall of Rome, comprised of young Christian boys who were taken from their families, educated, converted, and turned into Turks. These infantry units were called the "slaves of the Gate," the *Yandi Cheri* or Janissaries, and they were loyal only to the sultan. Later sultans such as Mehmet the Conqueror had as bodyguards former Christian boys who had been taken from their homes as children, guarding them as they slept and ready to place themselves in the way of the assassin's blade.

To the western world the prospect of little Balkan boys kidnapped by the monstrous, exotic Turks to be raised as brutalized soldiers was appalling. And yet there was much to admire in these people, even hostile European observers could see, in their tolerance, appreciation for art and beauty, their willingness to absorb foreign cultures. They adapted and adopted so much that over time the people changed too, developing today's Mediterranean appearance due to the large number of conquered peoples adopting Turkish culture. Modern genetic studies of the Turks place them much closer to southern Europeans ancestrally than to the original central Asian Turks.

Sultan Murad I took Gallopoli in 1353, a foothold into Europe that they would maintain for six centuries (the British Empire, famously, could not dislodge them from there in 1915). Soon Constantinople found itself surrounded, and it did not help that after its Emperor Cantacuzene left to become a monk, there was thirty-five years of characteristic bloody internecine fighting, with various members of the royal family deposed, imprisoned, or worse.

In 1365, Murad made Adrianopole (now Erdine), northwest of Constantinople, his new capital, and six years later he defeated the Serbs and Bulgars, cementing control over the Balkans. The French then led one last desperate attempt at holy war, which ended in disaster, although the Turks had bigger problems with the Mongols.

Although Genghis Khan caused a huge amount of death, he was nothing on Tamerlane, also called Timur, who ruled much of China, Russia, the Middle East, and India ("Mughal," the name for later Indian rulers, from which we get mogul, is a corruption of Mongol). When, in 1401, Tamerlane marched through what is now northern Iraq, sacking Baghdad, he ordered his men to produce two enemy skulls each or lose their own, and vast numbers of women were taken as slaves. More pyramids of heads were created as he swept through Asia Minor and emptied its cities, defeating the Turks in 1402 and taking the sultan prisoner, where he was kept as a captive in the back of a wagon so that he might watch the Mongols as they devastated his land. The experience killed him.

Later Tamerlane felt so guilty about the bloodshed he'd caused that he promised to atone by launching a new, this time holy, war, in the hope that this might cause God to forgive his earlier bloodshed. Luckily, he died soon after, having raised a huge army for the conquest of China, but the Mongol leader is still believed to have killed a higher proportion of the world's population than anyone else in history.

Despite this the Turkish advance continued, and Constantinople was near surrounded. And then came the year 1432, one of omens in Turkish legend: "Horses
produced a large number of twins; trees were bowed down with fruit; a long-tailed
comet appeared in the noonday sky over Constantinople."[11] On the night of March
20, Sultan Murat was in the palace at the capital in Edirne. His wife, a captured slave
most likely from Serbia, was in labor and, unable to sleep, he read the Koran and was
just reaching the "Victory *suras*," the parts that told the story of the promised triumph
over the unbelievers, when news came of a son, his third. Seeing it as a sign Murat
called him Mehmet, the Turkish for Mohammed, and he was indeed to be a forceful
leader—the day after becoming sultan Mehmet had his young half-brother murdered
in the bath.

The Turks had taken a tribute from Constantinople for some time, but the new
Emperor Constantine XI withheld it. He hoped for Western help, but after a century
of plague, famine, and war, the Latin Christians had lost interest in crusade; although
the Pope was open to aiding the Byzantines, the Western Church still insisted on
their recognizing Roman supremacy and to the Orthodox Christians this was
unthinkable. And the walls of Constantinople were increasingly a relic from another
era, before the new fire weapons.

Although gunpowder had followed traders, armies, and plague along the silk road
in the fourteenth century, its use had been limited. Big guns were difficult to cast
because, as iron was poured to make them, any tiny cracks were liable to expand when
they were in use and so cause the gun to explode.[12] However, a Hungarian called
Urban had approached Mehmet II with the offer of two new guns cast using improved
technology and capable of firing cannonballs of 1,000lb (450kg), four times the size
of the largest French projectile. Over three months they were dragged by sixty horses
and three hundred ships from Edirne to the banks of the Bosphorus facing Constantinople, a distance of 130 miles; Mehmet had amassed an army of two hundred thousand troops, while the Queen of Cities had only nine thousand men defending it.
Even Mehmet's own private entourage featured as many as thirty thousad people,
with sixty just to make cakes.

Constantinople had always been protected by the Virgin Mary, its people believed,
and the last of the Romans would need all the divine help they could muster. As the
Venetian Senate was told by a representative in 1452: "Constantinople is completely
surrounded by the troops and ships of Sultan Mehmet."[13]

In the summer of that year Mehmet was constructing a castle on the Bosporus with the aim of closing access to the Black Sea. The Ottomans called it Throat Cutter and it was armed with large bombs which could blast at any passing ship, further tightening the noose. On November 26, a Venetian merchant galley bringing supplies to the city from the Black Sea was sunk by Throat Cutter; its sailors made it to land where they were taken to the sultan and its courageous Captain Antonio Rizzo was impaled on a stake, along with forty of his crew, in full view of the city.

Inside Constantinople the people prepared for the worst. Its considerable Latin population, mostly Venetians, would support them until the bitter end, despite their difficult history; indeed, the Venetian flag of St Mark and the double-headed eagle of Rome flew side-by-side from the Blachernae Palace as the invaders surrounded them.

After the Turks had paraded the bodies of more captured blockade-runners, "the lamentation in the city for these young men was incalculable," reported Makarois Melissenos, a Greek bishop who collected many eyewitness accounts of the siege, but grief soon turned to anger.[14] The following day, 260 Ottoman prisoners were "savagely slaughtered" in full view of their compatriots.

The Byzantines had always been pious people, and morale was further damaged by unseasonable weather in May 1453, with wildly unusual storms occurring for that time of year. The most likely cause was an eruption of the volcanic island of Kuawe, 1,200 miles east of Australia, months earlier, producing "eight cubic miles of molten rock [that] were blasted into the stratosphere with a force two million times that of the Hiroshima bomb."[15] It dimmed the planet, blighting harvests across the Northern Hemisphere, at a time when the known world continued to get colder and colder. South of the Yangtze River, in southern China on the edge of the tropics, there was forty days of snow. Tree-ring records from England show dismal summers, just as the king was slipping into madness. In Constantinople that spring, the city was hit by rain, hail, fog, and snow, with strange, lurid sunsets and strange optical effects.

For a nearly-defeated people who for so long had survived only because of the blessing of the Virgin, it looked like a vision of Armageddon. Then on May 26, perhaps also because of the volcanic eruption, the city's Hagia Sophia cathedral was lit up with strange ribbons of fire.[16]

On the morning of May 29, 1453, Mehmet performed ritual prayers and donned the talismanic shirt, embroidered with the names of God and verses from the Koran.

The sultan set off on horseback, wearing his turban and caftan, with a sword at his waist, and surrounded by his commanders.

The Turks attacked from land and sea. After the guns bombarded the walls, the first assaults would be made by irregulars and foreign auxiliaries, the least import-ant of the troops, many of whom had been forced into battle or were there for the booty. Many were Christians, kept there by force, according to Nicolo Barbaro, a Venetian witness to events. "Greeks, Latins, Germans, Hungarians—people from all the Christian realms," according to Leonard,[17] another man who saw it.

People living in a besieged city always knew their fate would be grim if the men outside could not be stopped. When the Turks broke through the walls people were dragged from their chambers, and children were snatched from their parents; the old "slaughtered mercilessly," along with "the weak-minded . . . the lepers and the infirm" while "the newborn babies were hurled into the squares." Assorted groups of captives were tied together by their captors, "dragging them out savagely, driving them, tear-ing at them, manhandling them, herding them off disgracefully and shamefully into the crossroads, insulting them and doing terrible things."[18] Many women threw them-selves into wells rather than endure the nightmare, a course that is discussed in King's Landing when a similar fate awaits them. The Turks were not especially cruel, after all, this was just the fate that awaited all cities at the mercy of enemy armies.

Some of the invaders were killed fighting among themselves over the most beauti-ful girls. Churches and monasteries were ransacked, with those closest to the wall plundered; the icon of the Hodegetria, one of the most precious religious relics in the city, was cut into four pieces and divided among soldiers, for its frame. Crosses were smashed, and the tombs of saints thrown open for treasure, holy artifacts and golden robes were ransacked along with precious pearls, and churches emptied of gold. Afterward, corpses floated in the sea "like melons in a canal."[19]

As the assault had begun a small number had been able to escape; about a dozen Greek and Italian ships had made it out of Turkish-controlled waters and reached the safety of the West. The survivors, after the slaughter had died down, settled down to life in a new reality. Their last leader, Constantine XI, "in Christ true Emperor and Autocrat of the Romans," was last seen running into the thickest of the fighting, fall-ing with the empire he ruled. His body was never found.

KNOWLEDGE IS MY TRADE, MY LADY.

Today the tomb of Mehmet has the inscription: "Mehmet Chelebi—Sultan—may God fasten the strap of his authority to the pegs of eternity and reinforce the supports of his power until the predestined day!"

Such was the Ottoman way with words. The sixteenth century sultan Selim had given himself many titles, including "Marcher Lord of the Horizon," "Rock that Bestrides the Continents," and "Shadow of God on Earth."[20] When that the sultan's underling, the ruler of Crimea, wished to address the Russian Tsar he declared: "The immortal declaration of the Khan that concerns you is as follows."

To Europeans the Turks remained a source of exotic fascination and their practices were indeed strange. Back in 1389, the new Ottoman sultan Bayezid had ordered his brother, whom he regarded as a threat, to be publicly strangled, and this became something of a tradition; just as in Dothraki society a new Khal will have the old leader's children killed, so the Turks had a similar grizzly ritual. As Jorah says: "A khal who cannot ride is no khal. This isn't Westeros where men honor blood. Here they only honor strength; there'll be fighting after Drogo dies."[21]

In the sixteenth century, sultans began to purposefully impregnate their various mistresses, in order to sire a pool of potential successors, and a morbid system developed where the mother of the boy who succeeded would have all his half-brothers, sometimes mere infants, strangled with a silken cord by the head gardener. (Like the Mongols, the Turks had superstitions about spilling blood, in this case that if there was blood at death the soul would not go to heaven.)

The Turks institutionalized many other habits that to us seem quintessentially oriental, exotic, sensual, and sinister. A *harem* was originally just the name for the private area of the house, as opposed to the *selamlik*, or greeting area, but it grew to mean a house for the mistresses of the sultan. The harem was ruled by the Chief Black Eunuch of the Ottoman court, called the Kizlar Agha. This office was created in 1594 and was always held by African eunuchs, usually Nubians from upper Egypt or northern Sudan.

The Chief Black Eunuch was also tasked with running spy rings within the palace, since rulers—quite reasonably—viewed them as a nest of treason. The Kizlar Agha was usually close to the Valide Sultana, or Queen Mother, who "embedded him deeply in dynastic politics, supported by his network of spies, who were (primarily but not exclusively) the other black eunuchs."[22] The Black Eunuch was third in importance aftet the sultan, behind only the Grand Vizier and religious authority, the Sheikh ul-Islam. The Vizier was the chief minister, although the term literally means the sultan's foot, like the hand of the king. In contrast to the Chief Black Eunuch, his counterpart the Chief White Eunuch, who came from the Balkans or Caucasus, was in charge of male pages, a not-so-prestigious role that had less opportunity for plotting.

The brutal practice whereby the sultan's strongest son (or at least the son possessing the most cunning mother) took the throne did at least ensure that reasonably intelligent men would always rule. The European model meant that an heir without any of the necessary qualities might become king and the realm would be thrown into chaos—as happened first in France and then in England. The tradition of strangling all the new ruler's brothers survived for a couple of centuries, until one sultan in the late sixteenth century, Mehmet III, never fully recovered after his nineteen half-brothers were murdered. In the early seventeenth century, Sultan Ahmet I, a poet who patronized the arts, outlawed the practice. Although the country began a process of modernization in the late nineteenth century, accelerated by President Atatürk in the twentieth, the Turks remained figures of fascination and fear for European audiences for centuries—on the one hand seen as exotic, brutal oppressors of Christians, but also as hospitable, civilized, generous, and open-minded people whose culture bestrides east and west.

36
THE KINGS IN THE NORTH

During the Age of Heroes the Boltons used to flay the Starks and wear their skins as cloaks.

—JAIME LANNISTER

T he Percy-Neville feud burned slowly at first. As late as 1453 the two families were still working together against the Scots and dealing with administration in the north. But a changing balance of power is always dangerous, in families as with countries, and outside of the county of Northumberland the Nevilles had now gained the upper hand. The expansion of the Salisbury branch of the Neville family had also provoked increasing opposition from the other northern houses, among them the Clifford and Dacre families in Cumberland; Lord Dacre was also married to one of the daughters of Ralph Neville's first marriage who were embittered by their loss of their rightful inheritance.

The Percys had traditionally held prestigious positions, such as the Warden of the East, which have their corresponding equivalents in Westeros, where Ned Stark is Warden of the North, a role that entails protecting the realm from the Wildlings; Eastwatch in Westeros also corresponds to the East March in England.[1] Yet the Nevilles had since acquired the better paid position of Warden of the West, defending the Cumberland stretch of the border, much to their rivals' anger.

In Martin's world, the various houses trace their descent back to different groups of people who arrived in Westeros; most were originally Andals, although the Targareans and Baratheons were once Valyrian, and the Starks hail from the First Men (although presumably most are a mixture). In reality, all of the noble families in England were of Norman descent through the male line, since the Normans had effectively decapitated English society, killing thousands at Hastings and disinheriting the others, so that there were just two significant native landowners by the time of the Conqueror's death. The one exception were the Nevilles, who could trace their lineage back to the old kingdom of the North.

Ralph Neville came from a long line of de Nevilles, mostly called Robert or Geoffrey, but Ralph's paternal great-great-great-great-great-grandfather Sir Robert Fitz Meldred Raby had adopted the name after marrying an Isabella de Neville. Fitz Meldred was of Anglo-Saxon origin, his father's father being the far less French-sounding Dolfin, lord of Fitzuchred. Although born after the conquest, three of Dolfin's grandparents were Saxons, unusual for someone of such high status after 1066; his paternal grandfather was Gospatric, Earl of Northumbria, and his grand-mother Etheldreda, granddaughter of Edmund II, the last fully Saxon king of England. And way, way back into the mists of time, Gospatric's paternal ancestor was King Osberht of Northumbria, killed in battle in 867 fighting the Vikings. This marked the end of the old kingdom of the North, and when Northumbria was con-quered from the Vikings two generations later it would be the "South Angles" in charge, the former kings reduced to earls.

Fitz Meldred, through his mother, was also descended from Uchtred the Bold, Earl of Northumbria, whose family seat was Bamburgh, the northern kingdom's cap-ital and the site of a fortress and castle ever since. He was killed in 1016 in the war against the Norsemen.* Like the Starks, the Nevilles were descended from the old kings of the North, and like them could imagine their forefathers sitting on the same land under the same stars many centuries before. A Neville could look upon the land in Durham and Yorkshire and know the line of his forefathers went back to an age of kings, and as DNA analysis of the British population confirms that the Saxons took natives wives, so his family would go all the way to the first men of the island.

After Ralph Neville's death in 1425, his sons fell out over the inheritance of his estates, and from 1430 to 1443, increasing hostility between the children of his first and second marriages. The eldest from the former, John, had died prematurely and the inheritance taken up by his son Ralph, who became second Earl of Westmorland. He and his brothers and cousins were bitterly opposed to their half-Beaufort cousins, their anger growing even worse when Richard Neville, the Earl of Salisbury came into his wife's inheritance, too, making him vastly wealthier than his half-nephews.

---

*Uchtred is also the name of the Northumbrian protagonist in Bernard Cornwell's *Last Kingdom* series, who is supposed to come from the same family.

Salisbury and Alice Montagu had twelve children, the eldest of whom, another Richard, had been made immeasurably wealthy when, aged six, he was betrothed to another rich heiress, Anne Beauchamp, Countess of Warwick. Her father, the Earl of Warwick, was a fantastically rich and cultured man who had also burned Joan of Arc; Anne's mother Isabella le Despenser was descended from Edward II's infamous crony. At twenty-one, Warwick had already inherited lands larger in size than his father's, though poorer, and luckily for him a lot of wealthy female relatives died in a short space of time, including his aunt Cecily in 1450 and his wife's half-sister in 1448. But Warwick also had five younger brothers make it to adulthood, surplus males who added to the land- and status-hunger among the aristocracy.

The Percy clan were married into both branches of the Nevilles, with Henry Percy, the second Earl of Northumberland, wed to one of Salisbury's sisters and his sister Elizabeth married to Westmorland. Despite this, Percy found himself drawn into the conflict.

Henry Percy had six sons, at least two of whom were uncontrollably violent and possibly unstable. His second son Thomas was the worst, a notorious thug who was "quarrelsome, violent and contemptuous of all authority" and with "all the worst characteristics of a Percy for which his grandfather Hotspur was still a byword."[2] In King's Landing, Ned Stark is forced to listen to the pleas of the Riverlands folk after their homes and tenants are attacked by the monstrous Gregor Clegane, and in real life ordinary people often found themselves at the mercy of thugs with titles. In 1447, the twenty-five-year-old Thomas Percy and friends ended up in jail in Yorkshire after going on a rampage, but it was just the start of a litany of disorder. On another occasion Percy ordered his men to beat up the Sheriff of Cumberland because he was a Salisbury follower.

In 1449, Suffolk gave Thomas Percy the title of Baron Egremont partly in the hope that it would encourage him toward more civilized behavior, although it only had the opposite effect. Suffolk also wished to rebalance northern politics in favor of the Percys, but little could prevent the clan rivalry spiralling out of control.

Richard Percy, the earl's third son, was also a hooligan; he and a gang had once broken into a church in nearby Craven and seized a local bailiff while a priest said Mass and would have killed him were it not for the holy man's intervention. Another brother, William Percy, was made bishop of Carlisle in 1452, aged just twenty-four, but only used his position to help his siblings stir up trouble with the Nevilles.

Despite his bloodline, Egremont preferred to spend his time in the seedier taverns and inns of his native county, enjoying the company of the "artisans, tradesmen and the unemployed" whom he recruited as his own private gang.[3] Over the winter of 1452-3 he moved onto York, which was enduring hard times and had become a breeding ground for various resentments. The city was in between Neville territory centered on Sheriff Hutton and Sowerby, with Percy land to the west and north in Topcliffe, and thus was a natural flashpoint.

So, when in January 1453 three deputy sheriffs arrested Oliver Stockdale, a Percy tenant in the city, 120 locals came out to stop the arrests by asserting they could not do that in Percy land where the king's writ did not run. In Westminster, the Neville Earl of Salisbury informed the king of Egremont's worsening behavior; Thomas Percy was summoned to fight in France instead, but refused to come south. Instead Warwick's brother John Neville was sent to look for him, and a "cat and mouse game" followed, leaving a trail of vandalism and broken limbs across the region.[4] Neville, the third of Salisbury's sons, had from an early age experienced war and diplomacy, and grew to become an efficient and reliable commander, especially adept at flushing out rebels. Aged just eighteen, he was among a handful of men given the task of overseeing border defences, but he had little prospect of an inheritance while his brothers lived.

With escalating violence between the two men and their followers, the royal council in London ordered Neville to stop; three days later he threatened to hang tenants if they didn't tell him where Egremont was and the king sent orders to both men ordering them to cease the violence. Egremont had now formed an alliance with the even more unpleasant Duke of Exeter, a sadist rather than a simple thug, and the two men planned for Exeter to claim the duchy of Lancaster and challenge York's protectorate. In order to calm the waters, Richard of York went north in May 1453 where he had to retreat after learning of a plot to assassinate him.

In August, the Percy-Neville conflict broke out into open fighting, the spark being the inheritance of Wressle Castle in Yorkshire. Wressle had been in the hands of the Percys since the early fourteenth century and the wider area had once been their heartland before they moved further north. But after their failed rebellion against Henry IV, the estate had been confiscated and passed to the Duke of Bedford and had since been held by the crown and loaned out to favorites. The loss still hurt to a family in fear of decline.

On August 24, 1453, there came the marriage at Wressle of Salisbury's second son Sir Thomas Neville and Maud Stanhope, which would result in the castle passing to the Nevilles; it ended up as a battleground. There are records of 710 Percy men turning up, among them a wide range of social classes, including Oliver Stockdale, who like all the Percy tenants repaid their loyalty when called upon. Although this "Battle of Heworth" was described as the first skirmish of the War of the Roses, no one died— but that would change soon.

Two weeks later, John Neville and his gang smashed up a Percy house at Catton in Yorkshire, breaking doors and windows and writing threatening messages on the wall. The following day Richard Percy and forty-one "drunken rioters," twenty-nine of whom had been at the wedding battle, broke into the house of a vicar in Neville territory and stole all the wine, before beating up the local deputy sheriff and bailiffs. As often with civil conflicts, the eruption of out-and-out violence was often preceeded by lower level thuggery, a sign of growing disorder.

The two families slowly shifted sides in the wider dynastic dispute. The Percys had been bitter enemies of the House of Lancaster, but from 1453 the Nevilles began to align themselves with York, partly because of their marriage alliance but also Warwick's increasing hostility to his cousin Somerset. The two men were in dispute over the inheritance of their wives, half-sisters, who owned large tracts of land in south Wales. Northumberland, instead, moved toward the house that had killed his father and grandfather.

Queen Margaret gave birth to a prince at Westminster on October 13, 1453, named Edward, and afterward a great council was summoned; at some point it was decided that York should be invited, and on October 24, a letter was sent signed in the king's name to his "right trusty and well-beloved cousin" and the messenger was told to advise him to put aside his differences with Somerset. However, when the baby was presented to the king at Windsor, he showed no signs of recognition. Somerset stood as godfather, and there was muttering—like Cersei, Margaret was rumoured to have fathered a bastard behind her unsuspecting husband's back, a boy who grew into a monster and whom powerful enemies wished to disinherit.

With the king in a catatonic state, in January 1454 Margaret issued "a bill of five articles" in which she demanded "to have the whole rule of this land," to appoint officials and to have an income for her and Edward. Margaret, like the other women in her family, had experience ruling in the absence of men, but a powerful queen was always dangerous. MPs rejected her proposal.

The king could not be coaxed out of his slump, even when Archbishop of Canterbury Cardinal John Kemp died on March 22, 1454, after which twelve leading lords and bishops rode to Windsor to tell Henry. Three times Reginald Peacock, the scholalry Bishop of Chichester, tried to addresss him, but they could get no answer; two days later it was agreed that York should be appointed protector.

When Richard of York arrived in London, he persuaded Norfolk, now an ally, to launch an attack on Somerset at the council, once again accusing him of treason and demanding his imprisonment—a majority of lords this time agreed. John Mowbray, the third Duke of Norfolk, descended from the same Mowbray of Richard II's time. His father, like York, had had his wardship sold to Ralph Neville, who married him off to his daughter Katherine, making the current duke yet another scion of the prodigious Earl of Westmorland. Mowbray had 150 properties across twenty-five counties, but it was mostly concentrated in East Anglia, and only there could he gather an affinity.

Mowbray was in fierce competition with local rivals in the flatlands by the North Sea, which saw increasing use of force in property disputes. Mowbray's main competitor was Suffolk, but even after his downfall he found himself frustrated by rivals, mainly Viscount Beaumont—who was also his stepfather and in charge of one-third of Mowbray's patrimony. Originally loyal to the crown, Norfolk grew closer to York as the conflict escalated, largely because Beaumont sided with the queen.

The larger families had to decide whose side they were on. Humphrey Stafford, Duke of Buckingham, had a huge affinity and estates in twenty-two counties in 1455, producing five thousand pounds in revenue, around the same as York. He had fought with Henry V and been knighted, and later he served with York, who was nine years his junior and had no military experience yet had been appointed Lieutenant of Normandy nonetheless. He had married yet another of Ralph Neville's daughters and had so far remained neutral.

William FitzAlan, Earl of Arundel, was married to Salisbury's eldest daughter but he was cautious; so too was John Vere, Earl of Oxford, who was allied with Norfolk against Suffolk and disliked Somerset but remained neutral for now. There was Thomas, Lord de Ros, who had the oldest continuous title of nobility in the whole country, based in Helmsley in Yorkshire; his mother had married Somerset and they were locked into an almost interminable conflict over inheritance, but he remained loyal to the crown.

The council was now full of Yorkists: Warwick, Salisbury, and Lincolnshire baron Ralph Cromwell, while Exeter, Somerset, Northumberland, and Clifford had been excluded. As protector, York made himself Captain of Calais, on top of Lieutenant of Ireland, and he also appointed Richard Neville as chancellor, but despite such partisanship his rule was just, and he had also brought some semblance of peace to the vendetta in the North. He had also imprisoned his own son-in-law Henry Holland, Duke of Exeter, in Pontefract Castle, for his involvement in a local feud, against his oath as a lord. Queen Margaret, Buckingham, and the Tudor brothers all received lands or offices, while York's ally Warwick got nothing. His great enemy Somerset remained in the Tower, however.

York, in many ways an honest and honorable man, lacked the necessarily guile to rule the land; he failed to understand that many leading men were not like him and expected bribery and rewards. He seemed to possess an acute sense of what was right and just rather than expedient. In contrast, Somerset, who had wormed his way into the king's inner circle, was better at manipulation; he was also a spymaster, and in January 1454, even while imprisoned in the Tower, he still employed friars and seamen to act as his spies and "enter the house of each lord in the land."[5]

In May 1454, Salisbury and York ordered Northumberland as well as his brothers Thomas and Ralph to come to London to explain their actions. No Nevilles were asked, despite some of their depredations, and the Percys refused. Instead Egremont went to York where they held the mayor hostage; so, Richard of York went north and forced his submission.

York also succeeded in ending the violence between the Courtenays and Bonvilles, which had begun in October 1445. The feud had deteriorated to such an extent that one of the Courtenays, Sir Thomas, had arrived at the house of a Bonville affiliate, an MP called Nicholas Radford, and knocked him to the ground, after which one of his cronies cut the man's throat. But with York's firm hand the Realm saw some peace.

Then on Christmas Day, 1454, Henry left his catatonic state. Five days later he met his son, held his hand, and thanked God for this blessing; yet, he said, he could not remember the child ever being born, who must have been brought by the Holy Ghost. After eight years of a childless marriage this only further added fuel to rumor and speculation about the child's real father. York, who stood next in line, was certain the boy was really Somerset's bastard, or at least he had instructed his liegemen to say so.

The mad king released Somerset, and, on February 9, York was formally stripped of his role as protector and of his Calais position, which was given to Somerset. Salisbury was forced to abdicate the chancellorship and his son Warwick made to release Henry Holland—and so the Yorks and the Nevilles went north to raise an army.

Somerset arranged for a great council to meet in Leicester in the midlands, in which York and his allies were invited. But Salisbury had already recruited an army of five thousand from his family seat in Middleham in Yorkshire. In mid-May the king's men chose to meet instead at St Albans and ordered York, Salisbury, and Warwick to come with no more than five hundred men in total. They did not.

In Westeros, Jaime can raise thirty thousand men against Robb, and Tywin brings an equal number; Robb Stark can gather around twenty thousand. Standing armies are expensive, and only a few lords could raise anything like that many troops; outside Ware, a few miles from St Albans and just north of London, the king's force heard news that York was nearby with three thousand men, half raised as he marched south from Yorkshire, while the king had only two thousand.

Despite attempts to compromise by replacing Somerset as Constable of England with the more neutral Buckingham, the two groups were camped outside St Albans where York issued more demands on May 21. Then at ten o'clock the following morning Warwick launched an assault on the town where the king and his entourage were based.

Fighting in built up areas gives advantage to defenders, something the English learned in France, but such was the speed and surprise of the attack that many Lancastrians had not had time to put their armor on, and the battle lasted barely half an hour. During that time several thousand men fought with longbows, swords, maces, axes, and pole-axes through side streets and even houses, bludgeoning each other or swinging axes. Many would have brandished giant broadswords with two hands, and the muscles of regular soldiers were incredibly well-developed before the advent of modern warfare. A pole-axe, up to six feet in length, would also be used and could go through armor and rip bones and flesh. After a short space of time the men would have been exhausted.

The Earl of Northumberland, Hotspur's son, was struck down by Salisbury; Lord Clifford, Percy's cousin, was also slain. Somerset had killed four men in close combat outside an inn before, looking up, he noticed the sign outside—the Castle—and recalled the prophecy he was once told. Momentarilly distracted, he was stabbed and then dragged away and hacked to death. His son Henry, just nineteen, was seriously wounded and not expected to make it.

While this fighting played out the Mad King Henry sat by the royal banner in the market place, and at one point an arrow landed in his neck, and he cried out in pain— but the rebels could not kill the king, too much of a taboo even when all the other rules were being broken, for as it is said in the Old Testament: "The Lord forbid that I should stretch forth mine hand against the Lord's anointed."[6]

With most of the leading Lancastrians cut down, the king's men fled, leaving Henry sitting on the ground, dazed and wounded. The battle won, Warwick and York approached and called for a surgeon and afterwards the king was taken to the nearby abbey, where a Mass was said for the sixty men who had died that day. Among the fallen were the most powerful barons in the country, and their sons would do everything to get their revenge.

37
THE SONS OF
THE FIRST MEN

I've had an exciting life. I want my death to be boring.

—Bronn

The crushing of Glyndŵr's rebellion had ruined many once-proud native families, and it would be the last such uprising by the British, as the Welsh were still called at times by their neighbors. Many of their sons would therefore grow up in hardship and forced to make their own way in the world, among them Owain ap Maredudd. He had been born in one of the most remote regions of Wales, on the island of Anglesey which juts out into the Irish Sea; even today it has a large Welsh-speaking population and was then well inside *Pura Wallia*, "deep Wales" where English law did not run. Owain's grandfather had been Tudur ap Goronwy and the family was Welsh nobility, serving the princes of Gwynedd and later the English kings. They could trace their line back to Ednyfed Fychan ap Cynwrig, who fought against the armies of King John in the early thirteenth century and had brought the heads of three English lords to Llywelyn the Great, Prince of Gwynedd; Ednyfed had risen to become *seneschal*, that is chief minister, of the principality. Before that, they descended from Marchudd ap Cynan, lord of one of the fifteen tribes of Wales and still further traced their ancestry to Cadrawd Calchfynydd, a Brythonic king from the sixth century. These were indeed the first men of Britain, and DNA evidence shows that a quarter of fully-Welsh people are today descended in the male line from just twenty early medieval warlords.[1]

Owain's father Marududd ap Tudur, along with his brothers, had fought with Owain Glyndŵr, and been disinherited for their troubles; Owain was born around 1400, at a dangerous period when Glyndŵr's revolt began, and by the time he reached fighting age the family had nothing, its men killed or stripped of their land. Instead Owen Tudor, as his name was sometimes Anglicized, had risen solely by his soldiering ability and noted charisma, a humble soldier-for-hire with roguish charm and an eye for the ladies. He had served in France for Henry V, his father's enemy, and fought bravely enough at Agincourt to get noticed; by 1421 he was fighting for Sir Walter Hungerford, a veteran of the 1415 campaign who had become Admiral of the Fleet.

After Henry V's death, his widow Catherine of Valois had found herself isolated and alone. She had grown close to Edmund Beaufort, the future Duke of Somerset, who was five years her junior, but because Edmund was the nephew of Cardinal Henry Beaufort, Humphrey of Gloucester became alarmed that Catherine might marry one of his rivals and so increase the Beaufort's stranglehold on power. Instead in 1427, under Humphrey's influence, Parliament expressly forbade queens from remarrying without "special license" of an adult king; her son at the time was just six. Catherine now lived away from court life, lonely and forgotten.

There was always scope for a handsome and charming swordsman to better himself, and some time around 1430 the queen became close to Tudor, one of a number of her husband's retainers she had taken on. He was but a common soldier, her "sewer and servant" and his "kindred and country were objected . . . as most vile and barbarous."[2] Yet Tudor was "handsome and sympathetic and he would know how to sing sad Welsh songs to the sad Catherine. Soon he had sung himself into her bed."[3]

It is possible that being from across the sea she didn't realize how lowly his status was and was unaware that his people were seen as inferior. Penal laws against the Welsh from 1402 stated that they could not own property, hold royal office nor hold public meetings, or even testify against an Englishman in Wales, and all castles in the country had to be garrisoned by full-blooded Englishmen. Englishmen who married Welsh women were also subject to the laws.

Various stories attach themselves to their romance, so that she spotted Tudor bathing naked in a river and was consumed by passion; another recalled that he fell down drunk on her lap. They were married soon after, in secret and away from the dangers of court, but despite their best efforts it became a subject of gossip. Their firstborn was named Edmund; whispers in high places suggested that Beaufort was the real father.

Catherine eventually petitioned Parliament to have her husband's status recognized, with proof of his noble ancestry; Tudor was granted lands and citizenship, but his status and security depended on his wife and in 1436 she fell ill, perhaps from the same illness as her father and son. Over the winter of 1436-7 the ailing queen stayed at Bermondsey Abbey and in her will she wrote of "grievous malady, in which I have been long, and yet am, troubled and vexed."[4] This was the coldest decade of the millennium, a harsh winter when a "great, hard, biting frost . . . grieved the people wonder sore," and Catherine's condition deteriorated; she died on January 3, 1437, aged thirty-five. For her son the king, just fifteen, it was yet another blow.

Tudor, now in the midlands, knew he was in serious danger and was making his way west toward safer territory when he was caught and taken back to Westminster. Later he was brought to the king and declared his innocence of breaking the law by marrying his mother, and the merciful ruler allowed him to return to Wales, only for Tudor to be arrested again, and sent along with his servant to Newgate.

This grim jail on the western fringes of London was surrounded by a moat and the dank and polluted Fleet river, notoriously filled with excrement. Many here were placed in irons, and the dungeons, called the "less convenient chambers,"[5] were cramped, dangerous, dark, and filled with contagious diseases. But the prison was also corrupt and badly run, and in January 1438 Tudor broke out in a daring escape, injuring his jailor along the way. Although rearrested, Edmund Beaufort arranged for his transfer to Windsor Castle under the guard of his old captain Walter Hungerford. In July 1439, he was finally pardoned.

Tudor's sons Edmund and Jasper, now aged seven and six, went to live with Suffolk's sister Katherine de la Pole, abbess of Barking, and a godmother to the children of many wealthy families. The Tudor boys spent five years here during which they became closer to their half-brother the king; when they reached the age of manhood their blood connection to the monarch was formally recognized, and later they were raised to the peerage, with lands taken from the Yorkist Sir William Oldhall— which York could only take as a slight. To further add insult, Jasper Tudor was given appointments in Wales that York had traditionally held, and Edmund Tudor received the great prize of the young Margaret Beaufort, the richest heiress in the realm.

"POWER IS POWER"

After St Albans had come the victor's justice. The Percys were fined £6,050 for transgressions against the crown, conveniently close to the £6,000 they were already owed. York was reappointed protector on November 1455 and made Warwick captain of Calais while also giving him some of Somerset's land in Wales. However, York was forced out again the following February, having failed to pass an act that would have raised revenue for the crown by taking back land previously sold off. Many viewed him as an overmighty subject, and by the end of the year York's allies were replaced by those in Queen Margaret's affinity.

The queen was building up her powerbase in the midlands and north. She went to Coventry in Warwickshire, the very heart of England—and later Shakespeare's county—where the Lancastrians support was strongest and was greeted in verse by men dressed as Alexander the Great, St John the Baptist, and Edward the Confessor. Actors read lines praising Henry and Margaret and looking forward to Edward continuing the dynasty; in fact, many suggested that Margaret now wanted her husband to abdicate in favour of her son. Margaret appointed numerous allies to secure roles and gave others advantageous matches; she also began to arm, taking twenty-six long guns, or serpentines, from the Tower to her fortress of Kenilworth Castle in Warwickshire.

A growing role was now played by Salisbury's son, Warwick "Kingmaker,"[6] almost as absurdly rich as his father and far more arrogant. Warwick had been knighted at the age of sixteen and saw military service for the crown soon after. He had remained loyal to King Henry, but from 1453 had become rivals with Somerset over the Beauchamp inheritance, and the lordship of Glamorgan, which Warwick also claimed through his wife.

It was now that he became increasingly drawn to his uncle, York, and would prove a useful ally to make up for York's lack of political ability. Warwick was a brilliant politician with a talent for winning popular opinion, he was charismatic, and "a man of exceptional intelligence, personal charm and steely determination."[7] He was also a ruthless killer. Too important and rich to exclude, in October 1457 Warwick had been given the task of doing the king's enemies "all hurt and annoyance" at sea, which also meant keeping a third of the profits himself, so the role of pirate suited him fine.

In 1458, the king organized a "love day" for March 25, Lady Day, based on old judicial practices in which parties were ordered to try to reconcile their differences. It was hoped to bring Lancastrians and Yorkists together after St Albans, with Northumberland, Warwick, Salisbury, Somerset, Clifford, and York walking hand-in-hand to St Paul's cathedral. And yet each of the factions brought so many armed men—as many as four thousand in the small confines of the city—that archers had to be placed along the Thames with orders to fire if the two sides clashed. The two sides were separated by London's old walls, while the Mayor of London brought a force of five hundred—just as well, for the sons of those killed at St Albans had only revenge on their minds.

In November 1458, there was a scuffle in Westminster which began when one of Warwick's retainers struck a menial royal servant; someone, Warwick then claimed, tried to kill him and he escaped to Calais. When he returned to London to tell the council that only Parliament could relieve him of his job, he was attacked a second time, by Somerset and Wiltshire's men—but this time the queen was almost certainly behind it.

There was now a further build-up of arms on both sides. The Lancastrians ordered three thousand bows to be made at the royal arsenal, and for sheriffs of each shire to select men to fight. Queen Margaret tried to punish York through an Act of Attainder, which blamed him for all the kingdom's troubles. This took away his lands but also denied it to his heirs, an act against precedent, since the sons of traitors were given their father's lands after his death. The queen, in trying to hold the kingdom together, was becoming excessive; later that year she removed more Neville men from positions on the border.

Margaret was now entirely in charge. The following May, the queen and her supporters headed into their heartlands in the midlands and northwest, recruiting men into their service. There was quite clearly a war coming. A great council was called in June 1459, but York and the Nevilles refused to attend and the queen openly denounced them. The court in Coventry sent the elderly war veteran James Tuchet, Lord Audley, to arrest Salisbury, and with this action the kingdom exploded into violence.

Audley was a lord in the west midlands, and recruited men from Cheshire, Staffordshire, and Shropshire, perhaps twelve thousand in total, many of them cavalry armed with helmets, breastplates, and armor. Salisbury had raised an army of five thousand from his family seat of Middleham in Yorkshire, heading toward the Welsh borders. Across the West families were forced to choose their sides. In south Wales, the Gruffudd clan were pro-Lancastrian so their rivals the Dwnns of Kidwelly became Yorkists. Across the border in Shropshire the Kynaston and Eyton families were rivals of the pro-Lancastrian Talbots, and so supported York. The Skydmores of Herefordshire were opposed to York and Herbert, and the Pulestons of Denbeigh were rivals to Lord Grey of Ruthyn, so became attached to Margaret.

Audley and his troops got to Blore Heath, near Newcastle-under-Lyme in Stafford-shire, where Salisbury's men were waiting for them across the small river. The queen had a second army, some ten miles away, led by Lord Stanley, the most powerful magnate in Lancashire, and his brother William. On the morning of September 23, 1459, battle began when Salisbury tricked the enemy into coming out, unleashing their arrow volleys before being pinned down by return fire. The battle might have gone either way and yet Stanley—now forever known as "the late Lord Stanley"—held back to see which side would win.*

The Lancastrian Lord Audley, who had been born in the reign of King Richard, led the fighting and was struck down by Sir Roger Kynaston, one of York's bannermen from the Welsh marshes whose ancestors had originally been princes of Powys. After four hours, two thousand men lay dead and the Yorkists had won, but it would not last, as a fresh royal army was nearby. Salisbury proceeded south-west, meeting Warwick and York and swearing mutual oaths, and then on toward the border town of Ludlow in Shropshire, built on the wool and cloth trades, and home to numerous prosperous merchants. It was also York's base, and his wife and two youngest sons, George and Richard, were in the town. It was here that events now moved.

The most influential history of the War of the Roses was Edward Hall's *The Union of the Noble and Illustre Famelies of Lancastre and York*, published in 1548. This came to heavily influence Shakespeare's telling of events which in turn became the standard narrative. Hall's grandfather had been one of York's councilors and heard accounts directly from Salisbury's men arriving at Ludlow, which is how the history came to be passed down.

By early October, the Yorkists were camped by the River Teme, below Ludford Bridge; the Lancastrian army appeared on the 12th, among them Somerset, Bucking-ham, and Northumberland, and also in attendance was Henry Holland, Duke of Exeter. Despite being married to York's daughter Lady Anne, he had become a bitter enemy of the Yorkists as the conflict escalated. Various other earls and lords were camped with the royalist forces, the bulk of the aristocracy sticking with the mad king, while Henry and Margaret were in the rear. Even York's Welsh allies, the Herbert and Vaughan families, were pinned down in Pembrokeshire by Owain Tudor.

---

*Likewise, Walder Frey is the Late Lord Frey for a similar action.

In the night Andrew Trollope, one of Warwick's captains, led his troops across the river to submit, and so the rebel leaders, realizing they could now expect no pardon, snuck out of the camp, among them Warwick, Salisbury, York, and his two eldest sons Edward and Edmund, now of fighting age. They divided their forces, some to Ireland and others to the southwest and eventually Calais.

Ludlow was now sacked, all of this watched by Cecily Neville from the castle, her young sons, eleven and eight, by her side. Across the town the king's men helped themselves to wine and "went wete-schode in wyne" before they "defoulyd many wymmen."[8] Cecily walked through the streets with George and Richard but, it was said, when the troops found her, "The noble duches of York unmanly and cruelly was entreted and spoyled."[6] Mercifully, by this it was meant only that she was robbed rather than raped, but the ordeal would have been terrifying, and a lesson to the House of York about what happened when they crossed the queen. It seemed like Margaret had won.

38
THE BLACK DINNER

Explain to me why it is more noble to kill ten thousand men in battle than a dozen at dinner.

—Tywin Lannister

The queen was merciless to her enemies, ruining many Yorkist families in late 1459 during "the Parliament of Devils." York was denounced and all estates, honors, and dignities were removed from his affinity. Lancastrians such as Owen Tudor and his son Jasper were rewarded, while York was replaced as Lieutenant of Ireland by the loyal James, Earl of Wiltshire, veteran of the first St Albans—although he had actually run away. In reality, York, now residing in that western island, had the loyalty of the Anglo-Irish lords. Likewise, Henry Beaufort, who had inherited the Somerset title after his father's death at St Albans, was made captain of Calais but the port was now controlled by Warwick.

Calais remained for another century England's last outpost on the continent and after London it was the realm's second most important city; the entry point for the country's continental exports and home to its only permanent garrison.

While the queen was in the midlands on July 2, Salisbury marched on London with two thousand men, where they were met with widespread support. The Tower was controlled by Lord Scales, Edward of March's sixty-three-year-old godfather and former Yorkist. A tough old veteran of the French war, he ruthlessly turned on the city people, and a chronicler reports: "They that were within the Tower cast wildfire into the City, and shot in small guns, and burned and hurt men and women and children in the city."[1] However after a successful siege Scales surrendered with a promise of safe conduct—ignored by the city's rough watermen who ferried people across the river, and who beat him to death. Warwick stayed forty-eight hours in the city before his men split into two large armies, one led by Edward of March and Warwick, and the other by Fauconberg.

By now the country was irreversibly divided. The Lancastrians still had the vast majority of the higher nobility, including Northumberland, Buckingham, Shrewsbury, Beaumont, Egremont, Humphrey Stafford, John Talbot, Sir Thomas Percy, and Sir Edmund Grey, Lord of Ruthin. Among York's allies were Norfolk, Warwick, March, Bourchier, Abergavenny, Audley, Fauconberg, Say, and Scrope; on both sides choices were made either through family connections or in opposition to a local rival.

On July 10, Warwick's force met an army led by his uncle Buckingham just outside of Northampton, with John Talbot, Earl of Shrewsbury, and Thomas Percy also among the Lancastrian forces, who had the king with them. The queen's men took up position in the grounds of Delapre Abbey, along the River Nene, defended by a ditch layered with stakes. The Lancastrians had cannons and rejected peace overtures by Warwick.

Most of the soldiers would not have been heavily armed, locally raised men wearing only a jacket and a helmet, probably a kettle hat, and with odd bits of mail and other equipment stolen from the dead. As Talisa says of one of Robb's soldiers: "he's a fisherman's son—probably never held a spear until three months back."[2] When the fighting started at 2 p.m., the Yorkists were faced with both pouring rain and arrows, although the bad weather also neutralized the Lancastrian cannons. However, the battle was won with treachery, when Edmund Grey—another of Gaunt's descendents—took his men over to the Yorkist troops, in exchange for the Yorks supporting him in his dispute with the House of Holland. Those common soldiers wearing Grey's badge were spared.

The thuggish Thomas Percy met with a heroic end, falling alongside Buckingham and Shrewsbury while making a last stand in heavy armor outside the king's tent as they were surrounded by Warwick's Kentish soldiers. The king was taken prisoner, while Queen Margaret had fled to Wales with her son Edward.

Cecily Neville was staying with her sister Anne, the Duke of Buckingham's wife, when they heard the news of Buckingham's death at the hands of their nephew Warwick. Cecily had endured a turbulent year on the move; after the horror of Ludlow, a widow from London called Alice Martyn had taken in her sons George and Richard, keeping them safe from vengeful Lancastrians.

Like that of Catelyn Stark and her sister, the relationship between Cecily and Anne seems to have been difficult, as well as being complicated by the family politics of the time (although she didn't have a strange boy sucking at her breast). Cecily had been mercifully treated by the king, but her future was now uncertain; that of her sister even more so.

York now arrived in Westminster on October 10, 1460 with several hundred men, and the Parliament of Devils was overturned. The two factions had concentrated their forces at either side of the country, with the House of York controlling the south and the House of Lancaster the north and west.

Meanwhile, over the autumn of 1460, young Henry Percy, the third Earl of Northumberland since his father was killed five years earlier, was running the North as an independent kingdom. Henry VI had given him even greater powers there, and Percy ordered that all men between the ages of sixteen and sixty arm themselves to free the king and to attack Richard of York with a northern legion. The family were damned by the Yorkist Parliament "as ravagers and misdoers," but the House of York would have known that a Percy call to arms in the North would not be ignored.

And now Richard claimed the crown outright, for there was now nowhere else to go in this game of thrones—victory or death. In front of a stunned assembly at Parliament he sat down on the seat reserved only for the monarch, expecting to be proclaimed king. Instead there was stunned silence; even Warwick and Salisbury, and York's eldest son Edward, could not follow him in breaking the ultimate taboo.

As well as the corruption and intrigue at the heart of the queen's faction, York must also have now felt that the crown was his by right; he was, after all, through his mother's Mortimer line, the true heir to Edward III, by the king's second son Lionel of Antwerp; the House of Lancaster derived from his third son, John of Gaunt. And yet many noblemen were disturbed by the implication of York's action, for if he could disinherit the king's son could he or someone else not also do the same to their sons too?

Instead it was agreed that York be made heir, and Prince Edward disinherited; the queen, naturally, refused, but nevertheless on October 24, the Yorkist Parliament passed an act of Accord, making it so. All royal officers would now have to give their obedience to York, who was also given power to raise troops for any reason. Warwick remained in London, with the king in the Tower, while Edward of March went west to recruit more men, and York and his second son Edmund, Earl of Rutland, rode to Yorkshire to secure the north.

In November, Somerset and Devon arrived at the city of York where they met Percy and went south. That month Margaret took her son with her to Scotland, by ship, and it was bitterly cold when they arrived on December 3 at the church of Lincluden, a gothic twelfth century priory built by Uchtred mac Fergusa, Lord of Galloway, whose name reflects the mix of Scots and Anglian culture of the region. There they stayed with the dowager Queen Mary, regent for her young son James III. Mary of Guelders had been fifteen when she made the journey from her native Holland to marry James II of Scotland, arriving with a huge dowry of sixty thousand crowns, a fortune for the Scots and provided by her cousin Duke Philippe of Burgundy. With the money they had built Holyrood House to receive such a grand queen, which is today the official residence of the British monarch in Scotland. Alas James II had been killed that August while testing a new type of canon during the siege of Roxburgh Castle in a rather ill-conceived attempt to show off to his wife. Now Margaret and Mary negotiated a treaty by which Prince Edward would be married to James III's sister, securing the border for Margaret and allowing her to raise an army in the North, and even—to the horror of the kingdom—recruit Scots to come south.[3]

RED WEDDINGS

England had made peace with the Scots a century before, but with the overthrow of Richard II the men of the far north had found themselves increasingly drawn into the English and French political dramas. There was also continual conflict at home: Robert III had sent his twelve-year-old son James to France after his other son had died suspiciously in the custody of the king's brother, the Duke of Albany—also, confusingly, called Robert. Along the way the boy's ship was intercepted by English pirates, who handed him over to King Henry, and so poor James endured eighteen years in an English prison.

When James was finally released, eighteen years later and now married to John of Gaunt's granddaughter Joan Beaufort, he nursed many grievances.

By 1437 things had come to a head with a plot led by another member of the king's family, the Stuarts. The House ultimately traced its origins to a Breton knight, Alan fitz Flaad, who had come over to Britain with Henry I; his great-grandson Walter had become the "steward," or governor, of the Scottish throne, a position that became hereditary, until one of their line married the daughter of Robert the Bruce. Their son Robert II became the first of the House of Stewart (the spelling was later changed to Stuart to make it easier for French speakers to pronounce).

And yet there were many different Stewart sub-houses in conflict with each other. The plot to kill the king was led by his former ally, Walter Stewart, Earl of Atholl, who had lost two sons fighting for the monarch against his rivals, the Albany Stewarts, the two branches of the family nursing a deadly hatred against each other. However, King James had not rewarded Walter Stewart, nor certified the family's hold on titles and land, and Atholl was worried that when he died the king would take away his estates. So, when James was in Perth, Atholl's retainer Robert Graham conspired with their former enemies the Albany Stewarts to remove the monarch.

On the night of February 20, 1437, when King James went to bed, a band of thirty men stormed into his quarters, killed his page, and burst into the bedroom. But James had prised open some floorboards and escaped into the sewer, leaving his queen and ladies-in-waiting. The assassins were about to cut Joan's throat when one of their number, Thomas Graham, shouted "For shame . . . she is bot a woman." This was a mistake.

Unfortunately for the king, the sewer had recently been blocked up, and he found himself cornered; James killed two assassins but was felled by a third, Robert Graham. The king was bleeding now and cried for a priest, but Graham replied "Thou shalt never haue other confessore bot this same sword" and "smote hum thorogh the body." Three other assassins stabbed him sixteen times.

The king's six-year old son, James II, was installed on the throne, and his allies—having the testimony of the queen—had the conspirators hunted down and killed. Walter Stewart would be tortured for three days, and among his torments was being blinded by red-hot iron pincers and having his entrails removed and burned in front of him, before his heart was torn out.[4] Six successive monarchs of Scotland—James's I to V and Mary, Queen of Scots—all died violent deaths or as the result of war.

The new king was just seven and the realm was ruled by a regency led by Archibald Douglas, of the fabled Clan Douglas. Archibald Douglas died in 1439 and there followed a power struggle—and the inspiration for one of the most notorious scenes in the *Game of Thrones* saga. The new head of the clan, William Douglas, was only sixteen, and had inherited an array of titles including Lord of Galway, Selkirk, and Annandale, as well as Duke of Touraine in France. However rival magnates Sir

William Crichton, James Douglas, and Sir Alexander Livingston all wanted the Douglases excluded from power.

And so, in 1440, the young Earl of Douglas and his younger brother David were invited to Edinburgh Castle on behalf of the ten-year-old James II. In fact, the whole thing had been organized by Crichton, Lord Chancellor of Scotland, with the support of the Livingston family. Over supper at Edinburgh castle the young men had been joking and talking merrily when the head of a black bull was thrown onto the table, and a single drum beat was sounded. The two brothers were immediately dragged outside onto Castle Hill, told they were guilty of treason, and beheaded.

This notorious incident became known as the Black Dinner, and was the obvious inspiration for the Red Wedding, as Martin has himself said, where Robb Stark and his relations are murdered while under the hospitality of the Freys.[5] Such political violence was not unusual north of the border; indeed just twelve years later the eighth Earl Douglas, a cousin, was murdered by James II and his body thrown from a high window at Stirling Castle. King James had asked Earl Douglas to break with his allies; Douglas refused and so the king shouted, "False traitor, sen yow will nocht, I shall" and stabbed him twenty-six times, his brains splattered all over the wall and floor. Douglas's son fled south across the border.

Violence was shocking, but violence toward a guest was unforgivable. As in Westeros, the laws of hospitality were hugely important in all ancient and medieval societies. In classical Athens, Clesithenes was a popular politician but his family the Alcmacondids were believed to be polluted because generations before they had killed enemies who were supplicants; the shame and stigma stuck to the family for decades. Today the hospitality rule survives in societies which remain clannish; one of the difficulties the United States had with searching for Osama bin Laden was that his Pashtun hosts would not give him up, however high the reward or horrific the crimes he had committed, because he was their guest.

Such is the taboo about killing guests that recorded incidents were rare and shocking; back in the eleventh century, Mercian nobleman Eadric Streona was notorious for having murdered a rival while entertaining him, and then blinding both his sons. Having double-crossed Edmund Ironside to side with Canute, the Viking then had him executed because he had betrayed his master. The Scots even had a special law making such a crime worse than regular homicide, called "murder under trust." And yet Scotland also provides the other inspiration for the Red Wedding—the Glencoe massacre of 1692, in which up to 38 members of the MacDonald clan were murdered by their guests, the Campbells. All that would lie long in the future – but for now the Scots were being drawn into the finale of the conflict between Richard of York and Margaret, de facto head of the House of Lancaster.

39

THE YOUNG WOLF

He's a boy and he's never lost a battle.

—Tywin Lannister on Robb Stark

Percy was now raising an army alongside Clifford and Ross, the other northern barons loyal to the Queen, for what was to be the grand finale to Richard of York's rebellion against the mad king, and the bloodiest battle in Britain's history. It would mark the end of the first war between the Houses of Lancaster and York, although not the last. Queen Margaret sent messages to Somerset, Devon, and other supporters in the south, and issued a letter to the City of London condemning the rebels.

York and his second son Edmund, Earl of Rutland, had spent Christmas at the castle of Sandal in Yorkshire, and when he arrived there he found a kinsman, Lord John Neville of Raby, from the other branch of the Neville family. (Not to be confused with Warwick's brother, John Neville. To make matters confusing, this John Neville had recently married the widow of his nephew, another John Neville.) Lord John went to York to ask permission to raise troops in the area, to which he agreed; yet when later York saw fighting outside from inside the castle tower, he and his son were tricked into coming out to face a Lancastrian army. They soon learned that it was five thousand-strong, and included Somerset, Northumberland, Clifford, and Lord John Neville, who was indeed recruiting soldiers—for York's enemies.

Perhaps he now knew it was the end; York was outnumbered five to one, and after an hour of fighting sent his son Rutland to flee while he held off the Lancastrians. Richard of York was soon cut down, and his long battle to win the throne was over.

Now in desperate flight the young Rutland had reached nearby Wakefield Bridge when he was cornered by Baron Clifford, whose father had been slain at St Albans. John Clifford had been born in Conisbrough castle in Yorkshire and had the blood of all the leading families of the north; his mother was a Dacre and his grandmothers a Percy and a Neville, making Clifford a great-grandson of both Hotspur and Ralph de Neville, just as Rutland was a grandson. Yet when he learned of his captive's identity Clifford mercilessly killed him, York's blood spilled in return for his father's.[1] Salisbury's second son Thomas Neville also fell in the fighting and Salisbury himself was captured and beheaded the next day.

When the Queen arrived in York she saw the heads of York, Rutland, and Salisbury stuck over the gates of the city, and Clifford told her "Madam, your war is done, here is your king's ransom."[2] There was "much joy, and great rejoicing" among the camp and Margaret now ordered that a paper crown be placed on her enemy's head along with the sign "Let York overlook the town of York." For the Queen, who had endured so much, "it must have been exhilarating to have hundreds of fierce warriors wearing the Prince of Wales's livery kneel before them, with their enemies' heads grimacing down of them."[3] And yet perhaps she would live to regret these deaths and the humiliation she inflicted, and her joy might one day turn to ashes.

For Cecily of York it was now an even more deadly situation. She had lost one son already, and her younger boys George and Richard were in grave danger, smuggled to the coast and sent across the sea to Burgundy. Her eldest, now Edward, Duke of York, was in the West Country celebrating Christmas when he was told the devastating news. Edward of March had been raised in Ludlow on the Welsh border and was seen by the marcher men as one of their own. He and his brother Edmund were very close in age and had grown up together along with local boys, but his childhood was short and as the country headed toward civil war he would have been in training from a young age.

Robb Stark is only supposed to be fifteen when he leads his army to victory; in reality, York's son Edward of March was eighteen when he first commanded in battle, but he had been learning at his father's side for far longer, and eighteen is by no means exceptionally young for military experience. Testosterone levels in fourteen-year-old boys can reach as much as 1,200 ng/dL, higher than most adult men, which range between 270 and 1,070. That is partly why males at fifteen commit more violent crime than those over twenty-five, and violence peaks at the ages of eighteen-nineteen. Boy soldiers as young as Robb are therefore not unusual, since they are at the age when men most enjoy fighting; their brains' undeveloped frontal lobe also leads them to be more impulsive and unable to assess danger, and so brave but reckless.

Edward's ancestor Henry II had led an army against his cousin Stephen while aged just fourteen during the Anarchy, while two thousand years ago Octavius, the future Roman Emperor Augustus, headed a force at eighteen, and the following year was given command over the whole imperial army. Rome's most famous military hero, Scipio Africanus, fought from the age of sixteen and led an attack on the Carthaginians when he was just seventeen. King John's nephew Arthur was fifteen when he was in charge of an army fighting his own grandmother in one of the strangest dynastic conflicts of the era. Poland's King Wladyslaw III invaded Hungary at seventeen and just two years later, in 1444, led a force of twenty thousand Christians to take on the Turks. Faced with an army three times as large, the teenager led a cavalry charge against the Sultan Murad II which unfortunately ended up with his head being put on a pike.

Edward was very different to his father in appearance and temperament, which has added to speculation about his paternity, with his enemies accusing Cecily Neville of cuckolding her husband. Whereas York was short, dark-haired, and cold, even charm-less, Edward was very tall, perhaps 6'4", blond, good-looking and affable; he was a charmer and seducer, and even persuaded some Lancastrians to change sides when it was a better strategy than killing them. Following his father's death, the young warrior immediately faced his first challenge, as the now aging Owen Tudor brought eight thousand men east from Wales toward Worcester on the English side of the border. The two armies met at Mortimer's Cross, close to the frontier, March and his mostly local troops aiming to stop Tudor, with his Breton and Irish mercenaries, from joining with the main Lancastrian host heading south toward London. The battle took place in the depths of winter, on February 3, 1461, where "on the morning there was seen three suns rising." Edward's men were at first "aghast" at this strange and unnatural vision, but the new Duke of York took it as a good omen, signifying the three surviving "sons" of York. Shakespeare records it:

> Three glorious suns, each one a perfect sun;
> Not separated with the racking clouds,
> But sever'd in a pale clear-shining sky.
> See, see! they join, embrace, and seem to kiss,
> As if they vow'd some league inviolable:
> Now are they but one lamp, one light, one sun.
> In this the heaven figures some event. *Henry VI, Part 3, Act 2, Scene 1*

It was in fact a parhelion, or sun dog, a phenomenon which occurs during exceptionally cold weather when ice crystals refract the sun's rays, giving the appearance of three suns in the sky. Afterward, March took the symbol of the "Sun in Splendour" as his personal banner.

March came close to joining his brother that day, but the battle turned with the arrival of William Hastings, a former sheriff whose father had served the House of York for many years. Hastings's troops swung the fighting and afterwardthe Yorkists ran after their fleeing enemies, capturing the elderly Tudor and taking him to Hereford on Edward's orders. Tudor had fought for many years in France and knew everything there was about warfare, and now expected a return to imprisonment until hostages could be exchanged. And yet the age of chivalry was gone, and it was only as the buttons around his neck were being undone that the old soldier realized his fate. This ladies' man now lamented that the head that once lay on a queen's lap was now to lie on a block. Afterward that same head was mounted in the market place of the town where a mad old crone placed a hundred candles around it, combing the corpse's hair and washing off the blood.[4]

With her treaty in the northern kingdom, Margaret had raised an army to head south, bringing the terrifying prospect of a northern army bearing down on the south, and—even worse—a rabble of Scots with them too. Without the money to pay soldiers, she agreed that her troops could plunder once they had crossed the Trent into Yorkist territory in the east midlands. The northern army rumbled south along the king's road while Warwick raised men in London. As her northern and Scot troops moved further into alien land, more of them slipped away with their plunder; these stragglers held up progress as well reducing the numbers of fighting men, and alienating villagers along the way. As well as the Scots, the army also contained Welsh and Irish troops and French mercenaries, all of whom would have been a terrifying prospect to the people of the realm.[5]

Warwick led an army out of London with a group of leading nobles, including Norfolk; John de la Pole, married to his cousin Elizabeth; William FitzAlan, Earl of Arundel and Warwick's brother-in-law, who had been a Lancastrian but had now switched; and Warwick's brother John Neville and his uncle, Fauconberg. The two armies met on February 17, 1461, once again at St Albans, where Margaret had brought more than ten thousand and probably closer to fifteen thousand men; Warwick had as many as ten thousand, as well as the king as his prisoner. These armies were larger than any English city at the time other than London, and the amount of provisions they needed would have been awesome.

The killing went on until nightfall, and the Lancastrians were victorious. As prisoner, Henry had been treated well, but afterwards the mad king's former captors Lord Bonville and Sir Thomas Kyriell were brought before the Queen and seven-year-old Prince Edward. He was asked: "Fair son, by what manner of means shall these knights die?"[6]

"Let their heads be taken off." The boy got his wish.

Henry had guaranteed the safety of Bonville and Kyriel, but it was Margaret who ordered the executions, an unnecessary act of ruthlessness that showed either a cruel nature or simply the exhaustive stress of six years of conflict.

The Queen now descended on London, with Edward still in the Cotswolds. For the men of the south country the prospect of a northern army overrunning their lands was terrifying, not to mention what Scots or Frenchmen might do. A chronicler called the Prior of Croyland reported: "The duke [of York] being thus removed from this world, the northmen . . . swept onwards like a whirlwind from the north, and in the impulse of their fury attempted to overrun the whole of England . . . paupers and beggars flocked forth from those quarters in infinite numbers, just like so many mice rushing forth from their holes, and universally devoted themselves to spoil and rapine, without regard of place or person," attacking monasteries and "covering the whole surface area of the earth just like so many locusts."[7]

Songs of the period recall the threats of northern men violating southern women and of "the lords of the North" coming to "destroy the south country." Clement Patton, an East Anglian squire, told his brother John: "In this country [county] every man is willing to go with my lords here, and I hope God shall help them, for the people in the north rob and steal and are appointed to pillage all this country, and give away men's goods and livelihoods in the south country, and that will ask a mischief."[4]

Margaret's army ransacked the outer suburbs of the capital but, fearful that they would lose her any support in London, she now led her troops away from the city and headed north. It was a strategic mistake, for on February 26 Richard of York's son rolled in from the west, unopposed, and was proclaimed Edward IV.

THOSE ARE BRAVE MEN KNOCKING AT OUR DOOR. LET'S GO KILL THEM.

On March 3, 1461, bishops and lords assembled in Baynard's Castle on the western edge of London where they agreed to Edward of March's claim to the throne. Yet the Queen would not stay idle while her son was disinherited, and now followers of the great families were called up to fight for their lords, with the greatest battle ever fought on British soil about to unfold. The winters were still getting harsher as Europe went further into the Little Ice Age, and this climactic battle was fought amidst a snow blizzard just a week before Easter Sunday. Edward's army may have had as many as forty-eight thousand men, the Queen perhaps even sixty thousand, and although these figures seem exaggerated, when the two sides met just off the Great North Road, at Towton in north Yorkshire, the front lines were as long as eight hundred yards apiece, packed thick with men.

Alongside March were a group of lords linked by blood; Warwick and his brothers-in-law Worcester, FitzHugh, Stanley, Arundel and Bonville, along with his uncle by marriage, Norfolk. Warwick's bastard half-brother also joined him and was killed in the fighting. On the opposing side were most of the northern barons, including Percy, Clifford, Beaumont, and the Westmorland Nevilles, as well as Somerset.

Towton was turned into a gruesome pile of flesh, bones, and steel, and anywhere between nine thousand and twenty-eight thousand died over twenty-four hours of fighting in the snowfall. Some men were killed by small daggers driven into the eyes or brains, others by forty-inch broadswords. Many more were slain by arrow fire, and it was this that ground down the Lancastrian forces, who were shooting against the wind and whose arrows fell short.

The Lancastrian leadership was also decapitated. Edward had ordered men to go after his brother's killer, Clifford, but thinking himself away from his pursuers, he went to drink a glass of wine, took off his neck-guard, and was killed instantly by a sniper hiding in a tree. Andrew Trollope, who had betrayed the Yorkists at Ludlow and killed several men at Barnet, was also slain, as was another major baron, Lord Clifford's kinsman Randolph Dacre. Henry Percy, following his father, grandfather, and great-grandfather, also died in the fighting.

Before the battle, the Lancastrians had knocked down the only bridge to prevent their armies fleeing across the Cock Beck, a nearby stream. Now they were trapped and forced against the river on a spot that later became known as Bloody Meadow.[8]

Many jumped in the frozen water, and it was only when the river was dammed by a pile of dead men that anybody could escape over the corpses of their comrades, across this Bridge of Bodies as veterans later called it.

Recent archaeological work on the site has given historians a glimpse of the horror of that bitterly cold day as the Houses of York and Lancaster fought their climatic battle. Centuries later, in 1996, a pit was uncovered containing forty-three bodies, of which twenty-seven had multiple injuries, illustrating the ferocity and desperation of the fight: "One man received eight sharp-force traumas; one had nine sharp-force and two penetrative-force wounds; and another suffered ten sharp-force and three blunt-force traumas." Twenty-seven of twenty-eight heads found in one corner of the field showed injuries from "swords, daggers, maces, war hammers, staff weapons, longbow arrows, and possibly crossbow bolts" and are "consistent with fleeing infantry cut down by horsemen."[9] Another grave had thirty-seven bodies, of which one had five slashes to the head, and another had survived a previous battle in which his face had been cut in two with a wound across his mouth and jaw.

Following the battle, numerous atrocities were committed against survivors, as well as the mutilation of bodies, reported by contemporary accounts and proven by recent digs, with "injuries that are far in excess of those necessary to cause disability and death."[10]

The young King Edward was lucky to survive the day, his life saved by a Welsh knight, Sir David Ap Mathew, who was thereafter given permission to name the battle on the family crest as an honor, so that his posterity might always bask in the glory of his deed. Afterwards a trail of blood lined the twenty-three-mile road from Towton to York, and the victor marched on the city where he was greeted with the heads of his father and brother, now cut down and replaced by those of the defeated.

The boy had defeated his enemies, the House of Lancaster, those men who had cut his father's head from his shoulders, and the unpopular queen and her violent young son were forced to flee. And so began the reign of Edward IV, and the end of the House of Lancaster. The new king stayed in the north until May 1 when he witnessed the Earl of Wiltshire's beheading in Newcastle, one of several Lancastrian lords put to death, but soon the bloodlust ran out and he headed south for his coronation in June.

Across the sea Duke Philippe of Burgundy's attitude toward the exiled children of the Duke of York changed. They had been kept far away from court in Utrecht but were now brought to Sluys and entertained at Duke Philippe's home, and a banquet laid on. For the cunning and canny people across the sea—a stereotype of the Dutch that the English maintained for many years—the House of York were now their true friends.

Families who had sided with March now enjoyed the fruits of success. The Bourchier clan was rewarded, with its heir Henry becoming Earl of Essex. Sir John Wenlock, who had besieged the Tower of London for Edward and helped his entry into London, was made Knight of the Garter. William Hastings became Lord Hastings, chamberlain of the household and gatekeeper to the king's presence. Hastings, who would become Edward's priapic accomplice in drinking and whoring, commissioned a coat of arms for himself, one which showed a tiger with a grinning face, most likely Hastings himself, and an enormous erect penis. After the drabness of Henry's court, life would become interesting again under the young King Edward.

The king's uncle Fauconberg became Earl of Kent and his cousin John Neville was made Lord Montague and also Earl of Northumberland, the hereditary Percy title, illustrating their total defeat. Warwick was not made duke, however, despite there being no adult dukes left—perhaps a snub, and a sign of troubles to come.

For the losers there was retribution, with twelve peers and one hundred knights and squires made outlaws, while Percy's young son Henry was placed in the Tower and the family attained. Yet the young king was intelligent and understood that, as Tywin Lannister put it: "When your enemies defy you, you must serve them steel and fire. When they go to their knees, however, you must help them back to their feet. Elsewise no man will ever bend the knee to you."[11] Henry Stafford, the second son of the Duke of Buckingham, was pardoned despite fighting on the losing side. Henry Beaufort, the Duke of Somerset, was as ardent a Lancastrian as they came; he had fought and nearly died at the first battle of St Albans and watched his father slain by the Yorkists. Beaufort had seen action at Wakefield, the second St Albans and Towton, and when he was captured in 1462 he might well have expected the block. And yet Edward spared him, and indeed treated him like a friend. London mayor William Gregory wrote that Somerset "lodged with the king in his own bed many nights, and sometimes rode a-hunting behind the king, the king having about him not passing six horse[men] at the most and yet three were the duke's men."[12] Six months after his capture in 1462 his lands were all returned, and the two men became close, enjoying wenching together.

As for the Queen, following Towton she had escaped to exile in Scotland, where some colorful stories attached themselves to Margaret and her son Edward traveling along the road north over the mountainous, remote border country. One tells of them being separated from their group when a gang of cut-throats attacked and, when preparing to kill them, learned of their identity and instead swore to take them to safety. Another tale about Margaret's dramatic escape is described by Burgundian chronicler Jehan de Waurin:

> She and her son were caught, captured by thieves and murderers who wanted to kill them, but a great argument broke out over whom was to have her rings and jewels. While it pleased God that these murderers should be quarrelling with each other, taking her son in her arms she hid in the forest. Finally, overcome by hardship and exhaustion, she had no choice but to entrust her child to another brigand whom she encountered in the woods, saying 'Save your king's son.' Through this man she and her son escaped out of the hands of those robbers and murderers and got away.[13]

Whether these stories carry any truth, Margaret eventually arrived in Scotland, destitute and defeated and yet determined to carry on the fight. For some time afterward, the defeated King Henry remained loose in the far north, while Lancastrian rebels still held onto three Percy castles on the East March—Alnwick, Dunstanburgh, and Bamburgh—and for four years maintained the struggle in the border lands. Young Edward, after taking Bamburgh, had given the castles back to the Percys, a bold move and yet one in which he had no choice, for as contemporary John Hardyng had put it, the Percys "have the hearts of the people of the North and always have had." Instead the Percys handed the castles over to Queen Margaret, and then in November 1463 Somerset defected and made his way to the exiled King Henry at Bamburgh. "The king loved him well, but the duke thought treason under fair cheer and words," it was recorded, and yet in fairness to Somerset he was at heart a Lancastrian and always would be.

The Percys were finally defeated in 1464, and the late earl's brother Ralph was put in charge of his nephew and agreed to hand over Dunstanburgh to Edward IV. He wanted his nephew's lands returned and to be treated well, and he also had a family of his own, a wife, three boys, and a girl. Ralph Percy was pardoned soon after and given Dunstanburgh and Banburgh in return—yet once again the Percys handed over their castles to the Lancastrians.

It was a very frigid winter—"fervent colde" a chronicler said. Still the winters were getting colder, but it would be the last for the rebel lords. Finally, in April and May 1465, the rebellion was crushed when John Neville twice defeated Lancastrian armies, killing Ralph Percy at Hedgeley Moor and a much larger Lancastrian army led by Somerset at Hexham a month later. The last Lancastrian castle to hold out, Bamburgh, was besieged and when its defenders refused to surrender Warwick ordered the guns to fire—the ancient stronghold of the old kings of the north became a ruin, the first fortress in England heavily damaged by modern artillery. The medieval world of castles was coming to an end, and a terrifying new age of fierce weapons capable of devastation on a new scale was fast approaching.

Henry Beaufort had been captured at Hexham and the following month finally executed, and with the axes's blow the House of Beaufort was crushed. The House of Percy, too, lay ruined and defeated and with them the Lancastrian cause was finished, the mad king finally captured in 1465 and Margaret an exile in a foreign land. All three houses, of Lancaster, Percy, and Beaufort, had risen in the previous century, reaching the pinnacle of power in the realm, and all three now faced destruction, while the son of their arch-nemesis sat on the throne at Westminster. Such was fate, and the gulf between victory and defeat, when you play the game of thrones.

And yet there were ominious signs on the horizon for the House of York, for Fortune's wheel was always turning, and just as it raised some so might it bring about their downfall. Edward had headed north during this final rebellion to help his kinsmen, the Nevilles, destroy their mutual enemies, bringing with him destructive artillery capable of reducing a castle to rubble in minutes—but along the way he had done something hugely foolish and destructive to his network of alliances. He had married for love. As a chronicler of the time warned on hearing this news: "now take heed what love may do."[14] There would be trouble ahead.

BIBLIOGRAPHY

Ackroyd, Peter, *Foundations*

Albert, Edoardo and Tucker, Katie, *In Search of Alfred the Great*

Angela, Alberto, *A Day in the Life of Ancient Rome*

Asbridge, Thomas, *The Greatest Knight*

Ashley, Mike, *British Kings and Queens*

Attewell, Steven, *Race for the Iron Throne: Political and Historical Analysis of 'A Game of Thrones'*

Audley, Anselm, *Death Keeps His Court*

Barker, Juliet, *England, Arise!*

Bartlett, Robert, *England Under the Norman and Angevin Kings*
    The Making of Europe

Bergreen, Lawrence, *Marco Polo*

Bicheno, Hugh, *Battle Royal*

Bradbury, Jim, *Stephen and Matilda*

Braudel, Fernand, *The Identity of France*

Bridges, Antony, *The Crusades*

Brooke, Christopher, *The Saxons and Norman Kings*

Brown, Peter, *The Rise of Western Christendom*

Castor, Helen, *Blood and Roses*
    She-Wolves
    Joan of Arc

Clark, Gregory, *The Son Also Rises*

Clements, Jonathan, *Vikings*

Cochran, Gregory and Harpending, Henry, *The 10,000 Year Explosion: How Civilization Accelerated Human Evolution*

Crossley-Holland, Kevin, *The Anglo-Saxon World*

Crowley, Roger, *City of Fortune: How Venice Won and Lost a Naval Empire*
    Constantinople: The Last Great Siege, 1453

Danziger, Danny and Gillingham, John, *1215: The Year of Magna Carta*

Davies, Norman, *Vanished Kingdoms*

Druon, Maurice, *The Accursed Kings series*

Duby, Georges, *France in the Middle Ages*

Fischer, David Hackett, *Albion's Seed*

Fletcher, Richard, *Moorish Spain*

Foot, Sarah, *Athelstan: The First King of England*

Frankel, Valerie, *Winter is Coming*

Fraser, Antonia, *The Lives of the Kings and Queens of England*

Freeman, Charles, *A New History of Early Christianity*

Frankopan, Peter, *Silk Roads*

Gies, Joseph and Gies, Frances, *Life in a Medieval Castle*
    Life in a Medieval City
    Life in a Medieval Village

Gillingham, John, *Conquest, Catastrophe and Recovery*
    War of the Roses

Goodwin, George, *Fatal Colours*
    Fatal Rivalry

Haag, Michael, *The Templars*

Haimson Lushkov, Ayelet, *You Win or You Die*

Hall, Edith, *Introducing the Ancient Greeks*

Hannan, Daniel, *How We invented Freedom*

Hibbert, Christopher, *The English: A Social History*

Hindley, Geoffrey, *A Brief History of the Anglo-Saxons*
    Magna Carta

Holland, Tom, *Millennium*
    Persian Fire
    Rubicon

Holmes, George, *The Later Middle Ages 1272-1485*

Horne, Alistair, *Seven Ages of Paris*

Horspool, David, *Richard III*

Hourani, Albert, *A History of the Arab Peoples*

Jager, Eric, *The Last Duel*

Jones, Dan, *Realm Divided*
    The Hollow Crown
    The Plantagenets
    The Templars

Jones, Terry and Ereira, Alan, *Medieval Lives*

Kelly, John, *The Great Mortality*

Kendall Murray, Paul, *Richard the Third*

Kitto, H.D.F, *The Greeks*

Lacey, Robert, *Great Tales from English History (Parts One and Two)*

Larrington, Carolyn, *Winter is Coming*
Lewis, David Levering, *God's Crucible*
Lowder, James (ed), *Beyond the Wall: Exploring George R.R. Martin's A Song of Ice and Fire*
MacFarlane, Alan, *The Origins of English Individualism*
McKisack, May, *The Fourteenth Century*
McLynn, Frank, *Lionheart and Lackland*
Mallory, J.P., *The Origins of the Irish*
Manchester, William, *A World Lit Only By Fire*
Martin, George R.R., *A Game of Thrones*
   A Clash of Kings
   A Storm of Swords
   A Feast for Crows
   A Dance with Dragons
Martin, George R.R., Garcia, Elio M. Jr, Antonsson, Linda, *The World of Ice and Fire*
Morris, Marc, *A Great And Terrible King*
   King John
   The Norman Conquest
Mortimer, Ian, *The Perfect King: The Life of Edward III*
   The Time Travellers Guide to Medieval England
Myers, A.R., *England in the Late Middle Ages*
Neillands, Robin, *The War of the Roses*
Nixey, Catherine, *The Darkening Age: The Christian Destruction of the Classical World*
Norenzayan, Ara, *Big Gods: How Religion Transformed Cooperation and Conflict*
Norwich, John Julius, *Byzantium The Early Centuries*
   Byzantium The Apogee
   The Popes
Oliver, Neil, *A History of Ancient Britain*
Ormrod, W.M., *The Kings and Queen of England*
Palmer, Alan, *Kings and Queens of England*
Parker, Philip, *The Norseman's Fury*
Pollard, Justin, *Alfred the Great*
Poole, A. L., *Domesday to Magna Carta*
Price, Neil S., *The Viking Way: Religion and War in Late Iron Age Scandinavia*
Pye, Michael, *The Edge of the World*
Read, Piers Paul, *The Templars*
Reid, Peter, *A Brief History of Medieval Warfare*
Robb, Graham, *The Discovery of France*
Rose, Alexander, *Kings in the North*
Rosen, William, *The Third Horseman*
Royle, Trevor, *War of the Roses*
Saul, Nigel, *For Honour and Fame*
Schama, Simon, *A History of Britain*

Seward, Desmond, *The Demon's Brood*
    The Hundred Years War
    The War of the Roses
Skidmore, Chris, *Bosworth*
Speck, W.A., *A Concise History of Britain*
Stone, Norman, *Turkey: A Brief History*
Strathern, Paul, *A Brief History of Medicine*
Strong, Roy, *The Story of Britain*
Tombs, Robert, *The English and their History*
Tuchman, Barbara, *A Distant Mirror*
Weir, Alison, *Isabella, She-Wolf of France, Queen of England*
    Lancaster and York
White, R.J., *A Short History of England*
Whittock, Martyn, *A Brief History of Life in the Middle Ages*
Wickham, Chris, *The Inheritance of Rome*
Wilkinson, Toby, *The Rise and Fall of Ancient Egypt*
Wilson, Derek, *The Plantagents*
Wood, Harriet, *The Battle of Hastings*
Ziegler, Philip, *The Black Death*

WEBSITES

http://awoiaf.westeros.org/index.php/Main_Page
http://gameofthrones.wikia.com/wiki/Game_of_Thrones_Wiki
http://history-behind-game-of-thrones.com
https://northamptonfandom.wordpress.com/2015/07/07/lannisters-dont-act-like-fools
    -tywin-lannister-edward-i/
http://watchersonthewall.com/
http://wikiofthrones.com/
https://towerofthehand.com/
https://winteriscoming.net/
http://www.westeros.org/

ACKNOWLEDGMENTS

This book developed from a far smaller ebook in 2014 called *The Realm*. For all the help with both the original Kindle Single and the book, I'd like to thank Laura Rosenheim, Louise Greenberg, Jerrod MacFarlane, Caroline Russomanno, and Sean Goodwin.

NOTES

INTRODUCTION

1. Kendall, Paul Murray *Richard the Third*.
2. This is disputed, and the low estimate puts it at around 9,000, which would still make it the bloodiest battle on British soil. And indeed, the weather is hotly contested; besides which a British 'blizzard' might not impress many people from the Upper Midwest
3. Bryson, Bill *Mother Tongue*.
4. Pinker, Steven *Better Angels of Our Nature*.
5. http://www.westeros.org/Citadel/SSM/Entry/Influence_of_the_Wars_of_the_Roses.
6. http://uk.businessinsider.com/game-of-thrones-was-supposed-to-be-a-trilogy-2015-2.
7. Dan Jones, Sunday Times magazine, July 9, 2017.
8. https://www.lrb.co.uk/v35/n07/john-lanchester/when-did-you-get-hooked.
9. Lowder, James (ed) *Beyond the Wall*.
10. Obviously we know he's not really his bastard, but I don't want to spoil it.
11. Kendall, Paul Murray *Richard the Third*.
12. Season 1, Episode 7.

CHAPTER 1

1. The exact date of the barbican is unclear; whether it dated from the early 14th century or as late as the late 15th century.
2. Rose, Alexander *The Kings in the North*.
3. Rose, Alexander *The Kings in the North*.
4. Rose, Alexander *The Kings in the North*.
5. Ibid.
6. Ned Stark in *A Game of Thrones*.
7. Saul, Nigel *For Honour and Glory*.
8. Told by Walter of Guisborough, a 14th century canon, although many historians are skeptical of the story.
9. From the episode 'You Win or You Die.'
10. Bartlett, Robert England Under the Normans and Angevins.
11. Rose Alexander *The Kings in the North*.
12. Larrington, Carolyne *Winter is Coming*.
13. Geoffrey of Monmouth *History of the Kings of Britain*.
14. The contemporary *Gesta Stephani*.
15. The 15th century *Crowland Chronicles*.
16. *Chronicles of Froissart*.
17. Ibid.
18. Martin made the comparison himself https://winteriscoming.net/2017/07/15/game-of-thrones-as-myth-the-roots-of-the-white-walkers-the-others/.
19. *Polydore Vergil's English History*.
20. Tombs, Robert *The English and Their History*.

21. Saul, Nigel *For Honour and Glory*.
22. *A World of Ice and Fire*.
23. Court records from 1368.
24. Quoted in Kelly, John *The Great Mortality*.
25. Kelly, John *The Great Mortality*.
26. Andrew Boorde, an Elizabethan poet.
27. http://www.nytimes.com/1994/10/23/us/historical-study-of-homicide-and-cities-surprises
    -the-experts.html.
28. Tuchman Barbara *A Distant Mirror*.
29. Frankopan, Peter *Silk Roads*.
30. Bartlett, Robert *The Norman and Angevin Kings*.
31. Ibid.
32. Bergreen, Laurence *Marco Polo*.
33. Ibid.
34. Ibid.
35. Ibid.
36. Ibid.
37. Kelly, John *The Great Mortality*.

CHAPTER 2

1. *Chronicles of Froissart*.
2. Tuchman, Barbara *A Distant Mirror*.
3. Weir, Alison *Isabella, She-Wolf of France, Queen of England*.
4. This is all described in detail in Maurice Druon's novel *The Royal Succession*.
5. According to one theory, so-called because so many Jews were burned there during various persecutions.
6. Kelly, John *The Great Mortality*.
7. Horne, Alistair *The Seven Ages of Paris*.
8. No one called it 'Gothic' at the time, this was a much later term.
9. https://www.huffingtonpost.com/2015/06/19/westeros-europe_n_7565694.html.
10. As Martin said: 'King's Landing, that's the capital, is not quite so tropical—in the books it's more like medieval Paris or London and the north is more like Scotland.'
11. http://www.huffingtonpost.co.uk/entry/westeros-europe_n_7565694.
12. The famous Robert Browning poem, "How They Brought the Good News from Ghent to Aix," helps to portray the sheer vastness of the country. Having driven across the country several times, I feel their pain.
   http://de.reddit.com/r/MapPorn/comments/2pyu11/agricultural_land_use_in_france_oc
   _1266x1297/?utm_content=bufferb1a6f&utm_medium=social&utm_source=twitter
   .com&utm_campaign=buffer.
13. Duby, Georges *France in the Middle Ages*.
14. Larrington Carolyne *Winter is Coming*.
15. Jager, Eric *The Last Duel*.
16. Alternatively it's from *louver*, blockhouse, or *l'ouevre* work.
17. Manchester, William *A World Lit Only by Fire*.
18. Manchester, William *A World Lit Only by Fire*.
19. Horne, Alistair *Seven Ages of Paris*.
20. Duby, Georges *France in the Middle Ages*.
21. It may have been one of the other knights, as the witnesses couldn't be sure because of the sound of the fire and screaming. In fact this story dates to many centuries later so may be completely made up.

22. This is only first recorded many centuries later.
23. http://www.bbc.co.uk/news/magazine-26824993.

CHAPTER 3

1. *Sunday Times* magazine.
2. http://freepages.misc.rootsweb.ancestry.com/~byzantium/Mdv.html.
3. From an 18th description of the corpses buried at Westminster Abbey.
4. Seward, Desmond *Demon's Brood*.
5. This is at least the most popular theory.
6. The royal arms of England are 'gules, three lions passant guardants or,' in the language of heraldry, which translates as 'on a red field, three golden lions, facing outwards, with right foreleg raised.'
7. http://bestiary.ca/beasts/beast78.htm.
8. *The Bestiary*, translated by Richard Barber.
9. Morris, Marc *A Great and Terrible King*.
10. http://history-behind-game-of-thrones.com/medieval-scotland/longshanks.
11. Carpenter, David *Magna Carta*.
12. From the chronicles of the contemporary monk Matthew Paris.
13. Morris, Marc *A Great and Terrible King*.
14. Gillingham, John *Conquest, Catastrophe and Recovery*.
15. The contemporary *Flores Historiarum*, the *Flowers of History*.
16. Rose, Alexander *The Kings in the North*.
17. http://historyofengland.typepad.com/documents_in_english_hist/2012/10/the-song-of-lewes-1264.html.
    http://citeseerx.ist.psu.edu/viewdoc/download;jsessionid=AC9162D7FA5F3903BE48383CC8981A0F?doi=10.1.1.613.4151&rep=rep1&type=pdf.
18. Shahar, Shulamith: Childhood in the Middle Ages, translation by Chaya Galai. Routledge, 1990.
19. This story may have grown in the telling, to put it mildly, but at the very least it reflects their enduring romance.

CHAPTER 4

1. British Isles is a contentious name in Ireland, although no alternative name has ever been found to replace it.
2. Martin, George R.R., Garcia, Elio M. Jr., Antonsson, Linda *The World of Ice and Fire*.
3. Also called 'frozen fire.'
4. As written in *The World of Ice and Fire*, which is told as if in the style of a well-educated Renaissance man.
   These statistics, based on the skulls of those people unlucky to live between 4000 and 3200 BC, only include head wounds, and it is also likely that the natives used deer antlers to stab each other to death http://news.nationalgeographic.com/news/2006/05/060518-skulls.html.
5. http://www.ted.com/talks/steven_pinker_on_the_myth_of_violence/transcript?language=en.
6. Mallory, J.P. *The Origins of the Irish*.
7. http://biorxiv.org/content/early/2017/05/09/135962.
8. http://www.bbc.co.uk/news/science-environment-13082240.
9. The nature of Pictish is extremely disputed. It may have been Celtic, Germanic or indigenous.

10. There may be confusion because the Normans and French invaders of 1066 sometimes called themselves 'Romanz,' the concept of Frenchness having not really been established yet.
11. Martin, George R.R. *A Dange With Dragons*.

CHAPTER 5
1. A nice description of this can be found in Ian Mortimer's *A Time Traveller's Guide to Medieval England*.
2. Bergreen, Laurence *Marco Polo*.
3. Quoted by contemporary Walter of Guisborough.
4. Asbridge, Thomas *The Perfect Knight*.
5. The taxable revenue of Holy Island just out of the border went from £202 in 1296 to £21 in 1326. From 1299-1316 annual tithes in Norham went from £162 to £2.
6. Rose, Alexander *The Kings in the North*.
7. Martin, George R.R. *A Game of Thrones*.
8. Rosen, William *The Third Horseman*.
9. Ibid.
10. Ibid.
11. Quoted in Morris, Marc *A Great and Terrible King*.
12. According to *The Chronicle of Walter of Guisborough*, written around 1346.
13. Rosen, William *The Third Horseman*.
14. In his poem 'The Curse Upon Edward.'
15. Weir, Alison *Isabella*.
16. Rosen, William *The Third Horseman*.
17. The *Annales Paulini*.
18. Weir, Alison *Isabella*.
19. Weir, Alison *Isabella*.
20. Weir, Alison *Isabella*.
21. Horne, Alistair *Seven Ages of Paris*.

CHAPTER 6
1. This backstory is explained in a sort of fake history, *The World of Ice and Fire*, supposedly by a maestar although actually by George R.R. Martin, Elio M. Garcia and Linda Antonsson.
2. Literally 'to rule,' monarch meaning 'one ruler.'
3. Martin, George R.R., Garcia, Elio M. Jr., Antonsson, Linda *The World of Ice and Fire*.
4. http://www.sciencemag.org/news/2016/03/slaughter-bridge-uncovering-colossal-bronze-age-battle.
5. This point is made in Ayelet Haimson Luskkov's *You Win or You Die*, so I cannot claim credit for it.
6. Martin, George R.R. *A Dance With Dragons*.
7. The precise etymology of this word is disputed. It may refer to the name of one of the Messinian villages.
8. Hall, Edith *The Ancient Greeks*.
9. Ibid.
10. Told by the Roman Plutarch in his book *The Sayings of the Spartans*.
11. Two of the 300 actually made it home. One, Aristodemus, was half-blinded and so told to return home, where he was treated as a coward. Another was returning from being sent as an envoy and so missed the crucial battle, and so when he got home was also disgraced and hanged himself.

12. Hall, Edith *The Ancient Greeks*.
13. Plutarch.
14. Wilkinson, Toby *The Rise and Fall of Ancient Egypt*. He wrote: 'Indeed, it is remarkable that they were not afflicted by more serious congenital conditions.'

CHAPTER 7

1. Mary Beard estimates it as 13% while Alison Futrell, in *The Roman Games: Historical Sources in Translation*, puts it at 19%.
2. Holland, Tom *Dynasty*.
3. As Tom Holland wrote in Dynasty, he wished to 'rub the noses of the nobility in their own irrelevance and desuetude, there was nothing any longer to keep him from the greatest stage of all.'
4. Ibid.
5. Ibid.
6. Tacitus.
7. http://blogs.transparent.com/latin/game-of-thrones-ancient-rome-part-i/.
8. Tacitus's *Agricola*.
9. *Roman History* by Cassius Dio.
10. http://www.livescience.com/42838-european-hunter-gatherer-genome-sequenced.html.
11. A theory first suggested in *The 10,000 Year Explosion* by Gregory Cochran and Henry Harpending.
12. Tacitus's *Agricola*.
    This is a subject that remains controversial and attracts some pretty wild speculation. The full details can be summarized here: http://en.wikipedia.org/wiki/Legio_IX _Hispana.
13. From an interview with BBC Radio 4's 'Front Row' https://www.bbc.co.uk/programmes /p00t0cvx.
14. http://blog.english-heritage.org.uk/30-surprising-facts-hadrians-wall/.
15. *Roman History* by Cassius Dio.
16. The film in question is the 2004 King Arthur with Clive Owen and Kiera Knightley
17. This is at least the traditional explanation, although much debated by historians, some would say debunked.
18. Bowman, Alan. K (ed) *The Cambridge Ancient History, Volume 11*.
19. This is according to a source a century later who was admittedly anti-Persian. The true fate of the emperor is unknown. Valerian persecuted Christians and by the time of the writer the Persians were too, so it illustrated both Persian cruelty and the fact that a terrible fate awaited those who mistreated Christians. Other sources claim he was well-treated.
20. http://awoiaf.westeros.org/index.php/Doom_of_Valyria.
21. Recorded by Gildas, a sixth-century monk in his 'Ruin and Destruction of Britain.'

CHAPTER 8

1. Poole, A.F. *Domesday to Magna Carta*.
2. Bartlett, Robert *The Making of Europe*.
3. Ibid.
4. Ibid.
5. Ibid.
6. Ibid.
7. Bartlett, Robert *England under the Norman and Angevin Kings*.
8. Ibid.

9. From his *Orygynale Cronykil of Scotland*.
10. Gillingham, John *Conquest, Catastrophe and Recovery*.
11. Larrington, Carolyne *Winter is Coming*.
12. From the *Orkneyinga Saga*.
13. The cause of the dire wolves' extinction is still a cause for debate, although certainly they disappeared around the same time that humans turned up in the Americas.
14. Gillingham, John *Conquest, Catastrophe and Recovery*.
15. From his memoirs, *Commentaries*.
16. Rosen, William *The Third Horseman*.
17. Rosen, William *The Third Horseman*.

CHAPTER 9
1. Pliny's *Natural History*.
2. Frankel, Valerie Estelle *Winter is Coming*.
3. https://www.theatlantic.com/science/archive/2016/03/were-europes-mysterious-bog-people-human-sacrifices/472839/.
4. http://gameofthronesandnorsemythology.blogspot.co.uk/2013/05/ragnarok-song-of-ice-fire.html.
5. Parker, Philip *The Northmen's Fury*.
6. Whittock, Martyn *A Brief History of Life in the Middle Ages*.
7. Bartlett, Robert *England under the Norman and Angevin Kings*.
8. The always-skeptical William of Newburgh wrote 'one would not easily believe that corpses come out of their graves and wander around, animated by I don't know what spirit to terrorize or harm the living, unless there were cases in our times, supported by ample testimony.' He did not suffer bullshit easily.
9. Ibid.
10. Bartlett, Robert *England under the Norman and Angevin Kings*.
11. The *Chronicon Anglicanum*.
12. *A Game of Thrones*.
13. From the Anglo-Saxon poem 'The Battle of Brunanburh,' written sometime in the 10th century.
14. Frankel, Valerie Estelle *Winter is Coming*.
15. http://www.irelandseye.com/aarticles/culture/talk/banshees/werewolf.shtm.
16. Angela, Alberto *A Day in the Life of Ancient Rome*.
17. Frankopan, Peter *Silk Roads*.
18. Nigosian, Solomon *The Zoroastrian Faith: Tradition and Modern Research*.
19. First mentioned in Ziauddin Barani's *History of Firoz Shah*.
20. Van Woerkens, Martine *The Strangled Traveler: Colonial Imaginings and the Thugs of India*.

CHAPTER 10
1. Rosen, William *The Third Horseman*.
2. Kelly, John *The Great Mortality*.
3. Other sources suggest there may have been one or two days respite.
4. Rosen, William *The Third Horseman*.
5. Ibid.
6. Bartlett, Robert *England under the Norman and Angevin Kings*.
7. https://pseudoerasmus.com/2014/06/12/aside-angus-maddison/.
8. Kelly, John *The Great Mortality*.
9. Ibid.

10. Ibid.
11. Rosen, William *The Third Horseman*.
12. Horne, Alistair *Seven Ages of Paris*.
13. http://www.res.org.uk/details/mediabrief/10547499/ECONOMIC-ROOTS-OF -JEWISH-PERSECUTIONS-IN-MEDIEVAL-EUROPE.html.
14. Rosen, William *The Third Horseman*.
15. Ibid.
16. 'Mair fell than wes ony devill in hell', as a chronicler put it.
17. The evidence for this relationship is not so clear cut, it is fair to say. They certainly had an intimate friendship which damaged the king's marriage.
18. McKisack, May *The Fourteenth Century*.
19. Weir, Alison *Isabella*.
20. Weir, Alison *Isabella*.
21. Ibid.
22. Ibid.
23. Quoted in Ibid.
24. Castor, *She-Wolves*.
25. However it had an immunity clause that said his land should be spared if he was attacked, which rather calls into question his motive.
26. Well, possibly.
27. Weir, Alison *Isabella*.
28. This is the theory suggested by her biographer Alison Weir.
29. Frankel wrote in *Winter is Coming*: 'With her constant insistence on "courtesy as a lady's armor," Sansa demonstrates her love for medieval "courtesy books"—primers on proper behavior written mainly between the twelfth and fifteenth centuries.'
30. Rose, Alexander *The Kings in the North*.
31. There is probably some degree of artistic license involved in this story, which is otherwise the only thing most people know about him. It was also reported that in jail he was mistreated, mocked and made to shave off his hair and beard with cold water from a ditch, then dressed in old clothes, and made to swallow rotting food and a crown of hay placed on his head, the aim being to slowly kill him. However Alison Weir doubts the source.
32. Rose, Alexander *The Kings in the North*.

CHAPTER 11

1. Freeman, Charles *A New History of Early Christianity*.
2. *A Game of Thrones*.
3. http://www.onreligion.co.uk/religion-in-game-of-thrones/.
4. http://slatestarcodex.com/2017/10/15/were-there-dark-ages/.
5. Lewis, David Levering *God's Crucible*.
6. The contemporary Zacharias of Mytilene.
7. Kelly, John *The Great Mortality*.
8. The theory that Westeros equals Europe is here http://www.quora.com/Are-Westeros -Kingdoms-inspired-by-real-life-countries-and-peoples The Iron Islands are not the Viking kingdoms of the islands of Scotland, Man and Ireland, but Scandinavia itself. In this theory the North is eastern Europe, with White Harbor translating as St Petersburg; the Slavic lands of north-east Europe were the last to leave the old gods behind, with some parts of the Baltic remaining pagan until the 13th century. The Westerlands, rich in mines, serves as a substitute for Britain, which was enriched by tin and later coal; both also have lions as symbols. In this comparison the Riverlands are the Low Countries and the Rhineland region of Germany, a region dominated by rivers, with good

farming land that is nonetheless vulnerable to conquering armies. The Crownlands represent eastern Germany, forested land in the middle of continent that is often fought over.

9. Martin, George R.R., Garcia, Elio M. Jr., Antonsson, Linda *The World of Ice and Fire*.
10. Bartlett, Robert *England under the Norman and Angevin Kings*.

CHAPTER 12

1. Larrington, Carolyne *Winter is Coming*.
2. Martin, George R.R., Garcia, Elio M. Jr., Antonsson, Linda *The World of Ice and Fire*.
3. https://www.spectator.co.uk/2017/10/the-muslim-world-is-more-tolerant-of -homosexuality-than-you-think/.
4. Hourani, Albert *A History of the Arab Peoples* Quoted in the introduction by Malise Ruthven.
5. https://www.reddit.com/r/europe/comments/4kdvol/the_thirty_largest_cities_in_europe _by_population/.
6. A juicier description can be found in Fletcher, Richard *Moorish Spain*.
7. Lewis, David Levering *God's Crucible*.
8. http://gameofthrones.wikia.com/wiki/Long_Bridge.
9. Fletcher, Richard *Moorish Spain*.
10. Ibid.
11. Fletcher, Richard *Moorish Spain*.
12. It features in a Game of Thrones tour of Spain. http://www.designmena.com/thoughts /game-of-thrones-themed-tour-of-spains-moorish-architecture-on-offer.
13. Fletcher, Richard *Moorish Spain*.
14. This was apparently just a literary convention to show how romantic he was, although in Dubai today they can actually bring snow to the desert.
15. Fletcher, Richard *Moorish Spain*.
16. Lewis, David Levering *God's Crucible*.
17. Fletcher, Richard *Moorish Spain*.
18. The current sword was made for Charles I's coronation.
19. Fletcher, Richard *Moorish Spain*.

CHAPTER 13

1. Rose, Alexander *The Kings in the North*.
2. Seward, Desmond *Demon's Brood*.
3. (The term Warden of the March had first been used in 1309, a Clifford being the first.)
4. http://www.proto-english.org/o21.html He also said he 'felt free to mix armour styles from several different periods.'
5. This was related to the indigenous Gaullish language spoken there before the Romans and now, with French dominance, the region's Celtic language was being replaced by a Latin one for the second time.
6. As Froissart put it in his *Chronicles*.
7. Bartlett, Robert *The Making of Europe*.
8. As described by Gerald of Wales, a chronicler in the 12th century.
9. Reid, Peter *A Brief History of Medieval Warfare*.
10. Reid, Peter *A Brief History of Medieval Warfare*.
11. Rose, Alexander *The Kings in the North*.
12. Mortimer, Ian *A Time Traveller's Guide to Medieval England*.
13. De Charny's *Book of Chivalry*.
14. Ibid.

15. Tuchman, Barbara wrote in *A Distant Mirror:* 'To fight on horseback or foot wearing 55 pounds of plate armor, to crash in collision with an opponent at full gallop while holding horizontal an eighteen-foot lance half the length of an average telephone pole, to give and receive blows with sword or battle-ax that could cleave a skull or slice off a limb at a stroke, to spend half of life in the saddle through all weathers and for days at a time, was not a weakling's work.'
16. *A Storm of Swords.*
17. Keegan, John *The Illustrated Face of Battle.*
18. *A Game of Thrones.*
19. Harvey, John *The Plantagenets.*
20. Rose, Alexander *The Kings in the North.*
21. Ibid.
22. Ibid.
23. Appleby, John C *Outlaws in Medieval and Early Modern England.*
24. Froissart's *Chronicles.*
25. Larrington, Carolyne *Winter is Coming.*
26. Duby, Georges *France in the Middle Ages.*
27. Bartlett, Robert *England under the Norman and Angevin Kings.*
28. Poole, A.F. *Domesday to Magna Carta.*
29. Ackroyd, Peter *Foundations.*
30. Seward, Desmond *The Demon's Brood.*
31. Barker, Juliet *England Arise.*
32. Tuchman, Barbara *A Distant Mirror.*

CHAPTER 14

1. *A Dance with Dragons.*
2. Henry's *Historia Anglorum.*
3. This is the traditional theory; another possibility is that these eastern parts of Britain had always been Germanic-speaking - indeed that Boudicca was a sort of Saxon— although there are a number of problems with this idea.
4. Mortimer, Ian *Time Traveller's Guide to Elizabethan England.*
5. Martin, George R.R., Garcia, Elio M. Jr., Antonsson, Linda *The World of Ice and Fire*
6. This word was not used at the time, and only appeared much later.
7. http://www.nature.com/news/british-isles-mapped-out-by-genetic-ancestry-1.17136.
8. The degree to which the Angles and Saxons displaced the natives has always been hotly debated.
9. That is at least one theory. It may have been Mercia. Or East Anglia http://csis.pace.edu /grendel/projf20004d/History.html.
10. http://www.bbc.co.uk/culture/story/20140616-game-of-thrones-debt-to-tolkien.
11. http://www.bbc.com/culture/story/20140616-game-of-thrones-debt-to-tolkien.
12. https://twitter.com/ClerkofOxford/status/914396271506575360.

CHAPTER 15

1. http://alxlockwood.webs.com/plaguecomet1347.htm.
2. Although this came about over a confusion with the 1st century outbreak in Rome, which Seneca had so christened).
3. Kelly, John *The Great Mortality.*
4. Ziegler, Philip *The Black Death.*
5. Contemporary Gabriel de Mussis, in *The Great Dying of the Year of our Lord 1348.*
6. Ziegler, Philip *The Black Death.*

7. Ibid.

8. In the early 20th century the price of tarabagan skins quadrupled and Chinese hunters flooded into Manchuria to catch the rodent, causing an outbreak that killed 60,000 people within a year. The average survival time from onset of symptoms was just 14 hours 30 minutes.

9. Ziegler, Philip *The Black Death*.

10. https://www.standard.co.uk/news/uk/black-death-plague-spread-by-dirty-humans-and -not-rats-study-finds-a3741411.html.

11. Jean de Venette's *Chronicle of the Hundred Years War* (although not everyone is sure he wrote it).

12. Frederic C. Lane says plague killed 60 percent of Venice, or 72,000 people.

13. One possible legacy of the plague is the folk song "Ring a Ring a Roses," the children's rhyme that ends 'we all fall down', although this is heavily disputed and many people think it originated in the nineteenth century. This Plague link only appears after World War Two.

CHAPTER 16

1. Lewis, David Levering *God's Crucible*.

2. Brown, Peter *The Rise of Western Christendom*.

3. Jordanes's *Getica*.

4. Larrington, Carolyne *Winter is Coming*.

5. *A Clash of Kings*.

6. Clements, Jonathan *The Vikings*.

7. Wilkinson, Toby *The Rise and Fall of Ancient Egypt*.

8. Goldsworthy, Adrian *The Fall of the West*.

9. Parker, Philip *The Norsemens' Fury*.

10. Price, Neil S. *The Viking Way*.

11. Price, Neil S. *The Viking Way*.

12. Pye, Michael *The Edge of the World*.

13. Price, Neil S. *The Viking Way*.

14. Price, Neil S. *The Viking Way*.

15. Price, Neil S. *The Viking Way*.

    The Army of the Dead, or *das germanische Totenheer*, was according to Offo Hofler's 1934 book *Kultische Geheimbünde der Germanen* (Secret Cultic Societies of the Germanic Peoples) 'the mythological reflection of real warrior fraternities operating in the Iron Age among the Germanic peoples.' From Price, Neil S. *The Viking Way*.

16. Price, Neil S. *The Viking Way*.

17. Ibid.

18. *Historia de Gentibus Septentrionalibus*.

19. http://www.electrummagazine.com/2017/04/neanderthals-scandinavian-trolls-and -troglodytes/.

    The grave of a female Viking warrior was supposedly discovered in September 2017, but experts treat it with skepticism https://arstechnica.com/science/2017/09/have-we-finally -found-hard-evidence-for-viking-warrior-women/.

20. *A Dance with Dragons*.

21. *A Feast for Crows*.

22. This, of course, could have been a later rationalization after Ethelred's disastrous reign.

23. *A Feast for Crows*.

24. Larrington, Carolyne *Winter is Coming*.

25. Parker, Philip *The Norsemens' Fury*.

26. http://www.huffingtonpost.co.uk/2014/03/10/one-million-brits-viking-descendants_n_4933186.html.
27. Iceland's is older, but did not function for many years.

CHAPTER 17
1. 'Carolyne Larrington: there's no place for the High Septon on the Small Council, no communal prayers within the palace, no regular attendance at the equivalent of mass for the nobility or the knightly classes.'
2. Mortimer, Ian *A Time Traveller's Guide to Medieval England*.
3. This comparison is made by Carolyn Larrington. Among the other masters of the English middle ages were Eadmer, William of Malmesbury, Symeon of Durham, Henry of Huntingdon, Orderic Vitalis, William of Newburgh, Gervase of Canterbury, Ralph of Diceto, Roger of Howden and Ralph of Coggeshall, men who provide the bulk of sources we rely on.
4. Bartlett, Robert *England under the Norman and Angevin Kings*.
5. Ibid.
6. Horne, Alistair *Seven Ages of Paris*.
7. Gies, Frances and Joseph *Life in a Medieval Village*.
8. Hibbert, Christopher *The English, a Social History*.
9. *A Feast for Crows*.
10. Kelly, John *The Great Mortality*.
11. Ziegler, Philip *The Black Death*.
12. Ziegler, Philip *The Black Death*.
13. Tuchman, Barbara *A Distant Mirror*.
14. Ibid.
15. Tuchman, Barbara *A Distant Mirror*.
16. Ibid.
17. Gies, Frances and Joseph *Life in a Medieval City*.
18. https://twitter.com/douthatnyt/status/747584810693042176?lang=en.
19. http://www.dailymail.co.uk/news/article-201388/Gunpowder-Plot-ruined-city.html.

CHAPTER 18
1. Bergreen, Lawrence *Marco Polo*.
2. Tuchman, Barbara *A Distant Mirror*.
3. Mortimer, Ian *A Time Traveller's Guide to Medieval England*.
4. Crowley, Roger *City of Fortune*.
5. Ibid.
6. Reid, Peter *Medieval Warfare*.
7. Crowley, Roger *City of Fortune*.
8. Gies, Frances and Joseph *Life in a Medieval City*.
9. Martin, George R.R., Garcia, Elio M. Jr., Antonsson, Linda *The World of Ice and Fire*.
10. Tuchman, Barbara *A Distant Mirror*.
11. Bergreen, Lawrence *Marco Polo*.
12. Bergreen, Lawrence *Marco Polo*.
13. Larrington, Carolyne *Winter is Coming*.
14. Bergreen, Lawrence *Marco Polo*.
15. Crowley, Roger *City of Fortune*.
16. Bergreen, Lawrence *Marco Polo*.
17. Crowley, Roger *City of Fortune*.
18. Martin, George R.R., Garcia, Elio M. Jr., Antonsson, Linda *The World of Ice and Fire*.

19. http://kengarex.com/real-life-game-of-thrones-locations-you-can-actually-visit-23
    -photos/15/.
20. Larrington, Carolyne *Winter is Coming*.
21. http://www.oldpicsarchive.com/23-most-unusual-and-strange-sculptures-from-around
    -the-world/2/.
22. Bergreen, Lawrence *Marco Polo*.
23.. Bergreen, Lawrence *Marco Polo*.
24. Crowley, Roger *City of Fortune*.
    This sort of language test is known as shibboleth, from the Biblical story in which the
    Gileadites identified the Ephraimites by their inability to pronounce the word. Several
    such grizzly tests have marked groups down the years for death. If you're REALLY inter-
    ested you could learn more in my book *England in the Age of Chivalry*.

CHAPTER 19

1. Rose, Alexander *The Kings in the North*.
2. Ibid.
3. Castor, Helen *Joan of Arc*.
4. Poole A.L. *From Domesday Book to Magna Carta*.
5. Tuchman, Barbara *A Distant Mirror*.
6. Tuchman, Barbara *A Distant Mirror*.
7. Bartlett, Robert *England under the Norman and Angevin Kings*.
8. *A Clash of Kings*.
9. *A Dance with Dragons*.
   Of course a writer of fantasy is not constrained by this so it doesn't matter, and no doubt
   GRRM is aware its myth. But it has appeared in historical fiction, too, mostly famously
   in *Braveheart*.
10. Alan MacFarlane's *The Origins of English Individualism* changed the way many saw this
    period, making the idea of 'peasants' at the time seem obsolete.
11. This is a historical comparison made by Carolyn Larrington.
12. http://awoiaf.westeros.org/index.php/Smallfolk.
13. Braudel, Ferdinand *The Identity of France*.
14. Rosen, William *The Third Horseman*.
15. Kelly, John *The Great Mortality*.
16. Horne, Alistair *The Seven Ages of Paris*.
17. As Parliament described it in 1363.
18. Audley, Anselm *Death Keeps His Court*.
19. There hadn't been a coronation for 50 years so almost no one would know what to do
    from first-hand experience. The coronation's organizers used a book called *Liber Rega-
    lis*, written by Abbott Lytlyngton, which is still used for the coronation of British mon-
    archs today.
20. Rose, Alexander *The Kings in the North*.
21. Although mass break outs of medieval prisons were common, the prison at Bishop's
    Stortford had breakouts of 16 in 1392, of 18 in 1393 and ten in 1401, all by 'convicted
    clerks.'
22. Froissart's *Chronicle*.
23. Ibid.
24. Rose, Alexander *The Kings in the North*.
25. Or possibly Maidstone.
26. There is debate about the circumstances of Tyler's death, and who drew a weapon first
    and why. Suffice it to say that the meeting didn't go well for him.

CHAPTER 20

1. Crowley, Roger *1453*.
2. Crowley, Roger *1453*.
3. Ibid.
4. McLynn, Frank *1066*.
5. Petrus Gyllius's *De Topographia Constantinopoleos*.
6. Larrington 'a huge port city, owing its prosperity to the great guilds (the Ancient Guild of Spicers, the Tourmaline Brotherhood) and the merchant princes who trade in spices, saffron, silks and other exotic wares from further east beyond the Jade Sea."
7. Martin, George R.R. *A Clash of Kings*.
8. Larrington, Carolyne *Winter is Coming*.
9. http://awoiaf.westeros.org/index.php/Xaro_Xhoan_Daxos#cite_note-Racok 27.7B.7B.7B3.7D.7D.7D-0.
10. Martin, George R.R. *A Clash of Kings*.
11. Crowley, Roger *1453*.
12. Norwich, John Julius *Byzantium: The Apogee*.
13. Norwich, John Julius *Byzantium: The Apogee*.
14. Norwich, John Julius *Byzantium: The Apogee*.
15. Allegedly. Quite a suspicious large numbers of such items were running around at the time.
16. From his *Relatio de legatione Constantinopolitana ad Nicephorum Phocam*.
17. As Jaime Lannister put it.
18. Although she may also have been stabbed or scalded to death.
19. Norwich, John Julius *Byzantium: The Apogee*.
20. Norwich, John Julius *Byzantium: The Apogee*.
21. Frankopan, Peter *Silk Roads*.
22. Frankopan, Peter *Silk Roads*.
23. Bridges, Antony *The Crusades*.
24. Herrin, Judith *Byzantium*.
25. *A Clash of Kings*.
26. Jean de Joinville's *Life of St Louis*.
27. http://www.theguardian.com/tv-and-radio/2013/mar/24/game-of-thrones-realistic-history.
28. Herrin, Judith *Byzantium*.
29. Frankopan, Peter *Silk Roads*.
30. Frankopan, Peter *Silk Roads*.
31. Herrin, Judith *Byzantium*.
32. Norwich, John Julius *Byzantium: The Apogee*.
33. Martin, George R.R., Garcia, Elio M. Jr., Antonsson, Linda *The World of Ice and Fire* This is at least according to Harald's own sagas which were, in fairness, notoriously unreliable and filled improbable boasting, the sort of person who today would have claimed to be in the SAS.
34. This story may have not be 100 percent accurate, as with most of the stories told about Harald.

CHAPTER 21

1. The Thenns also acknowledge a lord and have discipline more typical of southern people, but in the television series, for simplicity reasons, they're conflated with the cannibalistic ice river clans.
2. Tuchman, Barbara *A Distant Mirror*.
3. Tuchman, Barbara *A Distant Mirror*.

4. Ibid.
5. Jager, Eric *The Last Duel*.
6. Tuchman, Barbara *A Distant Mirror*.
7. Rose, Alexander *The Kings in the North*.
8. Jager, Eric *The Last Duel*.
9. Tuchman, Barbara *A Distant Mirror*.
10. Jager, Eric *The Last Duel*.
11. Froissart's *Chronicles*.
12. *Chronique de Religieux de Saint-Denys, contenant le regne de Charles VI de 1380 a 1422*.
13. Tuchman, Barbara *A Distant Mirror*.
14. Ibid.
15. Tuchman, Barbara *A Distant Mirror*.
16. Tuchman, Barbara *A Distant Mirror*.
17. Hibbert, Christopher *The English, A Social History*.
18. Gies, Frances and Joseph *Life in a Medieval City*.
19. The *Vierzeiliger oberdeutscher Totentanz*, written around 1460.

CHAPTER 22

1. *The World of Ice and Fire*.
2. http://www.nature.com/scitable/blog/viruses101/hiv_resistant_mutation?isForcedMobile=Y
3. http://www.westeros.org/Citadel/SSM/Category/C91/P90.
4. Jager, Eric *The Last Duel*.
5. Bartlett, Robert *The Making of Europe*.
6. This is disputed by some historians, who suggest her father was actually quite respectable. At any rate people believed it, and later taunted William.
7. Borman, Tracy *Matilda*.
8. Wilkinson, Toby *The Rise and Fall of Ancient Egypt*.
9. Bridgeford, Andrew *1066: The Hidden History of the Bayeux Tapestry*.
10. William of Newburgh .
11. Gies, Joseph and Frances *Life in a Medieval Castle*.
12. Gies, Joseph and Frances *Life in a Medieval Castle*.
13. Duby, Georges *France in the Middle Ages*. One suspects that the entire system of medieval European civilization was largely designed by Frenchman to ensure that their supply of wine was safe.
14. Duby, Georges: 'Just as early medieval kings brought up the sons of their vassals, so the territorial princes made the sons of castellans welcome at their courts, and the castellans in turn took in and trained the sons of local knights.'
15. Gies, Joseph and Frances *Life in a Medieval Castle*.
16. *The Ecclestiastical History* of Orderic Vitalis.
17. Larrington, Carolyne *Winter is Coming* The names of the Houses reflect their environment; alongside the dominant House Reed are House Fenn, House Quagg, House Peat and House Boggs', named after artificial islands.
18. Larrington, Carolyne *Winter is Coming*.
19. This is one story. In truth very little is known about him.
20. Clark, Gregory *The Son Also Rises*.

CHAPTER 23

https://www.researchgate.net/publication/264402032_From_Swords_to_Words_Does
_Macro-Level_Change_in_Self-Control_Predict_Long-Term_Variation_in_Levels_of
_Homicide With thanks to Ben Southwood – @bswud – for the hat-tip.

21. The Real History behind Game of Thrones documentary with George R.R. Martin and historians https://www.youtube.com/watch?v=Odw3Nxdqq4o.
22. D'Elgin, Tershia *The Everything Bird Book: From Identification to Bird Care, Everything You Need to Know about our Feathered Friends.*
23. Or suffocated beneath a featherbed. The net effect was the same at any rate.
24. Ackroyd, Peter *Foundations.*

CHAPTER 24
1. https://www.oddee.com/item_96620.aspx.
2. Gies, Frances and Joseph *Life in a Medieval Castle.*
3. Bartlett, Robert *The Norman and Angevin Kings.*
4. Tuchman: 'As penetration by outsiders increased, so did snobbery until a day in the mid-15th century when a knight rode into the lists followed by a parade of pennants bearing no less than 32 coat-of-arms.'
5. Larrington, Carolyne *Winter is Coming.*
6. According to French medievalist Karl Uitti.'
7. The closest translation would be 'cunt', *con* being a very crude word.
8. Jones, Terry *Medieval Lives.*

CHAPTER 25
1. Hackett, David Fischer *Albion's Seed.*
2. Rose, Alexander *The Kings in the North.*
3. Ibid.
4. Larrington, Carolyne *Winter is Coming.*
5. Rose, Alexander *The Kings in the North.*
6. Goodwin, George *Fatal Rivalry.*
7. Rose, Alexander *The Kings in the North.*
8. Steven Attwell, Race for the Iron Throne, writes that in Westeros 'the Umbers don't get along with the Glovers; the Manderlys (who like to build public works at Stark expense), Tallharts, Flints, Karstarks, and Boltons are interested in expanding their territories at the expense of the Hornwoods; the Boltons have only been relatively recently brought under Stark control, and clearly require a strong hand to keep in check.'
9. Goodwin, George *Fatal Rivalry.*
10. From Walter Scott's *Poetical Works.*
11. Hackett, David Fischer *Albion's Seed.*
12. Hackett, David Fischer *Albion's Seed.*
13. Saul, Nigel *For Honour and Fame.*

CHAPTER 26
1. *History of William Marshal.*
2. Asbridge, Thomas *The Perfect Knight.*
3. There is only one reference to this, Marshal's own biography.
4. The Anglo-Saxon Chronicle.
5. http://gameofthrones.wikia.com/wiki/Red_Keep.
6. The second most recent Gilbert Leigh, born in 1884, was from the Norman-descended Grosvenor family, the grandson of the 2nd Marquess of Westminster.
7. Seward, Desmond *Demon's Brood.*
8. Frankel, Valerie *Winter is Coming.*
9. Castor, Helen *She-Wolves: The Women Who Ruled England before Elizabeth.*

10. http://www.nytimes.com/1993/01/03/nyregion/the-royal-family-tree-sprouts-unofficial-limbs.html?pagewanted=all.
11. Seward, Desmond *The Demon's Brood*.
12. Bradbury, Jim *Stephen and Matilda*.
13. Ibid.
14. Poole, A.F. *Domesday to Magna Carta*.
15. Ibid.
16. From his *Historia Anglorum*.
17. Ibid.
18. Bradbury, Jim *Battle of Hastings*.
19. Ibid.
20. https://ew.com/article/2014/04/13/george-r-r-martin-why-joffrey-killed/.
21. *The Peterborough Chronicle*.
22. Gies, Joseph and Frances *Life in a Medieval Castle*.

CHAPTER 27

1. The English account in the *Gesta Henrici* records: 'For when some of them, killed when battle was first joined, fall at the front, so great was the undisciplined violence and pressure of the mass of men behind them that the living fell on top of the dead, and others falling on top of the living were killed as well.'
2. *A Game of Thrones*.
3. Some believe he was also a Lollard, like Oldcastle.

CHAPTER 28

1. Or at least it was suspected.
2. Jones, Terry *Medieval Lives*.
3. Gies, Frances and Joseph *Life in a Medieval Castle*.
4. Hibbert, Christopher *The English, a Social History*.
5. Larrington, Carolyn *Winter is Coming*.
6. Hibbert, Christopher *The English, a Social History*.
7. Bartlett, Robert *The Norman and Angevin Kings*.
8. Ibid.
9. Ibid.
10. The evidence is mixed, however, and causal arrow not known.
11. Bartlett, Robert *The Norman and Angevin Kings* This is from an adventure involving Burnel the Ass, the main character in a fable written by Nigel, a monk in Canterbury.
12. In Britain alcohol consumption increased in the late 20th century, but is still nowhere near its 1800 rate, and has since declined sharply. In France the average person drinks one-third the amount of wine as 50 years ago.
13. Morris, Marc *King John*.
14. Horne, Alistair *The Seven Ages of Paris*.
15. Duby, Georges *France in the Middle Ages*.
16. For more—see my fantastic book *1215 and All That*.
17. Clause 39: 'No free man is to be arrested, or imprisoned, or disseised, or outlawed, or exiled, or in any other way ruined, nor will we go against him or send against him, except by the lawful judgment of his peers or by the law of the land.' Again, buy my book on the subject.
18. Bartlett.
19. This story is recalled in greater detail in Thomas Asbridge's *The Greatest Knight*.

CHAPTER 29

The institution, laws & ceremonies of the most noble Order of the Garter collected and digested into one body, Ashmole, Elias; Hollar, Wenceslaus; Sherwin, William, https://quod.lib.umich.edu/e/eebo/A26024.0001.001/1:10.3?rgn=div2;view=fulltext.

20. Frankel, Valerie *Winter is Coming*.
21. Froissart's *Chronicles*.
22. Larrington, Carolyne *Winter is Coming*.
23. Carolyne Larrington: 'Both women are warriors and are beautiful and in love with noble nights, Bradamante with Saracen Ruggiero, who she marries after he converts to Christianity, and Britomart with Artegall, who symbolises justice. Britomart rescues him from an enchantress. in line with Merlin's prophecies, she becomes ancestor to British kings.'
24. 'Brienne of Tarth and Joan of Arc share substance and style: they're both obsessively loyal, and they both know how to rock a suit of armor. Brienne swore her sword first to Renly Baratheon, then to Catelyn Stark, and finally to Jamie Lannister-- she's so devoted, she even named her sword "Oathkeeper."'
25. Castor, Helen *Joan of Arc*.
26. Ibid.
27. Ibid.
28. Ibid.
29. Ibid.
30. Tuchman, Barbara *A Distant Mirror*.
31. Wilson, Colin *The Occult*.

CHAPTER 30

1. Brothers of the Night's Watch weren't supposed to have sex either although it's ignored by quite a few of them.
2. We don't know for certain there were nine to start with or whether this was just a convention.
3. Read, Piers Paul *The Templars*.
4. Larrington, Carolyne *Winter is Coming*.
5. Read, Piers Paul *The Templars*.
6. *The Rule of the Templars*.
7. Ibid.
8. Haag, Michael *The Tragedy of the Templars*.
9. Ibid.
10. As Steven Attewell writes in Race for the Iron Throne: 'While the religious nature of these orders doesn't quite parallel, the strictness of the lifelong vows of the Night's Watch, especially in relation to chastity and inheritance, does have at least the flavor of monasticism that came with the militant Christian orders.
11. Larrington, Carolyne *Winter is Coming*.
12. Season 4, Episode 3.
13. Bridge, Antony *The Crusades*.
14. Read, Piers Paul *The Templars*.
15. Read, Piers Paul *The Templars*.
16. In 1274 Edward I repaid 27,974 livres with an extra 5,333 in expenses.
17. Frankopan, Peter *Silk Roads*.

CHAPTER 31

1. http://www.hist.unibe.ch/content/tagungen/the_coldest_decade_of_the_millennium/index_ger.html.
2. As 19th century historian Jacques Chartier wrote: 'The king of France imposed such good order on the conduct of his men-at-arms that it was a fine thing.'
3. https://neurosciencenews.com/schizophrenia-heritability-7672/?platform=hootsuite
4. Schizophrenia is far more common when both parents have it, and there is some suggestion that Henry V, a messianic figure whose behaviour was certainly on the cusp of deranged, carried risk factors.
5. Weir, Alison *Lancaster and York*.
6. Ibid.
7. Bicheno, Hugh *Battle Royal*.
8. Bicheno, Hugh *Battle Royal*.
9. Sewell, Desmond *Demon's Brood*.
10. Russian-American academic Peter Turchin cites 'elite overproduction' as a major cause of destabilization in numerous societies, and this may have played a factor.
11. Rose, Alexander *The Kings in the North*.
12. Harvey, John *The Plantagenets*.
13. Weir, Alison *Lancaster and York*.
14. *The Paston Letters*.
15. Frankel, Valerie *Winter is Coming*.
16. Royle, Trevor *The War of the Roses*.
17. Kendall, Paul Murray *Richard III*.
18. Huizinga, Johan The Waning of the Middle Ages.
19. Horspool, David *Richard III*.

CHAPTER 32

1. Jager, Eric *The Last Duel*.
2. Jager, Eric *The Last Duel*.
3. Ibid.
4. Jager, Eric *The Last Duel*.
5. Duby, Georges *France in the Middle Ages*.
6. Manchester, William *A World Lit only by Fire*.
7. http://www.thomas-morris.uk/roger-two-urinals-clerk/.
8. Jager, Eric *The Last Duel*.
9. *A Dance with Dragons*.
10. https://www.ft.com/content/5a3b661c-fc45-11e5-b5f5-070dca6d0a0d.
11. Pye, Michael *The Edge of the World*.
12. 'It was possession of the gallows that marked out those lords who claimed routine franchisal jurisdiction over thieves.'
13. Ackroyd, Peter *Foundations*.
14. Manchester, William *A World Lit only by Fire*.
15. Jager, Eric *The Last Duel*.
16. This may not be a true story.
17. Steven Pinker's *Better Angels of Our Nature* lists numerous such fights.

CHAPTER 33

1. Kelly, John *The Great Mortality*.
2. Larrington, Carolyne *Winter is Coming*.
3. Larrington, Carolyne *Winter is Coming*.

4. Larrington, Carolyne *Winter is Coming*.
5. Frankopan, Peter *Silk Roads*.
6. *A World of Ice and Fire*.
7. Attewell, Steven *Race for the Iron Throne*.
8. Frankopan, Peter *Silk Roads*.
9. Frankopan, Peter *Silk Roads*.
   The Dothraki language, created by David Peterson of the Language Creation Society, takes words from Turkish, Russian, Estonian (which belongs to the distant Ugric group of languages, not Indo-European), Inuktitut (spoken by Canadian Inuit) and Swahili. Peterson has said that 'Most people probably don't really know what Arabic actually sounds like, so to an untrained ear, it might sound like Arabic. To someone who knows Arabic, it doesn't. I tend to think of the sound as a mix between Arabic (minus the distinctive pharyngeals) and Spanish.' http://www.tor.com/blogs/2010/04/creating-dothraki-an-interview-with-david-j-peterson-and-sai-emrys.
10. Kelly, John *The Great Mortality*.
11. Ata Malik Juviani, a Persian alive at the time.
12. According to *The Secret Life of the Mongols*, Chinggis means strong.
13. A contemporary, quoted in Frankopan, Peter *Silk Roads*.
14. Stone, Norman *Turkey: A Short History*.
15. Frankopan, Peter *Silk Roads*.
16. Bergreen, Lawrence *Marco Polo*.
17. Ibid.
18. Ibid.
19. http://rstb.royalsocietypublishing.org/content/367/1589/657.
20. http://www.rationaloptimist.com/blog/polygamy-fuels-violence.aspx.
21. Bergreen, Lawrence *Marco Polo*.
22. Season 3, Episode 3.
23. Bergreen, Lawrence *Marco Polo*.
24. Ibid. A small branch of the Assassins did live on in Syria.
25. Haag, Michael *The Tragedy of the Templars*.

CHAPTER 34

1. Bicheno, Hugh *Battle Royal*.
2. Kendall, Paul Murray *Richard the Third*.
3. Royle, Trevor *The War of the Roses*.
4. Bicheno, Hugh *Battle Royal*.
5. Jones, Dan *The Hollow Crown*.
6. Huizinga, Johan *The Waning of the Middle Ages*.
7. Bicheno, Hugh *Battle Royal*.
8. Horspool, David *Richard III*.

CHAPTER 35

1. Crowley, Roger *1453*.
2. Stone, Norman *Turkey: A Short History*.
3. http://www.washingtonpost.com/blogs/worldviews/wp/2014/11/11/why-turkeys-military-wants-to-ban-game-of-thrones/.
4. Crowley, Roger *1453*.
5. Ibn Khaldun's *Muqaddimah*.
6. Frankpan, Peter *Silk Roads*.
7. Norwich, John Julius *Byzantium: The Apogee*.

8. Stone, Norman *Turkey: A Short History.*
9. Stone, Norman *Turkey: A Short History.*
10. Stone, Norman *Turkey: A Short History.*
11. Crowley, Roger *1453.*
12. Stone, Norman *Turkey: A Short History.*
13. Crowley, Roger *1453.*
14. Ibid.
15. Crowley, Roger *1453.*
16. Alternatively it was St Elmo's fire, which is caused by atmospheric electricity.
17. Ibid.
18. Crowley, Roger *1453.*
19. Crowley, Roger *City of Fortune.*
20. Stone, Norman *Turkey: A Short History.*
21. Season 1, Episode 9.
22. Larrington, Carolyne *Winter is Coming.*

CHAPTER 36

1. h/t to Dan Jackson, @northumbriana https://twitter.com/northumbriana/status/862745439619215360.
2. It is here that Maester Balder wrote *The Edge of the World*, a tale of legends.
3. In the words of historian R.L. Storey, Quoted in Rose, Alexander *The Kings in the North.*
4. Rose, Alexander *The Kings in the North.*
5. Rose, Alexander *The Kings in the North.*
6. Gillingham, John *The War of the Roses.*
7. 1 Samuel 26.

CHAPTER 37

1. http://www.walesonline.co.uk/news/wales-news/dna-survey-reveals-25-welsh-8308111.
2. Sir John Wynn, a late 16th century Welsh baronet. Quoted in Skidmore, Chris *Bosworth.*
3. Kendall, Paul Murray *Richard the Third.*
4. Bicheno, Hugh *Battle Royal.*
5. Jones, Dan *The Hollow Crown.*
6. No one called him that at the time. It was first coined by David Hume in the 18th century.
7. Bicheno, Hugh *Battle Royal.*
8. Horspool, David *Richard III.*
9. Ibid.

CHAPTER 38

1. Seward, Desmond *War of the Roses.*
2. Season 2, Episode 4.
3. Whether her army contained Scots is disputed.
4. http://www.medievalists.net/2015/07/top-10-medieval-assassinations/?utm_content=bufferf2c6b&utm_medium=social&utm_source=twitter.com&utm_campaign=buffer.
5. The telling of the Black Dinner may have got exaggerated down the years. There is no mention of the bull in the earliest account.

CHAPTER 39

1. Although the Shakespearean image of a man slaying a mere boy is misleading—Clifford was 25 and Rutland 17, and so considered fully a man.
2. Rose, Alexander *The Kings in the North*.
3. Bicheno, Hugh *Battle Royal*.
4. It was the feast of Candlemass, a Christian festival that also marked the coming of spring, and in which people brought candles to church.
5. Well, depending on who you believe.
6. Weir, Alison *Lancaster and York*.
7. *Chronicle of the Abbey of Croyland*.
8. *The Paston Letters*.
9. The Cock, since renamed the Wharfe, is a small and beautiful river that nevertheless contains perhaps the most dangerous stretch of river anywhere in the world, the Strid, due to its fast current and rocks.
10. http://www.dailymail.co.uk/travel/travel_news/article-3588584/Is-world-s-dangerous-stretch-water-innocent-looking-river-Yorkshire-Strid-s-currents-pulverise-falls-in.html. http://booksandjournals.brillonline.com/docserver/9789004306455_webready_content _s003.pdf?expires=1501162189&id=id&accname=guest&checksum =3D13AA69A5664112A1B45B0EEBE0514A.
11. Ibid.
12. *A Storm of Swords*.
13. http://www.british-history.ac.uk/camden-record-soc/vol17/pp210-239.
14. Seward, Desmond *War of the Roses*.
15. *The Chronicle of Gregory*, a contemporary writer.

INDEX